# Important addresses & Telephone numbers

*Emergency room* ______________________

______________________

*Poison control center* ______________________

______________________

*Ambulance* ______________________

______________________

*Family doctor* ______________________

______________________

*Pediatrician* ______________________

______________________

*Specialist* ______________________

______________________

*Dentist* ______________________

______________________

*Dental emergency number* ______________________

______________________

*Hospital* ______________________

______________________

*Other* ______________________

______________________

# TAKE CARE OF YOURSELF

**BOOKS BY THESE AUTHORS**

---

*Vitality and Aging*
by James F. Fries and Lawrence M. Crapo

*Taking Part: A Consumer's Guide to the Hospital*
by Donald M. Vickery

*Aging Well*
by James F. Fries

*Arthritis: A Comprehensive Guide*
by James F. Fries

*The Arthritis Helpbook*
by Kate Lorig and James F. Fries

*Lifeplan: Your Own Master Plan for Maintaining Health and Preventing Illness*
by Donald M. Vickery

*Taking Care of Your Child*
by Robert Pantell, James F. Fries, and Donald M. Vickery

# TAKE CARE OF YOURSELF

## The Complete Guide to Medical Self-Care

WINNER OF THE MEDICAL SELF-CARE AWARD

FIFTH EDITION

*Donald M. Vickery, M.D.*
*James F. Fries, M.D.*

ADDISON-WESLEY PUBLISHING COMPANY

Reading, Massachusetts ■ Menlo Park, California ■ New York
Don Mills, Ontario ■ Wokingham, England ■ Amsterdam ■ Bonn
Sydney ■ Singapore ■ Tokyo ■ Madrid ■ San Juan
Paris ■ Seoul ■ Milan ■ Mexico City ■ Taipei

Many of the designations used by manufacturers and sellers to distinguish their products are claimed as trademarks. Where those designations appear in this book and Addison-Wesley was aware of a trademark claim, the designations have been printed in initial capital letters (e.g., Excedrin).

**Library of Congress Cataloging-in-Publication Data**

Vickery, Donald M.
Take care of yourself : The complete guide to medical self-care /
Donald M. Vickery, James F. Fries.—5th ed.
p. cm.
Includes bibliographical references and index.
ISBN 0-201-63292-6
1. Medicine, Popular. 2. Self-care, Health. I. Fries, James F.
II. Title.
[DNLM: 1. Medicine—popular works. 2. Self-Care—popular works.
WB 120 V637t]
RC81.V5 1993
613—dc20
DNLM/DLC
for Library of Congress 92-48678
CIP



Text design: Editorial Design/Joy Dickinson
Production: Michael Bass & Associates
Electronic composition and page make-up: Publishers Design Studio/Jim Love

0-201-63294-6 0-201-62710-8
0-201-62496-6 0-201-62721-3
0-201-62497-4

3 4 5 6 7 8 9–MA–96959493

First Edition, 1976, Twenty-nine printings
Second Edition, 1981, Twenty-seven printings
Third Edition, 1986, Fourteen printings
Fourth Edition, 1989, Nineteen printings
Fifth Edition, Third printing, August 1993

Instructions on the abdominal-thrust maneuver for choking (pages 148–151) have been adapted from the National Safety Council publication *Family Safety and Health*, Winter 1986–1987.

The decision chart on alcoholism (page 395) has been adapted from J. A. Ewing, "Detecting Alcoholism: The CAGE Questionnaire," *JAMA*, 252(1984):1905.

Information on substance abuse (pages 392–398) has been adapted from *Lifeplan: Your Own Master Plan for Maintaining Health and Preventing Illness* by Donald M. Vickery (Reston, Va.: Vicktor, 1990).

# TO OUR READERS

This book is strong medicine. It can be of great help to you. The medical advice is as sound as we can make it, but it will not always work. Like advice from your doctor, it will not always be right for you. This is our problem: If we don't give you direct advice, we can't help you. If we do, we will sometimes be wrong. So here are some qualifications:

- If you are under the care of a doctor and receive advice contrary to this book, follow the doctor's advice; the individual characteristics of your problem can then be taken into account.
- If you have an allergy or a suspected allergy to a recommended medication, check with your doctor, at least by phone.
- Read medicine label directions carefully; instructions vary from year to year, and you should follow the most recent.
- If your problem persists beyond a reasonable period, you should usually see a doctor.

# CONTENTS

# PREFACE

"Au Revoir!" "Auf Wiedersehen!" "Take Care!" With these traditional parting phrases, we express our feelings for our friends. When I see you again, be healthy. Keep your health. We show our priorities with our parting salutation. Not "Be rich!" or "Be famous!" but "Take care of yourself!"

This book is about how to take care of yourself. For us, the phrase has four meanings. First, "take care of yourself" means maintaining the habits that lead to vigor and health. Your life-style is your most important guarantee of lifelong vigor, and you can postpone most serious chronic diseases by the right preventive health decisions.

Second, "take care of yourself" means periodic monitoring for those few diseases that can sneak up on you without clear warning, such as high blood pressure, cancer of the breast or cervix, glaucoma, or dental decay. In such cases, taking care of yourself may mean going to a health professional for assistance.

Third, "take care of yourself" means responding decisively to new medical problems that arise. Most often, your response should be self-care, and you can act as your own doctor. At other times, however, you need professional help. Responding decisively means that you pay particular attention to the decision about going, or not going, to see the doctor. This book helps you make that decision.

Many people think that all illness must be treated at the doctor's office, clinic, or hospital. In fact, over 80% of new problems are treated at home, and an even larger number could be. The public has had scant instruction in determining when outside help is needed and when it is not. In the United States, the average person sees a doctor slightly more than five times a year. Over 1.5 billion prescriptions are written each year, about eight for each man, woman, and child. Medical costs now average over $3,000 per person per year—over 12% of our gross national product. In total, $750 billion each year. Among the billions of different medical services used each year, some are life-saving, some result in great health improvement, and some give great comfort. But there are some that are totally unnecessary, and some that are even harmful.

In our national quest for a symptom-free existence, as many as 70% of all visits to doctors for new problems have been termed unnecessary. For example, 11% of such visits are for uncomplicated colds. Many others are for minor cuts that do not require stitches, for tetanus shots despite current immunizations, for minor ankle sprains, and for the other problems discussed in this book. But while you don't need a doctor to treat most coughs, you do for some. For every ten or so cuts that do not require stitches, there is one that does. For every type of problem, there are some instances in which you should decide to see the doctor and some for which you should not.

Consider how important these decisions are. If you delay a visit to the doctor when you really need it, you may suffer unnecessary discomfort or leave an illness untreated. On the other hand, if you go to the doctor when you don't need to, you waste time and you may lose money or lose dignity. More subtly, confidence in your own ability and in the healing power of your own body begins to erode. You can even suffer physical harm if you receive a drug that you don't need or a test that you don't require. Your doctor is in an uncomfortable position when you come in unnecessarily and may feel obligated to practice "defensive medicine" just in case you have a bad result and a good lawyer. This book, above all else, is intended to help you with these decisions. It provides you with a "second opinion" within easy reach on your bookshelf. It contains information to help you make sound judgments about your own health.

There is a fourth final intended meaning in the title of our book. Your health is *your* responsibility; it depends on *your* decisions. There is no other way. You have to decide how to live, whether to see a doctor, which doctor to see, how soon to go, whether to take the advice offered. No one else can make these decisions, and they profoundly direct the course of future events. To be healthy, you have to be in charge.

Take care of yourself!

Donald M. Vickery, M.D.
Evergreen, Colorado

James F. Fries, M.D.
Stanford, California

# ACKNOWLEDGMENTS

We are grateful to many people for their help with this fifth edition, including the thousands of readers who have written with suggestions and encouragement and the hundreds of health workers who have used previous editions in their programs and practices.

In particular, we would like to thank Dr. William Bremer, Rick Carlson, Dr. William Carter, Dr. Grace Chickadonz, Dr. Peter Collis, Charlotte Crenson, Ann Dilworth, Dr. Edgar Engleman, William Fisher, Sarah Fries, Jo Ann Gibely, Harry Harrington, Dr. Halsted Holman, Dr. Robert Huntley, Dr. Donald Iverson, Dr. Julius Krevans, Dr. Kenneth Larsen, Dr. Kate Lorig, Professor Nathan Maccoby, Florence Mahoney, Michael Manley, Lawrence McPhee, Dr. Dennis McShane, Dr. Eugene Overton, Dr. Robert H. Pantell, Charles L. Parcell, Christian Paul, Clarence Pearson, William Peterson, George Pfeiffer, Gene Fauro Pratt, Dr. Robert Quinnell, Nancy Richardson, Dr. Robert Rosenberg, Dr. Ralph Rosenthal, Craig Russell, Robert Shepard, Dr. Douglas Solomon, Dr. Michael Soper, John Staples, Judy Staples, Warren Stone, Dr. Richard Tompkins, Dr. William Watson, Douglas Weiss, and Dr. Craig Wright for their advice and support.

# INTRODUCTION

*You can do more for your health than your doctor can.*

We introduced the first edition of *Take Care of Yourself* in 1976 with this phrase. The concept that health is more a personal responsibility than a professional one was controversial at that time, although it can be found in the earlier writings of René Dubois, Victor Fuchs, and John Knowles, among others. But these ideas were still foreign to a society that was heavily dependent on experts of every kind and seemingly addicted to ever more complex gadgetry and medications.

What a difference a few years can make. In 1981, the Surgeon General of the United States released a carefully worded report, *Health Promotion and Disease Prevention,* with this statement: "You, the individual, can do more for your own health and well being than any doctor, any hospital, any drugs, any exotic medical devices." The report goes on to detail a strategy for improved national health based on personal effort. The federal government now has an Office of Health Promotion and Disease Prevention. The strategy of *Take Care of Yourself* is now a nationally accepted one. Your health depends on you. We are proud that this book has played a role in the changing national perception of health.

In 1991, the Department of Health and Human Services released an important document called *Healthy People 2000: National Health Promotion and Disease Prevention Objectives*. It laid out health goals for the nation for the year 2000; they have long been the goals of *Take Care of Yourself*. Some of the specific targets:

- Increase moderate daily physical activity to at least 30% of people (currently 23%)

- Reduce overweight problems to no more than 20% of people (currently 25%)
- Reduce dietary fat intake to an average of less than 30% of calories (currently 36%)
- Reduce cigarette smoking to less than 15% of adults (currently 29%)
- Reduce alcohol intake by 20% (from 2.54 to 2.0 gallons per year per person)
- Increase fiber intake to 5 servings a day on average (currently 2½ a day)

We are pleased to support these national goals fully, and you will find many specific suggestions in *Take Care of Yourself* for how to reduce your personal health risks in the direction of the national goals.

The first four editions of *Take Care of Yourself* have included 89 printings totaling nearly 7 million copies. It has been translated into 12 languages. It has been the central feature of many health-promotion programs sponsored by corporations, health insurance plans, and other institutions. Acceptance by professional review panels is testimony to the soundness of the medical advice provided here and is also a testament to far-sighted panels and program directors who saw the need for new approaches to health problems. The success of the first four editions was possible only because of the support of all these people.

## *Evidence That This Book Works*

But does *Take Care of Yourself* work? Can you improve your health with the aid of a book? Can you use the doctor less, use services more wisely, save money? Absolutely. *Take Care of Yourself* has been more carefully evaluated by critical scientists than any health book ever written, and the evaluations have been published in the major medical journals. The five largest studies involved an aggregate of many thousands of individuals and cost nearly $2 million in total to perform. The results of all the studies have been positive.

- A report in the *Journal of the American Medical Association* describes a randomized study conducted in Woodland, California. As determined by lot, 460 families were given *Take Care of Yourself*, and 239 were not. The number of visits to doctors by those who were given *Take Care of Yourself* was reduced by 7.5% as compared to those who were not given the book. Visits to doctors decreased 14% for upper respiratory tract infections (colds).
- A 1983 report in the *Journal of the American Medical Association* compared the use of *Take Care of Yourself* in a health maintenance organization with a random control group. Total medical visits were reduced 17%, and visits for minor illnesses were reduced 35%. This large study of 3,700 subjects, requiring 5 years, obtained its data directly from medical records, had a rigorous experimental design, and found statistically significant reductions in medical visits in both the Medicare and general populations.
- A major study reported in the journal *Medical Care* in 1985 reports an experiment in 29 work-site locations that reduced visitation rates for households of 5,200 employees by 14%—1.5 doctor visits per household per year—after distribution of *Take Care of Yourself.*
- People who were given *Take Care of Yourself* were asked how helpful they found it. In Middlebury, Vermont, responses to a questionnaire were tabulated for 359 people. Of these, 342 found *Take Care of Yourself* a good reference book, and 349 had used it for a problem at least once. Five out of every 6 felt that it improved the effectiveness and appropriateness of their medical care, and over half felt that they had saved money by using it. In Woodland, California, a telephone survey of 295 families indicated that 89% had read at least some of the book, and 40% had used it for one or more problems. Of those who used the book, approximately 3 times as many people decided *not* to go to the doctor as those who decided they would. No negative results from using the book were reported. Asked about their feelings, 55% said they were more personally confident about their health care. None reported loss of confidence.
- In 1992, the *Archives of Internal Medicine* reported a randomized 12-month controlled trial of nearly 6,000 Bank of America retirees. The people who received *Take Care of Yourself* and the Senior Healthtrac program reduced health risks by 15% compared with control groups. Furthermore, they saved about $150 per person.

- Also in 1992, a report in the *American Journal of Health Promotion* analyzed health risk changes in over 250,000 people given *Take Care of Yourself* and Healthtrac materials and followed their health for up to 30 months. A decrease of health risks was consistent, at about 10% per year, and applied equally to young and old age groups and to those with less or more education.

We, as a nation, are in the midst of a health care cost crisis. Costs now average $3,000 per person per year—more than double those of any other country. Many people can no longer afford insurance. The *Take Care of Yourself* solution is simple:

- Stay healthy and reduce your need for medical care.
- Be a good purchaser and purchase only the services you truly need.

For every heart attack prevented the system saves $50,000, and you may save your life. Your Living Will may save your family thousands of dollars and can increase the dignity of your care if you develop a terminal illness. Even that cold that you treat at home may save $100 or more of doctor bills, laboratory tests, X-rays, and medication.

Why should you work to reduce medical care costs when you have insurance? You paid for it; why not use it? We are reminded of the "tragedy of the commons." In a small mountainous village in Spain, each family had one goat, which represented their total wealth. The village goats grazed on the common land inside the circle of huts and provided milk and cheese. One man reasoned that if he had two goats he would be twice as wealthy, and the commons could surely support one more goat, so he raised two goats. Then another man did the same. And another. And another. Eventually the grass was all eaten up, the goats died, and the villagers starved.

The health care crisis can be controlled if we all work to decrease our need for and use of medical services. It is a time to work for the common good: to preserve common resources. Moreover, your good health is its own reward. A vigorous life-style, a continuing sense of adventure and excitement, exercising personal will, and accepting individual responsibility are essential to the healthy life. Take care of yourself. You will help the broader society. And your loved ones will thank you for it.

# *Take care of yourself*

# PART I

# *The Habit of Health*

CHAPTER 1

# *Avoiding Illness: Your Master Plans for Health*

You can do much more than any physician to maintain your health and well-being. But you have to get into the habit of health. You must have a plan. At the age of 50, individuals with good health habits can be physically 30 years younger than those with poor health habits; at age 50, you can have a physical age of 65 or 35. It's up to you. You will feel better and accomplish more if you develop the habit of health.

The major health problems in the United States are due to chronic, long-term illness in middle age and later, as well as to trauma at young ages. These problems cause nearly 90% of all deaths. They also account for about 90% of all sickness in the United States. About two-thirds of these illnesses can be prevented with present techniques. Even though we often think of these diseases as fatal, we are trying to prevent the sickness and the injuries even more than the deaths.

## *The Nature of Major Illness*

It is important to understand the basic nature of chronic illnesses such as atherosclerosis, emphysema, osteoarthritis, and cancer.

- These diseases are universal; we all have a tendency toward them. We differ from each other in how rapidly the tendency toward actual illness is increasing in our bodies.

- These conditions progress in our bodies, often for decades, before they cause any symptoms. You have the tendency toward them, but you don't feel sick. The conditions may begin in your 20s, 30s, or 40s and not be detected until perhaps 40 years later.
- These disease tendencies are slowly progressive unless they are prevented. The important factor is *how rapidly these conditions are progressing in you*.
- Diseases have "risk factors." Risk factors cause the progression to be more or less rapid than otherwise. Strictly speaking, risk factors do not cause diseases. They affect the *rate* of development of the disease.

Figure 1 shows these different patterns of disease development in different individuals. An individual who is developing a condition rapidly may progress to symptoms relatively early, and the individual may even die. If the condition progresses more slowly, symptoms are encountered much later in life. If it progresses slowly enough, there may never be any symptoms during the entire life span. It is important to remember the following principles:

1. *Prevention changes the rate of development of disease.*

   The goal is to change the rate of unseen progression from the steepest lines of Figure 1 toward a less rapid progression.

2. *Attention to health risk factors improves the* quality *of life more than the* quantity *of life.*

   Scientific evidence now suggests that even the best preventive practices will have less effect on the length of your life than previously thought. Healthy habits can prolong your predicted life expectancy but only by a relatively small amount, usually a year or so at most. Most important, if you reduce risks, you will have major improvement in your physical and emotional reserves and in how much you enjoy your life.

The illness and pain associated with disease are the real problem. These can be greatly reduced by a good plan for health. For example, after stopping cigarette smoking, you return to normal risk levels for heart attacks after only two years. After ten years you are at nearly normal risk for lung cancer. In only a few weeks, exercise programs begin to contribute to your health and well-being. For most diseases,

**FIGURE 1** *Patterns of Disease Development*

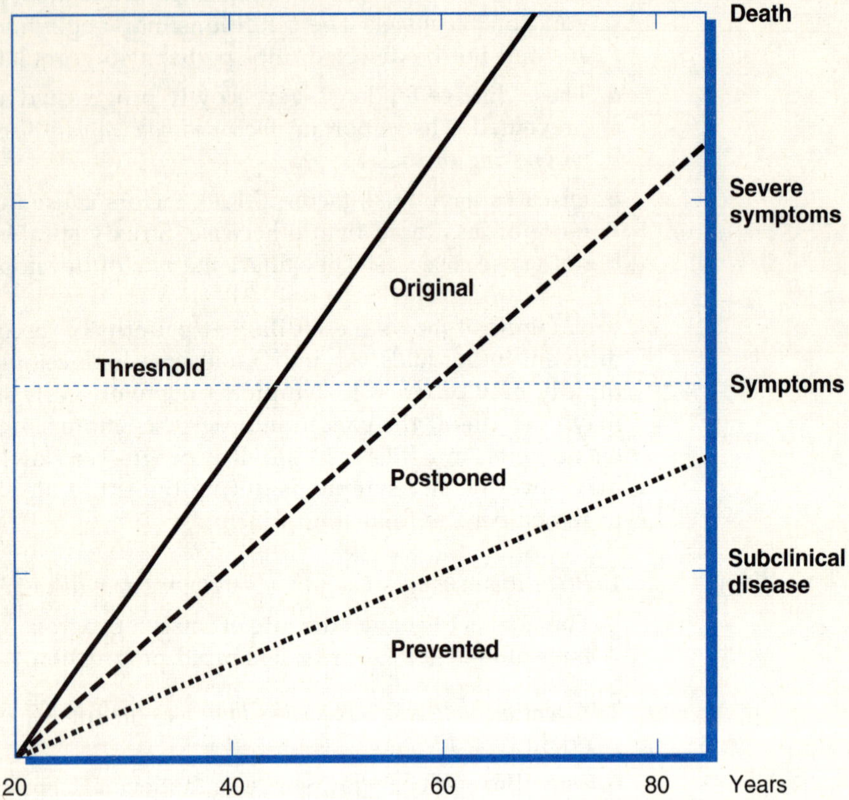


not only can you slow the rate of progression, but you can also reverse part of the damage. This means that by developing the habit of health, even after a condition has appeared, you can reduce the amount of illness you will have in your life.

You need three master plans for prevention. The plans are simple. First, you need to prevent the fatal illnesses. Second, prevent the non-fatal ones. Third, anticipate and prevent the problems of aging. The plans overlap, but each has its own purpose. This chapter summarizes these three plans and how they work. These discussions are intended to give you the "why" of disease prevention. Much of this information will be familiar to you, but we have tried to present it in an organized and reasonably detailed way for your reference. You may be surprised to learn how many different health problems can be prevented.

## *Avoiding Possibly Fatal Disease*

Table 1 summarizes your master plan for preventing fatal illnesses. Note that *there are only a few important risk factors that need attention.* The same few risk factors encourage disease in many categories. Your plan needs to include

1. A good diet
2. Exercise

**TABLE 1** *Your Master Plan for Primary Prevention of Fatal Disease*

| *Disease* | *Diet* | *Exercise* | *Weight Control* | *Avoid Smoking* | *Moderate Alcohol* | *Treat High Blood Pressure* | *Behave Safely* |
|---|---|---|---|---|---|---|---|
| **Atherosclerosis** | X | X | X | X | | X | |
| **Cancer** | | | | | | | |
| LUNG | | | | X | | | |
| BREAST | X | | X | | | | |
| COLON | X | X | | | | | |
| MOUTH | | | | X | | | |
| LIVER | | | | X | X | | |
| ESOPHAGUS | | | | X | X | | |
| **Emphysema** | | | | X | | | |
| **Cirrhosis** | | | | | X | | |
| **Diabetes** | X | X | X | | | | |
| **Trauma** | | | | | X | | X |

**3.** Avoidance of smoking

**4.** Alcohol moderation

**5.** Weight control

**6.** High blood pressure control and

**7.** Prudence (for example, using automobile seat belts)

The following pages show how these steps reduce the risk of the most common fatal diseases.

## ATHEROSCLEROSIS

### Process

Atherosclerosis contributes to nearly one-half of death and illness in the United States. About 40 feet of large and small arteries throughout the body, down to about the size of a soda straw, are the site of this problem. Small plaques (patches), made mostly of cholesterol, accumulate on the inside walls of these arteries. This results in narrowing of the arteries. The narrowed and irregular artery thus becomes susceptible to a sudden blood clot. This can cause a heart attack or stroke. Or atherosclerosis can result in so much narrowing of the artery that not enough oxygen-carrying blood can get through, causing angina or other problems. The various syndromes depend on the particular arteries involved and whether there is a sudden clot or a continually weak blood flow. Evidence now points out that atherosclerotic plaques that are already in place can shrink in size with diet and exercise.

Atherosclerotic deaths are usually due to **heart attack** or **stroke**. These can also be non-fatal problems, causing a great deal of pain and disability. They can result from sudden formation of a blood clot in the arteries of the heart or brain. There is increasingly good treatment for these clots immediately after they have formed, but not having the clot at all is far better.

Additionally, atherosclerosis causes many other non-fatal problems. **Angina pectoris** (heart pain) results from inadequate blood supply to the heart muscle. Pain results when exercise or other activities increase the heart's need for oxygen that cannot be supplied through the narrowed artery. **Intermittent claudication** is a similar condition involving the arteries to the legs. Pain in the legs comes during exercise when the leg muscles need more oxygen than they can receive. **Congestive heart failure** results when the heart is unable to pump as much blood as the body needs due to weakening or scarring of the heart muscle. **Transient ischemic attacks** are like little strokes in which short-lived clots form in the arteries that supply blood to the brain. **Multiple infarct dementia** results when recurrent small clots in the brain result in death of some brain tissue. This damages thinking and memory. **Kidney function** can break down when the arteries leading to the kidney become narrowed.

### Prevention

Diet is the most important single factor for prevention of atherosclerosis. The diet should be low in total fat and particularly low in saturated fats, found in eggs, ice cream, butter, and animal meats. As a simple rule, these fats usually are solid at room temperature. They are white or yellowish.

Smoking cigarettes, cigars, or pipes encourages spasm in the walls of the arteries. Not smoking can reduce a person's risk of atherosclerosis by as much as one-half.

Control of high blood pressure is also important. Higher blood pressure speeds the formation of atherosclerotic plaques and increases the chances that a weakened artery will blow out. **Hypertension** (high blood pressure) is a particularly strong risk factor for stroke. Too much salt holds water in the tissues and increases blood pressure; hence, moderation in salt intake is also important. Some people are particularly "salt sensitive"; their blood pressure is greatly elevated by high salt intake.

Exercise, to help avoid atherosclerosis, needs to be aerobic, or endurance, in type. That is, it needs to be maintained at least 12 minutes at a session and must be sufficient to raise the pulse rate by 30 to 50 points from resting. This helps teach the heart to become more effective at extracting oxygen from the blood. It also improves your heart reserve function to protect you even if a problem, such as a clot, does occur.

Excessive body weight contributes to higher blood cholesterol levels and decreased physical activity, and forces the heart to do additional work even at rest.

## CANCER

### Process

There are many theories of the development of cancer. In the simplest form, cancer results from *recurrent injury to the cells in a tissue over a long period of time,* often due to an irritant (carcinogen) such as cigarette tar. The injury causes death of some cells, requires increased cell division, and increases the chance of an error in that cell division so that a malignant (death-causing) cell line is born. With age, the immune surveillance system that usually destroys such malignant cells becomes less effective, allowing the malignant cell line to grow. As the cancer grows, it may directly interfere with local tissues or, commonly, may metastasize (spread) to other parts of the body.

Cancer causes about 20% of deaths in the United States. Cancer problems are related to the location of the main tumor but also include pain, weight loss, and problems at distant sites of the body. Complications of radiation treatment, surgery, or chemotherapy add to the illness burden.

Prevention is best. The much-heralded "war on cancer" begun over two decades ago is acknowledged to have been a failure to date. The problem? This "war" ignored prevention, instead focussing entirely on cure. Current estimates state that about two-thirds of cancers can be prevented with current knowledge! You can reduce your likelihood of getting cancer by *two-thirds!*

## Prevention

**Cancer of the Lung.** This needless problem is the leading cause of cancer death in both men and women. About 90% of lung cancer is caused directly by cigarette smoking. In men, lung cancer is now on the decline due to recent trends toward less frequent cigarette use.

**Cancer of the Breast.** Breast cancer frequency appears to be significantly increased by obesity and by high-fat diets. The mechanism is not entirely clear but appears to involve two factors: (1) There are greater amounts of breast tissue in which to develop a cancer, and (2) this makes it more difficult to detect an early cancer. Prevention involves weight control and lower-saturated fats in the diet. Secondary prevention (early detection) techniques include monthly breast self-examination and yearly physician examination. After age 50, yearly mammography (X-rays of the breasts) is recommended.

**Cancer of the Esophagus.** Cigarette, cigar, and pipe smoking greatly influence risk here, as does heavy alcohol intake.

**Cancer of the Mouth and Tongue.** Cigarette, pipe, and cigar smoking account for over 90% of these cancers. The cancers are often, but not always, preceded by development of **leukoplakia**, whitish patches on the throat or tongue. Smokers should stop; those who don't stop should inspect the inside of their mouth and throat with a flashlight at monthly intervals.

**Cancer of the Colon.** The dietary factors that influence development of colon cancer have been partly recognized. These factors account for about half of these tumors. The key factor for prevention of colon cancer is to eat enough dietary fiber. This is found in unrefined grains, fruits, and vegetables. Fiber in the diet helps regulate the bowels. It also helps lower the serum cholesterol. With sufficient fiber, there is less frequent development of pre-cancerous colon polyps and a greatly decreased likelihood of malignant change in the colon.

**Cancer of the Cervix.** Cancer of the cervix (mouth of the uterus) has been rapidly declining in women in most developed countries, probably because of improved hygiene. The Pap smear is critically important for secondary prevention (early detection) and actually acts in some ways as primary prevention by detecting pre-cancerous changes. For prevention, follow your doctor's recommendation for Pap smears. Usually, this will be every three years or so if smears are negative. After age 50, Pap smears should be done every one or two years.

**Cancer of the Uterus.** Risk factors are not well established for this cancer, but estrogen therapy appears to play at least a small role in some women.

**Cancer of the Liver.** Heavy alcohol intake greatly increases the likelihood of this very difficult-to-treat cancer.

**Cancer of the Skin.** The sun is the big culprit with these often minor cancers. Sun exposure, particularly in fair-skinned individuals, causes recurrent tissue irritation, pre-malignant changes, and then cancer, usually **basal cell** and **squamous cell cancer**. A more serious cancer, **malignant melanoma**, has been related to episodes of severe sunburn during the teenage years. Secondary prevention is reasonably simple but sometimes neglected. You need to watch your skin for development of new lumps, changes in color of warts or moles, or small sores that don't heal. Cure of basal cell and squamous cell cancer is almost automatic if you detect and treat these problems early enough. Melanoma is far more sneaky, but early detection is still important and effective.

**Other Cancers.** No definite risk factors have been identified for cancer of the stomach, pancreas, prostate, or brain. **Lymphomas** (cancers of the lymph system) and **leukemias** (cancers of the blood) may result from radiation exposure or from chemotherapy given for other cancers or other diseases.

## EMPHYSEMA

### Process

The breathing tubes (bronchi) are kept free of mucus and infection by small hairs (cilia). Cilia move the mucus continually toward the throat where it is swallowed. Cigarette smoking destroys these cilia so that the mucus cannot be cleared and bacteria can live within the lung. Partial blockage of the breathing tubes makes it difficult to exhale. The inflammation and the increased respiratory effort rupture the small air sacs in the lung; this causes loss of the surface area necessary for oxygen exchange. This results in slow oxygen starvation, great limitation in function, and usually leads to multiple hospitalizations. The side effects of treatment are often also major problems.

### Prevention

Over 90% of emphysema results from cigarette smoking. Pipe and cigar smoke (if not inhaled) does not increase risk of emphysema, but does increase the risk of lip and mouth cancer. Stopping smoking early in the process will allow stabilization. Although this condition does not reverse, stopping smoking at any point is helpful.

## CIRRHOSIS

### Process

Cirrhosis of the liver results from three factors: (1) repeated injury to the liver cells, (2) fatty change and death of many of these cells, and (3) accumulation of fibrous scar tissue that ultimately prevents function of the liver. The abdomen may fill up with fluid; this is called **ascites**. Jaundice (yellowing) may result from obstruction of small ducts in the liver or replacement of the normal liver tissue by scar tissue.

### Prevention

Cirrhosis can follow other kinds of injury, such as hepatitis; but long-term heavy alcohol intake, often accompanied by inadequate nutrition, directly causes 75% of the cases. If alcohol is causing liver damage, alcohol intake must be stopped entirely. In early stages, considerable recovery is possible. After heavy scarring of the liver has occurred, cirrhosis is not reversible.

## DIABETES

### Process

As we age or if we are overweight, our bodies are not able to handle a high sugar load. Glucose (sugar) stays in the blood in higher levels and for longer periods of time. The problem is greatly increased if exercise is inadequate. As a result of the high blood sugar, some of this sugar is wastefully excreted in the urine. This results in the typical early symptoms of frequent, heavy urination and thirst. Diabetes is a relative lack of insulin because insulin is required for uptake (absorption) of sugar by the cells. For reasons that are not entirely clear, diabetes itself becomes a risk factor for atherosclerosis. Diabetes also can cause complications affecting vision, kidney function, and nervous-system function.

### Prevention

Diabetic symptoms beginning for the first time after age 30 can frequently be reversed completely by simple non-medical treatment. Even with the more serious type of diabetes beginning early in life, these approaches help a great deal; however, insulin treatment is usually also necessary in early-onset diabetes.

First, weight loss is important because it decreases food need and intake. Exercise is very important because it helps the uptake of sugar by the cells from the blood.

A diet that stresses complex carbohydrates (such as whole-wheat grains, cereals, vegetables, and fruits) and that contains adequate fiber is important. Complex carbohydrates, as opposed to the pure white sugars, are broken down more slowly by the body. This evens out the rate at which the sugars enter the blood so that the body can handle them better.

## TRAUMA

### Process

Trauma is the result of direct injury to the body. It is not, strictly speaking, a disease, but it results in a large number of deaths and even more pain and suffering. It causes over 75% of serious illness and death between the ages of 15 and 25. Overwhelmingly, these injuries, whether injury is to driver, pedestrian, or occupant, are the result of an automobile accident. There are about ten serious injuries, often resulting in lifelong problems, for every death.

### Prevention

Seat-belt use is by far the most important single habit to develop. This is an easy habit, without cost, which reduces risk by over one-half. Remember that seat-belt use is for driver *and* passengers, in both the front and back seats. Air bags are a supplement for seat belts, not a replacement for them. Using seat belts is a way of achieving greater personal control over your destiny. You think ahead, you plan, and you avoid trouble. You choose, far more than you ever imagined, whether or not you stay healthy.

Alcohol or drug intoxication is responsible for nearly one-half of all accidents. Prescription drugs (and illegal drugs) are another frequent cause of impairment. Codeine, Valium, and a whole range of sedatives and tranquilizers can alter reflexes and judgment enough to cause accidents. Don't drive if you are impaired. Don't ride with anyone who is impaired. Teach your children to do the same.

Gunshot wounds are a major cause of death in our society, especially among young people. Adolescents with thoughts of suicide are much more likely to succeed in killing themselves if there is a gun available. Criminals, especially in the illegal drug trade, often use guns without regard for whom they injure. Use common sense to protect yourself from crime. Take extreme care in using and storing firearms.

## *The Limits of Prevention*

The conditions discussed above are not preventable in all instances. And sometimes you may be suffering from an illness that was caused by something you did early in life, perhaps even at a time when the effects of that action were not well understood. It is important to avoid "victim blaming" or, in this instance, "blaming yourself." The past is past, and you may never know for sure what was the cause of a current problem.

The important goal is that you work for the future. Work for primary prevention of diseases before they appear. Work for early detection and treatment of illnesses that are already there. If you already have one or more substantial medical problems, you especially need to work actively to prevent additional problems in other areas.

Finally, there are a number of major illnesses for which there is no known primary prevention. Some of these are listed in Table 2. Some of these eventually may turn out to be infectious diseases or the

**TABLE 2** *Diseases for Which There Is No Known Primary Prevention*

- Rheumatoid arthritis
- Ulcerative colitis
- Systemic lupus erythematosus
- Crohn's disease
- Multiple sclerosis
- Parkinson's disease
- Alzheimer's disease
- Polymyalgia rheumatica

aftermath of infections. Some may be the result of toxic exposures of an as yet unknown type. In some, there are hints that risk factors may exist; for example, one study found increased cigarette-smoking rates in Alzheimer's disease patients. Even with these diseases, there is a great deal that you can do to minimize the problem.

Improvement of risk factors at any age improves the quality of life. And it does so at essentially no cost (with the exception of medications required to treat high blood pressure). A good diet is of equal or lesser expense than a bad one. Junk food is expensive. A thin individual has lower food costs than if he or she were obese. Exercise is one of the least expensive uses of your time. Tobacco smoking and alcohol consumption are costly habits. Seat belts come free, and air bags are becoming standard in most cars.

The major goal of prevention is improvement of the quality of your life in all areas, from vigor and vitality to economic viability. The quality and pleasure of your life can be materially improved by your careful attention to these few critically important factors.

## *Avoiding Non-Fatal Disease*

More health problems come from non-fatal diseases than from fatal ones! Prevention of these problems is critical to your ability to live as well as you can. You probably noticed in the preceding section that even potentially fatal diseases (like atherosclerosis) cause most of their problems by non-fatal complications such as angina pectoris, non-fatal heart attacks, non-fatal strokes, intermittent claudication, and congestive heart failure. Accidents cause 20 times as many severe and lasting disabilities as they do deaths.

There are many additional disease conditions that are seldom, if ever, fatal but that cause immense pain and suffering. For example, osteoarthritis and related syndromes cause nearly one-half of the physical symptoms reported by older individuals. Little attention has been paid to prevention of these diseases. Yet, prevention is possible to nearly the same degree as with the fatal diseases. Secondary prevention of these conditions, after symptoms have begun, is often more difficult. Preventive measures won't always work completely, but they markedly improve your chances. They will nearly always help to some extent. By working to prevent problems from these conditions, you can strikingly improve symptom levels and the quality of life. Plan ahead.

Table 3 summarizes your master plan for preventing these non-fatal diseases. Again, note that the list of measures required is small and the list is closely similar to that required for control of the fatal diseases. The list is led by exercise and weight control; these are essential. A brief discussion of some common problems follows.

**TABLE 3** *Your Master Plan for Primary Prevention of Non-Fatal Illness*

| *Disease* | *Diet* | *Exercise* | *Weight Control* | *Avoid Smoking* | *Moderate Alcohol* | *Medication Restraint* |
|---|---|---|---|---|---|---|
| **Osteoarthritis** | | X | X | | | |
| **Back problems** | | X | X | | | |
| **Hernias** | | X | X | X | | |
| **Hemorrhoids** | X | X | X | | | |
| **Varicose veins** | | X | X | X | | |
| **Thrombophlebitis** | | X | X | X | | |
| **Gallbladder disease** | X | | X | | | |
| **Ulcers** | X | | | X | X | X |
| **Bladder infections** | | | | | X | |
| **Dental problems** | X | | | X | X | |

## OSTEOARTHRITIS

### Process

Osteoarthritis, the most common kind of arthritis, results from degeneration of the joint cartilage that lines the ends of the bones. As the cartilage becomes weaker, it fragments, and bony and knobby spurs develop at the edges of the joint. The joint becomes stiff and often painful. The syndrome is often compounded by exercise limitation and disuse effects (detraining).

### Prevention

Risk factors for osteoarthritis include obesity, inactivity and lack of exercise, and previous injury to the joint. Your preventive strategy is, first, to keep fit. Exercise increases the strength of the bones and the stability of ligaments and tendons. Exercise nourishes the joint cartilage by bringing nutrients to the cartilage and removing waste products. Regular, gently graded, permanent exercise programs are required.

Second, control your weight. Being overweight places unnecessary stress on joints by changing the angles at which the ligaments attach to the bone. Being overweight also puts additional stress on the feet, ankles, knees, hips, and lower back.

Third, protect your joints. Listen to the pain messages that your body sends and perform activities in the least stressful way. Be particularly careful with joints that were injured earlier in your life because these joints are at greatest risk. If you feel pain after a particular activity, do not take a pain pill and continue doing it. Listen to the pain message and change your activity to avoid it.

Note that osteoarthritis is not the same as rheumatoid arthritis, which cannot be prevented. Good treatment is available, however. The postponement or management of arthritis is a large and complex subject. We have written extensively about these problems in *Arthritis: A Comprehensive Guide* and in *The Arthritis Helpbook*. (See the reference section at the end of this book.)

## BACK PROBLEMS

### Process

Osteoarthritis also occurs in the joints of the spine and can be aggravated by collapse of spinal vertebrae (bones) due to osteoporosis. In younger individuals, problems with herniated (ruptured) intervertebral discs are common, but by the age of 50 or 60, the disc itself becomes more scarred and fibrous and less prone to rupture.

### Prevention

Exercise is required to keep the muscles that support the back strong. Weight-bearing exercise is important to keep the bone-mineral content high and the spinal bones strong. The abdominal muscles must also be strong because they too provide support for the spine.

Weight control is the second line of defense; back problems frequently occur in overweight individuals. With excess body fat, there are unusual and greater stresses, and often lack of exercise and reduced muscle strength.

Diet is important: calcium intake should be maintained at substantial levels. Take calcium supplements, if necessary, to help keep the bones strong, particularly in seniors.

Previous injury is another risk factor; and, if you have had recurrent back problems, attention to exercise and weight control is even more important. Learning to lift correctly, with the legs, helps reduce risk.

## HERNIAS

### Process

Hernias occur through a combination of weak abdominal muscles and increased pressure within the abdominal cavity. They can result from obesity or coughing. As a result, small parts of the bowel herniate (rupture) outward through the inguinal or femoral canals in the general area of the groin.

### Prevention

Exercise is critical to maintain the strength of the abdominal muscles. Walking, running, bicycling, and swimming are at least as important as direct exercises to strengthen the abdomen. Weight control helps improve muscle tone and decreases stress. Stopping smoking is extremely important because the chronic smoker's cough more than doubles the risk of a hernia.

## HEMORRHOIDS

### Process

This condition, as well as varicose veins and thrombophlebitis, comes from inadequate blood flow in the veins, not the arteries. With hemorrhoids, there is slowed flow of blood in the veins around the anus and the development of painful blood clots with surrounding inflammation.

### Prevention

Exercise programs are important because they keep the body toned and the blood flowing briskly. Sitting a great deal is bad. Being overweight contributes to slow flow through the veins in several ways. Pregnancy is a risk factor.

Local cleanliness around the anus decreases inflammation. Hot baths act to increase blood flow and reduce inflammation. Perhaps most important, straining at stool increases internal abdominal pressure and slows blood flow. Straining also causes local irritation and inflammation as hard stool passes through the rectum and anus. Singing or talking while on the toilet can help prevent straining—*never* hold your breath. Take your time; read the newspaper if you need something to occupy you.

Dietary fiber is a natural laxative and is a very important part of your diet. Whole-wheat breads, fresh fruits, and vegetables are extremely important for preventing hemorrhoids, as well as other problems discussed previously.

## VARICOSE VEINS

### Process

Varicose veins generally result from slow blood flow through the veins of the legs. The veins gradually stretch and become unsightly. Fluid leaking through the capillaries results in swelling of the lower legs and ankles and further aggravates the problems with blood flow. With time, additional veins develop, but these actually aggravate the problem of slow flow.

### Prevention

Lack of exercise and prolonged standing (without support stockings) are the major culprits. Pregnancy is a risk factor. After varicose veins have been present for a while, walking and other exercise is not as helpful as it was earlier, so early prevention is best. Smoking can contribute in an additional way to development of blood clots. Obesity is a substantial contributing factor in most cases because the extra weight requires a larger blood flow and puts pressure on the soft-walled veins. The larger blood flow and increased pressure prevent efficient return of the blood toward the heart. For prevention, lose some weight, walk, and use support hose.

## THROMBOPHLEBITIS

### Process

Here the stasis (slowing) of blood flow and swelling of the veins in the legs (whether visible as varicose veins or not) result in the development of clots in the leg veins. The blood backs up behind the clot, and then that blood also clots. When the condition is present in large, deep veins, it is particularly hazardous. Clots can break loose and travel through the circulation into the lungs; there they can cause a serious condition known as **pulmonary embolism**.

### Prevention

The preventive program is identical to that for controlling problems with varicose veins. Exercise helps stimulate the blood flow; obesity makes it worse. Support hose can help. Smoking causes a substantial increase in the likelihood of clots forming. If you have already had one or more episodes of thrombophlebitis, the veins will have sustained damage, and the likelihood of recurrence is greater; blood-thinning medications may be required to help prevent future episodes.

## GALLBLADDER DISEASE

### Process

The gallbladder stores the bile salts and cholesterol made in the liver. Bile salts are then discharged from the gallbladder into the intestine to help digest fats. These bile salts are "soapy" substances. They are produced in response to the amount of fat in the diet requiring digestion. Sometimes these salts can become stones within the gallbladder itself; the stones often contain substantial amounts of cholesterol. The stones cause local inflammation; if the muscular gallbladder tries to expel them, blockage of the bile ducts by the stone may cause pain, additional inflammation, or jaundice (yellowing).

### Prevention

Two risk factors for gallbladder disease increase the likelihood of disease by six to eight times. These are (1) heavy intake of saturated fat and cholesterol in the diet, which increases bile salt production, and (2) being overweight. Obesity not only greatly increases the frequency of the condition, but it also makes surgery to correct it more difficult and more hazardous.

## ULCERS

### Process

Excess stomach acid or other irritants in the stomach or intestine can result in formation of erosions and ulcer craters; often these are large enough to hold a good part of the surgeon's thumb. A breakdown of the protective mucous barrier of the stomach accelerates the damage. We all form small ulcers every now and again, but severe progressive ones can lead to pain and major hemorrhage (bleeding). Severe ulcers can even perforate (make holes) all the way through the wall of the stomach or small bowel.

### Prevention

Stress, in all its forms, is a frequent contributing factor. Smokers have several times the frequency of ulcers than do non-smokers. Smoking causes constriction (tightening) of the small vessels, and that prevents adequate nourishment to the wall of the stomach. Diets that have pepper or spices usually *don't* play much of a role; but irregular meal habits, by preventing the buffering (neutralization) of the acid by food, often can result in a dietary contribution to the problem. Alcohol, particularly hard spirits, can be a culprit.

Medications are frequent irritants. Non-steroidal anti-inflammatory agents, such as ibuprofen, indomethacin, piroxicam, naproxen, or aspirin, are often responsible; these now account for one-third or more of all bleeding ulcers. Much of the time, the medications that have resulted in ulcers are later found to have been medically unnecessary.

## BLADDER INFECTIONS

### Process

If bacteria breed and multiply in the bladder, they cause irritation, inflammation, and painful, frequent, and even bloody urination. The bacteria first have to get there, and this happens most frequently in females because the urethra is short and the bladder not far from the outside. Bacteria usually enter through the urethra. For bacteria to cause problems, they must be able to multiply more rapidly than they are flushed out of the bladder during urination.

### Prevention

Adequate fluid intake and the resulting relatively frequent need for urination is the best prevention. You should drink enough so that your urine is clear, colorless, and plentiful at least once every day.

Hygiene of the genital area is important because most of the bacteria come from the intestine via the anus. After using the toilet, females should wipe with toilet paper from front to back to avoid transfer of bacteria to the neighborhood of the urethral opening.

For early symptoms, drinking cranberry juice in substantial quantities is an excellent secondary prevention. Cranberry juice contains a natural antibiotic (mandelic acid) that slows the multiplication of the bacteria.

## DENTAL PROBLEMS

### Process

Bacteria growing inside your mouth contribute to plaque, dental decay, and gum disease. These problems can be inconvenient, or they can be excruciating! Fortunately, the development and prevention of dental problems are well understood.

### Prevention

Diet is important. The bacteria in your mouth need sugar and starch to survive, especially if they have burrowed through the enamel into your teeth. Go easy on foods that are high in refined sugar, especially those that stick to and between teeth, and brush after eating. You can also use diet to help clean your teeth because food that is high in roughage acts like a natural toothbrush. End your meals with an apple or with a salad, as many families in Europe do.

The next preventive step is a sound program of cleaning teeth in order to remove particles of food. Brush your teeth after eating with a soft toothbrush and a toothpaste that contains fluoride and is recommended by the American Dental Association. Periodically floss between teeth with unwaxed dental floss; such cleaning also encourages healthy gums. Water jets are effective at removing trapped particles, but flossing does a better job if done conscientiously.

Fluoride is a natural element that is extremely effective in preventing tooth decay in children. It is found naturally in many water supplies and vegetables, and most U. S. cities have chosen to fluoridate their water supply. If your water is not fluoridated, ask your dentist about fluoride tablets for children under the age of ten.

Finally, have your teeth cleaned by a dentist once or twice every year. A dental cleaning has been proven to be effective in preventing both tooth decay and gum disease. We believe dental X-rays are needed only about once every three to five years.

If you have dentures or a bridge, follow your dentist's instructions about keeping the device clean. Even if you don't have all of your original adult teeth, you still have the power to prevent new dental problems.

## *Preventing Surgery*

Not only can the pain and discomfort from the problems discussed above (and many others) be greatly reduced, but you also may avoid various types of surgical operations. Thus, without a hernia, you don't need a surgical hernia repair. Surgery for hemorrhoids isn't ever required if you don't have hemorrhoids. You can decrease the likelihood of gallbladder surgery. You can decrease the requirement for gastric resection or other complex operations for treating ulcers. You can decrease the likelihood of needing coronary artery bypass surgery. Surgical operations are expensive and uncomfortable, and always involve some degree of risk. Reducing the need for such treatment is a major bonus.

The popular press almost always emphasizes fatal diseases. To stay healthy, it is even more important to prevent the common illnesses that can give you a lot of trouble over a long period.

## *Avoiding Problems of Aging*

Some of the problems that occur as we age are part of the aging process itself. They result from the stiffening and scarring in our tissues that increase as we get older. They result in a relative frailty of our entire bodies and of particular body parts. Here too, you are in control. To a considerable degree, you can slow the aging process.

The line between problems of chronic disease and problems of aging is very blurred. For example, arthritis has some aspects of an aging process and some of a specific disease. In our arteries, the accumulation of fats on the inside of the arteries, called *athero*sclerosis, is generally felt to be a disease. On the other hand, *arterio*sclerosis, the stiffening and the loss of elasticity in the artery walls with age, appears more likely to be part of the aging process. Further, many health burdens—such as problems with memory, medications, or falls—are general concerns of aging. These are not really "diseases," but they cause many difficulties.

This section is intended to indicate, by use of a few examples, three points: First, there *are* solutions to problems of aging just as there are solutions for problems of disease; second, these solutions require advance planning; and, third, your plan can yield concrete, positive results.

Table 4 summarizes your master plan for preventing some frequent problems of aging. It includes some important modifications to the earlier prevention plans.

- The diet you need includes sufficient calcium in addition to the factors that we have discussed earlier—low fat, high fiber, and low salt.
- You need to undertake exercise that is not only physical but also mental, to jog the memory and strengthen the mind.

**TABLE 4** *Your Master Plan for Preventing General Problems of Aging*

| | *Diet* | *Exercise* | *Medical Checks* |
|---|---|---|---|
| **Osteoporosis** | X | X | |
| **Falls and fractures** | X | X | |
| **Medication side effects** | | | X |
| **Cataracts** | | | X |
| **Corneal opacification** | | | X |
| **Hearing loss** | | | X |
| **Memory loss** | | X | |
| **Multiple problems** | | | X |
| **Multiple medications** | | | X |

- The medical checks, which are important for early detection and appropriate treatment of some of these problems, need to be done by yourself and, in some instances, by health professionals.

## OSTEOPOROSIS

### Process

As we age, we gradually lose calcium from our bones. The bones become less strong, more brittle, and thus more prone to fracture. This process is called osteoporosis. It occurs particularly rapidly in women after menopause because estrogen seems to be important in maintaining bone strength. About 650,000 fractures occur each year in the United States as a result of osteoporosis.

### Prevention

Exercise and estrogen supplementation in some women are required for strong bones. Both work independently. Exercise must be weight-bearing so that it stresses the bones and gives a signal to the body to lay down more calcium and strengthen the bones. Walking, jogging, and even standing provide such stress. Strengthening the bones of the spine is particularly important because this is the site of over half of the osteoporotic fractures.

Calcium is as important as exercise, but in a secondary sense. Without exercise, calcium is not used by the body; so no matter how much calcium you take in, you don't get an effect. You need the signal from your bones to the metabolic systems of your body that more calcium is needed; then the calcium is absorbed by the small intestine, transported to the appropriate part of the body, and laid down as new strong bone. Your last two years of exercise are most important; within two years, people who stop exercising lose the benefits. On the other hand, sufficient exercise can maintain bone strength at the normal levels of younger life for an indefinite period.

## FALLS AND FRACTURES

### Process

Falls cause an astonishing amount of difficulty for older individuals. Falls may result from frailty, slowed reaction time, lack of conditioning, poor vision, poor hearing, presence of medical disease, or a whole variety of different problems that are common in older people. The key is to think of the impact as well as the fall. (It isn't the falling that is the problem; it is hitting the ground.) This means that you have to think about your environment as well as about your physical condition.

### Prevention

Certainly, you want strong bones; the approach to preventing osteoporosis has been outlined above. You want your whole body to be as strong as possible, and this entails all of the principles described throughout this book. Then you need to consider the dangers in your environment. Loose throw rugs, absence of good lighting, failure to use non-skid tape in the bathtub, absence of hand rails in difficult places, and other such factors are very important. What about your vision? Think through a typical day, imagine those places where it is most likely that you might fall, and make a plan to reduce the danger. Go through the same process for each person with whom you live—if they break something, it will decrease the quality of your life, too.

## MEDICATION SIDE EFFECTS

### Process

As we age, we tend to get more side effects from lesser amounts of drugs. This is because the body mechanisms that eliminate drugs from our system are less effective; our liver and kidneys do not work as quickly to excrete these substances from the body. Drug side effects become extremely common, and *most of them are not even recognized.* Instead, the side effects are thought of as problems in their own right. Common drugs like codeine can cause depression and sleepiness. Simple tranquilizers like Valium can muddy your thinking and your memory. Aspirin and other non-steroidal anti-inflammatory drugs become more irritating to your stomach, even though you may not feel the early symptoms as keenly. *Somewhere between 10 and 20% of hospital admissions for seniors are the direct result of medication side effects.* Most of the medications that cause the side effects were not medically required.

### Prevention

This potential problem needs constant attention. We tend to gradually accumulate an overflowing medicine chest. New drugs are started more frequently than older ones are discontinued. Your medication program is seldom reviewed as a whole, either by you or by your doctor.

There is only one sure way to avoid medication side effects, and that is to take no medications at all. At the most basic level, you should always ask yourself whether elimination of all medicines might be possible. If you think this might be possible, then talk it over with your doctor. At least, you and your doctor may develop a plan that involves many fewer medications, even if they cannot all be eliminated altogether.

You can stop taking over-the-counter drugs by yourself. Ask yourself if you really need the medication. Try for a while without it and see if any problems come up. Talk over any questions with your doctor. Repeat this process at least every six months and prune your medication list back to those that are truly essential.

## CATARACTS

### Process

The lens of the eye focuses the light on the retina and allows us to see well. As we age, the lens begins to accumulate scar tissue (cataracts), so that eventually, in many people, light does not penetrate through the lens as it should. Decreased vision, particularly at night, comes first. Ultimately, blindness can result. The same process is generally going on in both eyes, although often at quite different rates.

### Prevention

We don't know any way to prevent the scarring in the lens, although prolonged heavy exposure to bright sunlight without using sunglasses is suspected to speed the process. However, the medical problem of loss of vision can be effectively treated. Cataracts are treated by surgery. A surprising number of people do not notice the slow decrease in vision with cataracts and delay the corrective operations far too long. This results in needless decline in the quality of life. Be alert for loss of vision. Cover one eye and then the other and check to see if vision is equal. Be particularly alert for problems with depth perception or in seeing at twilight or after dark. Have a formal eye examination every few years, or more often if you seem to be having problems.

## CORNEAL OPACIFICATION

### Process

The cornea is the outer covering of the eye and is also a lens. The same things happen to it that happen to the lens of the eye, although usually later, and often less seriously. The process of the cornea becoming opaque (corneal opacification) can result in blindness.

### Prevention

There is no direct way to prevent corneal opacification. Fortunately, this is less common than cataracts of the lens. As with cataracts, you need to be alert for changes in vision, and you need to call these to the attention of a health professional. Corneal transplants and special types of contact lenses are very effective in countering this problem. The usual mistake is to wait too long for correction, thus decreasing the quality of life in the period before diagnosis and treatment.

## HEARING LOSS

### Process

The delicate hearing apparatus in the middle ear (and the eardrum itself) becomes stiffer with age, causing gradual loss of hearing in almost all individuals, with loss of high-tone hearing occurring before loss of lower-tone hearing. Loss of hearing obviously makes communication more difficult. Equally important, hearing loss decreases the input that you need to make your memory and your thinking work well. Many problems that are written off as "senility" turn out only to be problems with hearing loss.

### Prevention

There is no known way to prevent the occurrence of hearing loss (although once in a while the problem is only wax buildup in the ear canals). However, hearing aids and devices that restore hearing to essentially normal levels are readily available. Your task is to be sensitive to any loss of hearing and to take up the corrective measures early. Otherwise, a whole series of unnecessary problems of communication and apparent loss of intellect can result, and the quality of your life will be less than it should be.

## MEMORY LOSS

### Process

With age, the speed of transmission of impulses through our nerves slows. Our brains contain ever larger amounts of material to remember. We tend to lose the ability to concentrate as closely on new facts, names, and events. Many of the items in our memory will not have been remembered recently and thus will be in inactive parts of the brain for retrieval. Some medications affect memory. The sum of all these things results in occasional loss of memory, particularly for recent events. This is, unfortunately, usually ascribed just to "age." This then becomes a worrisome occurrence, resulting in fear that we are losing our minds and becoming senile.

### Prevention

The underlying physical processes are not preventable, but most of the manifestations are. Correcting hearing, decreasing medications that affect thinking, using lists to compensate, concentrating on new information by using specific techniques, and a variety of other approaches can help. You need to exercise your memory.

## MULTIPLE PROBLEMS

### Process

Most of the major diseases of our time are more common in the older patient. Diabetes, atherosclerosis, osteoarthritis, cancer, and the other major problems are more common with increasing age. And the older patient, with less organ reserve, may have several problems at once, thus creating special difficulties.

In Part IV, we have provided decision charts for dealing with the common problems that arise. The charts work almost all of the time for the young patient, but not as often for the patient who has more than one problem. If you already have one significant medical problem, a second one is more serious than if it occurred when you were in good health. Because the simple rules do not apply as well in this situation, you have to use more judgment. In general, a combination of problems is more serious than the sum of the problems dealt with by themselves.

### Prevention

One problem can easily complicate another. High blood pressure can increase kidney failure, which can increase blood pressure. A problem of breathlessness caused by the heart can complicate breathlessness caused by lung disease. Arthritis can increase inactivity, which leads to blood clots in the legs. Your approach to these problems must be a compromise in which all aspects of the situation are considered. You need a doctor to help you in these decisions much more often than in the uncomplicated, isolated illnesses of relative youth.

## MULTIPLE MEDICATIONS

### Process

In medical slang, using too many medications is called "polypharmacy." A patient may be taking a diuretic (water pill), a uricosuric to help eliminate the uric acid caused by the water pill, a tranquilizer for anxiety, a sedative to sleep, an antacid to settle the stomach, a hormone to replace lost glandular functions, a pain medication for arthritis, an anti-inflammatory agent for muscle aches, a laxative to help elimination, miscellaneous vitamins and minerals "just in case," iron for the blood, and additional medicines whenever a new problem comes up. This is polypharmacy, and it is often a prelude to disaster. It happens most often in an older patient, and usually the use of all the drugs has built up over a long time. Often the doctor prescribing a new agent is not even aware of the long list of drugs already being taken.

The side effects of these many medications add up and may cause illness. Even more important, the drugs may interact. Sedatives can dangerously slow the metabolism of coumadin, a blood-thinning drug. The action of the uric acid drug may be blocked by aspirin. Antacids can destroy the effectiveness of antibiotics. Anti-inflammatory drugs can cause retention of fluid, which requires a water pill, or diuretic, for relief. As we indicated, drug interactions are so complicated that no doctor or scientist fully understands them.

### Prevention

Use as few drugs as possible. No drug interactions can occur if only a single drug is taken. This is not possible for all patients at all times, but if your drug intake is minimal, your doctor can usually find combinations that are known to work well together.

These are our three general principles:

1. Avoid tranquilizers (nerve pills), sedatives (sleeping pills), and analgesics (pain pills) whenever possible. These drugs have many bad effects and often do not solve the problem.
2. Use lifestyle change instead of medication whenever possible. Avoiding salt in your diet is better than taking a "water pill," exercise programs can reduce the need for blood pressure medications, and weight reduction will usually work better than pills for diabetes. There are many other examples listed throughout this book.

3. Get rid of the optional medications. Crucial drugs make up less than 10% of all prescriptions in the United States. Over 1.5 billion prescriptions are written each year in our country; this represents eight prescriptions for every man, woman, and child. And the figure is much higher for the elderly.

In addition to tranquilizers, sedatives, and minor pain medications, optional drugs include anti-inflammatory drugs given in the absence of serious arthritis, allopurinol (Zyloprim) given for uric acid elevation without gout, diuretics (water pills) given for "fluid retention" in the absence of an actual disease, hormonal supplements that are not related to a disease, and the pills (oral hypoglycemics) given for adult diabetes. There are many others. This is not to say that these drugs are not beneficial on occasion, but more often they are not necessary. The decision to use them must be made with caution.

## *Principal Principles*

Your master plan for avoidance of problems of aging requires an underlying strategy, and a general strategy of six interrelated principles is outlined below.

### MAINTAIN INDEPENDENCE

Personal autonomy and confidence appear to be the underlying requirements for preservation of vitality. Psychologists have developed at least three theories to explain these observations.

- Health and avoidance of depression have been linked to the prevention of "helplessness," a feeling that there are no options, that nothing is worthwhile, and that there is no way to avoid the situation.
- A related theory uses the awkward term "locus of control" to differentiate those people who act as though they are in control of their environment (internal control) and those who act as though they are controlled by their environment (external locus of control).
- "Self-efficacy," the belief that you can control your own future in major ways, has been shown to improve health.

Whatever the theory, personal autonomy, planning for the future, looking forward, and taking care of yourself are all critically important.

### MODERATE YOUR HABITS

Healthy habits have already been discussed as a means to good health. They are even more important as a means of slowing the aging process. The cigarette smoker, heavy drinker, or fat person ages faster than his or her more moderate counterparts. And the avoidance of chronic diseases such as emphysema, cancer, and arteriosclerosis makes it much easier to maintain vigor in later life.

### KEEP ACTIVE

Exercise regularly and pleasurably, at least four days a week for at least 15 minutes a day. Use your muscles and build up your heart reserve. Your cells will become more efficient in the use of oxygen, and you will increase your stamina through the rest of the day. Stretching exercises will give you flexibility and help avoid muscle strain. Walk, jog, bicycle, or swim regularly. Play tennis or some other sport for fun. If you have a medical problem or if you are starting out in poor shape, take it slow and easy at first. There is no hurry, and you can take a year or more to get back into shape. But develop a lifelong habit and maintain it.

### BE ENTHUSIASTIC

The enthusiasm of youth is always tempered by the wisdom of years, and this is undoubtedly good in part. But it seems that our society sometimes places a value on passive acceptance of ill health. To stay young, you need to act young in some senses. This means that enthusiasm is perfectly permissible. What do you really want to do? Work, travel, participate in sports or a hobby? Do it. Plan ahead and savor the anticipation. Do new things, change hobbies, develop new skills. And enjoy them. You are not old as long as you look forward with real pleasure to anticipated events in the future.

### HAVE PRIDE

Psychologists use the term "self-image" in order to avoid some of the negative associations of the term "pride," but this is really what it is. "Pride" is a vice, but having a good "self-image" is a virtue. You must think well of yourself. Individuals with a low self-image are sick more often, become depressed, and appear to age more rapidly. Pride can take almost any form: such as pride in personal appearance, household maintenance, family, friends, work, a hobby, play. There are things that you do well. Be proud of what you do.

**BE INDIVIDUAL**

As you grow older, you are more and more unique. There is no one else with your particular set of life experiences, insights, and beliefs. These are your strengths, and they make you interesting to others. Cultivate this individuality. As you actively grow and change, your personal uniqueness increases. Your individuality is not set early in life but develops as you develop. Avoid conformity for its own sake, both with your peer group and with your own earlier behaviors and beliefs.

A frequent problem of increasing age is a monotony of inputs: the same newspaper, television programs, magazines, and set of acquaintances with pretty much the same opinions about everything. You need to vary your personal customs so that you are exposed to uncomfortable opinions, challenges to your established thinking, and new political input, so that your unique synthesis of the conflicting threads of our complex society can grow. This may entail new classes, seminars, hobbies, interest groups, or whatever. Don't let yourself become predictable. You are unique.

**CONCLUSION**

Avoiding and compensating for the declines of aging is in large part possible by use of your master plan. The independent senior life is the end of a chain of events, and you control most of the events in that chain. You want to seek optimal physical and mental health and thus achieve the life of your own choice. This is the essence of successful aging.

## *Avoiding AIDS and Other Infections*

The major infectious diseases of the past, such as smallpox and polio, have greatly decreased as national health problems. This is principally a result of preventive measures. Now, the major infectious disease threat to individuals below age 65 is a new disease, AIDS.

AIDS, the Acquired Immune Deficiency Syndrome, is caused by the Human Immunodeficiency Virus (HIV). This virus first was recognized to cause human illness in 1977. The virus attacks a particular group of the body's white blood cells (a subclass of the T lymphocytes) and persists for a long time in these cells. HIV destroys the cells' ability to fight off additional infections, and these infections are frequently fatal. This virus makes the important body defense mechanism, the immune system, deficient (unable to fight back). In contrast to immune deficiency syndromes that are present at birth, it is usually "acquired" during adult life when the individual becomes infected by HIV.

HIV is transmitted from person to person by body secretions—such as semen, vaginal secretions, or even breast milk—or by transfusion of infected blood. It can be transmitted to the fetus by an infected mother. Individuals infected with the virus are said to be "HIV-positive." In some, the immune system appears to remain intact; these individuals are not sick but still are able to infect others. In others, there are relatively minor symptoms such as fatigue and swollen lymph glands. Over time, the immune system is profoundly altered in the majority of infected individuals; after the first major infection, death will often follow within a year or two.

AIDS was first discovered in homosexual men who had had large numbers of sexual contacts. The frequency of sexual exposure greatly increases the probability of coming in contact with the virus. Seventy to 80% of all cases in North America continue to occur in gay men. Increasingly, however, cases are reported in intravenous drug abusers who become infected through contaminated needles and syringes, after heterosexual contacts with prostitutes, after other heterosexual contact, or in babies born to infected mothers.

Avoiding AIDS is largely a matter of avoiding "high-risk behaviors," such as taking illegal intravenous drugs. The number of different sexual contacts is critically important; the larger the number of possibilities for transmission of virus through different partners, the larger the risk. Gay men in stable, monogamous relationships are at little, if any, increased risk.

The problems with blood transfusions of a few years ago have been almost entirely eliminated because all blood is now tested for the presence of the virus before transfusion. The disease can *not* be transmitted by coughing or other non-intimate contact. Medical personnel do not appear to be at substantial risk, although they must take precautions, and the risk to patients from medical workers is extremely small.

Rapid progress in understanding AIDS is being made, but a vaccine or a cure is not yet available. A test that detects antibody to the virus with reasonable accuracy is available. Early studies with this test indicate that as many as 1 million people in the United States already have antibodies to the virus. This suggests that they have been exposed to and possibly infected by the AIDS virus—an alarming statistic for a virus that has been around for only a few years.

Control of this disease depends largely on quarantine of the virus through the collective health actions of individuals. We strongly urge the following three measures; they not only help prevent AIDS but also other sexually transmitted diseases and other serious infections such as hepatitis (inflammation of the liver) and septicemia (blood poisoning).

1. *Decrease the risk of sexual transmission.*

   Recognize that casual sexual activity, either homosexual or heterosexual, paid or free, can be hazardous and that the risk goes up with the number of different individuals involved. Avoid such promiscuity. Practice "safer sex." Regular and careful use of condoms (but not other birth control techniques) can greatly reduce but not eliminate the risk of infection.

2. *If you think you may have been at risk for infection, get tested.*

   The AIDS test actually detects the antibodies produced by someone infected with the virus. It takes up to 6 months for these antibodies to appear, so have yourself tested again if your result is negative, just to be sure. Do this not only for yourself but to avoid the tragedy of unknowingly spreading the disease.

3. *Lend your efforts to the war on drugs.*

   Do all that you can to influence friends and adolescents to avoid the many serious risks of these practices. Work with your community to decrease the overall risks.

CHAPTER 2

# *A Pound of Prevention: Five Keys to Health*

An ounce of prevention is better than a pound of cure. Think what a *pound* of prevention can do. Good news—there are only five major areas on which to work:

- Exercise
- Diet
- Smoking cessation
- Alcohol moderation
- Weight control

Actually, for most individuals, *you don't even need to worry about five areas, but fewer yet.* Probably, you are already a nonsmoker. Probably, your body weight is not too far from where it needs to be. Probably, your alcohol intake is already moderate. Probably, you already do some exercise, and, probably, you already have some good dietary practices. Make your own personal inventory of what needs attention. It may well be quite a short list. Make your choices, make your plan, and get along with it.

## *Exercise*

Exercise is the central ingredient of good health. It tones the muscles, strengthens the bones, makes the heart and lungs work better, and helps prevent constipation. It increases physical reserve and vitality. The increased reserve function helps you deal with crises. Exercise eases depression, aids sleep, and aids in every activity of daily life.

### THE THREE TYPES OF EXERCISE

There are stretching exercises, strengthening exercises, and aerobic (or endurance) exercises. You need to know the difference.

**Strengthening exercises** are the least important, and you can do them or not. These are the "body-building" exercises that build more bulky muscles. Squeezing balls, lifting weights, and doing push-ups or pull-ups are examples of strengthening exercises. These exercises can be very helpful in improving function in a particular body part after surgery (for example, knee surgery) where it is necessary to rebuild strength. Otherwise, do them only if you want to increase your strength.

It should go without saying, but you should never use steroids as part of a strengthening program; by so doing, you will damage your future health.

**Stretching exercises** are designed to keep you loose. These are a bit more important; everyone should do some of them, but they don't have many direct effects on health. As you age, you want to be careful not to overdo these exercises. Toe-touching exercises, for example, should be done gently. Do not bounce. Stretching should be done relatively slowly, to the point of early discomfort and just a little bit beyond.

Stretching exercises can be therapeutic in certain situations. If you have a joint that is stiff because of arthritis or injury, if you have just had surgery on a joint, or if you have a disease condition that results in stiffness, then stretching is usually important. There is nothing mysterious about the stretching process. Any body part that you cannot move through its full, normal range of motion needs to be repeatedly stretched. This enables you to slowly, often over weeks or months, regain motion of that part.

For most people, however, stretching exercises are useful mainly as a warm-up for aerobic (endurance) exercise activity. Gently stretching before you begin endurance exercise is important for three reasons: (1) It warms up the muscles, (2) it makes them looser, and (3) it decreases the chances of injury. Stretching afterward can help prevent stiffness.

**Aerobic (endurance) exercise** is the key to fitness. This is the most important kind of exercise. The word "aerobic" means that during the exercise period, the oxygen (air) that you breathe in balances the oxygen that you use up. During aerobic exercise, a number of body mechanisms come into play. Your heart speeds up to pump larger amounts of blood. You breathe more frequently and more deeply to increase the oxygen transfer from the lungs to the blood. Your body develops increased heat and compensates by sweating to keep your temperature normal. You build endurance.

During endurance exercise periods, the cells of the body develop the ability to extract a larger amount of oxygen from the blood. This increases function at the cellular level. As you become more fit, these effects persist. The heart becomes larger and stronger and can pump more blood with each stroke. The cells can take up oxygen more readily. As a result, your heart rate when you are resting doesn't need to be as rapid. This allows more time for the heart to repair itself between beats.

## YOUR AEROBIC PROGRAM

### Principles

Aerobic exercise is important for all ages. It is never too late to begin an aerobic exercise program and to experience the often dramatic benefits. There are, of course, a few difficulties in beginning a new exercise program. If you have been de-conditioned by avoiding exercise for some time, start at a lower level of physical activity than a more active person would. You may have an underlying medical condition that limits your choice of a particular exercise activity; if so, you should ask your doctor for advice about exactly how to proceed.

Some people worry (1) that exercise will increase their heart rates, (2) that they have only so many heartbeats in a lifetime, and (3) that they may be using them up. In fact, because of the decrease in their resting heart rates, fit individuals use 10 to 25% fewer heartbeats in the course of a day, even after allowing for the increase during exercise periods. Aerobic training also builds good muscle tone, improves reflexes, improves balance, burns fat, aids the bowels, and makes the bones stronger.

## Heart Rate

Much has been made of reaching a particular heart rate during exercise that avoids too much stress and yet provides the training effect. Cardiologists (heart specialists) often suggest that a desirable exercise heart rate is 220 minus your age times 75%. Table 5 lists these target values depending on your age. Usually, it is difficult to count your pulse while you are exercising; but you can check it by counting the pulse in your wrist for 15 seconds immediately after you stop exercising, and then multiply by 4.

More important, as your training progresses, you may wish to count your resting pulse, perhaps in bed in the morning before you get up. The goal here (if you do not have an underlying heart problem and are not taking a medication such as propranolol, which decreases the heart rate) is a resting heart rate of about 60 beats per minute. An individual who is not fit will typically have a resting heart rate of 75 or so.

We generally find this whole heart rate business a bit of a bother and somewhat artificial. There really are no good medical data to justify particular target heart rates. You may wish to check your pulse rate a few times just to get a feel for what is happening, but it doesn't have to be something you watch extremely carefully.

**TABLE 5** *Target Heart Rates During Exercise*

| *Age* | *Beats per Minute* | |
|---|---|---|
| 20 | 150 | |
| 30 | 142 | |
| 40 | 135 | |
| 50 | 128 | |
| 60 | 120 | (220 – your age) × 75% |
| 65 | 116 | |
| 70 | 112 | |
| 75 | 109 | |
| 80 | 105 | |
| 85+ | 101 | |

There are easier ways of telling how you are doing. Aerobic activity is a bit uncomfortable at first and then becomes quite comfortable as your training program persists. It is not "all-out." You should be able to carry on a conversation while you are exercising. On the other hand, you should sweat during each exercise period if the exercise is performed at normal temperatures of approximately 70°F or 20°C (except swimming, of course). Sweat indicates that the exercise has raised your internal body temperature.

Aerobic exercise is sustained activity for a period of time. You need at least 10 or 12 minutes of exercise each session. You can progress up to 200 minutes per week, spread out over five to seven sessions; beyond this amount, no further benefit seems to result.

## Aerobic Choices

Your choice of a particular aerobic activity depends on your own desires and your present level of fitness. The activity should be one that can be graded. That is, you should be able to easily and gradually increase the effort and the duration of the exercise.

Walking by itself is not often an aerobic exercise, but it provides very important health benefits. If you haven't been exercising at all, start by walking. A gradual increase in walking activity, up to a level of 100 to 200 minutes per week, usually should precede attempting a more aerobic program. Get in the habit of putting in the time first, then increase the effort. Walking briskly can be aerobic, but you need to push the pace quite a bit to break a sweat and get your heart rate up a bit. Walking uphill can quite quickly become aerobic.

Jogging, swimming, and brisk walking are appropriate for all ages. At home stationary bicycles or cross-country ski machines are good. We have seen people confined to bed using a specially designed stationary bicycle. Some individuals like to use radio earphones while they exercise; others exercise indoors while watching the evening news. Almost any activity from gardening to tennis can be aerobic for a few people, but remember that aerobic exercise can't be "start and stop." Aerobic activity can't come in bursts; it must be sustained for at least a 10- to 12-minute period.

## Cautions

If you have a serious underlying illness, particularly one involving the heart or the joints, or if you are over age 70, you should ask your doctor for specific advice. Advice from your doctor should always take precedence over recommendations in this book. For most people, however, a doctor's advice is not required in order to decide to start exercising. We recommend mentioning your exercise program to your doctor while on a routine visit for some other reason. A good doctor will encourage your exercise program and perhaps guide you in choosing goals and activities.

Some doctors will recommend that you have an electrocardiogram or an exercise electrocardiogram before you start exercising, particularly if you are over 50 years of age. It is difficult to see what this accomplishes because, (1) gentle, graded exercise is a treatment for heart problems anyway and, (2) the test produces 80% "false-positive" results. Many doctors (including us) don't think that these tests are necessary, regardless of age, unless there are specific, known problems. If a doctor recommends a coronary arteriogram before you begin an exercise program, you should seek a second opinion to see if this somewhat hazardous test is needed.

"Crash" exercise programs are always ill-advised. You have to start gently and go slowly. There is never a hurry, and there is some slight hazard in pushing yourself too far too fast. Age alone is *not* a deterrent to exercise. Many seniors who have achieved record levels of fitness, as indicated by world-class marathon times, have started exercising only in their 60s, 70s, or even 80s. Mount Fuji has been climbed by a man over 100 years of age.

## Getting Started

Assess your present level of activity. This is where you start from. Set goals for the level of fitness that you want to achieve. Your final goal should be at least one year away. You may want to develop in-between goals for what you would like to achieve at one, three, and six months. Select the aerobic activity you want to pursue. Choose a time of day for your exercise. Develop exercise as a routine part of your day. We like to see exercise regularly performed, every day, for at least five out of seven days of the week; this is more frequent than often recommended. If you exercise all seven days, take it easy one or two days each week. Younger individuals can frequently condition with exercise periods three times a week; but for seniors, more gentle activities performed daily are more beneficial and less likely to result in injury. You can make ordinary activities like walking or mowing the lawn aerobic by doing them at a faster and constant pace.

Start slowly and gently. Your total activity should not increase by more than about 10% each week. Each exercise period should be reasonably constant in effort. If you are walking, jogging, or whatever, you can use both distance and time to keep track of your progression. When starting out, it is a good idea to keep a brief diary of what you do each day to be sure you're on track. It is generally best to first slowly increase your weekly exercise time to a total of at least 90 or 100 minutes before you work to increase the effort level of the exercise. Get accustomed to the activity first and then begin to push it just a little bit. Again, progress slowly.

Be sure to loosen up (stretching exercises) before and after exercise periods and to wear sufficiently warm clothing to keep the muscles from getting cold and cramping. The bottom line is patience and common sense.

### Handling Setbacks

No exercise program ever progresses without any problems whatsoever. After all, you are asking your body to do something it hasn't done for a while. It will complain every now and again. Even after you have a well-established exercise program, there will be interruptions. You may be ill, take a vacation where it is difficult to exercise, or sustain an injury. Most people starting exercise programs have two or three minor injuries in the first year and thereafter have problems less frequently. Sprained ankles, tendinitis, falls, and even dog bites are common. There may be setbacks, but they shouldn't change your overall plan.

Common sense is the key to handling setbacks. Often you can substitute another activity for the one with which you are having trouble and thus maintain your fitness program. Sometimes you cannot, and you just have to lay off for a while.

When you start back again, don't try to start immediately at your previous level of activity; de-conditioning is a surprisingly rapid process. On the other hand, you don't have to start again at the beginning. The general rule is to take as long to get back to your previous level of activity as you were out. If you cannot exercise for two weeks, gradually increase activity over a two-week period to get back to your previous level.

### Topping Out

After your exercise program is well established, you need to make sure that it has become a habit you want to continue for a long time. As indicated, there is no medical evidence that more than 200 minutes a week of aerobic exercise is of additional value. This is about half-an-hour a day. Many people will not want to exercise this much, and that is perfectly fine. You can get most of the benefits with considerably less activity. At 100 minutes a week, you get almost 90% of the gain that you get with 200 minutes. At 60 minutes a week, a total of 1 hour, you get about 75% of the benefit that you get with 200 minutes. After you have a well-established exercise program, dropping the frequency back to three or four times a week is all right and will maintain fitness.

Exercise should be fun. Often it doesn't seem so at first, but after your exercise habits are well developed, you will wonder how you ever got along without them. Once you are fit, you can take advantage of your body's increased reserve to vary your activity a good bit more than you did during the early months. You can change exercise activities or alternate hard-exercise and easy-exercise days. At this point, we hope you are a convert to exercise programs. You then can work to introduce others to the same benefits.

## *Diet and Nutrition*

Several dietary considerations are important to a healthy life. In general, you should move slowly in making changes from your present diet. Most people don't like sudden, radical changes in diet, so they may give up such changes after a while. Instead, develop good dietary habits over a time span. The further you go, the greater the benefits. Table 6 provides a guideline for a healthy diet.

### FAT INTAKE

Excessive dietary fat and saturated fat comprise the worst food habit in the typical American diet. Saturated fat is the major cause of atherosclerosis, which leads to heart attacks and strokes. The government's *Healthy People 2000* goals are for people to reduce their total fat intake to less than 30% of the total calories they consume and their saturated fat intake to less than 10%. We think that many people should try for 20% and 7% since such stricter diets have been shown to *reverse* some

**TABLE 6** *Your Diet for Health*

| | |
|---|---|
| **Protein** | Slightly decrease total protein. Increase protein from whole-wheat grains, vegetables, poultry, and fish. |
| **Fat and Cholesterol** | Decrease total fat intake to less than 30% of total calories. Greatly decrease the saturated fats of whole milk, most cheeses, and red meat. Switch to vegetable oils, canola oil, soybean oil, corn oil, peanut oil, or olive oil. |
| **Carbohydrate** | Increase total carbohydrates, emphasizing whole-wheat grains, vegetables, cereals, fruit, pasta, and rice; these contain "complex" carbohydrates. |
| **Alcohol** | Moderate use or less; "moderate" is approximately 2 drinks daily. |
| **Fiber** | Increase fiber intake with emphasis on fresh vegetables and whole-wheat grains. |
| **Salt** | Decrease to about 4 grams (g) per day from the present average intake of 12g a day. Avoid added salt in cooking or at the table and heavily salted foods. Further decrease if medically recommended. |
| **Caffeine** | Limit to 300 milligrams (mg) a day or less, equivalent to 3 cups of coffee. |
| **Calcium** | Recommendations are at least 1000 mg per day for men and 1500 mg per day for women. Non-fat milk has 250 mg per glass. Use powdered non-fat milk in foods such as soup. If necessary, consider calcium supplementation as with calcium carbonate (Tums, Oscal). |

atherosclerotic plaques. In some cases, patches on the artery walls nearly disappear. Such improvements have been shown both in monkeys given high-fat diets and then normal diets and exercise, and by arteriographic studies (X-ray dye studies) of human hearts.

## Cholesterol

Serum cholesterol levels are one sign of a need to reduce dietary fat. A good level is 175 mg/dl or less. (Native Japanese on native diets average a serum cholesterol level of under 100!) This measurement is only a very rough guide to your dietary needs, however, and everyone will benefit from further decreasing fat intake. Serum cholesterol levels are only a very rough guide to your dietary needs, however. The actual chemistry of fats in the body is very complicated. The waxy white cholesterol is not only in your diet but is also manufactured by your liver. This production in turn is related to the various other fats in your diet. Attached to the cholesterol itself are high-density lipoproteins (HDL), which help *prevent* atherosclerosis, and low-density lipoproteins (LDL), which make serious problems much more likely. The LDL travels "outbound" from the liver and can deposit on the inside of vessel walls. The HDL takes cholesterol "inbound" back to the liver for excretion and can help remove plaque from arterial walls. Many laboratories measure serum cholesterol quite inaccurately. Hence, we are not too enthusiastic about using serum cholesterol levels as the sole measure of your own dietary needs.

You can simplify this whole complicated business by cutting down on the *largest* sources of the saturated fats in your diet. Fortunately, there are easy approaches to changing intake of these major foods.

- With **eggs**, you just have to cut down the number per week; two eggs a week is a good ration.
- For **butter**, use soft or liquid margarine instead. Some evidence suggests that solid margarines are not much different from butter.
- For **milk**, just use low-fat or non-fat milk. The calcium and other nutrients in milk are very good for you.
- For **animal fats**, don't eat these foods often. A good rule for many people is to avoid having red meat two days in a row. This is easy, and it gets variety into your diet. Remember, it is really the white fat in the red meat that is the problem. Pork, bacon, hot dogs, and sausage are not "red" but usually have a great deal of animal fat. When you do have meat, choose a less tender cut, trim the fat extensively before cooking, broil so that the fat burns or runs off during cooking, and cook the meat a little more well done.
- If at all possible, don't fry foods; this usually adds saturated fat. If you do fry, avoid saturated fats and palm oil and coconut oil; although vegetable oils, these two are also saturated fats and bad for your arteries. Monounsaturated fats—such as olive oil, peanut oil, and canola oil—may be actually good for you.

## PROTEIN

How to select good protein for your diet? Fish is excellent; you should plan at least two fish meals a week. Interestingly, the best fish for you are the high-fat fishes that live in cold water, such as salmon or mackerel. These contain a kind of fish oil that is good for your heart and actually lowers your serum cholesterol.

Chicken and other poultry are good neutral foods; they have less fat, although still some cholesterol. There is even less fat if you remove the skin. The official, national nutritional guidelines call for a substitution of complex carbohydrates (such as whole-wheat grains and cereals) for some of your fat intake and some of your protein intake.

## OTHER STEPS

What about other ways to lower your serum cholesterol and other blood lipids? There are some, and they are worth considering as you put together your own dietary plan. Fiber (as in vegetables, celery, apples, beans, whole-wheat grains, breads, and cereals) actually acts to lower serum cholesterol, as does Metamucil, by binding some cholesterol in the bowel. Adequate calcium intake, needed for strong bones, also lowers blood pressure and probably the blood lipids. Your exercise program lowers your total cholesterol and also increases the good HDL lipids in your blood. When you stop smoking, HDL goes up. Good health habits all seem to fit together.

What about fish-oil capsules? These contain the good fish oils such as those found in salmon and mackerel. Five capsules are about equivalent to one serving of salmon. They cost less than salmon. Thus, there is nothing really wrong with using them, but in general we're not much for taking pills. The capsules are big and hard to swallow, and the process is a bit artificial. Besides, cats may start to follow you around.

## DRUGS

What about taking one tablet of baby aspirin every other day to thin the blood? This should not replace dietary change! Despite the publicity, studies on the subject should be considered preliminary. There has been no decrease in total deaths between subjects taking aspirin every other day and control subjects. There has been a decrease in heart attacks, but this was compensated for by increases in other categories of sudden death, including strokes. We believe that this regimen should be undertaken only with your doctor's advice.

The same recommendation holds for new cholesterol-lowering drugs, as well as old ones like niacin and cholestyramine. We recommend people seriously discuss such medications with their doctor only if they continue to have high cholesterol and they are in one of the following groups:

- People who have already had a heart attack
- People with very high cholesterol levels, over 260 mg/dl
- People with a family member who had an early (before age 40) heart attack

Nevertheless, try a diet and exercise program first, second, and third. Medication is the fourth step if your doctor agrees.

### SALT INTAKE

Too much sodium (salt) in the system tends to retain fluid in the body, increasing the blood pressure and predisposing people to problems such as swelling of the legs. The heart has to work harder with the increased amount of blood volume. Thus, it is good to decrease salt intake.

The average person in the United States takes in about 12 grams (g) of sodium each day, one of the highest intakes in the world. Our convenience foods and our fast foods are usually loaded with salt. Salt is in ketchup, in most sauces, and in hidden form in many foods. You need to read the labels to find it: look for "sodium," not "salt." The recommended amount is 4 grams a day of salt for the typical person. You will get plenty without adding anything. Under a doctor's advice, patients with problems of high blood pressure, heart failure, or some other difficulties may need to reduce salt much more radically.

Do you have the typical craving for junk foods? Don't despair—there are healthy snacks! One of our favorites: popcorn, butterless, hot-air cooked, sprayed with butter-flavored PAM, and sprinkled with a little Parmesan cheese. Even better, try popcorn with olive oil instead of butter, unsalted peanuts in the shell, or French bread basted with olive oil and toasted with oregano or garlic.

### FIBER

Adequate fiber intake is one of the most popular recent health measures. It is much more than a fad. Fiber is the indigestible residue of food that passes through the entire bowel and is then eliminated in the stool. It is found in unrefined grains, cereals, vegetables—particularly celery—and some fruits.

The beneficial aspects of high-fiber intake come from the actions of the fiber as it passes through the bowel. Fiber attracts water and provides consistency to the stool so that it may pass easily. The increased regularity of bowel action that results turns out to be very important. It decreases the chances of **diverticulitis**, an inflammation of the colon wall. Diverticulitis results from excessive pressure in the colon and weakening of the wall. Fiber protects the bowel so that the development of pre-cancerous polyps is greatly reduced, as is the risk of cancer of the colon. Fiber also acts to decrease problems with constipation, hemorrhoids, tears in the rectal wall, and other minor problems as well as the big ones. Fiber binds cholesterol and helps eliminate it from the body.

We must emphasize that the natural-fiber or fiber-supplement approach to regularity of the bowel is *greatly* preferred over use of laxatives and bowel stimulants, which have none of the advantages of fiber. You need to get the fiber habit and avoid the stimulant and laxative habit.

## CALCIUM

Everybody needs enough calcium, and it is particularly important for seniors and even more important for senior women. Our national trend toward better health habits has decreased intake of calcium-containing milk and cheese. Hence, calcium intake for many people has dropped below what is desirable. Thus, calcium supplements are often needed. Women over age 50 should have at least 1500 milligrams (mg) of calcium each day and men over age 65 at least 1000 mg. A glass of non-fat milk contains about 250 mg of calcium. Add in the odds and ends of calcium in various foods and a typical daily intake is usually around 500 mg. Hence, many people need supplementation with calcium carbonate. The most popular forms are Tums and Oscal; each tablet contains 500 mg. One or two tablets a day will usually do it.

Remember the calcium "paradox" because it is important. Just taking the calcium in your diet doesn't really do anything. The reason is that the calcium is not, for the most part, absorbed from the bowel. You need both to take enough calcium *and* to provide the body a stimulus to *absorb* the calcium. For everybody, this stimulus should include weight-bearing exercise. For women after menopause, estrogen supplementation can be helpful, and this possible treatment should be discussed with your doctor.

## *Smoking*

Cigarette smoking kills 307,000 people in the United States each year. Lung cancer and emphysema are the best known and most miserable outcomes. However, accelerated development of atherosclerosis is numerically the most important problem resulting from smoking. This results in heart attacks and strokes, angina pectoris (heart pains), intermittent claudication (leg pains), and many other problems. Pipe and cigar smoking does not have the pulmonary (lung) consequences that cigarette smoking does, but can lead to cancer of the lips, tongue, and esophagus. Nicotine in any form has the same bad effects on the small blood vessels and thus advances the development of atherosclerosis.

It is never too late to quit. Only two years after stopping cigarette smoking, your risk of heart attack returns to average. It has actually decreased substantially the very next week! Most people have plenty of time to get major health benefits. After ten years, your risk for lung cancer is back to nearly normal. After only two years, there is a decrease in lung cancer risk by perhaps one-third. The development of emphysema is arrested for many people when they stop smoking, although this condition does not reverse.

Moreover, you will notice at once that your environment has become more friendly when you are not a smoker. A lot of the daily hassles that impair the quality of your life go away when you stop offending others by this habit.

Here are some tips for quitting:

- Decide firmly that you really want to do it. You need to believe that you can do it. Set a date on which you will stop smoking. Announce this date to your friends. When the day comes, stop.
- You can expect that the physical addiction to nicotine may make you nervous and irritable for a period of about 48 hours. After that, there is no further *physical* addiction. There is, of course, the psychological craving that sometimes lasts a very long period of time. Often, however, it is quite short.
- Reward yourself every week or so and buy something nice with what would have been cigarette money.

- Combine your stop-smoking program with an increase in your exercise program. The two changes fit together naturally. Exercise will take your mind off the smoking change, and it will decrease the tendency to gain weight in the early weeks after stopping smoking; this is the only negative consequence of stopping.

The immediate rewards include better-tasting food, happier friends, less cough, better stamina, more money, fewer holes in your clothes, and membership in a larger world.

Many health educators are skeptical about cutting down slowly and stress that you need to stop completely. We don't think this is always true. For some people, rationing is a good way to get their smoking down to a much lower level and then at that point it may be easier to stop entirely. For example, the simple decision not to smoke in public can help your health and decrease your daily hassles. To cut down, only keep in the cigarette pack those cigarettes that you are going to allow yourself that day. Smoke the cigarettes only halfway down before extinguishing them.

There are now many good stop-smoking courses being offered through the American Cancer Society, the American Lung Association, or your local hospital. Most people actually don't need these, but if you do, they can help you be successful. Try by yourself first. Then, if you still need help, there is a lot of it around.

Nicotine chewing gum can help some people quit, and your doctor can give you a prescription and advice. Don't plan on this as a long-term solution because the nicotine in the gum is just as bad for your arteries as the nicotine in cigarettes.

An example of your ability to make your own choices is afforded by the challenge to stop smoking. If you are trapped by your addictions, even the lesser ones, you can't make your own choices. Victory over smoking improves your mental health, in part because this is a difficult victory. It can open the door to success in other areas.

## *Alcohol*

Excessive alcohol intake is a serious problem for some people in every age group. Drinking too much leads to depression, danger, and disease. Among the potentially fatal complications are alcohol poisoning, damage to the liver and kidneys, delirium tremens (the DTs) from withdrawal, and accidents in which alcohol plays a role. There are many other problems that are not fatal but difficult to endure. A drinking problem also makes a person dependent on the next drink, interferes with emotions and thinking, and burdens loved ones, diminishing everyone's quality of life.

Fortunately, alcoholism is a disease from which many people recover, although it is a lifelong process. There are about a million recovered alcoholics in this country, and between half and three-quarters of the people who attempt rehabilitation succeed. Success depends on personal characteristics, early treatment, the quality of counselors or a support program, access to the right medical services, and the strong support of family, friends, and co-workers. Among some highly motivated groups, the success rate is much higher. For example, more than 90% of physicians and airline pilots who go into highly-structured, monitored programs stay in recovery.

We discuss the warning signs and treatment of alcoholism on page 392. Please refer to this section if you have any questions about drinking. Usually, this problem gets too little attention too late. Keep your mind open to problems in family and friends, express your concerns to them, and cooperate in helping them establish a program for alcohol control or elimination. You can save their lives, and perhaps even save your own.

## *Obesity*

Excessive body weight compounds many health problems. It stresses the heart, the muscles, and the bones. It increases the likelihood of hernias, hemorrhoids, gallbladder disease, varicose veins, and many other problems. Excess weight makes breathing more difficult. Additional weight slows you down, makes you less effective in personal encounters, and lowers your self-image. Fat people are hospitalized more frequently than are people with normal weight; they have more gallbladder problems, more surgical complications, more cases of breast cancer, more high blood pressure, more heart attacks, and more strokes.

Weight control is a difficult task. Think of "weight control" as "fat control," and it will fit in well with your other good health habits. Excess weight is very seldom due to thyroid disease or other specific illness. For most of us, the problem and the solution are personal, not medical. As with the other habits that change health, management of this problem begins with its recognition as a problem. Weight control requires continued attention. For those of us with a potential problem, the vigilance must be lifelong.

Increasingly, exercise is being seen as an important key to weight control. Part of every weight-control program should be an exercise program. Obesity is not just the result of overeating; obese people, when studied carefully, are found to move around less and therefore burn too few calories. There is nothing very mysterious about calories. Thirty-five hundred calories equals about one pound. If you take in 3500 calories less than you burn, you lose one pound. If you take in 3500 more than you burn, you gain one pound. If you want your horse to lose weight, you just give him less hay.

There are two important phases to weight control: the weight-reduction phase and the weight-maintenance phase. The **weight-reduction phase** is the easiest. Here, the method you use to lose weight doesn't matter too much, although you should check with your doctor if you plan to lose a large amount of weight quickly. You want to be sure that the diet you intend to follow is sound. During the weight-loss stage, many of your calories are provided by your own body fat and protein as they are being broken down. Thus, you need little or no fat and much less protein in your diet during this period. Complex carbohydrates are important to most sound diets. Diets usually have a gimmick of some kind that encourages you and helps you remember the diet.

Most people have some success in losing weight. If you set a target, tell people what you are trying to do, and stick with it for a while, you can probably lose weight. Remember that it has to go slowly; even a total fast will cause true weight loss of less than one pound a day. Rapid changes in weight are generally due to loss of fluid. When you eat less, you usually eat less salt as well. The first few days of a diet give you a false sense of accomplishment as you lose some of the fluid that the salt was retaining in your body. Then, when the rate of weight loss slows, you may think that the diet has failed. You have to be patient with the weight-loss phase. One pound a week is a reasonable goal. This requires elimination of the equivalent of one day's food each week.

The **weight-maintenance phase** involves staying at the desirable weight you have now achieved. This is more difficult, and it requires constant attention. Weigh yourself regularly and record the weight on a chart. Draw a red line at three pounds over your desired weight and maintain the weight below the line, using whatever method works best for you. Keep exercising. Accept no excuses for increasing weight; it is easier and healthier to make frequent small adjustments in what you eat than to try and counteract binges of overeating with dieting. Keep yourself off the dietary roller coaster.

## *Other Health Habits*

An old joke maintains that everything that is pleasurable is either illegal, immoral, or fattening. This is exactly the wrong idea. Health is pleasurable; ill health is miserable. Good health habits have their own immediate reward. If changes toward healthier behaviors are making you feel less well, you are doing something wrong. Exercise makes you feel better. Good diets make you feel better. Nicotine avoidance makes you feel better. Having a good body weight makes your life activities easier and more pleasurable.

Much that is written about healthy behaviors makes the whole process seem mysterious and very complicated. The tabloids in supermarkets are always reporting some new threat to your health. Here we have tried to emphasize only the important and the proven. Only five areas require your attention:

- Exercise
- Diet
- Smoking cessation
- Alcohol moderation
- Weight control

There is a long list of other possible threats to health, but they have two problems. First, they often are not adequately proven to be actual threats. Second, even if they do prove to be true, they aren't very important compared with the big five discussed above. Fix these five first. As for other concerns, common sense can help you keep your priorities right. We do suggest moderation in barbecued foods because of possible cancer-causing risks, but only if you are having such meals more than 30 times a year. And many people may find a benefit in controlling caffeine intake, particularly in the evening. Even these suggestions are not scientifically very well established, and changes here are of less importance than changes in the five major areas.

CHAPTER 3

# Professional Prevention

Most prevention is personal. But, to take care of yourself, you will also sometimes require professional help. Medicine in recent years has been oriented to "cure" rather than prevent, even though most of the greatest medical successes, such as eradication of smallpox and control of paralytic polio, have been achieved through preventive measures. We have been crisis-oriented: our approach has been to wait for a consequence to appear and then try to treat it.

Today, interest is appropriately focusing on preventive medicine. The most important part of preventive medicine, moderating health habits, was discussed in the first two chapters. The idea of preventive medicine also includes the following five strategies, which involve health professionals as well as you, and it is important to understand both their strengths and their limitations:

- The checkup or periodic health examination
- Multiphasic screening
- Early treatment
- Immunizations and other public health measures
- Health-risk appraisal

# *The Myths of the Annual Checkup*

The "annual checkup" is still recommended by some schools, camps, employers, and the army. However, doctors seldom go to each other for routine checkups, nor do they send their families. The complete "executive physical," made popular a few years ago by large corporations that wished to ensure the health of their most critical employees, is slowly being discontinued. Even these elaborate checkups do not detect treatable diseases early with any regularity, and they may raise false confidence. That is, they encourage the false belief that if you are regularly checked you do not need to concern yourself as much about personal health maintenance, the theme of this book.

Your primary interest is in finding conditions about which something can be done, and for this the checkup is unfortunately not very successful. If you use the techniques described in Chapters 1 and 2 and attend to new symptoms as discussed in Part IV, there are very few advantages to be gained from the annual checkup. Nearly everyone now agrees that an annual physical examination is not indicated; decreases in screening have recently been recommended by a national Canadian task force and by the American Cancer Society.

There are a few areas in which periodic screening is most necessary, and it is important to keep them in mind:

- **High blood pressure** is a significant medical condition that gives little warning of its presence. During adult life, it is advisable to have your blood pressure checked at least every year or so. This measurement can easily be done by a nurse, physician's assistant, or nurse's aide; a full examination is not required. If high blood pressure is found, a doctor should confirm it, and you should carefully attend to the measures needed to keep it under control (see "High Blood Pressure," page 207).
- If you are a woman over age 25, you should have a **Pap smear** taken every year or so. Some authorities now recommend beginning Pap-smear testing at the age of beginning sexual activity, decreasing frequency to every 3 to 5 years after the first 3 are negative, and again increasing the frequency to every 1 or 2 years after age 40. This test detects cancer of the womb (cervix), and in early stages this cancer is almost always curable. See Chapter P, "Women's Health," for more information on Pap smears and instructions on breast self-examination.

- Women over age 25 should practice **breast self-examination** monthly. Any suspicious changes should be checked out with a doctor; the great majority of breast cancers are first detected as suspicious lumps by the patient. Women with large breasts cannot practice self-examination with as much reliability as other women and may wish to discuss other screening procedures with their doctor. In general, we do not like to recommend mammography as a screening procedure for women below age 50, but others believe it should start at age 40. Women who have already had a breast tumor should follow their doctor's recommendation. Women with a strong history of breast cancer in their family should begin with mammography by age 40.
- A test for **glaucoma** (a treatable disease that can cause blindness) should be done every few years after age 40 if there is a family history of glaucoma. Most cases of this disease are discovered during eye examinations, so it is generally advisable that such examinations include a routine check for glaucoma.
- **Dental checks** can save teeth, and regular dental examinations are recommended. The primary purpose of an annual dental examination is to find and fill cavities and to correct early gum disease; the benefits of other aspects of the examination ritual are less well established. Of course, your own preventive care is the most important factor of all.
- Screening tests of urine, tests for blood in the stool after age 30, and regular sigmoidoscopy after age 50 are of more dubious value. Some doctors feel that these are worthwhile, and others do not.

The importance of these few examinations is underscored by their availability as a public service, free of charge, at many city and county clinics. These are the most crucial elements of periodic checks; others are optional and controversial. The National Blue Cross/Blue Shield Association recently commissioned 12 papers by leading experts to assess the clinical literature on screening procedures. Their recommendations are summarized in Table 7 and are closely similar to our feelings about screening.

Note that after age 40 or 50, there are screening tests that you should consider. Try to arrange these together with a doctor's visit for another reason so as not to require a special trip for screening.

**TABLE 7** *Recommended Adult Screening Procedures*

| *Procedure* | *Recommendation* |
|---|---|
| **Pap smear for cervical cancer** | Annually for 3 years starting at age 20, or when sexual activity begins, whichever is earlier. If these 3 tests are negative, every 2 to 3 years from then on. |
| **Fecal occult blood tests for colo-rectal cancer** | Annually after age 50 |
| **Sigmoidoscopy for colo-rectal cancer** | Every 3 to 5 years after age 50<br>If family history of colon cancer in parent or sibling, air-contrast barium enema and sigmoidoscopy every 3 to 5 years after age 40 |
| **Breast cancer screening** | Monthly self-examination<br>Yearly physician examination after age 40<br>Mammography annually after age 40 or 50; after age 40 if family history of breast cancer in mother or sister |
| **Lung cancer screening** | Screening *not recommended* |
| **Asymptomatic coronary artery disease screening** | Screening with exercise stress testing *not recommended*<br>Screening with resting electrocardiogram *not recommended* |
| **Serum cholesterol and triglycerides screening** | Cholesterol at intervals of 5 or more years to age 70<br>Screening serum triglycerides *not recommended* |
| **High blood pressure screening** | Recommended, incidental to other health-care services |
| **Diabetes screening** | A glucose tolerance test recommended for pregnant women between the 24th and 28th week of gestation or women with a family history of diabetes who are planning to become pregnant.<br>Otherwise *not recommended* |
| **Osteoporosis screening** | Screening *not recommended* |

Are "complete" checkups ever worthwhile? Yes. The first examination by a new doctor allows you to establish a relationship with the doctor. Increasingly, the periodic checkup is being used not as much for the detection of disease as for the opportunity to counsel the patient about the health habits described in Chapters 1 and 2, so that patients can do a better job of disease prevention. We applaud this change and look to doctors to further refine their skills at influencing their patients to take care of themselves.

## *Early Treatment*

An effective health maintenance strategy includes seeking medical care promptly whenever an important new problem or finding appears. You should seek medical attention without delay if you notice one of the following symptoms:

- A lump in your breast
- Unexplained weight loss
- A fever for more than a week
- You have begun to cough up blood

These may not represent true emergencies, but they do indicate that professional attention should be sought within a few days. Most times, nothing will be seriously wrong; on other occasions, however, an early cancer, tuberculosis, or other treatable disease will be found.

The guidelines of Part IV of this book can help you select those instances in which you should seek medical care. In many cases, you can take care of yourself with home treatment. However, you must respond appropriately when professional care is needed.

To ensure timely treatment, you need to have a plan. Think things through ahead of time.

- Do you have a doctor?
- If you need emergency care, where will you go? To an emergency hospital? To the emergency room of a general hospital? To the on-call physician of a local medical group?
- If you are not sure what to do after consulting this book, who can you call for further advice?
- Have you written down the phone numbers you need?

Only rarely will you need emergency services. But the time that you need them is not the time to begin wondering what to do. If you have a routine problem that requires medical care, where will you go? Is there a nearby doctor? Who has your medical records? Chapter 4, "Finding the Right Doctor," and Chapter 6, "Choosing the Right Medical Facility," will help you answer these questions. But plan ahead.

## *Immunizations*

Immunizations have had far greater positive impact on health in the developed nations than all of the other health services put together. Only a few years ago, smallpox, cholera, paralytic polio, diphtheria, whooping cough, and tetanus killed large numbers of people. These diseases are now effectively controlled by immunization in the United States and in most other developed nations. Smallpox has been eradicated from the entire world, and there is no longer any need for smallpox immunization. An incredible success story!

Frequent immunization is not needed now because these diseases occur less often and because we now know that the immunizations provide protection for a long time. Thus, tetanus boosters are only required every ten years for adults who have had the basic series of tetanus injections. As these conditions become rare, the problems of side effects from the inoculations are in some instances as great as the risk of the illness.

Keep a careful record of your immunizations in the back of this book. Do not allow yourself to be reinoculated just because you have lost records of previous immunizations. If you haven't had a tetanus shot for ten years or so, ask for a booster shot while visiting the doctor for another reason. You can save future trips to the doctor by being protected for the next ten years. In general, do not seek out the optional immunizations. Flu shots, for example, are only partially effective and often cause a degree of illness themselves; they are recommended only for the elderly and for those with severe major diseases. Table 8 lists the recommended immunization schedule.

**TABLE 8** *Recommended Immunization Schedule*

| *Age* | *Immunization* |
|---|---|
| **Newborn** | Hepatitis B (also as directed by doctor) |
| **2 months** | DPT (diphtheria, pertussis, tetanus), OPV (oral polio virus), and HIB (*hemophilus* influenza type B) |
| **4 months** | DPT, OPV, and HIB |
| **6 months** | DPT, OPV (in certain areas only, not in the United States), and HIB |
| **15 months** | Measles, Mumps, Rubella, and HIB |
| **18 months** | DPT and OPV |
| **4–6 years** | DT (diphtheria, tetanus) and OPV |
| **5–18 years** | Measles, Mumps, Rubella |
| **Every 10 years** | T(d) (adult tetanus, diphtheria) |

We recommend that the optional immunizations (including mumps, hepatitis, pneumovac, and flu) be taken only on the recommendation of your doctor. In general, do not demand these inoculations. They have a definite role for some people, but not for all.

## *Health-Risk Appraisal*

Your future health *is* largely determined by what you do now. As discussed in Chapter 1, your lifestyle and your habits have a dominant influence on how healthy you are, how healthy you will be, how much time you will spend in hospitals, and how rapidly you will "physiologically" age.

Recently, techniques have been developed for mathematically estimating your future health risks, and these techniques are variously termed "health-risk appraisal," "health-hazard appraisal," or "health assessment." You complete a questionnaire or otherwise provide information about your lifestyle and health habits. Your responses are mathematically combined to complete estimates of your likelihood of developing major medical problems such as heart disease and cancer. Other estimates such as your "physiologic" age also may be calculated. These techniques form an increasingly important part of comprehensive health-education programs, such as Healthtrac, Senior Healthtrac, and the Taking Care Program of the Center for Corporate Health Promotion. These techniques also have a potentially large role in helping you shape your own personal health program.

There are several things that you should know about health appraisals.

1. The results are only estimates. Even though based on the best medical studies, such as the Framingham study, data from these studies are incomplete and may not apply equally to all populations. In general, the estimates may be accurate to within 10 or 20%. Think of health-risk scores as similar to IQ or achievement-test scores; they are approximately correct but not exact.
2. The predictions are only averages, and some people will do better than predicted and others worse.
3. Any single assessment represents you at one point in time, while your actual risks depend on the changes that you make and your average lifetime health habits as well. Regular repeated assessments can help show your current status and the benefits you have achieved by lifestyle changes.
4. A good health-risk appraisal should be based only on those relatively few risk factors that are scientifically well established and that are associated with major health problems. These include cigarette smoking, exercise, automobile seat-belt use, alcohol intake, obesity, salt, fat intake, blood pressure, cholesterol levels, stress level, and dietary fiber.
5. The assessment itself provides no health benefits unless it results in changes in your health-related behaviors, and the assessment might even increase anxiety.

Therefore, these assessments are best used as part of a program that not only identifies risk, but educates, motivates for change, provides suggestions and recommendations, and reinforces positive effects.

We are enthusiastic about the growing role of health-promotion programs that focus attention on prevention of disease and about the use of good health-assessment tools. Well-designed programs are already having a large effect on decreasing human illness.

## *Summary*

- You don't need frequent checkups if you feel well, except for a few specific tests. Blood pressure, Pap smears, breast examination, glaucoma testing, and dental checks are the most important; most people will not even need all of these. Most of these procedures can be obtained through public health departments at city or county expense. Take your doctor's advice concerning the need for a urinalysis, urine culture, tests of the stool for blood, rectal examination, or sigmoidoscopy.
- Elaborate physical examinations or multiphasic screening may detect trivial abnormalities and thus worry you unnecessarily.
- Complete physical examinations should include counseling on health habits.
- You should have a plan for obtaining medical care before the need arises.
- You should be immunized according to recommended schedules, but you need "boosters" only occasionally in adult life.
- Health-risk appraisal, as part of a comprehensive health-promotion program, can be beneficial to your health.

If you follow these general principles and if you moderate your habits as discussed in the first two chapters, you are well on the way toward taking care of yourself.

# PART II

# *Working with Your Doctors*

CHAPTER 4

# Finding the Right Doctor

Who is the right doctor for you? There are all kinds of doctors, and the distinctions among them can be confusing. This chapter is designed to help you understand the different types of doctors and how they conduct their medical practices. This chapter contains some guidelines to help you choose the right doctor for you and your family.

## The Family Doctor

The primary-care physician, who used to be termed a "GP" or "general practitioner," is now commonly called a "family practitioner." The family practitioner is a specialist, too, and has had several years of advanced training in family practice. A specialist in internal medicine or pediatrics also often serves as a primary-care physician.

Primary-care physicians represent the initial contact between the patient and the medical establishment. They accept responsibility for the continued care of a patient or a family and perform a wide variety of services. Usually, they have had some training in internal medicine, pediatrics, and gynecology. In the past, primary-care physicians performed both major and minor surgery; but in recent years, this practice has become much less common, and the family doctor will usually refer major surgical problems to surgeons. Obstetrics and gynecology, the female specialties, are not always handled by primary-care physicians.

Family practitioners serve as the quarterbacks of the medical system, and may direct and coordinate activities they do not perform personally. Other than the patient, the primary-care physician makes the most important decisions in medicine by determining the nature and severity of the problem, as well as recommending approaches to its solution.

## *The Specialists*

The five major clinical specialties are:

- Internal medicine
- Surgery
- Pediatrics
- Obstetrics and gynecology
- Psychiatry

There are other specialties such as radiology, clinical pathology, and anesthesiology, but they are not included in Figure 1 because the patient seldom goes directly to such doctors.

The largest specialty is internal medicine. Doctors may refer to this specialty as "medicine" and to its practitioner as an "internist." The internist is sometimes confused with the "intern." An intern is a recent medical school graduate who is undergoing hospital apprenticeship in any specialty; an internist is a specialist in internal medicine and has usually completed three or more years of training after graduation from medical school. Each of the other specialties and family practice has a similar length of training. As noted, family practice is now a specialty as well, although often not referred to as such.

## *The Subspecialists*

Subspecialties have developed within the major specialty areas (*see* Figure 1). In **internal medicine**, there is a specialist for nearly every organ system. Thus, cardiologists specialize in the heart;

**FIGURE 1** *Types of Doctors*

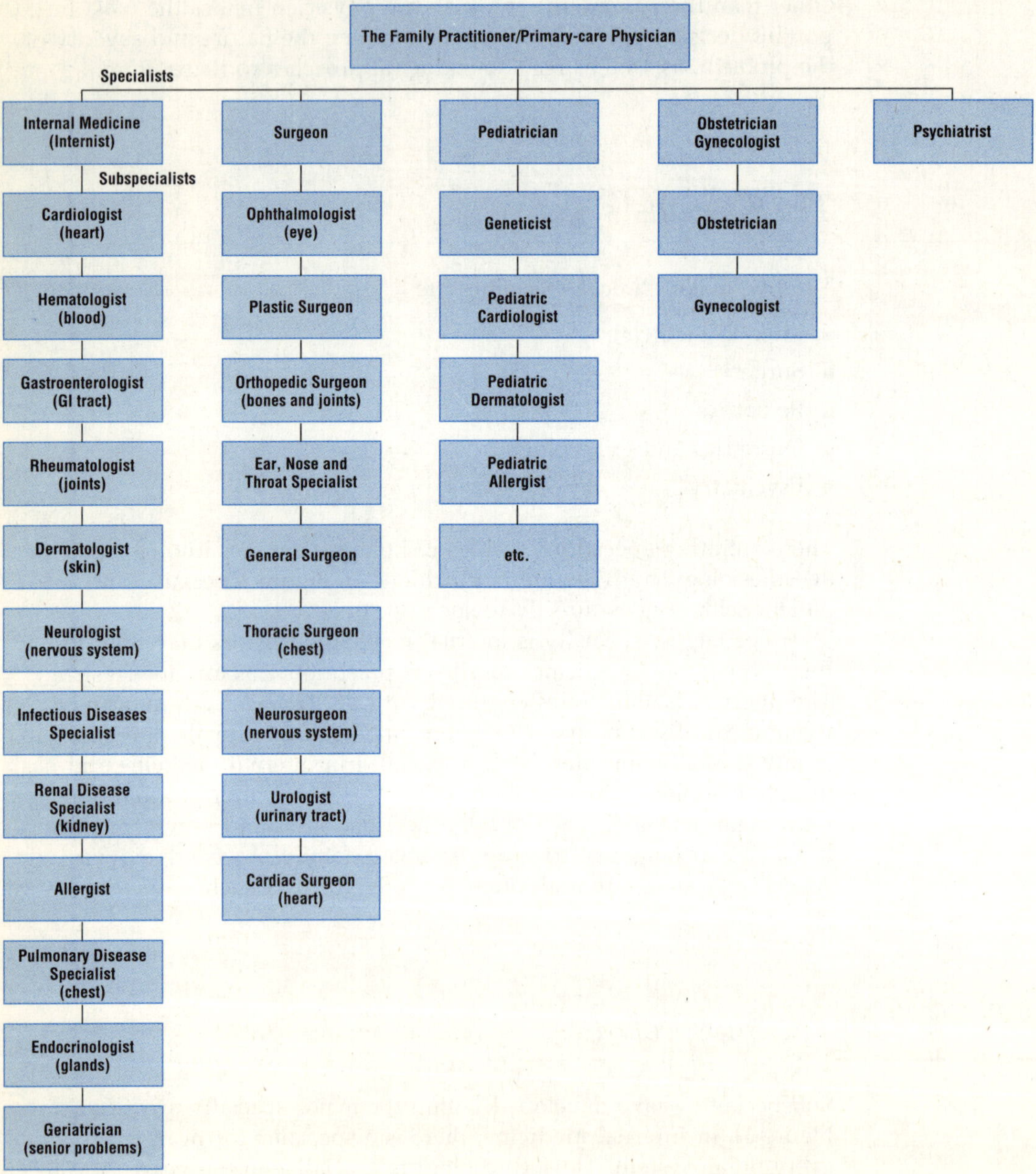

dermatologists, the skin; neurologists, the nervous system; renal disease specialists, the kidneys; and so forth. Dermatology and neurology are often separate departments now and are not necessarily included in the specialty of internal medicine.

Within **surgery**, different types of operations have defined the specialties. The ophthalmologist operates on the eyes; the ENT specialist on ears, nose, and throat; the thoracic surgeon in the chest; and the cardiac surgeon on the heart. The general surgeon operates in the abdominal cavity as well as other areas.

Within childhood medicine, or **pediatrics**, specialties have developed similar to those within adult internal medicine. In addition, because certain problems, particularly genetic and developmental ones, are more common in children, subspecialties unique to pediatrics have developed.

Increasingly, the specialty **obstetrics and gynecology** has been divided and is practiced by the obstetrician who delivers babies and the gynecologist who deals with diseases of the female organs.

**Psychiatry** does not have formal subspecialties, but a variety of schools of psychotherapy exist, such as Freudian and Jungian. Recently, obesity, alcoholism, and other specific problems have become subjects for separate disciplines within psychiatry.

There are other specialties and other names for doctors, and the full classification is more complicated than that which we show in Figure 1. For example, where does the podiatrist fit? The physiatrist? The chiropractor? But for most purposes you will find that Figure 1 is a good guide.

The different kinds of doctors provide their services under various arrangements: sometimes they practice alone, sometimes in groups, often under different financial conditions. You should know the strengths and weaknesses of each. By combining the right doctor with your medical and financial needs, you have a better chance of good medical care.

In recent years, busy solo practitioners have sometimes employed "nurse practitioners" or "physician's assistants" to enable them to care for a larger number of patients. Experience to date indicates that these health professionals, who are not doctors, provide excellent care in many areas of medicine.

## *Paying the Bill*

### FEE-FOR-SERVICE

The quality of medical care is not determined by the method of payment; nevertheless, there are psychological factors in payment arrangements that everyone should understand.

"Fee-for-service" is an awkward term that describes the traditional method of paying the doctor in the United States. A service is performed, and payment is given for that service. The more services provided, the higher the patient's bill and the higher the doctor's income. Nearly everyone else in the United States is paid by salary or by the hour, and piecework payment for physician services has been severely criticized by some.

When payment is determined by the number of services, customer satisfaction becomes important to the doctor. A good bedside manner may be developed, and extra services may be provided in response to special problems. Because considerable effort is expended in maintaining the relationship with the patient, respect of doctors by patients tends to be greatest in areas where doctors are paid for each service.

On the other hand, problems have been attributed to this payment system. It has been charged that patients have been seen too frequently, given too many medications and too many shots, had too many diagnostic procedures performed, and undergone too much surgery as a result of this financial incentive. Studies have suggested that doctors in the fee-for-service setting provide more services than doctors paid by salary. Controversy remains as to whether these additional services represent better care or simply greater expense.

### PRE-PAID PRACTICE

In pre-paid practice, a group of doctors offers a plan that looks like an insurance policy but actually represents a rearrangement of the traditional incentives. The patient knows in advance the medical expenses for the year. A set monthly amount is paid regardless of whether the medical facility is used frequently or not at all. When the patient needs a doctor, little or no additional expense is involved. The doctor is now given an incentive to minimize the number of services provided because the amount of money to be earned is already determined.

Advocates of pre-payment have argued that the doctor now has an incentive toward preventive medicine and will try to prevent illness rather then just treating it once it occurs. Some observers doubt that this is true; it is evident in some pre-paid group practices that little attention is given to preventive medicine. However, pre-paid group practices do decrease the overall cost of medical care, usually at a savings of approximately 20%; this is achieved by a lower use of expensive hospital care. Studies that compare the quality of medical care under the different payment conditions have not shown a difference. Many new kinds of prospective payment are currently under study. This kind of payment mechanism is rapidly becoming more frequent.

Of course, some patients are not happy with pre-paid group practices. The most common complaints are that it takes too long to get an appointment and that the choice of doctors is restricted. Pre-paid systems may be burdened by a few patients who overuse the system; 25% of the patients may use 75% of the services. The excessive services received by these few people increase the payments for the rest. The doctor is now given the incentive to minimize the number of services provided because the amount of money is already determined. The dedication of most doctors works to counteract these financial forces. Indeed, surveys indicate that patient satisfaction with pre-paid practice is about the same as with fee-for-service practice.

Many pre-paid plans now do not have a specific building or hospital. Rather, they are relatively loose associations of doctors who have agreed to practice under a pre-paid (capitation) mechanism. A doctor may be participating in several such plans. In principle, this may allow you to have your own doctor and to have a pre-paid plan, too, but in practice there are sometimes restrictions on the care that may be provided.

## *Managed Care*

You will hear more and more about managed care because it is at the heart of the debate over how to control medical care costs. Managed care may keep your premiums down and protect you against unnecessary surgery and hospitalization. On the other hand, some decisions are no longer solely up to you and your doctor, and payment depends on how you follow the health plan's guidelines. Regardless, managed care is here to stay and may be expected to increase in the future.

## HOW IS CARE MANAGED?

Although most managed care plans use financial incentives for doctors and hospitals to reduce medical care costs, they also use some combination of the following management techniques.

### Pretreatment Review and Authorization

Certain types of treatment plans, usually those involving surgery or hospitalization, must be reviewed before treatment begins. The review is usually done by a specially trained nurse who talks to both you and your doctor. Restrictions may be placed on the treatment: For example, laboratory testing must be done before entering the hospital, the number of hospital days is limited, or surgery must be done on an outpatient basis. Occasionally, the treatment may be rejected as inappropriate. If you don't obtain a pretreatment review and comply with the terms of the authorization, the plan usually pays less or nothing for the treatment.

### Concurrent Review

The plan reviews treatment and/or hospitalization while it goes on. This review can take into account changes that have occurred since treatment began, such as surgical complications, infections acquired in the hospital, or problems occurring in a mother or child after birth. You may not be aware of a concurrent review since the specialized nurses who perform it rely primarily on hospital records and talking to the physician. This review may result in a change to the authorized treatment plan, such as more days in the hospital. Again, failure to comply with the terms of the authorization usually results in the plan paying less for treatment.

### Case Management

In prolonged, complex, and expensive treatments, a case manager, usually a nurse, may be assigned to give individual and continuing attention to the case. Examples of such cases are premature infants and individuals who require rehabilitation while recovering from severe stroke or injuries. The case manager's goal is to make sure all the resources available are used wisely so that the patient gets the best result at the least cost. Case managers are bound by fewer rules than are preadmission and concurrent reviewers and may authorize payment for services not usually contemplated by the medical plan. For example, a case manager might authorize payment for homemaking services or construction of a wheelchair ramp so that rehabilitation might be done at home rather than in a hospital or convalescent facility.

**Retrospective Review**

Care is reviewed after it has been given. While the care of a single individual may be reviewed, often many cases involving a particular doctor or a group of doctors is reviewed. This allows the medical plan to offer a more accurate picture of the kind of care being given and to provide useful feedback to the doctors involved. It is unlikely that you will be aware of retrospective reviews, but it is very important for doctors to receive this kind of review if they are to improve the quality of the care that they give.

These managed care techniques may be used in either fee-for-service or pre-paid medical plans. The carrot (or stick, depending on how you look at it) is the same: compliance with the management techniques means that a greater portion of your medical care costs will be paid.

## *Types of Medical Plans*

A somewhat bewildering variety of medical plans can be created by combining various managed-care techniques with either the fee-for-service or prepayment method of paying for medical care. Here are the major types of medical plans that have emerged.

**TRADITIONAL INDEMNITY**

Your medical care charges are paid at a specified rate. No managed-care techniques are used. Often there are deductibles (you must pay for a certain amount on your own before coverage begins) and co-payments (you must pay a certain percentage of charges up to a specified limit) as a part of these plans. This is the traditional type of medical insurance.

**MANAGED INDEMNITY**

This combines traditional fee-for-service indemnity with managed-care techniques.

**PREFERRED PROVIDER ORGANIZATION (PPO)**

The medical plan provides a list of "preferred providers." If you use one of these preferred providers, you will pay less than if you used a doctor or hospital not on the list because those on the list charge the medical plan less. Charges are on a fee-for-service basis.

**EXCLUSIVE PROVIDER ORGANIZATION (EPO)**

This is essentially the same as a PPO except that you will pay essentially all the medical costs if you do not use a doctor or hospital on the exclusive provider list given by the medical plan.

**HEALTH MAINTENANCE ORGANIZATION (HMO)**

This is the original form of pre-paid medical care. Virtually all HMOs today combine prepayment with heavy use of managed-care techniques. Physicians who provide care for HMOs may be employed exclusively by the HMO or they may contract to provide care for HMO patients while still providing care for patients in other medical plans. HMOs will not pay for any care given by physicians or hospitals that are not a part of their system except in emergencies or when you are traveling.

**POINT-OF-SERVICE PLANS**

Recognizing that choice is important to many people, some plans will let you choose between plans when you go for care, i.e., at the point of service. In other words, you can wait until you need care to decide whether you will use traditional indemnity, an EPO, etc. You do not escape the consequences of the choice, however. If you choose a type of plan that costs the medical plan more, you will pay more. Each point-of-service plan has its own rules for how choices are made, what the consequences are, and how long you must stick with those choices, so be sure you *get a complete explanation* when considering such a plan.

Interestingly, there is considerable debate over the costs associated with each type of plan. For many years, it has been assumed that HMOs were the least costly type of plan. Some research now indicates that some managed indemnity plans may cost little more and perhaps even less than PPOs, EPOs, or HMOs.

## *Which Doctor Is Right for You?*

You should have one personal doctor in whom you have trust and confidence. This doctor should be your advocate and your guide through the complicated medical care system. A consultant may be required from time to time, and his or her recommendations should be interpreted and coordinated by your personal doctor. Good medical care usually does not result from an arrangement whereby you have a different doctor for every organ of your body. Someone has to have the whole picture, to know everything that is going on. Having too many doctors working in an uncoordinated manner often results in too many medications, too many medical procedures, too many side effects, and sometimes in opposing approaches to treatment. Your personal doctor doesn't need to be an expert in everything; he or she should readily seek advice from others when needed. He or she can help guide you to other appropriate health professionals. Someone needs to take responsibility for putting all the information together and making sure that nothing has been left out.

What kind of doctor should your personal doctor be? He or she might appropriately be:

- A family practitioner (specialist in family medicine)
- An internist (specialist in internal medicine)
- A gynecologist
- A geriatrician (specialist in the medical care of older people)

The family practitioner and the general internist are trained in dealing with the "whole patient" and in appropriate use of other consultants as required. Geriatrics is a relatively new specialty with practice limited to the senior population, and its practitioners take pride in recognizing the needs of the whole patient as well. Most internal medicine problems now occur after the age of 65, so the general internist has become, in large part, a geriatrician.

If you have a particular major disease, such as heart disease or rheumatoid arthritis, it may be inefficient to have a general doctor who frequently has to refer you to a specialist. See if it makes sense for the specialist to serve as your primary doctor. As noted above, it is not a good idea to have two or more primary doctors at the same time.

## ATTRIBUTES OF A GOOD PRIMARY PHYSICIAN

The most important qualities that you want in a primary care doctor center around *communication* and *anticipation*. Communication is the human side of medicine. A good primary physician:

- **Takes time to listen.** Help your doctor by explaining your problems clearly, as described at the beginning of Chapter 5.
- **Takes time to talk.** The doctor will explain his or her suggested course of action clearly.

- **Plans ahead to prevent problems.** A substantial part of your conversation should be about how to prevent future illnesses. Problems will be anticipated and plans made before they become severe.
- **Prescribes medicine carefully and reluctantly.** Prevention includes anticipating and minimizing the risks of possible side effects from drugs.
- **Reviews your total health program regularly.**
- **Has your trust and confidence.** If you can't communicate with your doctor, try another. Often two people just happen to be operating on different frequencies. You want to keep the same doctor for a long period of time, so if a relationship with a particular doctor is not working out, find a new one early on. When you find the right doctor, stay with him or her unless there is a substantial change in your medical needs so that you require a doctor with different skills.
- **Is available by phone.**
- **Makes house calls.**

## *Technical Skills*

There is a technical side of medicine too, and for some individuals this will represent the most important part of modern medicine. Perhaps you need an operation on your blood vessels or your brain. Perhaps you need surgery inside your middle ear. Perhaps you need replacement of your hip, you require kidney dialysis, or you need an organ transplant. In these situations, your standards for excellence in your consulting doctor are a little different. You are still interested in anticipation and communication, but you also want to pay a great deal of attention to the *technical skill* of the individual.

You would like to know if this particular surgeon, for example, gets better or worse results than average. This is often a little hard to judge, but there are two key tests that you can apply.

- Does the specialist have the complete confidence and approval of your primary doctor? Talk with your primary doctor about possible alternatives and ask about the advantages and disadvantages of each.

- Ask how frequently the specialist performs the particular procedure. Technical results are generally better at institutions and with doctors who perform the procedure frequently. As a general rule, results are substantially better where the procedure is done at least 50 times each year, and not as good where the procedure is only done occasionally.

These considerations do not apply only to surgical specialists. Increasingly the line between surgery and medicine has become blurred. There are now "invasive cardiologists" who perform marvelous but sometimes hazardous tasks through long tubes manipulated through your blood vessels under X-ray control. The gastrointestinal "endoscopist" can now use long, flexible, lighted tubes to look at (and sometimes treat) a surprising amount of your insides from the outside. An arthroscopist can perform surgery inside the joint; only a small cut in the skin is required to admit a lighted tube with which to see the inside of the joint. Arteriographers, often radiologists, use dye injected through long catheters to visualize your blood vessels on X-ray film. New X-ray techniques include computed axial tomography (CAT scans) and nuclear magnetic resonance (NMR) imagery. These techniques require skill both for performing the procedure and for interpretation of the results. Again, apply your two tests. Does the specialist who will do the procedure have the full agreement and confidence of your primary doctor? Does the specialist perform the procedure frequently?

## *Effects of the Doctor Surplus*

By most measures, we already have "too many" doctors in the United States; the number of doctors continues to rise in relation to the population each year and will for some time to come. In some subspecialties of medicine and surgery, we may have twice as many doctors in the year 2000 as are required.

On the positive side, this has greatly improved access to doctors; the poor now go to doctors even more frequently than the middle class. Well-trained specialists are now available in smaller cities. Increased competition for patients tends to provide better service and to hold costs down. We hope doctors will have and will take more time to talk with patients. More doctors may become interested in useful new activities, such as preventive health counseling and health promotion.

On the negative side, there may be pressure to introduce expensive new diagnostic and treatment techniques of questionable medical value, so as to occupy the extra medical personnel. As the doctor surplus grows, patients may have more alternatives but will also have to exercise more care in their choices. They may feel increasing pressure to accept additional, perhaps unneeded, services.

## *How to Detect Poor Medical Service*

There are some tip-offs to poor medical practices. If you are taking three or more different medicines daily, you may be receiving poor advice, unless you have a serious medical problem. If nearly every visit to the doctor results in an injection or a new prescription, there may be a problem. Be wary if the doctor recommends a costly service when you are not aware of any problem. Ask about any tests you do not understand. If your questions remain unanswered or if the doctor fails to perform any physical examination at all, it's time to worry.

Under each of the medical problems in Part IV, we give you an idea of what to expect at the doctor's office. If the doctor does not perform these actions, there is cause for some questioning. Expectations noted in this book are conservative and should be met in large part by most good doctors.

Free choice of doctors is available in the United States. For the "free market" to work effectively, you must be willing to "vote with your feet." In other words, if you cannot communicate effectively with your doctor, seek another. If your questions are not adequately answered, go somewhere else. If practice does not live up to your expectations and to the guidelines of this book, select another doctor.

But remember that your doctor is human, too. The doctor is faced with a continual barrage of complaints of problems that cannot be solved coming from patients who demand solutions. Don't use the doctor for trivial problems. Don't erode medical ethics by requests for misleading insurance claims or exaggerated disability statements. The high ethical standards of our profession continue to impress us; still, human is human, and sometimes problems begin with subconscious manipulation by the patient.

Support good medical practices and become a committed medical consumer. If you believe that women should be in medicine, don't avoid female doctors when you seek your own personal care. If you would like to see more family physicians, don't seek a specialist to direct your own care. If you like house calls, respect the doctor who will make them. If you want doctors to settle in your geographical area, patronize the doctor closest to your home. If cost is important to you, compare the charges of several doctors.

"Doctor-shopping"—going from one doctor to another to find one who will give you the treatment you want even if it is not warranted—will almost certainly result in poor care. Find a doctor who suits you, even if you must change doctors several times. But when you find a satisfactory situation, stay with it. Change early but not often.

## CHAPTER 5

# *Working with Your Doctor*

Many factors affect the quality of your medical care, but two are clearly the most important:

- Your ability to communicate with your doctor
- Your and your doctor's ability to share decisions

You and your doctor must be able to listen, explain, ask questions, understand each other, and choose options wisely. Put simply, you and your doctor must be able to talk and work together as partners.

## *The Medical History: Telling It Like It Is*

Your ability to give a concise, organized description of your illness is essential. The patient who rambles on about irrelevant details and doesn't mention real fears and problems is his or her own worst enemy. An inability to give a good medical history is expensive in terms of your health and your dollars.

Most people do not realize that every doctor uses a similar process to learn a patient's medical history. Obviously, the doctor must organize information in order to be able to remember it accurately and to reason correctly. Knowledge of the organization can help you give accurate information to your doctor. The doctor organizes information under five headings.

- The chief complaint

- The present illness
- The past medical history
- The review of systems
- The social history

The last three topics will usually not be discussed unless this is a first visit or comprehensive evaluation. On repeat visits, your primary physician will already know this background. Doctors will not always request information in the same order, but the following descriptions will help you understand the purposes of the medical interview in which you are participating.

## THE CHIEF COMPLAINT

Following the initial greeting, the "chief complaint" is usually the first information sought by the doctor. This question may take several forms: "What bothers you the most?" "What brings you here today?" "What's the trouble?" or "What is your biggest problem?" The purpose of such questions is to establish the priorities for the rest of the medical history process. Be sure you express your problem clearly. Know in advance how to state your chief complaint: "I have a sore throat." "I have a pain in my lower right side." Any of the problems listed in Part IV may be your chief complaint, and there are hundreds of less common problems.

Think of the "chief complaint" as the title for the story you are about to tell the doctor. Do not give the details of your illness at this time. Instead, title your illness appropriately and provide the doctor with a heading under which to understand your problem.

Sometimes you may go to the doctor with more than one problem, and you may not know if the problems are related. Identify this situation for the doctor. "I seem to have three problems: sore throat, skin rash, and cloudy urine." The doctor can then investigate each of these areas.

Tell it like it is. If you want to report a sexual problem, do not say that your chief complaint is that you're "tired and run down." If you are afraid that you have cancer, do not say that you came for a "checkup." If you mislead the doctor because of embarrassment, the real reason for your visit may never be determined. You will compromise the doctor's ability to be of assistance. An honest description is your best guarantee that your problems will be attended to correctly.

## THE PRESENT ILLNESS

Next, your doctor will want to hear the story behind your chief complaint. This section of the interview will be introduced by a question such as: "When did this problem begin?" "When were you last entirely well?" or "How long has this been going on?"

The first fact the doctor wants to establish is how long you have had the problem. Be sure that you know the answer to this question in advance: "Yesterday." "On June 4th." "About the middle of May." If you are uncertain about the date that the problem began, state the uncertainty and tell what you can. "I am not sure when these problems began. I began to feel tired in the middle of February, but the pain in the joints did not begin until the end of April." The doctor can then determine the starting point for the illness.

After you define the starting point for the problem, the doctor will want to establish the sequence of events from that time until the present. Tell the story in the order it occurred. Try not to use "flashbacks"; you will only confuse yourself and your doctor. If possible, avoid irrelevant occurrences in your family or social situation. Your cause is not aided by reference to the relatives who were visiting you at the time, the purchases you made at the shopping center, or the state of international affairs. If you confuse your story, the chances for a successful solution to your problems are decreased.

As you recount the sequence of the problem, sketch the highlights as you perceive them.

*I was well until I developed a sore throat four weeks ago. I had a fever and some swollen glands in my neck. This lasted about a week, and then I felt better although still tired. One week ago, the fever returned. I began to have pains in my joints, beginning with the right knee. The joint pain moved around from one joint to another, and I had pain in the shoulders, elbows, knees, and ankles. Over the last three days, I have had a red rash over much of my body. I have not taken any medications except aspirin, which helps a little.*

The doctor may interrupt the story to ask specific questions. At the end of the story, questions may be asked about problems that you have not mentioned. By making your account well organized and then allowing the doctor to ask additional questions, you provide information in the most effective way.

Supporting information can be extremely important. Know which medications you have taken before and during the course of the illness. Often it is helpful to bring the medication bottles to the doctor. Mention any allergic reactions that you have to drugs. If you are pregnant or could be pregnant, tell the doctor. If X-ray studies or laboratory tests have been performed during the course of the illness, attempt to make these materials or a report of the results available to the doctor. If other doctors have been consulted, bring those medical records with you. Be a careful observer of your own illness. Your observations, if carefully made and recounted, are more valuable than any other source of information.

## THE PAST MEDICAL HISTORY

After hearing about your chief complaint and a history of your medical problem, your doctor may want more background information about your general health. At this point, information that did not appear important earlier may be relevant. The doctor will ask specific questions; you can assist by giving direct, reasonably brief answers. You will be asked about your general health, hospitalizations, operative procedures, allergies, and medications. The doctor may be interested in childhood illnesses as well as those occurring during adult life. (Record this information in Part V so it will be readily available.)

The subjects most frequently misreported are allergies and medications. If you report a drug "allergy," describe the specific reaction you experienced. Many drug side effects (such as nausea, vomiting, or ringing in the ears) are *not* allergic reactions. Doctors are rightfully wary of prescribing drugs to which an allergy has been reported. If you report an allergy to a drug to which you are not allergic, you may deprive yourself of a useful method of treatment.

Be thorough when reporting medications. Birth control pills, vitamins, aspirin, and laxatives are medications that are frequently not reported. On occasion, each of these may be important in diagnosis or treatment of your medical problem.

## THE REVIEW OF SYSTEMS

Your doctor will usually review symptoms related to the different body systems; there are standard questions for each system. Your doctor may begin with questions about the skin; then ask about the head, eyes, ears, nose, and throat; and then begin to move down the body. Questions about the lymph glands, the lungs, and the heart are followed by questions about the stomach, intestines, and urinary system. Finally there will be questions about muscles, bones, and the nervous system. In this questioning, the doctor is looking for information that may have been missed previously and for additional factors that may influence the choice of therapy.

**THE SOCIAL HISTORY**

Finally, questions relating to your "social history" are addressed. Here, the doctor may wish to know about your job, family, and interpersonal stresses. Questions may concern smoking, drinking, use of drugs, and sexual activity. Knowledge of exposures to chemical or toxic substances may be sought. Questions are sometimes intensely personal. However, the answers can be of the utmost importance in determining your illness and how it can be best treated. A detailed social history should be expected only in a complete health examination.

## *Learn to Observe Yourself*

The careful physical examination requires skill and experience. Some important observations can be made at home. If you can report accurate information on these points, you can further help your doctor and yourself.

**TEMPERATURE**

Don't say "fever" or "running a temperature" or "burning up." Buy a thermometer, read the instructions, practice shaking the thermometer down, and be able to report the exact temperature. If you have a small child, buy a rectal thermometer and learn how to use it.

**PULSE**

If the problem involves a rapid or forceful heartbeat, know exactly how fast it is beating. Feel a pulse in the arm or throat, or put an ear to the chest. Count the exact number of beats occurring in one minute, or have someone do this for you.

If there is a problem with the pulse, determine whether the beat is regular or irregular. Is the heart "skipping a beat," "turning flip-flops," "missing every other beat," or is it "completely irregular"? A pulse irregularity is often gone by the time you reach the doctor. If you can describe it accurately, your doctor may be able to understand what happened. For more information, refer to **Palpitations**, page 404.

**BREAST**

The mammary tissue is normally a bit lumpy. Adult women should carefully examine their breasts every month in order to detect changes. Press the breast tissue against the chest wall, not between the fingers.

Try several positions—lying down, sitting, and with the arm on the side being examined raised over the head. Look particularly for differences between the two breasts. If you note a suspicious lump, see the doctor immediately. Many women delay out of fear. Please don't. Very few lumps are cancerous, but if the lump is malignant, it is important that it be removed early. Often the patient can feel a lump that the doctor misses; help the doctor locate the problem area. Detailed instructions for a self-examination can be found in Chapter P, "Women's Health."

**WEIGHT**

Changes in weight are often important. Know what your normal weight is. If your weight changes, know by how much and over what period it changed.

**OTHER FINDINGS**

Know your body. When something changes, report it accurately. A change in skin color, a lymph gland on the back of the neck, an increase in swelling in the legs, and many other new events are easily observed. Just as important, knowledge of your body will help you avoid reporting silly things. The "Adam's apple" is not a tumor. "Knobs" on the lower ribs or pelvis are usually normal. The vertebra (bone) at the lower neck normally sticks out. There is a normal bump at the back of the head—the "knowledge bump." We have known patients to report each of these as emergencies.

## *Choosing a Course of Treatment*

The old rituals of medicine with the authoritative doctor and the passive patient are undergoing re-evaluation. In the old relationship, the doctor would ask a series of questions, and you answered. The doctor carefully examined all parts of your body. Perhaps the doctor ordered tests. Then you were given a prescription and you left. These traditional parts of the doctor-patient encounter are still important, but they are no longer enough by themselves. They should not take up all the available time during your encounter.

You need to talk, too. You need to ask what to anticipate and how to prevent problems. You need to discuss your goals and values. The doctor needs to know how you feel about the benefits that various treatments might provide versus the side effects that might come from these treatments.

This last point is very important. Sensible decisions about treatment cannot be made unless you have a chance to put a value on the benefit and risk of each option. The basis for a decision is always the same: Which option offers the greatest benefit for the least risk and cost? It is the doctor's job to provide information on the probability that each option will provide a particular benefit or side effect, but only you can determine how much that benefit is worth to you or how much you fear that side effect.

For example, if you have a cataract, the doctor can tell you the probability that a particular operation will restore vision to a certain level as well as the risks of making vision worse or losing sight altogether. Only you can decide how much the improved vision would be worth or whether the risks of decreased vision are acceptable. If the cataract isn't bothering you very much, there may be no point in accepting any risk or pain associated with an operation. On the other hand, if the cataract is interfering constantly with your life and making you miserable, you may have a very different view of the benefit you hope to gain from the operation and regard the risks and discomfort of that procedure in a very different light. Remember that the ultimate goal of talking with your doctor is always to help you choose the option that, *in your opinion*, offers the greatest benefit for the least risk and cost.

## ASKING QUESTIONS

To use time effectively, make a list of your questions before the doctor visit and take it with you. Write out your questions. Date the list. Leave space to jot down answers while you are talking with the doctor. If someone is accompanying you on the visit, perhaps he or she can write down the answers for you. Ask the doctor each question. Go over the list and the answers again after you get home. Save the list as part of your own records.

Table 9 gives you some suggestions for questions that you may want to include on your list. Run through this list and see which questions you may want to include as you make up your list for a particular visit. There are many other questions that you may want to include as well, but the table can help you get started.

TABLE 9 *A Question List*

- What is my problem?
- Is it a common problem?
- What does the diagnosis mean?
- Can you tell me what the words (any words you don't understand) mean?
- Could the problem be anything else?
- How likely is that?
- **What are my options for the next step?**
- **What are the benefits, risks, and cost of each option?**

**If tests are an option:**

- What will be learned from these tests?
- Should I expect any discomfort from them?
- Do I need to make special arrangements (such as fasting before the test or planning transportation home)?

**If medication is an option:**

- How does the medication help?
- Does it have any side effects I should know about?
- Is it available in a generic form?
- Are there interactions with other drugs or with foods?
- What can I expect in the next few weeks and also over the long term?

**If a procedure is an option:**

- What are the risks of this procedure?
- How frequently does this procedure relieve my problem?
- Must the procedure be done right away?
- If it has to be done right away, why?
- How frequently do you do this procedure?
- I would feel more comfortable with another opinion. Could you recommend someone for me to check with?
- Can this procedure be done safely as an outpatient?

**If hospitalization is an option:**

- Can the tests or treatment be done as an outpatient?
- What are the risks of being in the hospital?
- Which hospital do you suggest and why?
- Does the hospital staff perform this treatment frequently?
- Can I recover at home and shorten the hospital stay?
- What should I do at home?
- Is there anything I shouldn't do?
- When should I check back with you?

**TABLE 10** *Problem List for Dr. Johanson, June 19, 1993*

| *Questions* | *Answers* |
|---|---|
| **1.** Dizziness when standing? | Low blood pressure. Decrease Aldomet to two a day. Will check blood counts. |
| **2.** Wonder about aspirin or fish oil capsules for heart attacks? | Not yet. Diet first. Will check cholesterol. |
| **3.** Leg cramps at night? | Warm baths and massage. |
| **4.** Gray splotches on skin? | Just age spots. O.K. |
| **5.** Move to Arizona for joint pains? | Probably not. Try a vacation to a hot, dry area first; see if feels better. |
| **6.** Cost of blood pressure pills? | Reducing dose anyway because of dizziness. Try AARP (American Association of Retired Persons) pharmacy services. |

Table 10 shows what the list might look like if you made a visit to Dr. Johanson because of a problem with dizziness when standing. Your list on the left will probably be handwritten and the answers on the right jotted down, but this example will give you a general idea of the process.

It is not necessary to limit a valuable doctor's appointment only to your current problems. You may have a lot of questions. The doctor visit is a good place to begin thinking, together with a knowledgeable

**TABLE 11** *Some Subjects to Discuss*

- Exercise
- Diet
- Calcium
- Estrogen for women
- Mammography for women
- Sexual problems
- Weight control
- Smoking
- Drug or alcohol use
- Medication program

professional, about solutions. (A list of possible discussion areas is shown in Table 11.) You also want to make the doctor's time count. You may only have a few minutes. You want the doctor to be efficient during his or her time with you so that you can get the most out of it.

## *Carrying Out Your Treatment Program*

Choosing the best treatment for yourself is just the start of getting the most out of your medical care.

You must understand any instructions given to you. If you are confused, ask questions: "Could you go over that again?" "I don't understand how to use this medication." "How long should I apply the ice pack?" "Are there any risks to this?" Ask your doctor to write out the instructions.

Understand the importance of each drug. In some instances it does not matter if you take the medicine regularly; in these circumstances the drug gives only symptomatic relief and should be discontinued as soon as possible. Be sure that you understand whether or not it is necessary to continue the medication after you feel well.

Consider the entire prescribed program. You may have difficulties not known to your doctor. Perhaps you have trouble taking a medication at work, or you anticipate trouble with a prescribed diet. Perhaps reasons unknown to your doctor prevent you from undertaking the recommended activity. If more than one medication has been prescribed initially, it may be more desirable for you to take them all at once. When such questions arise, ask in advance. Frequently, if you raise these questions with your doctor, your treatment program can be modified so that you feel more comfortable. Be frank. Don't say that you will do something that you know you will not do. Express your worries. You don't have to be a "perfect patient."

After an agreed program has been established, follow it closely. If you notice side effects from the program, call the doctor and inquire. If the side effects are serious, return for an examination. Make a chart of the days of the week and the times when medications are to be taken. Note on the chart when you take the medicines. This is not an insult to your intelligence; this practice is universally used in hospitals by trained personnel to ensure that medication schedules are maintained accurately. At home, you and your family are the custodians of your health. Do not view this task more lightly than it is viewed by professionals. More importantly, if you find that you cannot carry out the program, another option must be chosen.

When pills remain at the end of a course of therapy, flush them down the toilet. A medicine chest containing old prescription medicines presents multiple hazards. Every year, children and adults die from taking leftover drugs. Children take birth control pills, adults brush their teeth with steroid creams, and the wrong medication is taken because one bottle was mistaken for another. If you give your leftover tetracycline to your children with their next cold, you may cause mottling (gray spotting) of their teeth. If tetracycline becomes outdated and is subsequently used, dangerous liver damage may result. When a new illness occurs, the situation becomes confusing if you have already taken leftover medications. Sometimes it will be impossible to make an accurate identification of a bacterium by culture, or the clinical picture of the disease may be distorted.

The doctor-patient encounter is your most reliable protection against serious illness. Value the opportunity for such attention, use it effectively, and follow the program that you and your doctor develop to the maximum extent possible.

CHAPTER 6

# Choosing the Right Medical Facility

A wide variety of medical facilities is available to prospective patients—hospitals, emergency rooms, nursing homes, doctor's offices, and clinics. There are sufficient choices to satisfy most individual preferences. It's important to know the facilities in your area and to make your choices before you need the services.

To select the best facilities, you will need to understand the terms "primary," "secondary," and "tertiary" care.

- **Primary medical care** is provided by a doctor at the office or at an emergency room or clinic. This care may be obtained by a patient without the referral of another doctor. It is often called "ambulatory care" or "outpatient care."
- **Secondary care** is that provided by the typical community hospital, and the doctors involved may be specialists or subspecialists. As a rule, access to this care requires a doctor's referral. Much secondary care is "inpatient" or hospital care.
- **Tertiary care** includes special and extraordinary procedures such as kidney dialysis, open-heart surgery, and sophisticated treatment of rare diseases. This type of care is found at university-affiliated hospitals and regional referral centers.

When you select a medical facility, you want close primary care with good access to secondary care. Tertiary care can be located a considerable distance from your home because you may never need it.

## *Hospitals*

**Community hospitals** are the most common hospital facilities in the United States. These hospitals are either profit or nonprofit and generally contain 50 to 400 beds. Sometimes they have been financed with funds from doctors practicing in the area. More frequently, nonprofit organizations aided by government funds for hospital construction have financed the facility. The quality of care in these institutions largely depends on the doctor in charge of your case. Relatively few doctors' actions come under serious review. A doctor is not always present in the hospital at all times. Nevertheless, private hospitals usually give personalized, high-quality care. The hospital is quiet and orderly. In the great majority of cases, facilities are adequate for the care required.

**Public hospitals** include city, county, public health service, military, and Veterans Administration hospitals. These hospitals are generally large, with from 400 to 1000 beds. They have permanent full-time staff, and doctors are present in the hospital at all times. Usually, they have a "house staff," with interns and resident doctors always available. As befits their larger size, they offer more services and frequently have associated rehabilitation units or nursing homes. Activities in the public hospital are more visible, and the efforts of each doctor are scrutinized by others. The quality of care you receive depends in great part on the overall quality of the institution. The presence of interns and residents may pose some minor inconveniences to you as a patient, but their presence is an excellent guarantee of good care. The doctor-in-training has hospital-patient care as his or her primary responsibility and is not greatly involved with office practice and administrative tasks.

Many public hospitals have the reputation for providing service to the poorer economic classes. Within the community, they are often perceived as offering substandard service. These accusations are usually grossly unfair. While not always quiet and orderly, and often not physically attractive, these hospitals give dependable and excellent care. When available, they should be seriously considered by individuals of all economic classes.

**Teaching hospitals** are associated with a medical school. Teaching hospitals are large and have from 300 to 2000 beds. These hospitals always have interns and residents as well as medical students on the hospital wards. They have superb technical resources, and it is here that the most extraordinary events of medicine take place. Open-heart surgery, transplantation of organs, elaborate nurseries for the newborn, support and management of rare blood diseases, and other marvels are all available here. Dozens of people may be concerned with the well-being of a particular patient. Crucial medical decisions are thoroughly discussed, presented at conferences, and reviewed by many personnel.

On the other hand, the quality of personal relationships at teaching hospitals is variable. Many patients feel that they are treated in an impersonal way and that their laboratory tests receive more attention than their human and social problems. Because these institutions are on the frontier of medicine, there is a tendency to emphasize the new and elaborate procedures, when older and more modest ones might serve just as well. With the inexperience of some members of the care team, there is a tendency to order more laboratory tests than would have been considered necessary for the same condition in a private hospital. The sick patient is sometimes confused by having to relate to a large number of doctors and students. Medical educators are concerned with such criticisms and have moved to correct some of the problems. However, excesses of technological medicine still occur in these institutions.

## *Know When to Use the Hospital*

The hospital is expensive. It is not home or hotel. Lives are saved and lost. The hospital must be used, and it must be avoided. To manage these contradictions, the need for hospitalization for you or a member of your family must be carefully considered in each instance.

Don't use the hospital if services can be performed elsewhere. The acute (short-term) general hospital provides acute general medicine; it does not perform other functions well.

Don't use the hospital for a rest; it is not a good place to go for rest. It is busy, noisy, unfamiliar, and populated with unfamiliar roommates. Its nights are punctuated with interruptions, and it has an unusual time schedule. It has many employees, a few of whom will be less thoughtful than others.

Don't use the hospital for the "convenience" of having a number of tests done in a few days. It does not provide tests in the most efficient manner; indeed, most laboratories and X-ray facilities are not open on the weekend, and special procedures may require several days just to be scheduled.

Over a century ago, the Hungarian physician Inaz Philipp Semmelweiss (1818–65) noted two events: (1) Mothers giving birth at home and their infants fared better than those in the hospital, and (2) the existence of the often fatal "childbed fever" was one of the risks of the hospital. This problem, due to poor hygiene in the delivery rooms, has long since been corrected. But in our present age, new evidence suggests that for many conditions home treatment may work better than treatment in the hospital. For example, home treatment for minor heart attacks in the elderly has been reported as possibly better than hospital treatment. It is apparent to most hospital visitors that the crisis atmosphere of the short-term acute hospital does not promote the calmest state of mind for the patient. Many therapeutic features of the home cannot be duplicated in the hospital.

The hospice movement attempts to provide humane, caring, medically sound treatment with a minimum of the technological trappings of the hospital. Hospice and home-care programs are growing rapidly and are very worthwhile.

## *Emergency Rooms*

The emergency room has become the "doctor" for many patients. Patients who cannot find a doctor at night, or who don't know where else to go, are increasingly coming to emergency rooms. Thus, the typical emergency room is now filled with non-emergency cases. The various problems are all mixed together: trivial illnesses that could have been treated with the aid of this book, routine problems more easily and economically handled in a doctor's office, specialized problems that should have been dealt with at a time when the hospital facilities were fully available, and true emergencies. Even though the emergency room is not designed for the purpose it now serves, it does a surprisingly good job of delivering adequate care.

However, there are five major disadvantages to using an emergency room as your sole medical contact.

- Emergency rooms make little or no provision for continued care. You will usually be seen by a different doctor each time. The emergency room doctor will attend to the chief problem reported by the patient but seldom has sufficient time to complete a full examination or to deal with underlying problems.
- Although simple X-ray facilities are available, procedures such as gallbladder studies and upper G.I. series are arranged with difficulty. Thus, evaluation of a complicated problem is not handled well by emergency-room facilities.
- When a true emergency occurs, patients with less urgent problems are shunted aside. You cannot estimate with any certainty how long you will have to wait for treatment in an emergency room.
- Emergency-room fees, because they support equipment required to handle true emergencies, are higher than those of standard office visits.
- Emergency-room services are not always covered by medical insurance, even when the policy states that the costs of emergency care are included. With many policies, the nature of the illness determines whether or not it is covered. You may end up paying a large bill if you go to the emergency room with a sore throat.

The smoothly functioning emergency room is a dramatic place and provides one of the finest examples of a service profession at work. Using the procedures outlined in this book, you can use this valuable resource appropriately.

## *Other Medical Facilities*

### SHORT-TERM SURGERY CENTERS

Recently, a number of facilities specially designed for short-term surgery (requiring only a short stay, overnight at the most) have appeared. Obviously, such surgery is minor, and the patient must basically be in good health. Because such centers can avoid some of the overhead of a hospital, they often charge less for the use of their facilities. But because they do not have the capability to handle difficult cases or complications, you should use them only for minor procedures. The growing experience with these centers has been positive.

## WALK-IN CLINICS

Similarly, some medical problems can be managed at walk-in or "drop-in" clinics. If you have a new, uncomplicated problem (for example, sore throat or minor injury), such clinics can be excellent. The decision charts in Part IV will help you determine if a visit to the doctor is indicated. Appointments are not usually necessary, and service is swift and efficient. Often these clinics are open for long hours, including evenings and weekends. When available, such clinics should be used for non-emergency care in preference to emergency rooms. The problem with these clinics is with follow-up and sometimes cost. Costs are rising and now approach those of emergency rooms. If your problem has been with you for more than six weeks, or if you expect that the problem will require multiple visits and more than six weeks to clear up, we think you should see your regular physician.

## CONVALESCENT FACILITIES

Nursing homes and various types of rehabilitation facilities provide for the patient who does not require hospital care but cannot be adequately managed at home. The quality of these facilities ranges from horrible to superb. In the best circumstances, with dedicated nursing and regular doctor attendance, a comfortable and home-like situation for the patient can accelerate the healing process. In other cases, disinterested personnel, inadequate facilities, and minimal care are the rule. Before suggesting or accepting referral to a nursing-home facility, visit the facility or have a friend or relative visit it for you. In the convalescent setting, your comfort with the arrangements is essential. The same checkout practice should be used for a hospice; most are good, but some are not.

# *The Marketing of Medical Services*

Increased competition in medicine is here. With nostalgia, we note a certain loss of dignity. Hospitals compete with other hospitals for patients. Health insurance plans compete with other plans. Doctors compete with doctors. There are advertisements and direct marketing to consumers.

You need to be aware of these changes because once-conservative institutions are now trying to influence your choices. A new phenomenon, the hospital "chain," with facilities in many cities and national marketing practices, has developed. Payment for spectacular new technologies, such as the artificial heart, may be internally justified, at least in part, because it calls attention to the merits of particular companies. Marketing directors, or their equivalent, have been hired at many hospitals, even small ones. The hospital public relations director interacts with the media, and regular press releases as well as attractive brochures are prepared.

To an extent, marketing educates people, making them aware of the features of alternative choices. But beware of hype and jargon. The guidelines of this book are a more effective means of finding good-quality care than are slick brochures and press releases.

An increasing problem is the marketing of "procedures": CT scans, MRI scans, endoscopy, angiography, and others. These are high-profit items both for hospitals and for doctors. They are expensive and may not help. They can be hazardous. Listen, question, discuss—then decide.

CHAPTER 7

# Avoiding Medical Fraud

At least $20 billion yearly is spent on frauds, hoaxes, and false cures. You probably contribute to this windfall. When you buy worthless drugs as a result of television advertisements, take massive amounts of the vitamin-of-the-month, or send away for "cures" advertised in the back of magazines, you are paying part of this bill. You are being hustled.

You can recognize a hustle. There are four questions, one or more of which will usually identify the dishonest marketer.

- What is the motive?
- What are the promises and claims?
- Do experts use the service?
- Does the proposed service make sense?

## *What Is the Motive?*

Make some rough estimates of the proposed service as a business. Is it a revolving-door operation, where people walk in one door with their money and soon thereafter leave without it? What is the average fee paid by the patient? How many patients are seen each hour? The product of these two numbers represents the hourly income of the operation. If this gross amount exceeds $400 per professional employee, watch out. Many patients have paid hundreds of dollars to have their arthritis "treated" with ordinary "flu shots," which should cost a trivial amount. Medicines may be repackaged and marked up and misrepresented. The hustler is doing it for the money. Don't be misled by a "loss leader" advertisement that seems to be a bargain. Look at the total cost over the long term.

## *What Are the Promises and Claims?*

Are they vague? Misleading? A typical advertisement urges purchase of a product "containing an ingredient recommended by doctors." This is clearly intended to deceive; the advertiser knows that if the ingredient were named, you would recognize it to be relatively ineffective for the problem or readily available at less expense.

Beware of testimonials, coupons, and guarantees. If a product or service is advertised by testimonial, it is probably of marginal value or less. A testimonial may consist of "before-and-after" pictures. It may be a story told by a presumed patient relating success with the treatment. On occasion, testimonials will be totally fabricated. However, even if the testimonial is accurate, it provides no reliable information. Your interest is not whether the proposed service has *ever* helped anyone but whether it is likely to help *you*.

Coupons are another clue to bad services. Worthwhile treatments are not marketed through magazine and newspaper coupons. "Guarantees" in medicine are almost a guarantee that the product or service is worthless. In medicine, a guarantee is not possible. There are always exceptions, as well as the possibility of unfortunate results. No worthwhile medical service is accompanied by a money-back guarantee. Thus, it isn't that the guarantee will not be honored (which is probably also the case) but that the offer itself strongly suggests a suspicious product.

## *Do Experts Use the Service?*

Does your doctor take the vitamin you are considering? Does the doctor's family? Do arthritis doctors who have arthritis wear copper bracelets? Do cancer doctors use laetrile when they or their spouses have cancer? Doctors (and their families) get cancer and other diseases just as frequently as anybody else. If any treatment had the remotest chance of benefiting one of these serious conditions, the doctor would use that product. In fact, doctors do not use these marginal services. Instead, doctors have decreased their cigarette smoking. They have taken up jogging and other regular forms of exercise. They have not endorsed mega-vitamin therapy, diet fads, and other popular fancies by their own use, except in unusual instances.

**Who, if anyone, endorses the service?** Is it endorsed by a national professional organization? Or by a national consumer organization? Direct product endorsement by such organizations is rare but of great value if given. Endorsement of toothpaste containing stannous fluoride by the American Dental Association is an example. Consumers Union and its magazine *Consumer Reports* may be relied on for thoughtful discussions of the medical issues of the day.

## *Does the Proposed Service Make Sense?*

This is the final test. Frequently, frauds and promotion of false cures are successful because no one really asks whether they make common sense. Do you really think that creams will improve your bust line? Or that you can lose weight only in the hips? Or that a vitamin will help your sex life? Or that a lamb's embryo will keep you young? By definition, a false cure has false reasoning. This reasoning is often weak and is easily identified as such.

# *Three Examples: Obesity, Arthritis, Cancer*

Three of the oldest and largest medical rackets victimize people who have the problems of obesity, arthritis, or cancer.

## OBESITY

Overweight people appear to be particularly willing victims for the fringe health entrepreneur. As we noted in Chapter 2, successful weight control is achieved gradually, through moderate programs, and must be sustained for a lifetime. A weight-loss program has merit when it projects its program for a prolonged period. There is negligible medical benefit (and quite possibly harm) in weight loss that occurs abruptly and lasts only a few weeks or months. Individuals with a significant weight problem face a very difficult task requiring intense commitment, long-term discipline, and considerable emotional distress. We applaud the courage of those who undertake such a program and the fortitude of those able to maintain an important but difficult task.

The fraudulent approach is to promise a shortcut. A gadget of some type, massage, a miracle diet, an appetite suppressant, a food supplement, or some other mechanism is promoted as a way to "lose weight fast and easy." "Fast" and "easy" do not describe safe and effective weight-loss programs.

The facts are relatively straightforward. Most overweight people do not succeed in both losing weight and maintaining a steady, desirable level under any program. The best results have been obtained under medically supervised programs and with reputable, long-term programs that emphasize exercise such as Weight Watchers. Spot-reducing (reduction of fat at only one point in the body such as the hips or legs) does not work. Massage is not an effective way to lose weight. Appetite suppressants have not been successful over the long term. A brief period of weight loss frequently occurs with any technique promoted. Almost any program has an occasional success, but it is the individual and not the fad that is responsible for this improvement.

## ARTHRITIS

Arthritis is another very frequent subject for exploitation. Arthritis problems are often chronic and discouraging. A widespread myth exists that arthritis cannot be treated by traditional medicine. But the tragedy of false fads in arthritis is aggravated by this myth because good treatment is available for almost all patients. Patients are often unnecessarily crippled because they avoided sound, established medical approaches. The fourth test for recognizing a hustle in the area of arthritis is, Does it make sense? Take, for example, a diet for arthritis. You can understand a diet for losing weight, but what does it have to do with pain in the joints? Vinegar and honey for arthritis? Copper bracelets?

A legend persists that other countries have better drugs for arthritis than the United States. It is true that the Food and Drug Administration has rather carefully limited approval of new therapies for arthritis. There have been, at most points in recent years, several drugs available in Mexico, Canada, and Europe that are not yet licensed in the United States. However, none of these drugs is a major addition to existing therapy. The position of the Food and Drug Administration has been to ensure as carefully as possible the safety of new medications before allowing them to enter the market. There are no magical new drugs.

The legend of dramatic new treatments has led to fraudulent medical operations just over the Mexican border. (Such operations should not be confused with the very fine medicine available at many locations in Mexico.) These "arthritis mills" attract patients who come long distances to be seen briefly and then return to the United States with bags and boxes full of medications. Patients are told a variety of things about these medications, but it is usually suggested that they are being given drugs not available in the United States. We have occasionally analyzed the contents of such medications, and the active ingredient has uniformly been a drug related to cortisone; a drug called phenylbutazone is often present also. Both are available and frequently prescribed in the United States, but they are hazardous and have resulted in fatalities. Ill-conceived therapies with such drugs often make patients feel better over the first few days and weeks; such short-term improvement is what keeps the waiting rooms of the arthritis mills full. Over the longer term, increased disability and even death can result. Common sense suggests that the best medical care in the world is unlikely to be found in Mexican border towns. When you suspend common sense, you can lose more than money.

Acupuncture has received great publicity and is under intensive evaluation as a treatment for arthritis. The early studies suggest a minor effect in pain relief, less strong than the effect of aspirin. However, final information is not yet available. Other fad cures, such as cocaine or flu shots or bee venom, have already been definitely discredited.

Dimethylsulfoxide (DMSO) is a special case. This drug was removed from medical testing programs because of fears of toxicity but now is back as a legal remedy in some states, with limited distribution. We have studied it, and as a liniment, it is good. But it is not an active medication against arthritis. It will not help rheumatoid arthritis or osteoarthritis. Inaccurate claims are being advanced for this drug, which is an industrial solvent. Don't believe everything that you hear.

## CANCER

Cancer is the area of the cruelest hoaxes. In some cases, when cancer has already spread throughout the body, orthodox medicine cannot help the patient very much. In this setting, the vultures move in. "What have you got to lose?" is their call. The answer is that you may lose courage, dignity, and money. The tragedy of quack cancer treatments is that you have nothing to gain.

Cancer is not one but many diseases, requiring many different approaches to treatment. Very effective treatment is available for some cancers, and new techniques are being applied as fast as they can be proven effective. The great majority of cancer patients can be helped by present medical treatment. Many agencies and patients are working very hard to contribute to knowledge in cancer. This is a sophisticated field, with many minds working toward solutions. It is highly unlikely that significant discoveries will come in the form of apricot pits or horse serum. In our own experience, we have seen hundreds of patients take dozens of different "cures"; not a single one has received benefit.

You are hustled because you want to believe. Your wish that the claims might be true does not make them become so.

PART III

# *Managing Your Medicines*

CHAPTER 8

# *Reducing Medication Costs*

Legal drugs are a multi-billion-dollar industry. Your contribution to this industry is largely voluntary. The size of the contribution is determined by your doctor, your pharmacy, and yourself.

Drugs are life-saving, dangerous, curative, painful, pain-relieving, and easy to misuse. Most drugs act to block one or more of the natural body defense mechanisms, such as pain, cough, inflammation, or diarrhea. Drugs can interact with other drugs, causing hazardous chemical reactions. They can have direct toxic reactions on the stomach lining and elsewhere in the body. They can cause allergic rashes and shock. They can have severe toxic effects when taken in excess. Some drugs can decrease the ability of the body to fight infections.

If you do *not* receive a prescription or a sample package of medication from your physician, consider this good news rather than rejection or disinterest. Take the fewest possible drugs for the shortest possible time. It is best *not* to take medications unless they are truly necessary. When drugs are prescribed, take them regularly and as directed, but expect that your medication program will be thoroughly reviewed every time you see your doctor.

Most drugs are given as "symptomatic medications"—that is, they do not cure your problem but give only partial relief for the symptoms of the problem. If you report a different symptom every time you see your doctor and urgently request relief from the symptom, you will probably be given additional medications. You are unlikely to feel much better as a result, and you are nearly certain to function at a lower level. Unless you have a serious illness, you will seldom need to take more than one or two medications at a time. Many perceptive observers have argued that the present practice of using drugs to control symptoms is only a temporary phase in the history of medicine.

## *Your Doctor Can Save You Money on Drugs*

Your doctor plays a major role in the cost of drugs by choosing the drugs to be prescribed. For example, if you have an infection due to bacteria, you may be given tetracycline or erythromycin. Tetracycline costs about 10¢ a capsule, whereas erythromycin costs about 80¢. At the doctor's option, a steroid prescription for asthma may be prednisone at 8¢ per tablet or methylprednisolone at 50¢ per tablet. Medically, such drug choices are between agents of similar effectiveness. If your doctor prescribes a drug by its trade name, in many states the pharmacist must fill the prescription with that particular brand-name product. The brand-name product frequently costs many times more than its generic equivalent. Does your doctor know the relative cost of alternative drugs? Many doctors do not.

The drug-prescribing habits of different doctors can be divided into two groups: the "additive" and the "substitutive." With each visit to an "additive" doctor, you receive a medication in addition to those you already have. With a "substitutive" doctor, the medication you were previously taking is discontinued and a new medicine is substituted. Usually the "substitutive" practice is advantageous to your health as well as your pocketbook.

Most of the time, medication can be taken orally. Sometimes medication is given by injection because of the physician's uncertainty that you will take it as prescribed. However, as a thoughtful and reliable patient, you can assure your doctor that you will comply with an oral regimen. Taking medication orally is less painful, less likely to result in an allergic reaction, and far less expensive. There are exceptions, but whenever possible you should take medication by mouth rather than by injection.

If it is clear that you must take a medication for a prolonged period, ask the doctor to allow refills on the prescription. With many drugs, it is not necessary to incur the expense of an additional doctor visit just to get a prescription written. However, under some circumstances, the doctor may prefer to examine you before deciding whether the drug can be safely continued or is still required. Ask your doctor if refills on the prescription are permitted.

The careful doctor will ensure that you fully understand each drug that you are taking, the reasons you are taking it, the side effects that may arise, and the expected length of time that you will be taking the medication. A daily medication schedule will be arranged so that it is convenient as well as medically effective. If the program is confusing, ask for written instructions. It is crucial that you understand the why and how of your drug therapy. Do not leave the doctor's office for the pharmacy without understanding your medications.

## *Reducing Costs at the Pharmacy*

Studies indicate that the pharmacy you choose is a very important factor in drug costs. For the most part, the pharmacist no longer weighs and measures individual chemical formulations. Much of the activity in the pharmacy consists of relabeling and dispensing manufactured medication. Medication is thus usually identical at different pharmacies; you should choose the least expensive and the most convenient place.

Comparison shop. Discount stores often sell the same medication at significantly lower prices. If a considerable sum of money is involved, you should compare prices by telephone before purchasing the medication. Don't buy from a pharmacy that won't give you price information over the phone.

Unfortunately, even though your doctor writes a prescription by generic name rather than brand name, the pharmacist is usually not required to give you the cheapest of the equivalent alternatives. The pharmacy often stocks only one manufacturer's formulation of each drug. Thus, even though your doctor has been careful to prescribe a less expensive preparation, the pharmacist may substitute the more expensive alternative that is in stock. There is no way to detect this problem except to get direct price quotes from different pharmacies.

The majority of pharmacies charge a percentage markup. Their pricing is determined by the wholesale price; that price is multiplied by a fixed profit figure. A sliding scale may be used, but profit is largest on the largest sales. Other pharmacies work on a specific charge per prescription. These pharmacies add a constant fee to the wholesale price. With a small drug bill, you will be better off with the percentage markup formulas. If you are buying a significant quantity of expensive medication, application of the one-time fixed charge may be less costly. Knowledge of these practices and aggressive comparison shopping is essential for you to control costs.

## *Eliminating Some Drug Costs*

In this age, visits to the doctor frequently are requests for medication. If your satisfaction with the doctor depends on whether or not you are given medication, you are working against your own best interest. If you go to a doctor because of a cold and request a "shot of penicillin," you are asking for poor medical practice. Penicillin should only infrequently be given by injection, and it should not be given for uncomplicated colds. Your doctor knows this but may give in to your pressure.

The most frequently prescribed medications in the United States, making up the bulk of drug costs, are tranquilizers, minor pain relievers, and sedatives. These drugs cause the greatest number of side reactions. These are not scientifically important medications. This prescription pattern arose, at least in part, because of ill-advised consumer demand. You can decrease the cost of medications by using some of the techniques discussed previously; you can eliminate them almost completely by decreasing your pressure to receive and take medications that you do not require.

CHAPTER 9

# The Home Pharmacy

To effectively treat the minor illnesses that appear from time to time in your family, you need to have some medications on hand and know where to obtain others as you need them. Your stock should include only the most inexpensive and frequently needed medications. They will deteriorate with time and should be replaced at least every three years.

Table 12 lists the essential products for a home medical shelf; Table 13 gives a more complete list of agents that may sometimes be needed. The guidelines for common medical problems in Part IV indicate when and why to use each medication. In this chapter, we discuss drug dosage and side effects; because these are subject to changes, you should carefully read the instructions that come with the medication. Our discussion will add some perspective to the manufacturers' statements.

Note that only five items appear in Table 12 for the adult subject, and only the first two are drugs that are taken internally. You do not need most of the items that are currently in your medicine cabinet. It is best to dispose of them.

Always remember:

- Used in effective dosages, all drugs have the potential for side effects. Many common drugs have some side effects, such as drowsiness, that are impossible to avoid at effective dosages.
- Misuse of over-the-counter drugs can have serious consequences. Do not assume that a product is automatically safe because it does not require a prescription.

**TABLE 12** *Your Home Pharmacy*

| Medicine | Use |
|---|---|
| ■ Acetaminophen, aspirin, or ibuprofen | For fever, headache, minor pain |
| ■ Antacid | For stomach upset |
| ■ Adhesive tape and bandages | For minor wounds |
| ■ Hydrogen peroxide | For cleansing wounds |
| ■ Sodium bicarbonate | For soaking and soothing |
| ■ Liquid acetaminophen* | For pain and fever in small children |
| ■ Syrup of ipecac* | To induce vomiting |

**For families with children under 12 years of age.*

The rational approach to this dilemma is for you to learn something about the drugs that may be useful to you. This is the purpose of this chapter.

There are hundreds of over-the-counter medicines available at your supermarket or drugstore. For most purposes, there are several medicines that are almost identical. This has posed a problem for us in the organization of this chapter; if we discuss drugs by chemical name, the terms are long and confusing; if we use the brand name, we may appear to favor the product of a particular manufacturer when there are equally satisfactory alternatives. We have decided, instead, to give some clues to reading the list of ingredients on the package so that you can figure out what the drug is likely to do. We do not include all available drugs, but we do mention some representative alternatives. The brand names listed in this chapter are vigorously marketed and should be available almost everywhere. They are *not* necessarily superior to alternatives, which contain similar formulas, that are not listed. Remember, these drugs only act to control symptoms. They do not do anything basic to change the problem. If you can get along without them, it is usually best to do so.

The expanded list in Table 13 contains medicines that not all people will need. Nearly all of the home treatment recommended in this book may be carried out with the use of these agents.

**TABLE 13** *Medications for Sometime Use*

| Use | Medicine |
|---|---|
| ■ For Allergy | Antihistamines<br>Nose drops and sprays |
| ■ Antiseptic | Hydrogen peroxide, iodine |
| ■ For colds and coughs | Cold tablets, cough syrups |
| ■ For constipation | Bulk laxatives, milk of magnesia |
| ■ For dental problems (preventive) | Sodium fluoride |
| ■ For diarrhea | Bismuth subsalicylate, attapulgite |
| ■ For eye irritations | Eye drops and artificial tears |
| ■ For fungus | Antifungal preparations |
| ■ For hemorrhoids | Hemorrhoid preparations |
| ■ For pain and fever | |
| in adults: | Aspirin, acetaminophen, ibuprofen |
| in children and teenagers:* | Acetaminophen |
| ■ For poisoning (to induce vomiting) | Syrup of ipecac |
| ■ For skin rashes<br>(soaking and soothing) | Hydrocortisone cream<br>Sodium bicarbonate (baking soda) |
| ■ For sprains | Elastic bandages |
| ■ For sunburn (preventive) | Sunscreen agents |
| ■ For upset stomach | Antacid (nonabsorbable) |
| ■ For wounds (minor) | Adhesive tape, bandages |

**See page 122 for discussion of Reye's syndrome, associated with the use of aspirin when treating children and teenagers with chicken pox or influenza.*

## For Allergy

**ANTIHISTAMINE AND DECONGESTANT COMPOUNDS**

Allerest, Sine-Off, Chlor-Trimeton, Sinarest, Sinutab, and Dristan are among the over-the-counter drugs designed for treatment of minor allergic symptoms. They are similar to the cold compounds described below, but they less frequently contain pain and fever agents like aspirin, acetaminophen, or ibuprofen. Usually, these drug compounds contain an antihistamine and a decongestant agent. These can be identified from the label. You can purchase the ingredients of the compound separately, and we advise you to do so.

If you tolerate one of these drugs well and get good relief, you may continue to take it for several weeks (for example, through a hay fever season) without seeing a doctor. The same sort of drug taken as nose drops or nasal spray should be used more sparingly and only for short periods, as detailed below in "Nose Drops and Sprays."

### Reading the Labels

The decongestant is often phenylephrine, ephedrine, or phenylpropanolamine. If the compound name is not familiar, the suffix "ephrine" or "edrine" will usually identify this component of the compound. The antihistamine is often chlorpheniramine (Chlor-Trimeton, etc.) or pyrilamine. If not, the antihistamine is sometimes (but not always) identifiable on the label by the suffix "amine."

### Dosage

Take according to product directions. Reduce dose if side effects are noted, or try another compound.

### Side Effects

These are usually minor and disappear after the drug is stopped or decreased in dose. Agitation and insomnia usually indicate too much of the decongestant component. Drowsiness usually indicates too much antihistamine. If you can avoid the substance to which you are allergic, it is far superior to taking drugs. Drugs, to a certain degree, inevitably impair your functioning.

## NOSE DROPS AND SPRAYS

Afrin, Neo-Synephrine, Dristan, and others treat a runny nose. A runny nose is often the worst symptom of a cold or allergy. Because this complaint is so common, remedies are big business, and there are many advertised as decreasing nasal drips. Many of these preparations are "topical," like nose drops and sprays, and act directly on the inflamed tissue. There are some problems associated with the use of these compounds.

The active ingredient in these compounds is a decongestant drug—ephedrine or phenylephrine. When applied, you can feel the membranes shrinking down and "drawing," and you will note a decrease in the amount of secretion. In other words, the medication is effective and can relieve symptoms.

The major drawback is that the relief is temporary. Usually the symptoms return in a couple of hours, and you need to repeat the dose. This is fine for a while. But these drugs work by causing the muscle in the walls of the blood vessels to constrict (shrink), decreasing blood flow. After many applications, these small muscles become fatigued and fail to respond. Finally, they are so fatigued that they relax entirely, and the situation becomes worse than it was in the beginning. This is medically termed "rebound vasodilation." This can occur if you use these drugs steadily for three days or more. Many patients interpret these increased symptoms as a need for more medication. Taking more only makes the problem increasingly worse. Therefore, use nose drops or sprays only for a few days at a time. After several days' rest, they may be used again for a few days.

### Dosage

These drugs are almost always used in the wrong way. If you can taste the drug, you have applied it to the wrong area. If you don't bathe the swollen membranes on the side surface of the inner nose, you won't get the desired effect. Apply small amounts to one nostril while lying down on that side for a few minutes so that the medicine will bathe the membranes. Then apply the agent to the other side while lying on that side. Treat four times a day if needed, but do not continue for more than three days without interrupting the therapy.

### Side Effects

Rebound vasodilation from prolonged use is the most common problem. If you apply these agents incorrectly and swallow a large amount of the drug, you may experience a rapid heart rate and an uneasy, agitated feeling. The drying effect of the drug can result in nosebleeds. Try to avoid the substances to which you are allergic rather than treating the consequences of exposure. Often simple measures like changing a furnace filter, using a vaporizer, or using an air conditioner to filter the air will improve symptoms.

# *For Colds and Coughs*

## COLD TABLETS

Coricidin, Dristan, Triaminic, Contac, and dozens of other products are widely advertised as being effective against the common cold. The choice is confusing. Surprisingly, many give satisfactory symptomatic relief. We do not feel that these compounds add much to standard treatment with aspirin and fluids, but many patients feel otherwise, and we do not discourage their use for short periods.

These compounds usually have three basic ingredients. The most important is aspirin, acetaminophen, or ibuprofen, to reduce fever and pain. In addition, there is a decongestant drug to shrink the swollen membranes and the small blood vessels, and an antihistamine to block any allergy and dry the mucus.

### Reading the Labels

The decongestant is often phenylephrine, ephedrine, or phenylpropanolamine. If the compound name is not familiar, the suffix "-ephrine" or "-edrine" will usually identify this component of the compound. The antihistamine is often chlorpheniramine (Chlor-Trimeton, etc.) or pyrilamine. If not, the antihistamine is usually (but not always) identifiable on the label by the suffix "-amine."

Occasionally, a "belladonna alkaloid" is added to these compounds to enhance other actions and reduce stomach spasms. In the small doses used, there is little effect from these drugs. These are listed as "scopolamine," "belladonna," or something similar. Other ingredients that may be listed contribute little. Do not use products with caffeine if you have heart trouble or difficulty sleeping. Do not use products with phenacetin over a long period because kidney damage has been reported.

These products, then, contain the much promoted "combination-of-ingredients" approach. As a general rule, single drugs are preferable to combinations of drugs; they allow you to be more selective in treatment of symptoms, and consequently you take fewer drugs. The ingredients in combination products are available alone and should be considered as alternatives. The major ingredient, aspirin, is discussed below. Pseudoephedrine is an excellent decongestant and is available without prescription in 30-mg (milligram) and 60-mg tablets.

Chlorpheniramine, a strong antihistamine, is now available without prescription in the standard 4-mg size. When possible, consider applying medicine directly to the affected area, as with nose drops or sprays for a runny nose.

Finally, note that the commonly prescribed cold medicines (Sudafed, Actifed, Dimetapp) are really just more concentrated and expensive formulations of the same type of drugs (and often even the same names) that are available over the counter. Is it worth a trip to the doctor just for that?

### Dosage

Try the recommended dosage. If no effect is noted, you may increase the dosage by one-half. Do not exceed twice the recommended dosage. Remember that you are trying to find a compromise between desired effects and side effects. Increasing the dosage gives some chance of increased beneficial effects, but it guarantees a greater probability of side effects.

### Side Effects

Drugs that put one person to sleep will keep another awake. The most frequent side effects of cold tablets are drowsiness and agitation. The drowsiness is usually caused by the antihistamine component, and the insomnia or agitation results from the decongestant component. You can try another compound that has less or none of the offending chemical, or you can reduce the dose. There are no frequent serious side effects; the most dangerous is drowsiness if you intend to drive or operate machinery. Rarely, the "belladonna" component will cause dryness of mouth, blurring of vision, or inability to urinate. Aspirin's usual side effects—upset stomach or ringing in the ears—may also be experienced. More rarely, bleeding from the stomach may occur.

## COUGH SYRUPS IN GENERAL

This is a confusing area, with many products. To simplify, consider only two major categories of cough medication:

- **Expectorants** are usually preferable because they liquefy the secretions and allow the body's defenses to get rid of the material.
- **Cough suppressants** should be avoided if the cough is bringing up any material or if there is a lot of mucus. In the late stages of a cough, when it is dry and hacking, compounds containing a suppressant may be useful.

We prefer compounds that do not contain an antihistamine because the drying effect on the mucus can harm as much as help.

### Reading the Labels

Guaifenesin, potassium iodide, and several other frequently used chemicals cause an expectorant action.

Cough-suppressant action comes principally from narcotics, such as codeine. Over-the-counter cough suppressants cannot contain codeine. They often contain dextromethorphan hydrobromide, which is not a narcotic but is a close chemical relative.

Many commercial mixtures contain a little of everything and may have some of the ingredients of the cold compounds as well. We will discuss only guaifenesin (Robitussin, Naldecon CX, etc.) and dextromethorphan (Vicks Formula 44, Robitussin-DM, etc.) specifically; follow the label instructions for other agents.

## GUAIFENESIN

Guaifenesin acts to draw more liquid into the mucus that triggers a cough. Thus, the cough medicine liquefies these mucus secretions so that they may be coughed free. The resulting cough is easier and less irritating. For a dry, hacking cough remaining after a cold, the lubrication alone often soothes the inflamed area. Guaifenesin does not suppress the cough reflex but encourages the natural defense mechanisms of the body. There is controversy over its effectiveness, but it appears to be safe. It is not as powerful as the codeine-containing preparations, but for routine use we prefer it to prescription drugs. Pepper and garlic, usually not thought of as medicines, have a similar effect.

### Reading the Labels

These drugs are also available in combination with decongestants and cough suppressants; the decongestants may carry a "-PE" suffix for "phenylephrine" and the cough suppressants a "-DM" for "dextromethorphan."

### Dosage

Follow directions on the label. Call your doctor if you have a sick and coughing child less than 1 year old.

**Side Effects**

No significant problems have been reported. If preparations containing other drugs are used, side effects from the other components of the combination may occur.

### DEXTROMETHORPHAN

Robitussin-DM, St. Joseph's for Children, Vicks Formula 44, and others contain dextromethorphan, a drug that "calms the cough center." The drug makes the areas of the brain that control coughs less sensitive to the stimuli that trigger coughs. No matter how much is used, it will seldom decrease a cough by more than 50%. Thus, you cannot totally suppress a cough; this is actually beneficial because the cough is a protective reflex. This drug may be used with dry, hacking coughs that are preventing sleep or work.

**Dosage**

See directions on the label. Adults may require up to twice the recommended dosage to obtain any effect, but do not exceed this amount. A higher dose may produce problems, not further benefit.

**Side Effects**

Drowsiness is the only side effect that has been reliably reported.

## *For Constipation*

We prefer a natural diet, with natural vegetable-fiber residue, to the use of any laxative. But if you must use a laxative, the most attractive alternatives are psyllium as a bulk laxative or milk of magnesia to hold water in the bowel and soften the stool.

### BULK (PSYLLIUM-CONTAINING) LAXATIVES

Metamucil, Effer-Syllium, and similar preparations contain substances refined from the psyllium seed. They can help both diarrhea and constipation. Psyllium draws water into the stool, forms a gel or thick solution, and thus provides bulk. It is not absorbed by the digestive tract but only passes through; thus, it is a natural product and essentially has no contraindications or side effects. However, it doesn't always work; a similar effect probably can be obtained by eating enough celery. Psyllium has been recommended as a weight-reduction aid when taken before meals because it induces a feeling of fullness that may reduce appetite; however, it doesn't seem very effective in this role.

### Dosage

One teaspoonful, stirred in a glass of water, taken twice daily is a typical dose. A second glass of water or juice should also be taken. Psyllium is also available in more expensive, individual-dose packets, for times when you don't have a teaspoon. The effervescent versions mix a bit more rapidly and taste better to some people.

### Side Effects

If the bulk laxative is taken without sufficient water, the gel that is formed could conceivably lodge in the esophagus (the tube that leads from the mouth to the stomach). Sufficient liquid will prevent this problem.

## MILK OF MAGNESIA

This home remedy has been on most bathroom shelves since the days of our grandparents. Milk of magnesia has two actions: (1) as a laxative, it causes fluid to be retained within the bowel and in the feces; (2) as an antacid, it neutralizes the acid in the stomach. It is an effective antacid, but unfortunately, when taken in a sufficient dose to help an ulcer patient it causes quite severe diarrhea. A single dose is relatively well tolerated, so a mild upset stomach may be treated with milk of magnesia.

Magnesium is the active ingredient in milk of magnesia. Although milk of magnesia cannot be termed a "natural" laxative, it is mild and less subject to abuse than many alternatives.

### Dosage

For the adult, two tablespoons may be taken at bedtime as a laxative or up to once daily, as required, to quiet stomach upset. It produces its laxative effect in approximately eight hours. If the stomach is not soothed, use another antacid more frequently. Give one-half dose to children of ages 6 to 12, one-fourth dose to children of ages 3 to 6. As with other antacids, two tablets are roughly equal in chemical content to two tablespoons liquid. However, the liquid is more effective as an antacid.

**Side Effects**

Milk of magnesia is difficult to misuse because it causes diarrhea before any more serious effects. Too much magnesium is harmful to the body, but you won't ingest that much unless you use a bottle a day. There is some salt present, so be careful if you are on a low-salt diet. Milk of magnesia is a "non-absorbable" antacid, so it does not greatly affect the acidity of the body. However, it should never be used by people who have kidney disease.

## *For Dental Care*

Take care of your teeth; they help you chew. There is good evidence that preventive measures can save teeth. Brush your teeth as recommended, and use dental floss to clean between the teeth. Many doctors feel that flossing is the most important prevention against adult tooth decay. Adult tooth loss is usually due to plaque buildup, gum disease, and bone loss. Water jets (such as Waterpic) remove food products from between the teeth, but they are less effective than proper flossing.

### SODIUM FLUORIDE

If your water supply is fluoridated, your fluoride intake is adequate and you do not need to supplement your diet. The ground water in many areas is naturally fluoridated. Find out if your water is fluoridated or not, whether naturally or by chemical treatment; your local health department usually has the answer. If it is not fluoridated, it is important for you to supplement your children's diet with fluoride. Arguments remain about whether fluoride is needed after the teeth have been formed, but all authorities agree that fluoride is needed through age ten. Adults probably do not require dietary fluoride, although painting teeth with sodium fluoride paste by the dentist is still felt to be helpful, as is use of a stannous fluoride toothpaste.

**Dosage**

Fortunately, it is relatively easy to supplement with fluoride when the water supply is not treated. Buy a large bottle of fluoride tablets in a soluble form. Most tablets are 2.2 mg and contain 2 mg of fluoride; the rest is a soluble sugar. A child under the age of 3 needs approximately

0.5 mg (one-fourth tablet) per day, and a child between the ages of 3 and 10 needs 1 mg, or one-half tablet. The tablets can be chewed or swallowed. They may also be taken in milk; they do not alter the taste. In states where fluoride is available only by prescription, request a prescription from your doctor or dentist on a routine visit.

**Side Effects**

Too much fluoride will mottle (make gray spots) the teeth and will not give additional strength, so do not exceed the recommended dosage. At the recommended dosage, there are no known side effects; fluoride is a natural mineral present in many natural water supplies.

## *For Diarrhea*

For occasional loose stools, no medication is required. A clear liquid diet (for example, water or ginger ale) is the first remedy for any diarrhea; it rests the bowel and replaces lost fluid. When diarrhea persists, products with kaolin, pectin, or bismuth are often helpful. If these do not control the diarrhea, stronger agents containing substances such as paregoric may be prescribed. Long-term or severe diarrhea may require the help of a doctor and antibiotic treatments.

### ATTAPULGITE

Kaopectate, Diasorb, Rheaban, and similar medicines contain a mineral called attapulgite. This ingredient has a gelling effect that helps form a solid stool.

**Dosage**

Follow the directions on the label. For children below age three, call your doctor to ask for the correct dosage. In general, more severe diarrhea is treated more vigorously, whereas minor problems require less medicine.

**Side Effects**

None have been reported.

**BISMUTH SUBSALICYLATE (PEPTO-BISMOL)**

**Dosage** Follow label directions. For children below age three, call the doctor for dosage.

**Side Effects** Bismuth may cause a temporary, harmless darkening of the tongue and/or stool.

**PSYLLIUM HYDROPHILIC MUCILLOID**

Metamucil, Effer-Syllium, and similar products contain a substance (refined from the psyllium seed) that can help with both diarrhea and constipation. It draws water into the stool, forms a gel or thick solution, and thus provides bulk (see page 114).

## *For Eye Irritations*

The tear mechanism normally soothes, cleans, and lubricates the eye. Occasionally, the environment can overwhelm this mechanism, or the tear flow may be insufficient. In these cases, the eye becomes "tired," feels dry or gritty, and may itch. A number of compounds that may aid this problem are available.

**MURINE, VISINE, PREFRIN, AND OTHERS**

There are two general types of eye preparations. One class contains compounds intended to soothe the eye (Murine, Refresh, Liquifilm, etc.). Added to the compounds may be substances that shrink blood vessels and thus "get the red out" (Visine, Murine Plus, Visine AC); these substances are decongestants. Their capacity to soothe is debatable. The use of decongestants to get rid of a bloodshot appearance is totally cosmetic. It is possible that such preparations can actually interfere with the normal healing process, although this is unlikely.

**METHYLCELLULOSE EYEDROPS**

The second group of preparations makes no claims of special soothing effects and contains no decongestants. They are solutions with concentrations like those of the body so that no irritation occurs. Their purpose is to lubricate the eye, to be "artificial tears." These are the preparations preferred by ophthalmologists for minor eye irritation. Methylcellulose eyedrops are one example.

**Dosage**

Use as frequently as needed in the quantity required. You can't use too much, although usually a few drops give just as much relief as a bottleful. If your problem of dry eyes is constant, you should check it out with the doctor because an underlying problem could be present. Usually, the symptom of dry eyes lasts only a few hours and is readily relieved. Too much sun, wind, or dust usually causes the minor irritation.

**Side Effects**

No serious side effects have been reported. Visine and other drugs containing decongestants tend to sting a bit.

None of these drugs treats eye infections or injuries or removes foreign bodies from the eye. In Part IV, we give instructions for more severe eye complaints. Refer to:

**Foreign Body in Eye**, page 211
**Eye Pain**, page 213
**Decreased Vision**, page 215
**Eye Burning, Itching, and Discharge**, page 217

## *For Hemorrhoids*

### ZINC OXIDE POWDERS AND CREAMS

These agents aren't magic, but they are good for ordinary problems. The creams soothe the irritated area while the body heals the inflamed vein. They also help toughen the skin over the hemorrhoids so that they are less easily irritated. Don't trap bacteria beneath the creams; apply them after a bath when the area has been carefully cleaned and dried.

**Reading the Labels**

We do not advocate the use of creams that contain ingredients identified by the suffix "-caine" because repeated use of these local anesthetics can cause further irritation. The other heavily advertised products, in our opinion, offer little advantage over zinc oxide.

**Dosage**

Apply as needed, following label directions.

**Side Effects**

Essentially none.

## *For Pain and Fever: Adults*

There are three major over-the-counter drugs in this class: aspirin, acetaminophen, and ibuprofen. Acetaminophen is the safest of the three; both aspirin and ibuprofen can cause severe or even fatal bleeding of the stomach, although only rarely if just a few tablets are taken. On the other hand, acetaminophen does not reduce inflammation. Aspirin and ibuprofen do, if taken in substantial dosage. Ibuprofen is better than the other two for relief of menstrual cramps.

Most of the time, the manufacturer conceals the key drug in the fine print under "active ingredients" and refers obliquely to the amount of "analgesic," or "pain reliever," present in each tablet.

The reason is there are really only three drugs and many manufacturers. Each manufacturer wants his product to seem unique in a crowded marketplace, so they produce many minor variations on a similar theme. Anacin is aspirin and caffeine, Anacin 3 is acetaminophen. Excedrin is half aspirin and half acetaminophen. Caffeine may be added (for example, in Anacin and Excedrin); this improves pain relief but may make you jittery. An antacid may be added (for example, in Bufferin or Ascriptin) in an attempt to cut down on stomach distress. Other than these variations, there is little reason for a medical preference in most cases. If you like a particular formulation well enough, use it. If you want to save money, read the labels carefully and look for the best buys.

## ASPIRIN

Expensive aspirin preparations use coated tablets for easier swallowing and they dissolve faster, but this does not make them more effective than cheaper brands. If the bottle contains a vinegary odor when opened, the aspirin has begun to deteriorate and should be discarded. Aspirin usually has a shelf life of about three years, although shorter periods are sometimes quoted. (Note: U.S.P. stands for "United States Pharmacopeia." Although not an absolute guarantee that the drug is the best, it does mean that the drug has met certain standards in composition and physical characteristics. The same is true of the designation N.F., which stands for "National Formulary.")

### Dosage

In adults, the standard dose for pain relief is two tablets taken every three to four hours as required. The maximum effect occurs in about two hours. Each standard tablet is 5 grains (325 mg or 0.325 gram). If you use a non-standard concoction, you will have to do the arithmetic to calculate equivalent doses. The terms "extra-strength," "arthritis pain formula," and the like merely indicate a greater amount of aspirin per tablet. This is medically trivial. You can take more tablets of the cheaper aspirin and still save money. When you read that a product "contains more of the ingredient that doctors recommend most," you may be sure that the product contains a little bit more aspirin per tablet; perhaps 400 to 500 mg instead of 325.

Here are some hints for good aspirin usage. Aspirin treats symptoms; it does not cure problems. Thus, for symptoms such as headache or muscle pain or menstrual cramps, don't take it unless you hurt. On the other hand, for control of fever, you will be more comfortable if you repeat the dose every three to four hours during the day because this prevents fever from moving up and down. The afternoon and evening are the worst, so try not to miss a dose during these hours. If you need aspirin for relief from some symptom over a prolonged period, check the symptom with your doctor. Relief from pain or fever is not very different if you increase the dose, and you are more likely to irritate your stomach, so take the standard dose even if you still have some discomfort.

For control of inflammation, as in serious arthritis, the dose of aspirin must be high, often 16 to 20 tablets daily, and must be continued over a prolonged period. A doctor should monitor such treatment; it is relatively safe, but problems sometimes occur.

To be safe, avoid using aspirin for children or teenagers with a fever because of the possibility of causing **Reye's syndrome**. If you do use aspirin for children, a dose of about 1 grain (65 mg) for each year of age is appropriate, with an adult dose for children over 10 years old. Children's aspirin comes in 1.25-grain (81-mg) tablets that taste good; please do not allow them to be taken as candy by a small child.

To prevent heart attacks or complications of high blood pressure in pregnancy the dose is very low; 81 mg (one baby aspirin) every other day.

## Side Effects

In addition to Reye's syndrome, an upset stomach or ringing in the ears can be caused by aspirin. If your ears ring, reduce the dose—you are taking too much.

Serious gastrointestinal hemorrhage or a perforated (ruptured) stomach can occur; aspirin more than doubles your risk of a bleeding ulcer. If the stomach is upset, try taking aspirin a half-hour after meals, when the food in the stomach will act as a buffer. Coated aspirin (such as Ecotrin) can help protect the stomach. However, some people do not digest the coated aspirin and so receive no benefit. Buffering is sometimes added to aspirin to protect the stomach and may help a little. If you take a lot of aspirin and desire a buffered preparation, we recommend a combination made with a non-absorbable antacid (as in Ascriptin or Bufferin) rather than an absorbable antacid, as in some buffered aspirins. Non-absorbable antacids are much easier on your system. Over the short term, the buffering makes little difference, and there is controversy as to whether it works anyway.

Asthma, nasal polyps, deafness, serious bleeding from the digestive tract, ulcers, and other major problems have been associated with aspirin. However, such problems are unusual and usually disappear after the aspirin is stopped. Conversely, some studies suggest that aspirin might be good treatment for preventing heart attacks. If so, a tablet a day, or even a tablet a week, seems to be plenty of aspirin for the blood-thinning effects. In high risk pregnancies aspirin can reduce the risk of miscarriage or low birth-weight babies; here the dose is two baby aspirin (162 mg) per day during the second and third trimester.

Aspirin comes in combination with many other remedies not described in this book, most frequently caffeine and phenacetin ("APC Tabs"). Some scientists think these agents increase the pain-killing effects; others dispute this. They do increase the side effects, and we find little use for them. Do not use products with caffeine if you have heart trouble or difficulty in sleeping; do not use products with phenacetin over a long period because kidney damage has been reported.

## ACETAMINOPHEN

Aspirin is the drug of first choice in adults for treatment of minor pains and fever. Acetaminophen, available in several brand-name preparations—Tylenol, Datril, Liquiprin, and Tempra—is the second choice for adults and first choice for children and teenagers. It is slightly less predictable than aspirin, somewhat less powerful, and does not have the anti-inflammatory action that makes aspirin so valuable in treatment of arthritis and some other diseases. On the other hand, it does not cause ringing in the ears or upset the stomach—common side effects with aspirin. It does not cause Reye's syndrome. Most pediatricians feel that acetaminophen is preferable for use by children for these reasons. In the British Commonwealth, this drug is known as paracetamol.

### Dosage

Acetaminophen is used in doses identical to those of aspirin. For adults, two 5-grain tablets every three to four hours is the standard dose. In children, 1 grain per year of age every four hours is satisfactory. There is never a reason to exceed these doses because there is no additional benefit in taking higher amounts. Acetaminophen is available in liquid preparations that are palatable for small children. These are usually administered by a dropper, and the package insert gives the amount for each age range.

### Side Effects

These are seldom experienced. If you suspect a side effect, call your doctor. A variety of rare toxic effects have been reported, but none are definitely related to the use of this drug. A truly major overdose can cause liver failure, particularly in children, and this can be fatal. Keep the bottle where children can not get at it. Like aspirin, acetaminophen comes in multiple combination products that offer little advantage.

## IBUPROFEN

Ibuprofen (Advil, Nuprin, etc.) was long used as a prescription drug for rheumatoid arthritis and osteoarthritis and has recently been approved for over-the-counter use. Compared with aspirin or acetaminophen, the advantages and disadvantages pretty well cancel out. Ibuprofen is about as toxic to the stomach as aspirin, and more so than acetaminophen. It doesn't cause ringing of the ears like aspirin or severe liver disease (rare) like acetaminophen. It appears to be almost impossible to commit suicide by overdose with this drug. But concern has been raised about kidney problems (mild and reversible), and it is sometimes more expensive. Therapeutically, it is effective for pain and fever. It is particularly effective for menstrual cramps and is the best over-the-counter preparation for this problem.

**Dosage**

Ibuprofen comes in 200-mg tablets, and the maximum recommended dose is 1200 mg (six tablets) per day. This is about one-half the recommended dose for the prescription equivalent, but this dose is effective for minor problems and should not be exceeded without a doctor's advice.

**Side Effects**

Gastrointestinal upset is the most frequent problem and is reason to stop or to call the doctor. Serious gastrointestinal hemorrhage or a perforated stomach can result. In the rare patient with aspirin allergy, there can be cross-reactivity. Read the label carefully. This drug has been prescribed to millions of patients but is still relatively new as an over-the-counter preparation.

## *For Pain and Fever: Children*

The principles and drugs used to control minor pain and fever in the child are the same as in the adult, but there are differences in the importance of treatment and in the method of administration. In the child, fever comes on more rapidly and may rise much higher, even with a minor virus. The fever must be controlled; high fever can lead to a frightening temporary epilepsy, with seizures or "fits." Thus, while control of the fever in an adult is principally for the comfort of the patient, fever control in the child actually prevents serious complications. It can be difficult to get a sick small child to take medication; thus, different methods of administration are sometimes needed.

If the child has a rash, a stiff neck, difficulty in breathing, is lethargic, or looks very ill, call or visit the doctor. Be particularly careful with children under one year of age. Phone advice is graciously available in most areas; don't hesitate to call if you have a question. Many times, despite a high fever, the child will look fine and not even be very irritable. In such cases, treatment and observation at home are adequate. Doctors frequently prefer a phone call to a visit, because if the visit can be avoided, other children in the waiting room or office are not exposed to the virus.

Children who take aspirin when they have chicken pox or the flu have a higher risk of developing Reye's syndrome, a rare but serious disease of the brain and liver. Because it is hard to recognize chicken pox and flu in their early stages, we recommend that parents always give children and teenagers **acetaminophen** instead of aspirin. It does not carry the risk of Reye's syndrome and is slightly milder on the stomach than ibuprofen.

## LIQUID ACETAMINOPHEN

Most pediatricians prefer liquid acetaminophen or sodium salicylate to aspirin for the small child, because these liquid preparations are easier to administer and are better tolerated by the stomach. (If vomiting makes it impossible to keep even these liquid medicines down, the use of rectal suppositories of aspirin can be very helpful.)

### Dosage

For liquid acetaminophen preparations, follow the label advice. Administer every four hours. During the period from noon to midnight, awaken the child if necessary. After midnight, the fever will usually break by itself and become less of a problem; so if you miss a dose, it is less important. But check the child's temperature at least once during the night to make sure. Remember, these drugs last only about four hours in the body, and you must keep repeating the dose or you will lose the effect.

## ASPIRIN RECTAL SUPPOSITORIES

Aspirin rectal suppositories are available only by prescription in most localities. The dose is the same as by mouth—1 grain (65 mg) for each year of age per 4 hours; after age 10 use the adult dose. One-grain suppositories are manufactured but are sometimes difficult to find. If necessary, cut the larger 5-grain suppositories to make an approximate equivalent to the dose needed. Use a warm knife and cut them lengthwise. Ask your doctor for a prescription for aspirin rectal suppositories on a routine visit if you can't get them over the counter. Keep them in stock at home. Use them only when vomiting prevents retention of any oral intake, and do not exceed 3 doses for any one illness without contacting your doctor.

Use of suppositories confuses many parents. The idea is to allow the medicine to be absorbed through the mucous membranes of the rectum. Remove the wrapper before use! When inserting the suppository, firm but gentle pressure will cause the muscles to relax around the rectum. Be patient. In small children, the buttocks may need to be held or taped together to prevent expulsion of the suppository.

**Side Effects**

Rectal aspirin can irritate the rectum and cause local bleeding; therefore, it should only be used if the ordinary routes of administration are impossible—even then, if more than two or three doses seem to be required, call your doctor for advice. Because recent information indicates an association with a rare but serious problem known as Reye's syndrome, *aspirin should not be used for children or teenagers who might have chicken pox or influenza.*

**OTHER MEASURES**

Cool or lukewarm baths are also useful in keeping a fever down. During the bath, wet the hair as well. Keep the patient in a cool room, wearing little or no clothing.

## *For Poisoning*

**TO INDUCE VOMITING**

Syrup of ipecac causes vomiting. Keep this traditional remedy handy if you have small children. Vomiting should be induced immediately when poisoning is due to a plant or a drug. This will empty the stomach of any poison that has not already been absorbed.

Do *not* use ipecac or any agent to cause vomiting if the poison swallowed is a petroleum-based compound or a strong acid or alkali (see page 153).

It is far better to keep toxic chemicals out of a child's reach than to have to use ipecac. When you buy ipecac, use the purchase as a reminder to check the house for toxic materials that a child might reach; move them to a safer place. If your child does swallow something, the sooner the stomach is emptied, the milder the problem will be, with the exceptions listed above. There is no time to buy ipecac after your child has swallowed poison; therefore, you should have it on hand—just in case it's ever needed.

**Dosage**

One tablespoon of ipecac may suffice for a small child; 2 tablespoons are necessary for older children and adults. Follow the dose with as much warm water as can be given, until vomiting occurs. Repeat the dose in 15 minutes if you haven't had any results.

**Side Effects**

This is an uncomfortable medication, but it is not hazardous unless vomiting causes material to be thrown down the windpipe into the lungs. This can cause pneumonia, so do not induce vomiting in a patient who is unconscious or nearly unconscious. Do not cause vomiting of volatile materials that can be inhaled into the lung and cause damage. Call the local poison control center in any potentially severe poisoning. In this situation, giving ipecac on the way to the hospital may be helpful and even can be lifesaving, but the experts at the poison control center can tell you for sure. Poisoning from medicine or a poisonous plant should be treated with ipecac.

## *For Skin Dryness*

### MOISTURIZING CREAMS AND LOTIONS

There is little to be said about the various artificial materials—for example, Lubriderm, Vaseline, Corn Huskers, Nivea, and Noxzema—that people apply to their skin in the attempt to temporarily improve its appearance or retard its aging. The various claims are not scientifically based, and possible long-term benefits have not been demonstrated. In some areas, it has been postulated that they are harmful rather than beneficial.

Sometimes, dry skin can actually cause symptoms, thus becoming a medical problem. Remember that bathing or exposure to detergents may contribute to the drying of skin. Decreasing the frequency of baths or showers, wearing gloves when working with cleansing agents, and other similar measures are more important than using any lotion or cream. Moisturizing creams and lotions may make your skin feel better to you. Note that some people are sensitive to the lanolin contained in some of these products.

**Dosage** Use per product label.

**Side Effects** Essentially none except for the rare lanolin sensitivity mentioned above.

## *For Skin Rashes*

### ALUMINUM SULPHATE SOLUTION

This is also called Burow's solution. It is sold under the brand names Bluboro, BurVeen, and Domeboro, and it contains calcium acetate. To relieve itching caused by rashes and bacterial infections such as impetigo, wet dressings prepared with Burow's solution will help cool, soothe, clean, and combat the inflammatory process.

**Dosage** Dilute 1 part Burow's solution with 10 to 40 parts water. Apply on skin. Do not cover with plastic or rubber. Change dressing every 5 to 15 minutes for up to 8 changes in 2 hours.

**Side Effects** This can irritate skin if not diluted.

### HYDROCORTISONE CREAMS

For temporary relief of skin itching and rashes such as poison ivy and poison oak, hydrocortisone cream is available over the counter. Brand names are Cortaid, Dermolate, Lanacort, and CaldeCORT. This is a strong, local anti-inflammatory preparation; in general, it is as effective as anything that your doctor can prescribe. Used for a short period of time, these creams are safe and almost totally non-toxic. They will clear up many minor rashes, but they "suppress" a condition rather than "cure" it.

**Dosage** Rub a very small amount into the rash. If you can see any cream remaining on the skin, you have used too much. Repeat frequently as needed, which often is every two to four hours.

**Side Effects**

Over the long term, these creams can cause skin atrophy and wasting, so limit their use to a two-week period. Beyond this time, check with your doctor. Theoretically, these creams can make an infection worse, so be careful about using them if the "rash" seems as though it might be infected. Don't use these creams around the eyes, and do not take them by mouth.

## *For Skin Fungus*

**ANTIFUNGAL PREPARATIONS**

Fungal infections of the skin are not serious, so treatment is not urgent. In general, the fungus needs moist, undisturbed areas to grow and will often disappear with regular cleansing, drying, and application of powder to keep the area dry. Cleansing should be performed twice daily.

If you need a medication, there are effective non-toxic agents available. For athlete's foot, try one of the zinc undecylenate creams or powders, such as Desenex. In difficult cases, tolnaftate (Tinactin, etc.), clotrimazole (Lotrimin, etc.), and miconazole (Micatin, etc.) are effective. These agents are useful for almost all skin fungus problems, but are more expensive.

**Dosage**

For athlete's foot, use as directed on the label. For other skin problems, selenium sulfide is available by prescription in a 2.5% solution. Over the counter, a 1% solution is available as Selsun Blue shampoo. Use the shampoo as a cream and let it dry on the lesions; repeat several times a day to compensate for the weaker strength.

**Side Effects**

There are very few. Selenium sulfide can burn the skin if used to excess, so decrease application if you notice any irritation. Selenium may discolor hair and will stain clothes. Be very careful when applying any of these products around the eyes. And don't take them by mouth.

## *For Sunburn Prevention*

**SUNSCREEN PRODUCTS**

Dermatologists continually remind us that sun is bad for the skin. Exposure to the sun accelerates the skin-aging process and increases the chance of skin cancer. Advertisements, on the other hand, continually extol the virtues of a suntan. As a nation, we spend much of our youth trying to achieve a pleasing skin tone, with disregard for the later consequences of solar radiation. Sunscreen agents can be used to prevent burning but allow you to be in the sun. If the skin is unusually sensitive to the sun's effects, a more complete block of the rays is best; this is achieved with a strong agent, like Pre-sun, or any PABA-containing agent with a high sunscreen number. Suntan lotions that are not sunscreen agents block relatively little solar radiation. The ratings on the label are a good guide to the blocking power of the different agents. (The higher the rating, the better the blocking power.)

**Dosage**

Apply evenly to exposed areas of skin as directed on the label.

**Side Effects**

Very rare skin irritation and allergy have been reported.

## *For Sprains*

**ELASTIC BANDAGES**

Elastic (Ace, etc.) bandages are periodically needed in any family. You will probably need both a narrow and a broader width. If problems are recurrent, the one-piece devices designed specifically for knee and ankle are sometimes more convenient. All these bandages primarily provide gentle support, but they also act to reduce swelling. Elastic bandages should be used if they make the injured part feel better. The support given is minimal, and re-injury is possible, despite the bandage. Thus, it is not a substitute for a splint, a cast, or a proper adhesive-type dressing. Perhaps the most important function of these bandages is as a reminder that you have a problem so that you are less likely to re-injure the part.

**Dosage**

Support should be continued well past the time of active discomfort to allow complete healing and to help prevent re-injury; this usually requires about six weeks. During the latter part of this period, use of the bandages may be discontinued except during activities that will likely stress the injured part. Remember that re-injury is still possible while these bandages are being used.

**Side Effects**

The simple elastic bandage can cause trouble when not properly applied. Problems arise because the bandage is applied too tightly, and circulation in the limb beyond the bandage is impaired. The bandage should be firm but not tight. The limb should not swell, hurt, or be cooler beyond the bandage. There should not be any blueness or purple color to the limb.

When wrapping the bandage, start at the most distant area to be bandaged and work toward the trunk of the body, making each loop a little looser than the one before. Thus, a knee bandage should be tighter below the knee than above, and an ankle bandage should be tighter on the foot than on the lower leg. Many people think that because a bandage is elastic it must be stretched. This is not the case. The stretching is for when you move. Simply wrap the bandage as you would a roll of gauze.

## *For Upset Stomach*

### NON-ABSORBABLE ANTACIDS

Maalox, Gelusil, Mylanta, Di-Gel, Amphogel, WinGel, and Riopan are examples of non-absorbable antacids. They are an important part of the home pharmacy. They help neutralize stomach acid and thus decrease heartburn, ulcer pain, gas pains, and stomach upset. Because they are not absorbed by the body, they usually do not upset the acid-base balance of the body and are quite safe.

Almost all these antacids are available in both liquid and tablet form. For most purposes, the liquid form is superior. It coats more of the surface area of the gullet and stomach than the tablets do. Indeed, if not well chewed, tablets may be almost worthless. Still, during work or play, a bottle can be cumbersome, and a few tablets in a shirt pocket or handbag may help out with midday doses.

## ABSORBABLE ANTACIDS

Baking soda, Alka-Seltzer, Rolaids, and Tums contain absorbable antacids. The main ingredient in these products is sodium bicarbonate (Alka-Seltzer, baking soda), dihydroxyaluminum sodium carbonate (Rolaids), or calcium carbonate (Tums), which neutralizes acid. They are more powerful neutralizers than non-absorbable antacids and come in convenient tablet form. However, they are absorbed through the walls of the stomach, and this may cause problems. The sodium in sodium bicarbonate and dihydroxyaluminum sodium carbonate may be a threat to those with high blood pressure or heart disease. For this reason, we tend to recommend the non-absorbable antacids or a combination of non-absorbable and absorbable antacids. Note that calcium carbonate is an excellent source of supplemental calcium.

### Reading the Labels

Non-absorbable antacids contain magnesium or aluminum, or both. As a general rule, magnesium causes diarrhea and aluminum causes constipation. Different brands are slightly different mixtures of the salts of these two metals, designed to avoid both diarrhea and constipation. A few brands also contain calcium, which is mildly constipating; in general, the calcium-containing preparations should be avoided.

Different products differ in taste. While there are some differences in potency, most people will ultimately select the particular antacid that has a taste they can tolerate and that doesn't upset their bowels. Keep trying different brands until you are satisfied.

### Dosage

Two tablespoons or 2 tablets, well-chewed, are the standard adult dose. Use one-half the adult dose for children of ages 6 to 12, and one-fourth the adult dose for children of ages 3 to 6. The frequency of the dose depends on the severity of the problem. For stomach upset or heartburn, 1 or 2 doses may often suffice. For gastritis, several doses a day for several days may be needed. For ulcers, 6 weeks or more may be needed, with the medication taken as frequently as every hour or so; this type of program should be supervised by a doctor.

### Side Effects

In general, the only problem is the effect on the bowel movements. Maalox tends to loosen the stools slightly, Mylanta and Gelusil are about average, and Amphogel and Aludrox (with more aluminum) tend to be more constipating. Adjust the dose and change brands as needed. Check with your doctor before using these compounds if you have kidney disease, heart disease, or high blood pressure. Some brands contain significant quantities of salt and should be avoided by people on a low-salt diet. Riopan and Di-Gel have the lowest salt content of the popular brands.

## *For Warts*

**WART REMOVERS**

Warts are a curious little problem. The capricious way in which they form and disappear has led to countless myths and home therapies. They can be surgically removed, burned off, or frozen off, but they also will go away by themselves or after treatment by hypnosis. Warts are caused by a virus and are a reaction to a minor local viral infection. If you get one, you are likely to get more. When one disappears, the others often follow. The exception is plantar warts, on the sole of the foot, which will not go away by themselves and not always with home treatment; the doctor may be needed.

Over-the-counter chemicals, such as Compound W and Wart-off, for treatment of warts are moderately effective. They contain a mild skin irritant. By repeated application the top layers of the wart are slowly burned off and eventually the virus is destroyed.

**Dosage**

Apply repeatedly, as directed on the product label. Persistence is necessary.

**Side Effects**

These products are effective because they are caustic to the skin. Be careful to apply them only to the wart, and be very careful around your eyes or mouth.

## *For Wounds (Minor)*

**ADHESIVE TAPE AND BANDAGES**

Bandages really don't "make it better." Sometimes leaving a minor wound open to the air is preferable to covering it. Still, a home medical shelf wouldn't be complete without a tin of assorted adhesive bandages. To fashion larger bandages, you also need adhesive tape and gauze. Bandages are useful for covering tender blisters, keeping dirt out of wounds, and keeping the edges of a cut together. They have some value in keeping the wound out of sight and thus are of cosmetic importance.

### Dosage

For smaller cuts and sores, use a bandage from the tin. Leaving the bandage on for a day or so is usually long enough; change the bandage if you wish to keep the wound covered longer. For cuts, apply the bandage perpendicular to the cut, and draw the skin toward the cut from both sides to relax skin tension before applying the bandage. The bandage should then act to keep the edges together during healing. For larger injuries, make a bandage from a roll of sterile gauze or from sterile 2" × 2" or 4" × 4" gauze pads, and firmly tape it in place with adhesive tape. Change the bandage daily. If you see white fat protruding from the cut, see your doctor.

### Side Effects

If the wound isn't clean when you cover it with a bandage, you may hide a developing infection from early discovery. Clean the wound and keep it clean. The bandage should be changed if it becomes wet. Some people are allergic to adhesive tape; they should use non-allergenic paper tape. If adhesive tape is left on for a week or so, it will irritate almost anyone's skin, so give the skin a rest.

Some patients leave a bandage on too long because they are afraid of the pain as they remove the bandage—particularly if there is hair caught in the tape. For painless removal, soak the adhesive tape in nail-polish remover (applied from the back) for five minutes. This will dissolve the adhesive and release both the skin and hair.

## ANTISEPTICS AND CLEANSERS

A dirty wound often becomes infected. If dirt or foreign bodies are trapped beneath the skin, they can fester and delay wound healing. Only a few germs are introduced at the time of a wound, but they may multiply to a very large number over several days. Antiseptic removes the dirt and kills the germs. Most of the time, the cleansing action is more important because many antiseptic solutions (hydrogen peroxide, benzalkonium chloride, povidone-iodine, etc.) really aren't very good at killing germs. Antibiotic creams (such as Bacitracin and Neosporin) are expensive, usually not necessary, and of questionable effectiveness. Hydrogen peroxide, which foams and cleans as you work it in the wound, is a good cleansing agent, and iodine is a reasonably good agent with which to kill germs.

Scrupulous attention to the initial cleaning of a wound and scrubbing out any embedded dirt particles are crucial to healing. Do this even though it hurts and bleeds. For small, clean cuts, use soap and water followed by iodine and then soap and water again. For larger wounds, use hydrogen peroxide with vigorous scrubbing. Betadine is a non-stinging iodine preparation. First-aid sprays are a waste of money.

### Dosage

Do not use hydrogen peroxide that is stronger than 3%, such as that used for bleaching hair. Most hydrogen peroxide is sold at the 3% strength and may be used at full strength. Pour it on and scrub with a rough cloth. Wash it off and repeat. Continue until there is no dirt visible beneath the level of the skin. If you can't get it clean, go to a doctor.

Iodine is painted or wiped onto the wound and the surrounding area. Wash it off within a few minutes, leaving a trace of the iodine color on the skin.

### Side Effects

Iodine will burn the skin if left on full strength, so be careful. Iodine is also poisonous if swallowed; keep it away from children. Hydrogen peroxide is safe to the skin but can bleach hair and clothing, so try not to spill it. Some people are allergic to iodine; discontinue use if you get a rash.

## SOAKING AGENT

Sodium bicarbonate (baking soda, $NaHCO_3$) is a very useful household chemical. It has three principal medical uses:

- As a strong solution, it will draw fluid and swelling out of a wound and will act to soak and clean the wound at the same time.
- As a weaker solution, it acts to soothe the skin and reduce itching; thus, it is helpful in conditions ranging from sunburn to poison oak to chicken pox.
- If taken by mouth, it serves as an antacid and may help alleviate heartburn or stomach upset.

**Dosage**

To soak a wound use one tablespoon to a cup of warm water. If a finger or toe is injured, it may be placed in the cup. For other wounds, a wash cloth should be saturated with the solution and placed over the wound as a compress. Generally, a wound should be soaked for five to ten minutes at a time, three times a day. If the skin is puckered and "water-logged" after the soak, it has been soaked too long. A cellophane or plastic wrap may be placed over the cloth compress to retain heat and moisture longer.

To soothe the skin use from two tablespoons to a half-cup in a bath of warm water. Blot gently after the bath and allow to dry on the skin. Repeat this procedure as often as necessary.

As an antacid, use one teaspoonful in a glass of water, every four hours as needed—but only occasionally.

**Side Effects**

There are none as long as the baking soda is only applied to the skin. Be careful if you take it by mouth. First, there is a lot of sodium in it. If you have heart trouble, high blood pressure, or are on a low-salt diet, you can get into a lot of trouble. Second, if you take it for many months on a regular basis, there is some evidence that it may result in calcium deposits in the kidneys and thus in kidney damage. As an antacid, it is absorbable and is thus potentially more hazardous than non-absorbable antacids.

## *For Vitamin Deficiency*

### VITAMIN PREPARATIONS

Americans are said to have the most expensive urine in the world. Much of its added worth comes from unneeded, unabsorbed vitamins that are excreted in the urine and cannot aid the body. Most vitamins are chemically known as co-enzymes. They are essential to normal function but are required in only very small amounts. With an ordinary diet, many times the required amounts of vitamins are provided. Vitamin supplementation is needed only by severe alcoholics or by people with unusually limited diets. For exceptions, follow your doctor's advice for infants, children under age two, and pregnant or nursing women.

Mega-vitamin doses, providing many times the known requirements for vitamin C, vitamin E, and other vitamins, have been advocated by a few people. There is some evidence that adequate intake of the "antioxidant" vitamins (A, C, and E) are associated with decreased risk of some kinds of problems. However, extra vitamins have not been shown to decrease common colds, improve sex life, restore lost energy, or cure cancer or arthritis.

Unless a doctor documents a vitamin deficiency and recommends a supplement, use of vitamins is entirely optional. It's your money. If you want to buy vitamins, select the cheaper "house" brands that are not heavily advertised.

**Dosage**

As specified by a doctor for the individual's use.

**Side Effects**

Vitamin A, vitamin D, and vitamin $B_6$ (pyridoxine) can cause severe problems when excessively large doses are taken. Large doses of vitamin C have been reported to be associated with kidney problems in very unusual circumstances (total parenteral nutrition), but there is no convincing evidence that this is a problem at other times. Other vitamins have not been as well studied, but serious side effects appear to be rare.

PART IV

# *The Patient and the Common Complaint: Specific Advice for 120 Problems*

## CHAPTER A

# *How to Use Part IV*

In this part of *Take Care of Yourself* you will find information and decision charts that show you how to deal with 120 common medical problems. The general information describes possible causes of the problems, methods for treating them at home, and what to expect at the doctor's office if you need to go. The decision charts summarize this information, helping you decide whether to use home treatment or consult a physician. Consider these six steps when using this part.

**1. Is emergency action necessary?**

Usually the answer is obvious. The most common emergency signs are listed in the box on page 143. More advice on these problems is found starting on page 145. It is a good idea to read Chapter B, "Emergencies," *now* so that you're prepared for an emergency if one occurs. Fortunately, the great majority of complaints don't require emergency treatment.

**2. Find the section that covers your medical problem.**

Determine your chief complaint or symptom—a cough, an earache, dizziness. Don't jump to conclusions about the cause of the problem: chest pain, for instance, may indicate indigestion rather than a heart attack. Look that problem up under **Chest Pain**.

Use the list of chapters on page 143 to find the appropriate chapter. The first page of each chapter lists the problems it covers, organized by type of complaint or by area of the body: neck pain, shoulder pain, arm pain, and so on.

You can also look up a symptom in the contents or the index. They may help you skip directly to the section you need.

**3. If in doubt, turn to the section for your worst problem first.**

You may have more than one problem, such as abdominal pain, nausea, and diarrhea. In such cases, look up the most serious complaint first, then the next most serious, and so on.

You may notice some duplication of questions in the decision charts, especially when the symptoms are closely related. If you use more than one chart, play it safe: if one chart recommends home treatment and the other advises a call to the doctor, then call the doctor.

**4. Read all of the general information in the section.**

The general material gives you important information about interpreting the decision chart. If you ignore it, you may inadvertently select the wrong course of action.

**5. Go through the decision chart.**

Start at the top. Answer every question, following the arrows indicated by your answers. Don't skip around: that may result in errors. Each question assumes that you've answered the previous question.

**6. Follow the treatment indicated.**

Sometimes there will be an instruction to go to another section, or a description or diagram of what to do. More often you will find one of the instruction boxes shown below and on the next page.

Don't assume that an instruction to use home treatment guarantees that the problem is trivial and may be ignored. Home therapy must be used conscientiously if it is to work. Also, as with all treatments, home therapy may not be effective in a particular case, so don't hesitate to visit a doctor's office if the problem doesn't improve.

Similarly, if the chart indicates that you should consult a doctor, it does not necessarily mean that the illness is serious or dangerous. Often a physical examination is necessary to diagnose the cause of the problem, or you will benefit from certain facilities of the doctor's office.

The charts usually recommend one of the following actions:

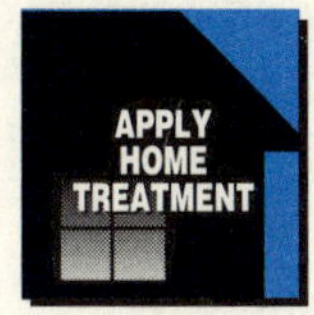


- **Apply home treatment**
  Follow the instructions for home treatment closely, and keep it up. These steps are what most doctors recommend as a first approach to these problems.

  If over-the-counter medications are suggested, look them up in the index and read about dosage and side effects in Chapter 9 before you use them.

  There are times when home treatment is not effective despite conscientious application. Think the problem through again, using the decision chart. The length of time you should wait before calling your doctor can be found in the general information in most sections. If you become seriously worried about your condition, call the doctor.

- **See Doctor Now**
  Go to your doctor or health-care facility right away. In the general information we try to give you the medical terminology related to each problem so that you can "translate" the terms your doctor may use during your conversation.

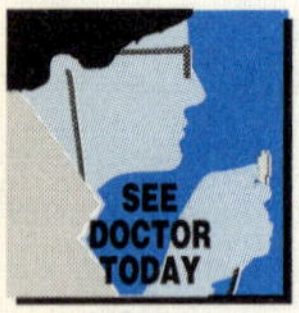


- **See Doctor Today**
  Call your doctor's office and say that you are coming in. Describe your problem over the phone as clearly as you can.

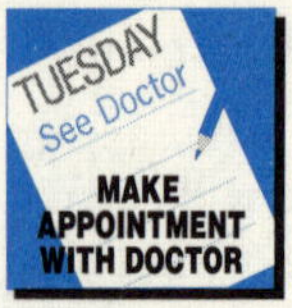


- **Make Appointment with Doctor**
  Schedule a visit to your doctor's office any time during the next few days.

- **Call Doctor Today**
  Often a phone call will enable you and your doctor or nurse to avoid unnecessary visits, using medical care more wisely. Remember that most doctors do not charge for telephone advice but regard it as part of their service to regular patients. Don't abuse this service in an attempt to avoid paying for necessary medical care.

  If every call results in a recommendation for a visit, your doctor is probably sending you a message: come in and don't call. This is unfortunate, and you may want to look for a doctor willing to put the telephone to good use.

With these guidelines, you will be able to use the following sections to quickly locate the information you need, while not burdening yourself with information that you don't require. Examine some of the charts now; you will quickly learn how to find the answers to health problems.

## HOW TO USE THE DECISION CHARTS

Does the patient show any of these Emergency Signs?

- Major injury
- No pulse or breath
- Unconsciousness
- Active bleeding
- Stupor or drowsiness
- Disorientation
- Shortness of breath while resting
- Cold sweats
- Severe pain

**yes** → Go to the emergency room or call for help immediately. Turn to Emergencies, page 144, for more instructions.

**no** ↓

Is the patient choking, and unable to speak or cry out?

**yes** → Turn to page 149 for instructions in the abdominal-thrust maneuver.

**no** ↓

Has the patient swallowed poison?

**yes** → Identify the poison, call the Poison Control Center, and turn to page 153 for more instructions.

**no** ↓

Read the list of problems below and turn to the appropriate chapter:

## CHAPTER B

# *Emergencies*



Emergencies require prompt action, not panic. What action you should take depends on the facilities available and the nature of the problem.

If there are massive injuries or if the patient is unconscious, you must get help immediately. Go to the emergency room if it is close. Have someone call ahead if you can.

If you can't reach the emergency room quickly, you can often obtain help by calling an emergency room or the rescue squad. Calling for help is especially important if you think that someone has swallowed poison. Poison control centers and emergency rooms can often tell you over the phone how to counteract the poison, thus beginning treatment as early as possible. See Chapter C, "Poisons," page 152.

**Work out a procedure for medical emergencies. Develop and test it before an actual emergency arises. If you plan emergency action ahead of time, you will decrease the likelihood of panic and increase the probability of receiving the proper care quickly.**

The most important thing is to *be prepared.* Record the phone numbers of the nearest emergency facility, poison control center, and rescue squad in the front of this book. Know the best way to reach the emergency room by car. Learn these procedures *before* an actual emergency arises.

## WHEN TO CALL AN AMBULANCE

An ambulance is not always the fastest way to reach a medical facility. It must travel both ways and often is not twice as fast as a private car. If the patient can readily move or be moved, and a private car is available, use the car and have someone call ahead. An ambulance is expensive and may be needed more urgently at another location, so engage it with care.

On the other hand, the ambulance brings with it a trained crew, who know how to lift a patient to minimize chance of further injury. Intravenous fluids and oxygen are usually available; splints and bandages are provided; and in some instances, life-saving resuscitation may be employed on the way to the hospital. Thus, care by ambulance attendants may greatly benefit a patient who:

- Is gravely ill
- May have a back or head injury
- May have a serious heart attack
- Is severely short of breath

In our experience, ambulances are too often used as expensive taxis. The type of accident or illness, the facilities available, and the distance involved are all important factors in deciding whether an ambulance should be used. Your trained EMT program can be a great community resource—use it wisely.

## EMERGENCY SIGNS

The instruction charts in the rest of this book assume that no emergency signs are present. Emergency signs overrule the charts and dictate that medical help be sought immediately. Be familiar with the following emergency signs.

### Major injury

Common sense tells us that the patient with a broken leg or large chest wound deserves immediate attention. Emergency facilities exist to take care of major injuries. They should be used promptly.

### No pulse or breath

Again, someone whose heart or lungs are not working needs help right away. Call for help. If you know CPR, start it after you call for help.

### Unconsciousness

The patient who is unconscious needs emergency care immediately.

### Active bleeding

Most cuts will stop bleeding if pressure is applied to the wound. This is the most important part of first aid for such wounds. Unless the bleeding is obviously minor, a wound that continues to bleed despite the application of pressure requires attention in order to prevent unnecessary loss of blood. The average adult can tolerate the loss of several cups of blood with little ill effect, but children can tolerate only smaller amounts, proportionate to their body size.

### Stupor or drowsiness

A decreased level of mental activity, short of unconsciousness, is termed "stupor." A practical way of determining if the severity of stupor or drowsiness warrants urgent treatment is to note the patient's ability to answer questions. If the patient is not sufficiently awake to answer questions concerning what has happened, then urgent action is necessary. Children are difficult to judge, but the child who cannot be aroused needs immediate attention.

### Disorientation

In medicine, disorientation is described and gauged in terms of time, place, and person. This simply means whether the person can answer these questions correctly:

- What is the date?
- Where are we?
- Who are you?

A person who doesn't know his or her identity is in more trouble than a person who does not know where he or she is, and that person is in more trouble than a person who cannot give the correct date.

Disorientation may be part of a variety of illnesses and is especially common when a high fever is present. The patient who previously has been alert and then becomes disoriented and confused deserves immediate medical attention.

### Shortness of breath

Shortness of breath is described more extensively on page 402. As a general rule, immediate attention is needed if the patient is short of breath even though resting. However, in young adults the most frequent cause of shortness of breath at rest is the hyperventilation syndrome, which is not a serious concern (see page 386). Nevertheless, if it cannot be confidently determined that shortness of breath is due to the hyperventilation syndrome, then the reasonable course of action is to seek immediate aid.

### Cold sweats

As an isolated symptom, sweating is not likely to be serious. It is the normal response to elevated temperature. It is also the natural response to stress, either psychological or physical. Most people have experienced sweaty palms when "put on the spot" or stressed psychologically.

In contrast, a cold sweat in a patient complaining of chest pain, abdominal pain, or light-headedness indicates a need for immediate attention. It is a common effect of severe pain or serious illness. Remember, however, that aspirin often causes sweating in lowering a fever. Sweating associated with the breaking of a fever is not the "cold sweat" referred to here.

### Severe pain

Surprisingly enough, severe pain is rarely the symptom that determines if a problem is serious and urgent. Most often pain is associated with other symptoms that indicate the nature of the condition. The most obvious example is pain associated with major injury—like a broken leg—which itself clearly requires urgent care.

The severity of pain is subjective and depends on the particular patient; often the magnitude of the pain is altered by emotional and psychological factors. Nevertheless, severe pain demands urgent medical attention, if for no other reason than to relieve the pain.

Much of the art and science of medicine is directed at the relief of pain, and the use of emergency procedures to secure this relief is justified even if the cause of the pain eventually proves to be minor. However, the patient who frequently complains of severe pain from minor causes is in much the same situation as the boy who cried "wolf"; calls for help will inevitably be taken less and less seriously by the doctor. This situation is a dangerous one, for the patient may have difficulty obtaining help when it is most needed.

**We have not attempted to teach complex first-aid procedures such as cardiopulmonary resuscitation (CPR) in this chapter. To use such procedures correctly, you need instruction and an opportunity to practice the skills. Community organizations such as the American Red Cross and the American Heart Association offer training in these procedures.**

# Choking

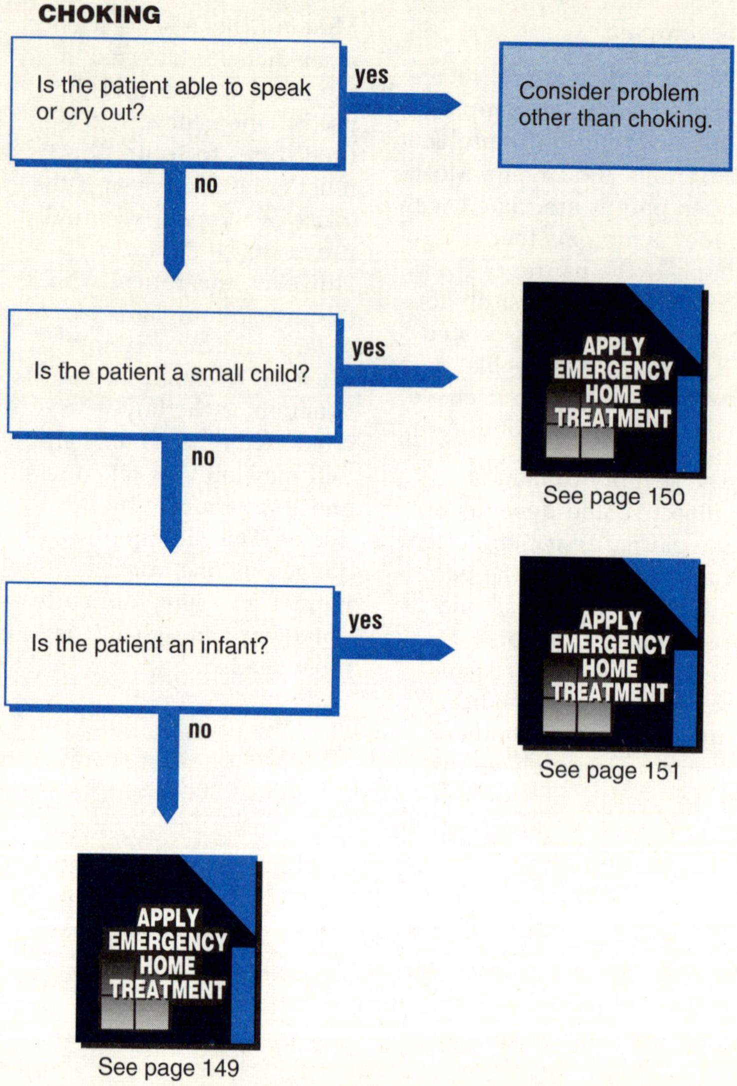


Your dinner companion can't breathe, can't talk, and is turning blue. He is gasping for air and puts his hand to his throat. These signs tell you he is choking. Do you know what to do?

Choking on a foreign object, usually food, is all too common. The most common setting for choking in adults is the evening meal, often in a restaurant or at a party. This situation increases the risk of choking in several ways: First, the victim is likely to have been drinking alcoholic beverages, and this may slow the reflexes that normally keep food from going down the wrong way. Second, the victim is likely to be distracted from the business of eating by conversation or entertainment. Finally, this is the most likely time that solid meats such as steak are to be eaten, and these are usually the culprits in adult choking.

Children stick a much wider variety of objects into their mouths, are likely to do so at any time of the day or night, and are much less likely to complicate the situation with alcohol. Nevertheless, a child is still most likely to choke on food. The most likely foods are hot dogs, grapes, peanuts, and hard candy.

## HOME TREATMENT

Choking is an emergency situation, but emergency medical services—doctors, EMTs, ambulances, emergency rooms, hospitals—play virtually no role in its treatment. The victim's fate will be decided by the time they can respond in almost every case. Either someone steps forward and relieves the choking, or there is a very good chance that there will be a fatal outcome.

You can be that someone. The most effective way to relieve choking is with the abdominal-thrust, or Heimlich, maneuver. Pushing on the lungs from below rapidly raises the air pressure inside the lungs and behind the foreign object causing the choking. This results in the forceful expulsion of the food from the throat back into the mouth. Done properly, an abdominal-thrust maneuver does not pose great risk of doing harm. Still, it's not the kind of thing that you want to do to someone who will not benefit from it. The most important indication of choking that will respond to the abdominal-thrust maneuver is the inability to talk. If the person in difficulty can speak, forget about the abdominal-thrust maneuver.

### FOR ADULTS

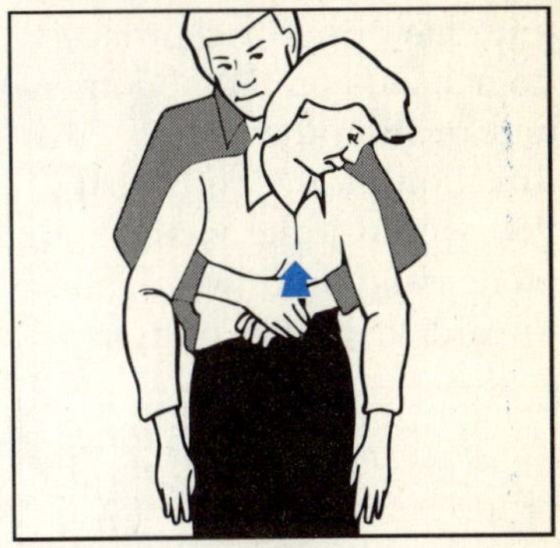

**1.** Stand behind the patient and place your arms around him or her. Make a fist and place it against the patient's abdomen, thumb side in, between the navel and the breastbone.

**2.** Hold the fist with your other hand, and push upward and inward, four times quickly.

**If the patient is pregnant or obese**, place your arms around his or her chest and your hands over the middle of the breastbone. Give four quick chest thrusts.

**If the patient is lying down**, roll the patient over onto his or her back. Place your hands on the abdomen and push in the same direction on the body that you would if the victim were standing (inward, and toward the upper body).

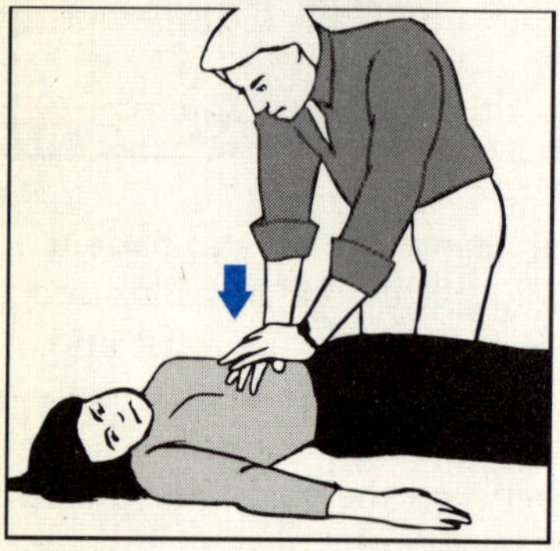

**3.** If the patient does not start to breathe, open the mouth by moving the jaw and tongue, and look for the swallowed object. *If you can see the object,* sweep it out with your little finger. If you try to remove an object you can't see, you may only push it in more tightly.

**4.** If the victim does not begin to breathe after the object has been removed from the air passage, use mouth-to-mouth resuscitation.

**5.** Call for help, and repeat these steps until the object is dislodged and the victim is breathing normally.

## FOR SMALL CHILDREN

**1.** Kneel next to the child who should be lying on his or her back.

**2.** Position the heel of one hand on the child's abdomen between the navel and the breastbone. Deliver six to ten thrusts inward and toward the upper body.

**3.** If this doesn't work, open the mouth by moving the jaw and tongue and look for the swallowed object. *If you can see the object,* sweep it out of the throat using your little finger.

**4.** If the patient does not begin to breathe after the object has been removed, use mouth-to-mouth resuscitation.

**5.** Call for assistance, and repeat these steps until the object is dislodged and the patient is breathing normally or until help arrives.

## FOR INFANTS

**1.** Hold the infant along your forearm, face down, so that the head is lower than the feet.

**2.** Deliver four rapid blows to the back, between the shoulder blades, with the heel of your hand.

**3.** If this doesn't work, turn the baby over and, using two fingers, give four quick thrusts to the chest.

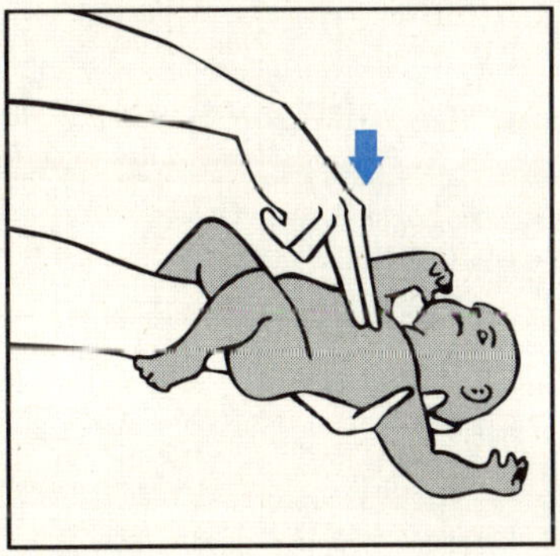

**4.** If you're still not successful, look for the swallowed object in the throat the same way you would for an adult or small child. *If you can see it,* try to sweep it out gently with your finger.

**5.** If the infant doesn't begin to breathe after the object has been removed, use mouth-to-nose-and-mouth resuscitation.

**6.** Call for assistance, and repeat these steps until the object is dislodged and the patient is breathing normally.

In the past, we have been uncertain whether the abdominal-thrust (Heimlich) maneuver for choking could be learned simply by reading about it. We are no longer uncertain. On January 17, 1988, Carolyn Tubbs used the abdominal-thrust maneuver to successfully dislodge a piece of food from the throat of her husband, Eddie. Eddie was in real trouble, and we believe that Carolyn's quick action saved his life. Carolyn's only knowledge of this maneuver came from reading a self-care newsletter. We are quite confident of the facts in this episode because Carolyn was secretary to one of us (DMV) at the time.

CHAPTER C

# Poisons



***Write down these phone numbers now:***

**POISON CONTROL CENTER**

____________________________

**EMERGENCY ROOM**

____________________________

Write them down in the front of this book as well, and keep them by your phone.

# Poisoning

Although poisons may be inhaled or absorbed through the skin, for the most part they are swallowed. The term *ingestion* refers to swallowing.

Most poisoning can be prevented. Children almost always swallow poison accidentally. Don't allow children to reach potentially harmful substances like these:

- Medications
- Insecticides
- Caustic cleansers
- Organic solvents
- Fuels
- Furniture polishes
- Antifreezes
- Drain cleaners

The last item is the most damaging: drain cleaners like Drano are strong alkali solutions that can destroy any tissue they touch.

### Identifying the Problem

Treatment must be prompt to be effective, but identifying the poison is as important as speed. *Don't panic.* Try to identify the swallowed substance without taking up too much time. If you cannot or if the victim is unconscious, go to the emergency room right away. If you can identify the poison, call the doctor or poison control center immediately and get advice on what to do. Always bring the container with you to the hospital. Life-support measures come first in the case of an unconscious victim, but the ingested substance must be identified before proper therapy can begin.

Many significant medication overdoses are due to suicide attempts. Any suicide attempt is an indication that help is needed, even if the patient has physically recovered and is in no immediate danger. Most successful suicides are preceded by unsuccessful attempts.

## HOME TREATMENT

*All cases of poisoning require professional help.* Someone should call for help immediately. If the patient is conscious and alert and the ingredients swallowed are known, there are two types of treatment: those in which vomiting should be induced, and those in which it should not.

Do *not* induce vomiting if the patient has swallowed any of the following:

- Acids—battery acid, sulfuric acid, hydrochloric acid, bleach, hair straightener, etc.
- Alkalis—Drano, drain cleaners, oven cleaners, etc.
- Petroleum products—gasoline, furniture polish, kerosene, lighter fluid, etc.

These substances can destroy the esophagus or damage the lungs as they are vomited. Neutralize them with milk while contacting the physician. If you don't have milk, use water or milk of magnesia.

Vomiting is a safe way to remove medications, plants, and suspicious materials from the stomach. It is more effective and safer than using a stomach pump and does not require the doctor's help. Vomiting can sometimes be achieved immediately by touching the back of the throat with a finger. This is usually the fastest way, and time is important.

Another way to induce vomiting is to give 2 to 4 teaspoons of **syrup** (not extract) of **ipecac**, followed by as much liquid as the patient can drink. Vomiting usually follows within 20 minutes. Mustard mixed with warm water also works. If there is no vomiting within 25 minutes, repeat the dose. Collect what comes up so that it can be examined by the doctor.

Before, during, and after first aid for poisoning, contact a doctor.

If an accidental poisoning has occurred, make sure that it doesn't happen again. Put poisons where children cannot reach them. Flush old medications down the toilet.

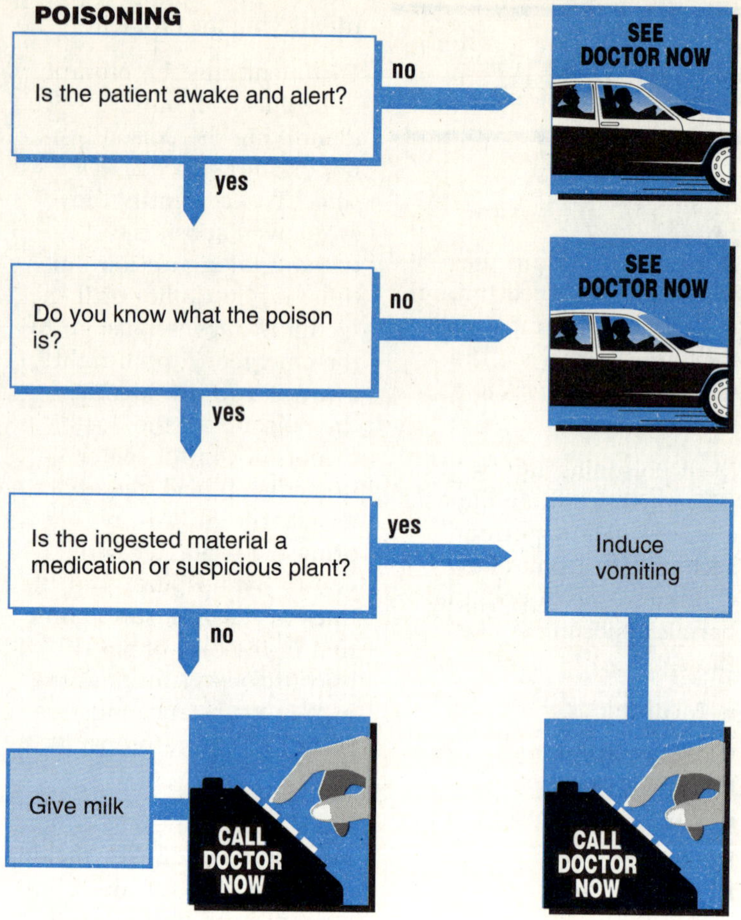


## WHAT TO EXPECT AT THE DOCTOR'S OFFICE

Significant poisoning is best managed at the emergency room. Treatment of the conscious patient depends on the particular poison and whether vomiting has been successfully achieved. If indicated, the stomach will be evacuated by vomiting or by the use of a stomach pump. Patients who are unconscious or have swallowed a strong acid or alkali will require admission to the hospital.

CHAPTER D

# *Common Injuries*

# Cuts (Lacerations)

Most cuts affect only the skin and the fatty tissue beneath it, and heal without permanent damage. However, injury to internal structures such as muscles, tendons, blood vessels, ligaments, or nerves presents the possibility of permanent damage. Your doctor can decrease this likelihood.

### Deeper Damage

It may be difficult for you to determine whether major blood vessels, nerves, or tendons have been damaged. These are the signs that normally call for examination by a doctor:

- Bleeding that cannot be controlled with pressure
- Numbness or weakness in the limb beyond the wound
- Inability to move fingers or toes

Signs of infection—such as pus oozing from the wound, fever, extensive redness and swelling—will not appear for at least 24 hours. Bacteria need time to grow and multiply. If these signs do appear, a doctor must be consulted.

### Stitches

Stitching (suturing) a laceration is a ritual in our society. The only purpose in suturing a wound is to pull the edges together to hasten healing and minimize scarring. Stitches are not recommended if the wound can be held closed without them because they injure tissue to some extent. Stitching should be done within eight hours of the injury. Otherwise the edges of the wound are less likely to heal together and germs are more likely to be trapped under the skin. Stitching is often required in young children who are apt to pull off bandages, or in areas that are subject to a great deal of motion, such as the fingers or joints.

### Difficult Cuts

A cut on the face, chest, abdomen, or back is potentially more serious than one on an extremity. Cuts on the trunk or face should be examined by a doctor unless the injury is very small or shallow. A call to the doctor's office will help you decide if the doctor's help is needed.

Facial wounds in a young child who drools are often too wet to treat with bandages, so the doctor's help is often needed. Because of potential disfigurement, all but minor facial wounds should be treated professionally. Cuts in the palm that become infected can be difficult to treat, so consult your doctor unless the cut is shallow.

**CUTS**

Is there a possibility of damage to major blood vessels or nerves, or is there fever, pus, or extensive redness and swelling?

yes →

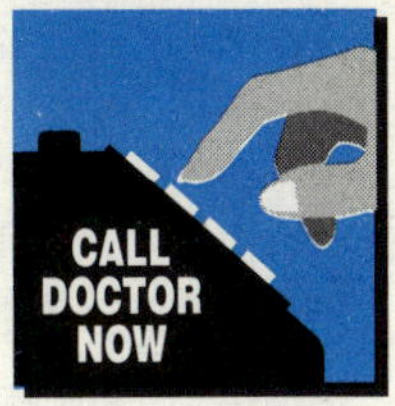


no ↓

Can the edges of the wound be brought together easily?

no →

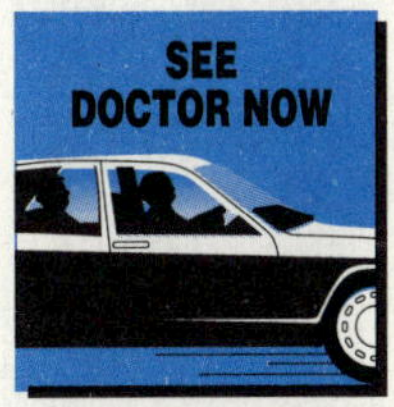


yes ↓

Is the cut on face, chest, abdomen, back, or palm?

yes →

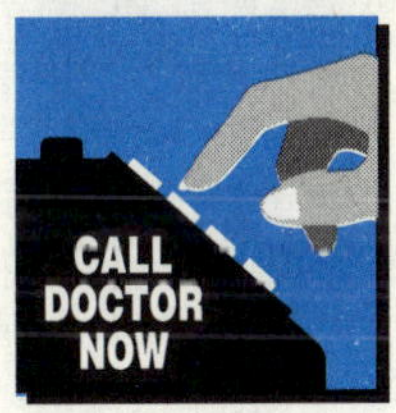


no ↓

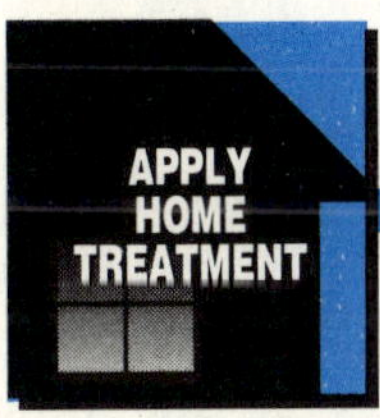


*See:* **Tetanus Shots**, page 165.

## HOME TREATMENT

Cleanse the wound. Soap and water will do, but be vigorous. Hydrogen peroxide (3%) may also be used. Make sure that no dirt, glass, or other foreign material remains in the wound. Antiseptics such as Mercurochrome and Merthiolate are unlikely to help, and some are painful. Iodine will kill germs, but it is not really needed and is also painful. (Betadine is a modified iodine preparation that is painless but more costly.)

The edges of a clean, minor cut can usually be held together by "butterfly" bandages or, preferably, "steristrips"—strips of sterile paper tape. Apply either of these bandages so that the edges of the wound join without "rolling under."

See the doctor if the edges of the wound cannot be kept together, if signs of infection appear (pus, fever, extensive redness and swelling), or if the cut is not healing well within two weeks.

### WHAT TO EXPECT AT THE DOCTOR'S OFFICE

The wound will be thoroughly cleansed and explored to be sure that no foreign particles are left and that blood vessels, nerves, and tendons are undamaged. Since the doctor may use an anesthetic to numb the area, report any possible allergy to local anesthetics (Xylocaine, for example). A tetanus shot and antibiotics will be given if needed.

Lacerations that may require a surgical specialist include those with injury to tendons or major vessels, especially in the hand and those on the face, if a good cosmetic result appears difficult to obtain.

**Your doctor will tell you when the stitches are to be removed. Unless there is some other reason to return to the doctor, you can perform this simple procedure.**

**1. Clean the skin and the stitches. Sometimes a scab must be removed by soaking.**

**2. Gently lift the stitch away from the skin by grasping a loose end of the knot.**

**3. Cut the stitch at the far end as close to the skin as possible and pull it out. A pair of small, sharp scissors or a fingernail clipper works well. It is important to get close to the skin so that a minimum amount of the stitch that was outside the skin is pulled through. This reduces the chance of contamination and infection.**

# Puncture Wounds

Puncture wounds are those caused by nails, pins, tacks, and other sharp objects. Usually, the most important question is whether a tetanus shot is needed. See **Tetanus Shots**, page 165, anytime a puncture wound occurs.

### Signs to Call the Doctor

Most minor puncture wounds are located in the extremities, particularly in the feet. If the puncture wound is located elsewhere, a hidden internal injury may have occurred. Call the doctor for advice.

Many doctors feel that puncture wounds of the hand, if not very minor, should be treated with antibiotics. Once started, infections deep in the hand are difficult to treat and may lead to loss of function. Call the doctor.

Injury to a tendon, nerve, or major blood vessel is rare but can be serious:

- Injury to an **artery** may be indicated by blood pumping vigorously from the wound
- Injury to a **nerve** usually causes numbness or tingling in the wounded limb beyond the site of the wound
- Injury to a **tendon** causes difficulty in moving the limb (usually fingers or toes) beyond the wound

Major injuries such as these occur more often from a nail, ice pick, or large instrument than from a narrow implement such as a needle.

### Infection

To avoid infection, be absolutely sure that nothing has been left in the wound. Sometimes, for example, part of a needle will break off and remain in the foot. If there is any question of a foreign body remaining, the wound should be examined by the doctor.

Signs of infection do not occur immediately at the time of injury. They usually take at least 24 hours to develop. The formation of pus, a fever, and severe redness and swelling are indications that you should see a doctor.

## HOME TREATMENT

Clean the wound with soap and water or hydrogen peroxide (3%). Let it bleed as much as possible to carry foreign material outside because you cannot scrub the inside of a puncture wound. Do not apply pressure to stop the bleeding unless there is a large amount of blood loss or a "pumping" type of bleeding.

## PUNCTURE WOUNDS

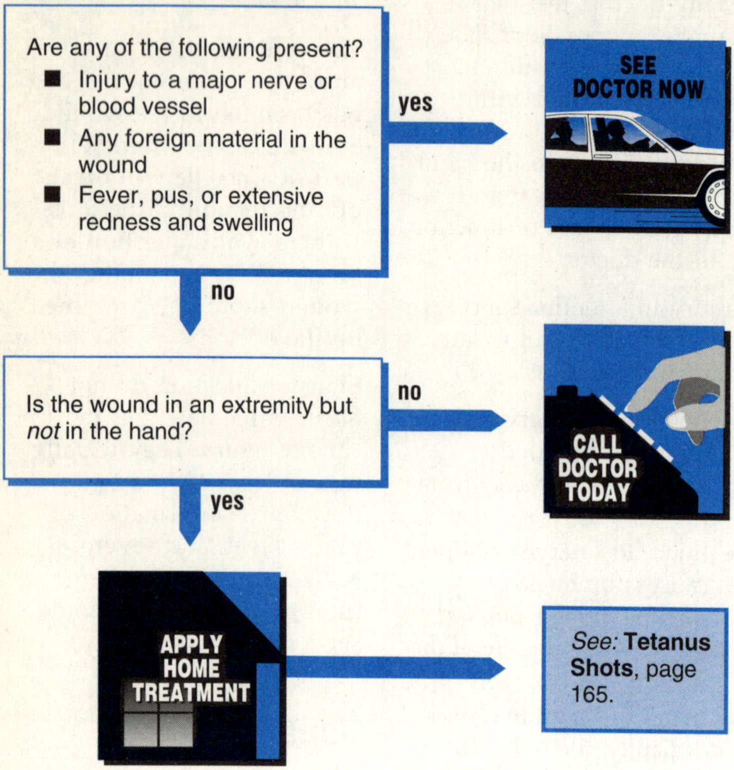


### WHAT TO EXPECT AT THE DOCTOR'S OFFICE

The doctor will answer the questions on the chart opposite from the patient's history and examination. If a metallic foreign body is suspected, X-rays may be taken; glass and wood do not show up on X-rays and may be difficult to locate. Be prepared to tell the doctor of possible allergies to local anesthetics (Xylocaine, for example). The wound will be surgically explored if necessary. Most doctors will recommend home treatment. Antibiotics are only rarely suggested.

Soak the wound in warm water several times a day for four to five days. The object of the soaking is to keep the skin puncture open as long as possible so that any germs or foreign debris can drain from the open wound. If the wound closes, an infection may form beneath the skin but not become apparent for several days.

See the doctor if there are signs of infection or if the wound has not healed within two weeks.

# Animal Bites

The question of rabies is of uppermost concern following an animal bite. The main carriers of rabies are skunks, foxes, bats, raccoons, and opossums. Rabies is also carried—though rarely—by cattle, dogs, and cats, and it is extremely rare in squirrels, chipmunks, rats, and mice. Although 3000 to 4000 animals with rabies are found in the United States each year, only one or two people contract the disease. Rabid animals act strangely, attack without provocation, and may drool or "foam at the mouth."

Any bite by an animal other than a pet dog or cat requires consultation with the doctor as to whether or not an anti-rabies vaccine is required. If the bite is by a dog or a cat, the animal is being reliably observed for sickness by its owner, and its immunizations are up to date, then consultation with the doctor is not required.

If the bite has left a wound that might require stitching or other treatment, consult **Cuts**, page 156, or **Puncture Wounds**, page 159. Although tetanus from an animal bite is rare, you should also check **Tetanus Shots**, page 165.

## HOME TREATMENT

An animal whose immunizations are up to date is, of course, unlikely to have rabies. However, arrange for the animal to be observed for the next 15 days to make sure that it does not develop rabies. Most often, the owners of the animal can be relied on to observe it. If the owners cannot be trusted, then the animal must be kept for observation by the local public agency charged with that responsibility. Many localities require that animal bites be reported to the health department. If the animal should develop rabies during this time, a serious situation exists and treatment must be started immediately.

Treat bites as you would other cuts or puncture wounds.

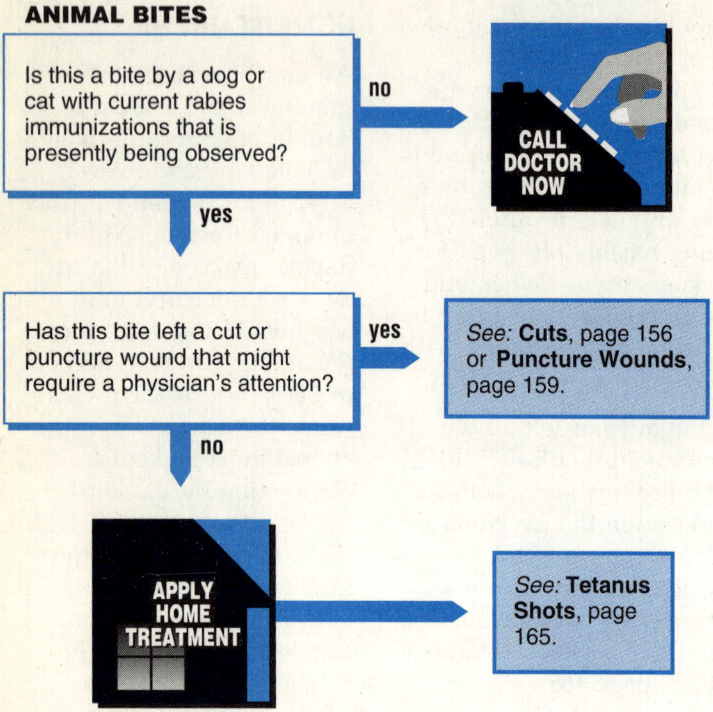


Rabies vaccine is administered in 5 injections, one as soon as possible and 4 over the next 28 days. The vaccine may cause local skin reactions as well as fever, headache, and nausea. Severe reactions to the vaccine are rare. The anti-rabies serum, unfortunately, has a high risk of serious reactions. The serum is given both directly into the wound and by intramuscular injection.

Many physicians give a tetanus shot if the patient is not "up to date" because tetanus bacteria can rarely be introduced by an animal bite. Antibiotics are usually not needed.

## WHAT TO EXPECT AT THE DOCTOR'S OFFICE

The doctor must balance the generally remote possibility of exposure to rabies against the hazards of rabies vaccine and anti-rabies serum. An unprovoked attack by a wild animal or a bite from an animal that appears to have rabies may require both the rabies vaccine and the anti-rabies serum. The extent and location of the wounds also play a part in this decision; severe wounds of the head are the most dangerous. A bite caused by an animal that has since escaped presents a dilemma, and may require treatment to be safe.

# Scrapes and Abrasions

Scrapes and abrasions are shallow wounds. Several layers of the skin may be torn or even totally scraped off, but the wound does not go far beneath the skin. Abrasions are usually caused by falls onto the hands, elbows, or knees, but skateboard and bicycle riders can get abrasions on just about any part of the body. Because abrasions expose millions of nerve endings, all of which send pain impulses to the brain, they are usually much more painful than cuts.

## HOME TREATMENT

Remove all dirt and foreign matter. Washing the wound with soap and warm water is the most important step in treatment. Hydrogen peroxide (3%) can also be used to cleanse the wound. Most scrapes will scab rather quickly; this is nature's way of "dressing" the wound. Using Mercurochrome, iodine, and other antiseptics does little good and is sometimes painful.

Adhesive bandages may be used as necessary for a wound that continues to ooze blood; they must be removed if they get wet. Antibacterial ointments (Neosporin, Bacitracin, etc.) are optional; their main advantage is in keeping bandages from sticking to the wound.

Loose skin flaps, if they are not dirty, may be left to help form a natural dressing. If the skin flap is dirty, cut it off carefully with nail scissors. (If it hurts, stop! You're cutting the wrong tissue.)

Watch the wound for signs of infection—pus, fever, or severe redness or swelling—but don't be worried by redness around the edges; this is an indication of normal healing. Infection will not be obvious in the first 24 hours; fever may indicate a serious infection.

Pain can be treated for the first few minutes with an ice pack in a plastic bag or towel applied over the wounds as needed. The worst pain subsides fairly quickly, and aspirin, ibuprofen, or acetaminophen can then be used as needed.

See the doctor if signs of infection appear or if the scrape or abrasion is not healed within two weeks.

### SCRAPES

Can dirt and foreign matter be removed?

no →

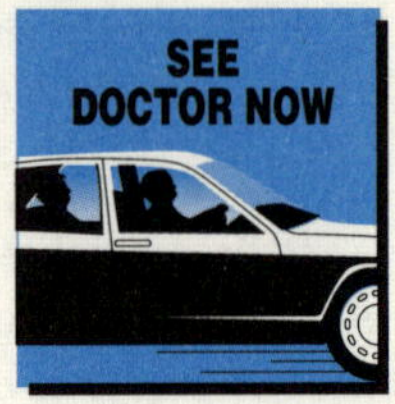


yes ↓

Are there signs of infection, such as fever, a big lump in part of the wound, or drainage of thick, smelly pus?

yes →

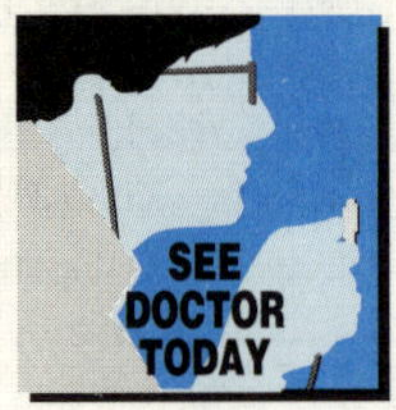


no ↓

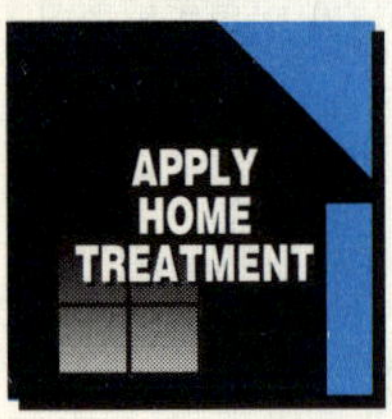


## WHAT TO EXPECT AT THE DOCTOR'S OFFICE

The doctor will make sure that the wound is free of dirt and foreign matter. Soap and water and hydrogen peroxide (3%) will often be used. Sometimes a local anesthetic is required to reduce the pain of the cleansing process.

An antibacterial ointment such as Neosporin or Bacitracin is sometimes applied after cleansing the wound. Betadine is a painless iodine preparation that is also occasionally used. Tetanus shots are not required for simple scrapes, but if the patient is overdue, it is a good chance to get caught up.

# Tetanus Shots

Patients may come to the doctor's office or emergency room to get a tetanus shot even though it is not needed. The chart on page 166 illustrates the essentials of the current U.S. Public Health Service recommendations. It can save you and your family several visits to the doctor.

The question of whether or not a wound is "clean" and "minor" may be troublesome. Wounds caused by sharp, clean objects such as knives or razor blades have less chance of becoming infected than those in which dirt or foreign bodies have penetrated and lodged beneath the skin. Abrasions and minor burns will not result in tetanus. The tetanus germ cannot grow in the presence of air, so the skin must be cut or punctured for the germ to reach an airless location.

## IMMUNIZATION

If you have never received a basic series of three tetanus shots, you should see your doctor. Sometimes a different kind of tetanus shot is required if you have not been adequately immunized. This shot is called "tetanus immune globulin" and is used when immunization is not complete and there is a significant risk of tetanus. It is more expensive, more painful, and more likely to cause an allergic reaction than the tetanus booster. So keep a record of your family's immunizations in the back of this book and know the dates.

During the first tetanus shots (usually a series of three injections given in early childhood), immunity to tetanus develops over a three-week period. This immunity then slowly declines over many months. After each booster, immunity develops more rapidly and lasts longer. If you have had an initial series of five tetanus injections, immunity will usually last at least ten years after every booster injection. Nevertheless, if a wound has contaminated material beneath the skin and is not exposed to the air, and if you have not had a tetanus shot within the past five years, a booster shot is advised to keep the level of immunity as high as possible.

## TETANUS SHOTS

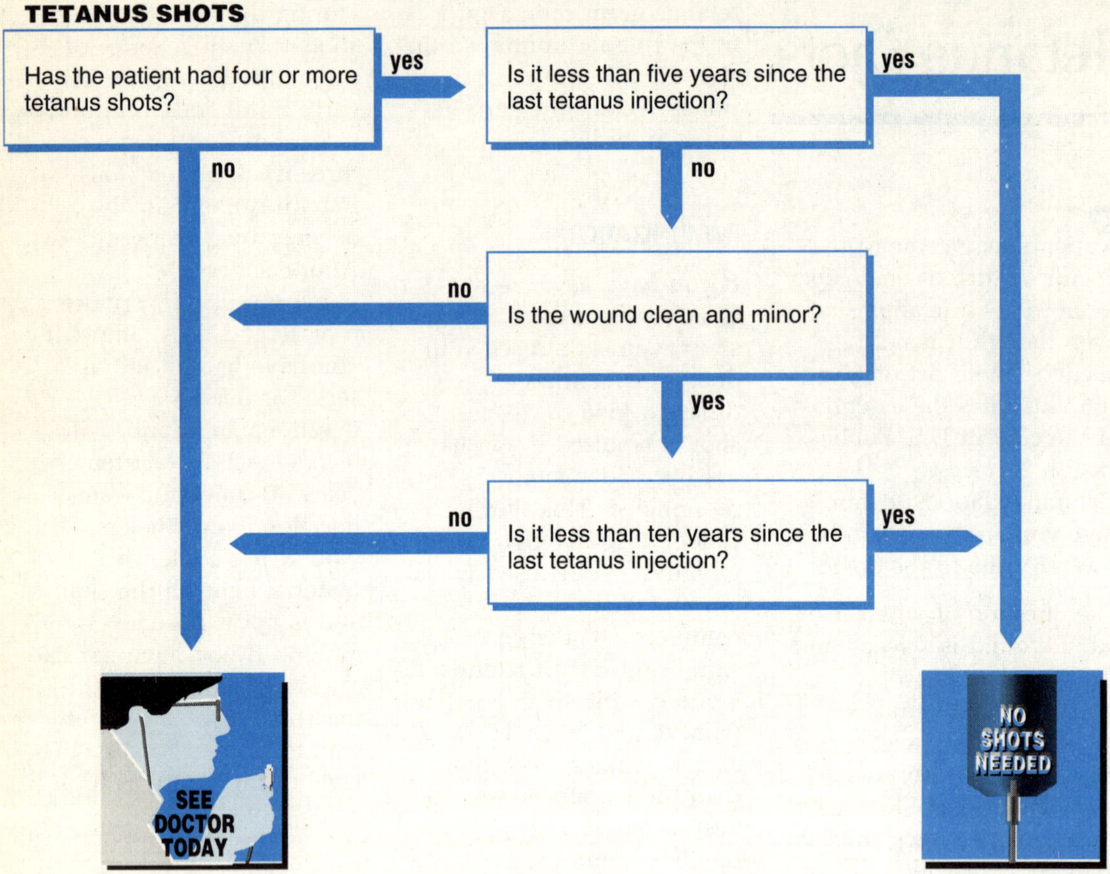


Tetanus immunization is very important because the tetanus germ is quite common and the disease (lockjaw) is so severe. Be absolutely sure that each of your children has had the basic series of three injections and appropriate boosters. Because the immunity lasts so long, adults usually get away with a long period between boosters, but immunization of children should be "by the book."

# Broken Bone?

Neither patient nor doctor can always tell by eye whether or not a bone is broken. On the other hand, bone fragments in most fractures are already aligned and setting is not required. Thus, prompt manipulation of the fragments is not necessary. If the injured part is protected and rested, a delay of several days before casting does no harm. Remember that the cast does not have healing properties; it just keeps the fragments from getting joggled too much during the healing process.

Possible fractures are discussed further in **Ankle Injuries**, page 170, **Knee Injuries**, page 172, **Arm Injuries**, page 174, and **Head Injuries**, page 176.

### Serious Fractures

A fracture that injures nearby nerves and arteries may result in a limb that is cold, blue, or numb. Fractures of the pelvis or thigh may be particularly serious. Fortunately, these fractures are relatively rare except when great force is involved, as in automobile accidents. In these situations, the need for immediate help is usually obvious.

Paleness, sweating, dizziness, and thirst can indicate shock, and immediate attention is needed.

Although broken ribs are generally diagnosed with X-rays, no particular treatment, other than binding and resting the affected ribs, is indicated. If you experience shortness of breath associated with a chest injury, there may have been an injury to the lung and a visit to the doctor is recommended; see **Shortness of Breath**, page 402.

A crooked limb is an obvious reason to check for fracture. Pain that prevents any use of the injured limb suggests the need for an X-ray. Soft-tissue injuries usually allow some use of the limb, although a bad sprain may cause more pain than a fracture.

Although large bruises under the skin are usually caused by soft-tissue injuries alone, marked bruising makes a fracture more likely.

Common sense tells us that when great force is involved the possibility of a broken bone is increased. An automobile accident or a fall from the roof raises our suspicion.

Young bones lengthen through growth plates at their ends. An injury to a bone near the end, that is, near a joint, must be treated more cautiously because growth plate damage may stop limb growth.

## HOME TREATMENT

Apply ice packs. The immediate application of cold will help decrease swelling and inflammation. If a broken bone is possible, the involved limb should be protected and rested for at least 48 hours. To rest a bone effectively, the joint above and below the bone should be immobilized. For example, if you suspect a fracture of the lower arm, you should prevent the wrist and elbow from moving. Magazines, cardboard, or rolled newspaper can be used as splints. Do not wrap tightly or circulation will be cut off. During this time, the limb should be cautiously tested to determine persistence of pain with movement and the return of function. A limb that cannot be used at all is more likely to be broken.

Any injury that is still painful after 48 hours should be examined by a doctor. Minutes and hours are *not* crucial unless the limb is crooked or there is injury to arteries or nerves. A limb that is adequately protected and rested is likely to have a good outcome even if a fracture is present and casting or splinting is delayed. Aspirin, ibuprofen, or acetaminophen can be used for pain.

## WHAT TO EXPECT AT THE DOCTOR'S OFFICE

Usually an X-ray will be required. In many offices and emergency rooms, a nurse or doctor's assistant will order the X-ray before the patient is even seen by a doctor. A crooked limb must be set, which sometimes requires general anesthesia. Pinning the fragments together surgically so that they will heal well is required for certain fractures.

## BROKEN BONE

Are any of the following conditions present?

- The limb is cold, blue, or numb
- The possible fracture is in the pelvis or thigh
- The patient is sweaty, pale, dizzy, or thirsty

yes →

no ↓

Is the limb crooked?

yes →

no ↓

Is the limb not usable and unable to bear weight?

yes →

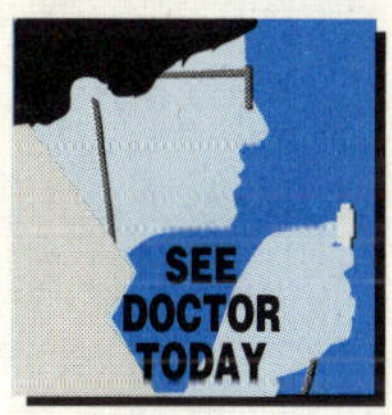


no ↓

Is there a great deal of bleeding and bruising in the area; was the injury the result of a severe blow; or is the possible fracture near a joint in a child?

yes →

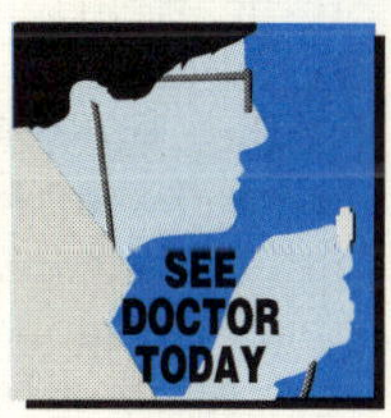


no ↓

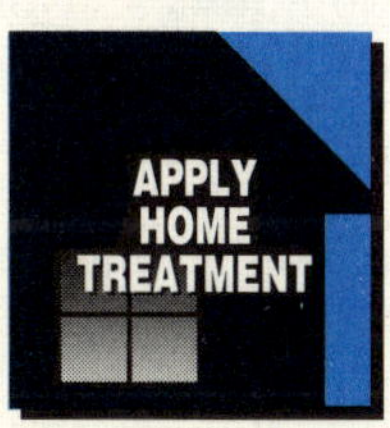

# Ankle Injuries

Ligaments are tissues that connect the bones of a joint to provide stability during the joint's action. When the ankle is twisted severely, either the ligament or the bone must give way. If the ligaments give way, they may be stretched (strained), partially torn (sprained), or completely torn (torn ligaments). If the ligaments do not give way, one of the bones around the ankle will break (fracture).

Strains, sprains, and even some minor fractures of the ankle will heal well with home treatment. Some torn ligaments do well without a great deal of medical care; operations to repair them are rare. For practical purposes, the immediate attention of the doctor is necessary only when the injury has been severe enough to cause obvious fracture to the bones around the ankle or to cause a completely torn ligament. This is indicated by a deformed joint with abnormal motion.

### Swelling

The typical ankle sprain swells either around the bony bump at the outside of the ankle or about two inches in front of and below it. The amount of swelling does not differentiate between sprains, tears, and fractures. The common chip fractures around the ankle often cause less swelling than a sprain. Sprains and torn ligaments usually swell quickly because there is bleeding into the tissue around the ankle. The skin will turn blue-black in the area as the blood is broken down by the body.

A swollen ankle that is not deformed does not need prolonged rest, casting, or X-rays. Home treatment should be started promptly. Detection of any damage to the ligaments may be difficult immediately after the injury if much swelling is present. Because it is easier to do an adequate examination of the foot after the swelling has gone down and because no damage is done by resting a mild fracture or torn ligament, there is no need to rush to the doctor.

### Pain

Pain tells you what to do and not do. If it hurts, don't do it. If pain prevents *any* standing on the ankle after 24 hours, see a doctor. If little progress is being made so that pain makes weight bearing difficult at 72 hours, see the doctor.

## HOME TREATMENT

RIP is the key word:

- Rest
- Ice
- Protection

Rest the ankle and keep it elevated. Apply ice in a towel to the injured area and leave it there for at least 30 minutes. If there is any evidence of swelling after the first 30 minutes, then ice should be applied for 30 minutes on and 15 minutes off through the next few hours. If pain

**ANKLE INJURIES**

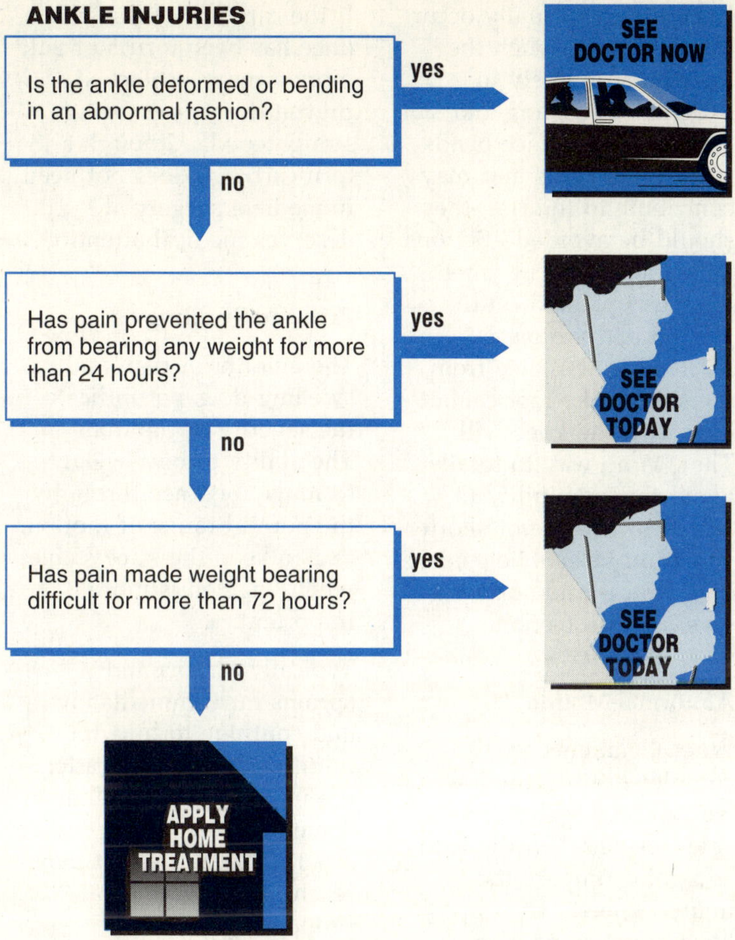


subsides in the elevated position, weight bearing may be attempted cautiously. If pain is present when bearing weight, weight bearing should be avoided for the first 24 hours. Heat may be applied, but only after 24 hours.

An elastic bandage can help but will not prevent reinjury if full activity is resumed. Do not stretch the bandage so that it is very tight and interferes with blood circulation. Taping generally should not be attempted on children; if it is done incorrectly, it may cut off circulation to the foot.

The ankle should feel relatively normal in about ten days. Be warned, however, that full healing will not take place for four to six weeks. If strenuous activity, such as organized athletics, is to be pursued during this time, the ankle should be taped by someone experienced in this technique.

## WHAT TO EXPECT AT THE DOCTOR'S OFFICE

The doctor will examine the motions of the ankle to see if they are abnormal and may have an X-ray taken. If there is no fracture or only a minor chip fracture, it is likely that a continuation of home treatment will be recommended. For other fractures, a cast will be necessary or, rarely, an operation to put the bones back together. Depending on the nature of a ligament injury, an operation may be required to repair a completely torn ligament.

# Knee Injuries

The ligaments of the knee may be stretched (strained), partially torn (sprained), or completely torn (torn ligament). Unlike the ankle, torn ligaments in the knee need to be repaired surgically as soon as possible after the injury occurs. If surgery is delayed, the operation is more difficult and less likely to be successful. For this reason, the approach to knee injuries is more cautious than for ankle injuries. If there is any possibility of a torn ligament, go to the doctor.

Fractures in the area of the knee are less common than around the ankle; they always need to be cared for by a doctor.

Knee injuries usually occur during sports, when the knee is more likely to experience twisting and side contact. (Deep knee bends stretch ligaments and may contribute to injuries; they should be avoided.) Serious knee injuries occur when the leg is planted on the ground and a blow is received to the knee from the side. If the foot cannot give way, the knee will. There is no way to totally avoid this possibility in athletics. The use of shorter spikes and cleats helps, but knee braces and supports give little protection.

### Abnormal Motion

When ligaments are completely torn, the lower leg can be wiggled from side to side when the leg is straight. Compare the injured knee to the opposite knee to get some idea of what amount of side-to-side motion is normal. Wiggling front to back (the drawer sign) is even more serious, since it suggests a tear of the ligament in the front of the knee. If you think that the motion may be abnormally loose, see a doctor.

If the cartilage within the knee has been torn, normal motion may be blocked, preventing it from being straightened. Although a torn cartilage does not need immediate surgery, it deserves medical attention.

### Pain and Swelling

The amount of pain and swelling does not indicate the severity of the injury. The ability to bear weight, to move the knee through the normal range of motion, and to keep the knee stable when wiggled is more important.

Typically, strains and sprains hurt immediately and continue to hurt for hours and even days after the injury. Swelling tends to come on rather slowly over a period of hours, but may reach rather large proportions. When a ligament is completely torn, there is intense pain immediately, which subsides until the knee may hurt little or not at all for a while. Usually, there is significant bleeding into the tissues around the joint when a ligament is torn; swelling tends to come on quickly and be of impressive dimensions.

**KNEE INJURIES**

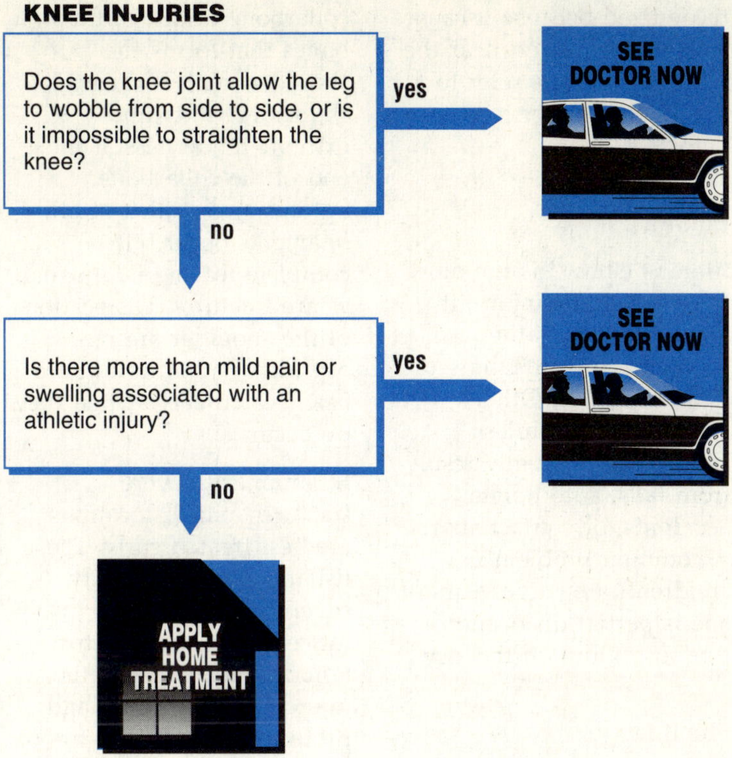


The best policy when there is a potential injury to the ligament is to avoid any major activity until it is clear that this is a minor strain or sprain. Home treatment is intended only for minor strains and sprains.

## HOME TREATMENT

RIP is again the key word—rest, ice, and protection. Rest the knee and elevate it. Apply an ice pack for at least 30 minutes to minimize swelling. If there is more than slight swelling or pain, despite the fact that the knee was immediately rested and ice was applied, see the doctor. If this is not the case, apply the ice treatment on the knee for 30 minutes and then off for 15 minutes for the next several hours. Limited weight bearing may be attempted during this time with a close watch for increased swelling and pain.

Heat can be applied after 24 hours. By then, the knee should look and feel relatively normal; after 72 hours, this should clearly be the case. Remember, however, that a strain or sprain is not completely healed for 4 to 6 weeks and requires protection during this healing period. Elastic bandages will not prevent reinjury but will ease symptoms a bit and remind the patient to be careful with the knee.

## WHAT TO EXPECT AT THE DOCTOR'S OFFICE

The knee will be examined for abnormal motion. A massively swollen knee may have blood removed from the joint with a needle. Torn ligaments need surgical repair. X-rays may be taken but usually are not helpful. For injuries that appear minor, home treatment will be advised. Pain medications are sometimes, but not often, required.

# Arm Injuries

The ligaments of the wrist, shoulder, and elbow joints may be stretched (strained) or partially torn (sprained), but complete tears are rare. Fractures may occur at the wrist, are less frequent around the elbow, and are uncommon around the shoulder. Injuries often occur during a fall, when the weight of the body is caught on the outstretched arm.

### Wrists

The wrist is the most frequently injured joint in the arm. Strains and sprains are common, and the small bones in the wrist may be fractured. Fractures of these small bones may be difficult to see on an X-ray. The most frequent fracture of the wrist involves the ends of the long bones of the forearm and is easily recognized because it causes an unnatural bend near the wrist. Physicians refer to this as the "silver fork deformity."

### Elbows

"Tennis elbow" is the most frequent elbow injury; if you think this is the problem, consult **Elbow Pain**, page 348. Other injuries are much less frequent and usually result from falls, automobile accidents, or contact sports. A common problem in children under five years of age is partial dislocations due to pulling on the arm.

### Shoulders

The collarbone (clavicle) is a frequently fractured bone; fortunately, it has remarkable healing powers. An inability to raise the arm on the affected side is common; the shoulders may also appear uneven. Bandaging the arm to the chest is the only treatment required.

Shoulder separation, often seen in athletes, is perhaps the most common injury of the shoulder. It is a stretching or tearing of the ligament that attaches the collarbone to one of the bones that forms the shoulder joint. It causes a slight deformity and extreme tenderness at the end of the collarbone. Sprains and strains of other ligaments occur but complete tearing is unusual, as are fractures. Dislocations of the shoulder are rare outside of athletics but are best treated early when they do occur.

In summary, severe fractures and dislocations are best treated early. These usually cause deformity, severe pain, and limit movement. Other fractures will not be harmed if the injured limb is rested and protected. Complete tears of ligaments are rare; strains and sprains will heal with home treatment.

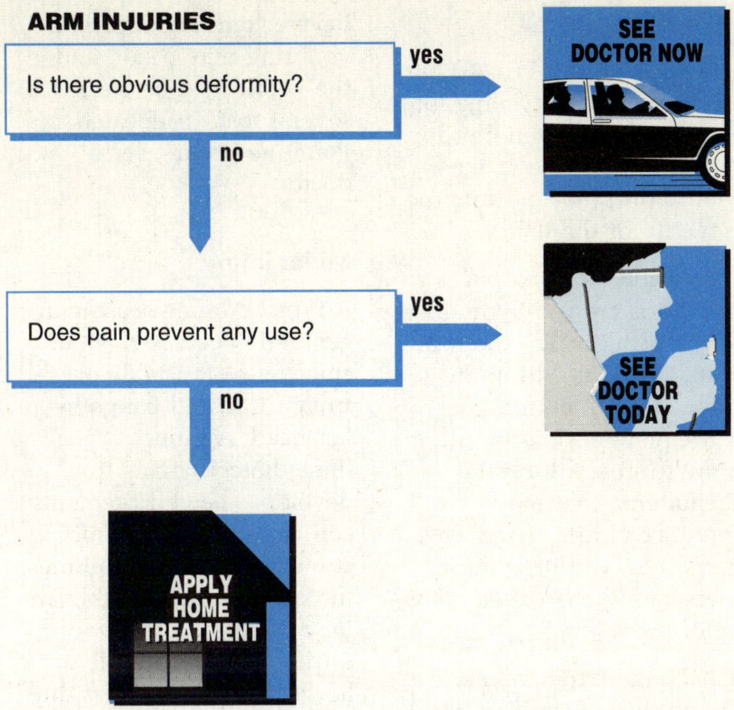


## HOME TREATMENT

RIP is the key word—rest, ice, and protection. Rest the arm and apply ice wrapped in a towel for at least 30 minutes. If the pain is gone and there is no swelling at the end of this time, the ice treatment can be discontinued. A sling for shoulder and elbow injuries and a partial splint for wrist injuries will give protection and rest to the injury while allowing the patient to move around. Continue ice treatment for 30 minutes on and 15 minutes off through the first 8 hours if swelling appears.

Heat can be applied after 24 hours. The injured joint should be usable with little pain within 24 hours and should be almost normal by 72 hours. If not, see the doctor. Complete healing takes from 4 to 6 weeks, and activities with a likelihood of reinjury should be avoided during this time.

## WHAT TO EXPECT AT THE DOCTOR'S OFFICE

An examination and sometimes X-rays will be performed. A cast or sling can be applied. Pain medication is sometimes given, but aspirin or acetaminophen is usually adequate. Certain fractures, especially those around the elbow, may require surgery.

# Head Injuries

Head injuries are potentially serious, but few lead to problems. The major concern in a head injury in which the skull is not clearly and obviously damaged is the occurrence of bleeding inside the skull. The accumulation of blood inside the skull may eventually put pressure on the brain and cause damage. Fortunately the valuable contents of the skull are carefully cushioned. Careful observation is the most valuable tool for diagnosing serious head injury. Usually, this can be done as well at home as in the hospital; there is some risk either way, so it is your choice.

The questions in the decision chart will help you distinguish between a **brain injury**, which can be serious, and a **head injury**, which usually is not.

## HOME TREATMENT

Ice applied to a bruised area may minimize swelling, but "goose eggs" often develop anyway. The size of the bump does not indicate the severity of the injury.

The initial observation period is crucial. Symptoms of bleeding inside the head usually occur within the first 24 to 72 hours. Infrequently, slow bleeding may form a **subdural hematoma** that may produce chronic headache, persistent vomiting, or personality changes months after the injury.

Check the patient every 2 hours during the first 24 hours, every 4 hours during the second 24, and every 8 hours during the third. Look for the following symptoms.

**Loss of alertness:** Increasing lethargy, unresponsiveness, and *abnormally* deep sleep can precede coma.

**Unequal pupil size:** About 25% of people normally have pupils that are slightly unequal all the time. If pupils become unequal *after* the injury, this is a serious sign.

**Severe vomiting:** Forceful vomiting may occur, and the vomit may be ejected several feet. If repeated vomiting occurs, see a doctor.

### Minor Injury

A typical minor head injury generally occurs when a child falls off a table or from a tree and bangs his or her head. A bump immediately begins to develop. The child remains conscious, although initially stunned. For a few minutes, the child is inconsolable and may vomit once or twice during the first couple of hours. Some sleepiness due to the excitement may be noted; the child may nap but is easily aroused. Neither pupil is enlarged and the vomiting ceases shortly. Within eight hours, the child is back to normal except for the tender and often prominent "goose egg."

## HEAD INJURIES

Have any of the following occurred?

- Unconsciousness
- Patient cannot remember injury
- Seizure

yes → **SEE DOCTOR NOW**

no ↓

Are any of the following present?

- Visual problems
- Bleeding from eyes, ears, or mouth
- Change in behavior (sleep, irritability, lethargy)
- Fluid draining from nose
- Persistent vomiting
- Irregular breathing or heart rate
- Child under age 2
- Patient under influence of alcohol or drugs
- Possible child abuse

yes → **SEE DOCTOR NOW**

no ↓

Is there a cut?

yes → *See:* **Cuts**, page 156.

no ↓

**APPLY HOME TREATMENT**

### Severe Injury

In a more severe head injury, symptoms usually take longer to develop. Two or more of the danger signs often are present at the same time. The patient remains lethargic and is not easily aroused. A pupil may enlarge. Vomiting is usually forceful, repeated, and progressively worse.

A critical sign of a serious complication will not be present one minute and gone the next. But, if in doubt, call your doctor.

Because most accidents occur in the evening hours, patients will generally be asleep several hours after most accidents. You can look in on them periodically to check their pulse, pupils, and arousability if you are concerned. With minor head bumps, and no signs of brain injury, nighttime checking is usually not necessary.

### WHAT TO EXPECT AT THE DOCTOR'S OFFICE

The diagnosis of bleeding within the skull cannot be made with great accuracy. Skull X-rays are seldom helpful except in detecting whether a fragment of bone from the skull has been pushed into the brain, but this situation is rare. A CT scan or MRI can be helpful but is expensive and may miss early accumulations of blood. With severe injuries, neck X-rays may be required.

The doctor will ask for a complete description of the accident, assess the patient's general appearance, and take repeated blood pressures and pulse rates. In addition, the head, eyes, ears, nose, throat, neck, and nervous system will be examined. The doctor will also check for other possible sites of injury such as the chest, abdomen, and arms and legs. When internal bleeding is possible but not certain, the patient may be hospitalized for observation. During this observation period, the pulse, pupils, and blood pressure will be checked periodically. In short, the doctor will observe and wait, much as would be done at home. Use of medications, which may obscure symptoms, will be avoided.

# Burns

How can you tell how bad a burn is? Burns are classified according to depth.

### First-Degree Burns

First-degree burns are superficial and cause the skin to turn red. A sunburn is usually a first-degree burn.

First-degree burns may cause a lot of pain but are not a major medical problem. Even when they are extensive, they seldom result in lasting problems and seldom need a doctor's attention.

### Second-Degree Burns

Second-degree burns are deeper and result in splitting of the skin layers or blistering. Scalding with hot water and a very severe sunburn with blisters are common instances of second-degree burns.

Second-degree burns are also painful and, if extensive, may cause significant fluid loss. Scarring, however, is usually minimal, and infection usually is not a problem.

Second-degree burns can be treated at home if they are not extensive. Any second-degree burn that involves an area larger than the patient's hand should be seen by a doctor. In addition, a second-degree burn that involves the face or hands should be seen by a doctor. It might result in cosmetic problems or loss of function.

### Third-Degree Burns

Third-degree burns destroy all layers of the skin and extend into the deeper tissues. Such areas are *painless* because nerve endings have been destroyed. Charring of the burned tissue is usually obvious.

Third-degree burns result in scarring and present problems with infection and fluid loss. The more extensive the burn, the more difficult these problems. All third-degree burns should be seen by a doctor because of these problems and because skin grafts are often needed.

## HOME TREATMENT

**Apply cold water or ice immediately.** This reduces the amount of skin damage caused by the burn and also eases pain. The cold should be applied for at least five minutes and continued until pain is relieved or for one hour, whichever comes first. Be careful not to apply cold so long that the burned area turns numb because frostbite can occur! Reapply treatment if pain returns. Aspirin, ibuprofen, or acetaminophen may be used to reduce pain.

## BURNS

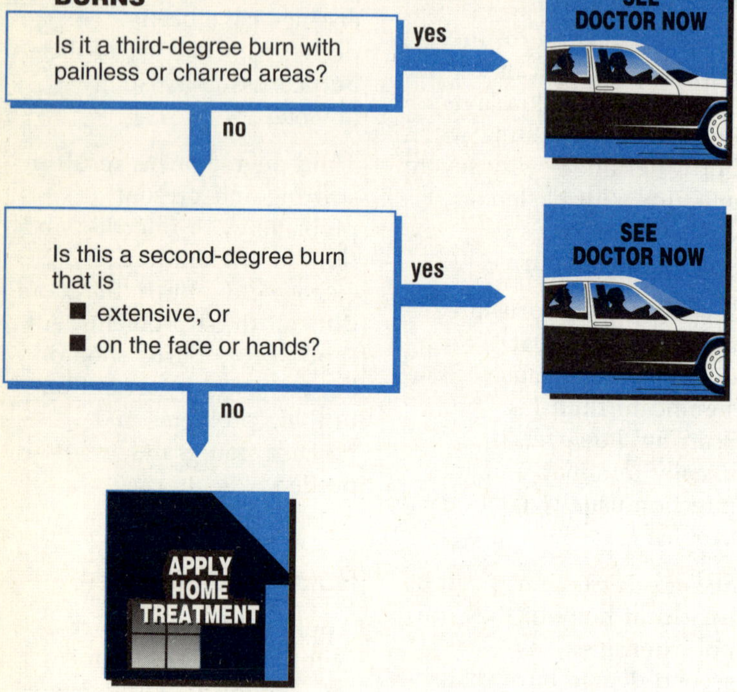


Any burn that continues to be painful for more than 48 hours should be seen by a doctor.

### WHAT TO EXPECT AT THE DOCTOR'S OFFICE

The doctor will establish the extent and degree of the burn and will determine the need for antibiotics, hospitalization, and skin grafting. A dressing with an antibacterial ointment will often be recommended; it must be frequently changed while checking the burn for infection. Extensive burns may require hospitalization, and third-degree burns may eventually require skin grafts.

Blisters should not be broken. If they burst by themselves, as they often do, the overlying skin should be allowed to remain as a wet dressing. Let the skin underneath toughen up, keep the area clean, and protect yourself next time.

The use of local anesthetic creams or sprays is not recommended because they may slow healing. Also, some patients develop an irritation or allergy to these drugs. Do not use butter, cream, or ointments (such as Vaseline). They may slow healing and increase the possibility of infection. Antibiotic creams (Neosporin, Bacitracin, etc.) probably neither help nor hurt minor burns.

# Infected Wounds and Blood Poisoning

To a doctor, blood poisoning means bacterial infection in the bloodstream and is termed *septicemia.* This is a serious condition. Fever is an indication of this rare complication of an infected wound. The patient usually feels terrible, not simply because of the pain from the wound.

An infected wound usually festers beneath the surface of the skin, resulting in pain and swelling. Bacterial infection requires at least a day, and usually two or three days, to develop. Therefore, a late increase in pain or swelling is a legitimate cause for concern. If the festering wound bursts open, pus will drain out. This is good, and the wound will usually heal well. Still, this demonstrates that an infection was present, and a doctor should evaluate the situation unless it is clearly minor.

An explanation of normal wound healing will be helpful.

**1.** The body pours out serum into a wound area. Serum is yellowish and clear, and later turns into a scab. *Serum is frequently mistaken for pus. Pus is thick, cheesy, smelly, and never seen in the first day or so.*

**2.** The edges of a wound will be pink or red, and the wound area may be warm. Such inflammation is normal.

**3.** The lymphatic system helps remove dead cells from the wound. Thus, pain along lymph channels or in the lymph nodes can occur *without* infection.

**There is a folk saying that red streaks running up the arm or leg from a wound are blood poisoning and that the patient will die when the streaks reach the heart. In fact, such streaks are only an inflammation of the lymph channels carrying away the debris from the wound. They will stop when they reach local lymph nodes in the armpit or groin and do not, by themselves, indicate blood poisoning.**

## INFECTED WOUNDS

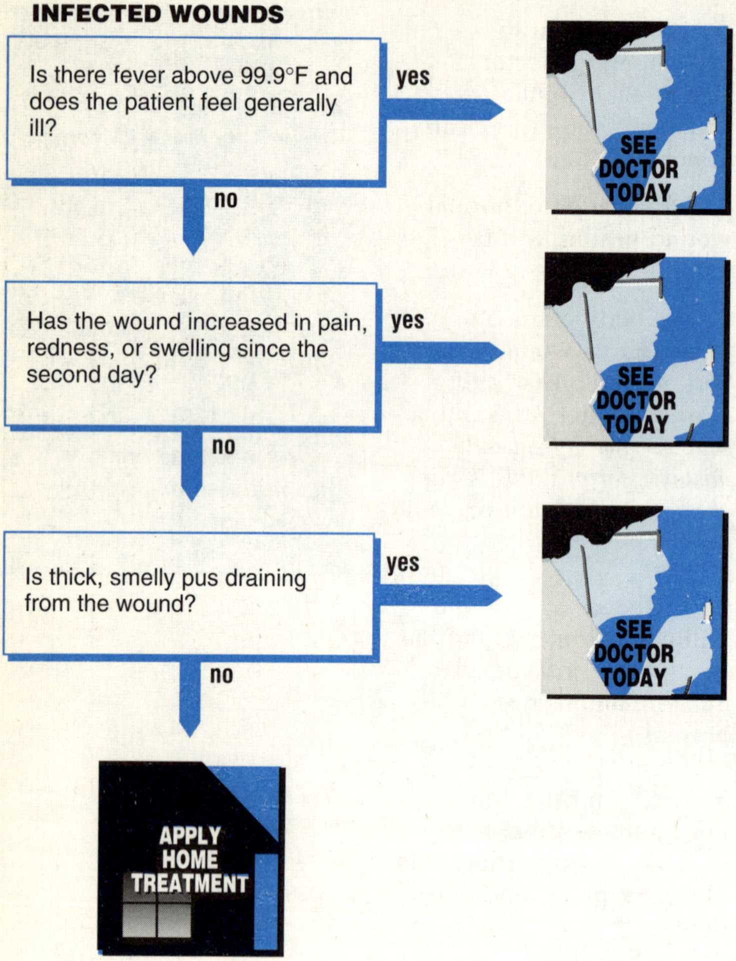


### HOME TREATMENT

Keep the wound clean. Leave it open to the air unless it is unsightly, oozes blood or serum, or gets dirty easily. If so, bandage it, but change the bandage daily. Soak and clean the wound gently with warm water for short periods, 3 or 4 times daily, to remove debris and keep the scab soft. Children like to pick at scabs and often fall on a scab. In these instances, a bandage is useful. The simplest wound of the face requires 3 to 5 days for healing. The healing period for the chest and arms is 5 to 9 days, for the legs it is 7 to 12 days. Larger wounds, or those that have gaped open and must heal across a space, require correspondingly longer periods to heal. Children heal more rapidly than adults. If a wound fails to heal within the expected time, call the doctor.

### WHAT TO EXPECT AT THE DOCTOR'S OFFICE

An examination of the wound and regional lymph nodes will be done, and the patient's temperature will be taken. Sometimes cultures of the blood or the wound are performed, and antibiotics may be prescribed. If there is a suspicion of bacterial infection, cultures may be taken before the antibiotics are given. If a wound is festering, it may be drained either with a needle or a scalpel. This is not very painful and actually relieves discomfort. For severe wound infections, hospitalization may be needed.

# Insect Bites or Stings

Most insect bites are trivial, but some bites or stings may cause reactions. **Local reactions** consist of pain, swelling, and redness at the site of the bite or sting. They are uncomfortable but do not pose a serious hazard. In contrast, **systemic reactions** may occasionally be serious and may require emergency treatment.

There are three types of systemic reactions. All are rare.

- An **asthma attack** is the most common, causing difficulty in breathing and perhaps audible wheezing.
- **Hives** or extensive skin rashes following insect bites are less serious but indicate that a reaction has occurred and that a more severe reaction might occur if the patient is bitten or stung again.
- **Fainting** or loss of consciousness may occur rarely. If the patient has lost consciousness, you must assume that the collapse is due to an allergic reaction. This is an emergency.

If the patient has had any of these reactions in the past, he or she should be taken immediately to a medical facility if stung or bitten.

If the local reaction to a bite or sting is severe or a deep sore is developing, a doctor should be consulted by telephone. Children frequently have more severe local reactions than adults.

### Spider Bites

Bites from poisonous spiders are rare. The female black widow spider accounts for many of them. This spider is glossy black with a body approximately one-half inch in diameter, a leg span of about two inches, and a characteristic red hourglass mark on the abdomen. The **black widow spider** is found in woodpiles, sheds, basements, or outdoor privies. The bite is often painless, and the first sign may be cramping abdominal pain. The abdomen becomes hard and boardlike as the waves of pain become severe. Breathing is difficult and accompanied by grunting. There may be nausea, vomiting, headaches, sweating, twitching, shaking, and tingling sensations of the hands. The bite itself may not be prominent and may be overshadowed by the systemic reaction.

**Brown recluse spiders,** which are slightly smaller than black widows and have a white violin pattern on their backs, cause painful bites and serious local reactions but are not as dangerous as black widows.

**Tick Bites**

Tick bites are common. The tick lives in tall grass or low shrubs and hops on and off passing mammals, such as deer or dogs. In some localities, ticks may carry Rocky Mountain spotted fever and in other regions Lyme disease. Most tick bites are not complicated by subsequent illness. Ticks will commonly be found in the scalp. Consult **Ticks**, page 310.

## HOME TREATMENT

Apply something cold promptly, such as ice or cold packs. Delay in cold applications results in a more severe local reaction. Aspirin or other pain relievers may be used. Antihistamines, such as chlorpheniramine or diphenhydramine, can be helpful in relieving the itch somewhat. If the reaction is severe or if pain does not diminish in 48 hours, consult with the doctor by telephone.

## WHAT TO EXPECT AT THE DOCTOR'S OFFICE

The doctor will ask what sort of insect or spider has inflicted the wound and will look for signs of systemic reaction. If a systemic reaction is present, adrenalin by injection is usually necessary. Rarely, measures to support breathing or blood pressure will be needed; these measures require the facilities of an emergency room or hospital.

If the problem is a local reaction, the doctor will examine the wound for signs of death of tissue or infection. Occasionally, surgical drainage of the wound will be needed. In other cases, pain relievers or antihistamines may make the patient more comfortable. Adrenalin injections are occasionally used for very severe local reactions.

If a systemic reaction has occurred, desensitization shots may be initiated. In addition, emergency kits can be purchased to help the person with a serious allergy.

## INSECT BITES

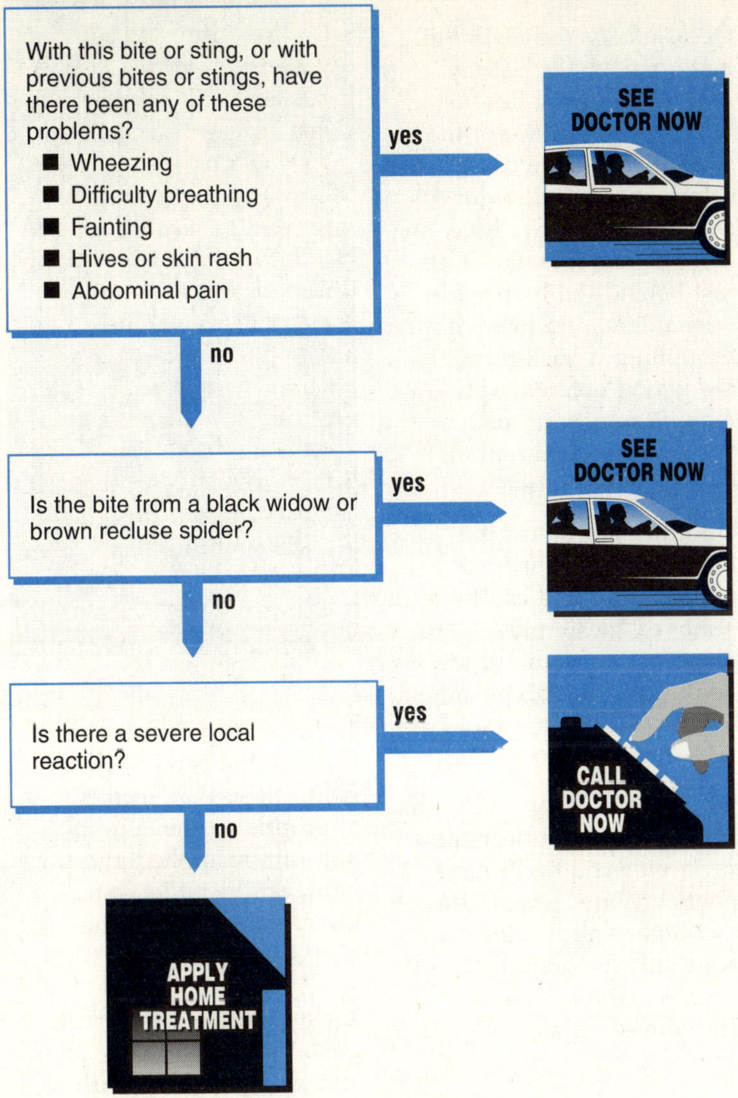

# Fishhooks

The problem with fishhooks is, of course, the barb. Meant to keep the fish hooked, it has the same effect when people are caught. Nevertheless, a fishhook usually can be removed without a doctor's help, unless it is in someone's eye. No attempt should be made to remove hooks that have actually penetrated the eyeball; this is a job for the doctor.

The patient's confidence and cooperation are needed in order to avoid a visit to the doctor. A pair of electrician's pliers with a wire-cutting blade should be part of your fishing equipment. The advantage of the doctor's office is the availability of a local anesthetic.

## HOME TREATMENT

Occasionally, the hook will have moved all the way around so that it lies just beneath the surface of the skin. If this is the case, often the best technique is simply to push the hook on through the skin, cut it off just behind the barb with wirecutters, and remove it by pulling it back through the way it entered. This may be somewhat painful; the average child may not be able to tolerate it.

On other occasions, the hook will be embedded only slightly and can be removed by simply grasping the shank of the hook (pliers help), pushing slightly forward and away from the barb, and then pulling it out.

If the barb is not near the surface or you don't have pliers or wire cutters, use the method illustrated on page 187; the hook is usually removed quickly and almost painlessly.

**A splinter under the skin can often be pulled out with tweezers. If some material remains, you can usually dislodge it by picking away at the overlying skin with a clean needle. Sterilize the needle first by dipping it in rubbing alcohol or holding it in a match flame. Another option is to soak the area of skin twice a day in a cup of very warm, but not hot, water mixed with one teaspoon of baking soda; the splinter will probably come out by itself in a day or two. Don't let a splinter wound become infected.**

**1.** Put a loop of fish line through the bend of the fishhook so that, at the appropriate time, a quick jerk can be applied and the hook can be pulled out directly in line with the shaft of the hook.

**2.** Holding onto the shaft, push the hook slightly in and away from the barb so as to disengage the barb (see figure *a*, page 187).

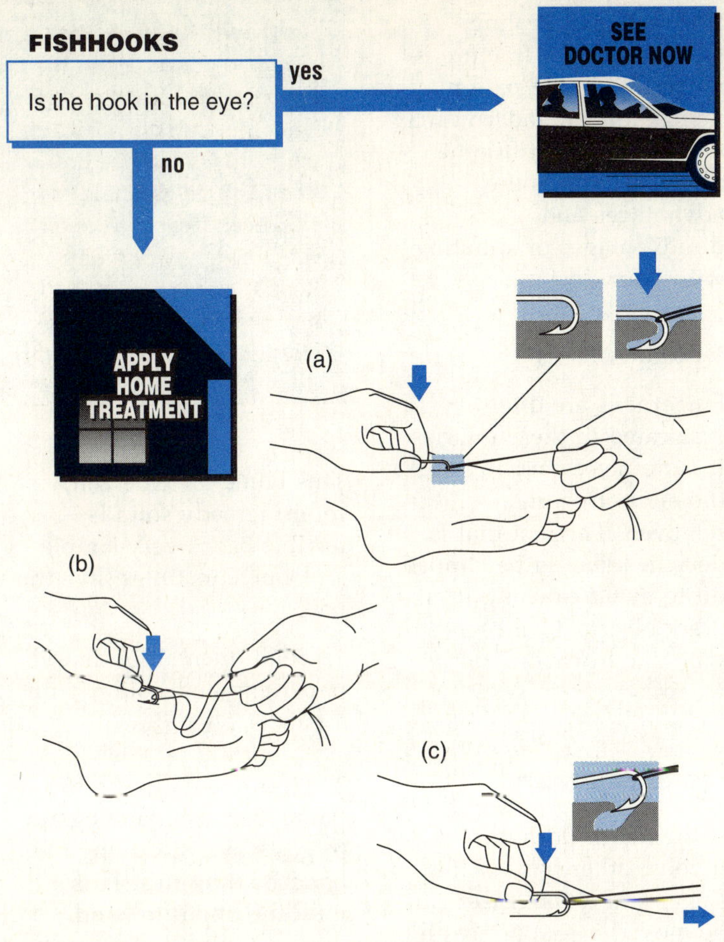


Drawing adapted from George Hill, *Outpatient Surgery*. Philadelphia: Saunders, 1973.

**3.** Holding this pressure constant to keep the barb disengaged, give a quick jerk on the fish line and the hook will pop out (see *b* and *c*, above).

If you are not successful, push the hook all the way through and out so that the barb can be cut off with wire cutters as described on page 186.

Be sure that the patient's tetanus shots are up to date (see **Tetanus Shots,** page 165). Treat the wound as in the home treatment section for **Puncture Wounds**, page 159. If all else fails, a visit to the doctor should solve the problem.

## WHAT TO EXPECT AT THE DOCTOR'S OFFICE

The doctor will use one of the three methods above to remove the hook. If necessary, the area around the hook can be infiltrated with a local anesthetic before the hook is removed. Often the injection of a local anesthetic is more painful than just removing the hook without the anesthetic.

If the hook is in the eye, it is likely that the help of an eye specialist or ophthalmologist will be needed, and it may be necessary to remove the hook in the operating room.

# Smashed Fingers

Smashing fingers in car doors or desk drawers, or with hammers or baseballs, is all too common. If the injury involves only the end segment of the finger (the terminal phalanx) and does not involve a significant cut, the help of a doctor is seldom needed. Blood under the fingernail (subungual hematoma) is a painful problem that you can treat.

### Joint Fractures

Fractures of the bone in the end segment of the finger are not treated unless they involve the joint. Many doctors feel that it is unwise to splint the finger even if there is a fracture of the joint. Although the splint will decrease pain, it may also increase the stiffness of the joint after healing. However, if the fracture is not splinted, the pain may persist longer, and you may end up with a stiff joint anyway. Discuss the advantages and disadvantages of splinting with your doctor.

### Dislocated Nails

Fingernails are often dislocated in these injuries. It is not necessary to have the entire fingernail removed. The nail that is detached should be clipped off to avoid catching it on other objects. Nail regrowth will take from four to six weeks.

## HOME TREATMENT

If the injury does not involve other parts of the finger and if the finger can be moved easily, apply an ice pack for swelling and use aspirin, ibuprofen, or acetaminophen for pain.

### Blood Under a Nail

Pain caused by a large amount of blood under the fingernail can often be relieved simply.

**Ingrown nails** can be treated at home. Cut the nail straight across so that its corner can grow outside the skin. Let the nail grow free by firmly pushing the skin back from the corner with a Q-tip twice a day. Keep the area clean. For **hangnails**, keep them clean. Don't chew on them.

This home (or emergency room) remedy sounds terrible but is very simple and can sometimes save the nail.

**1.** Bend open an ordinary paper clip and hold it with a pair of pliers.

**2.** Heat one end with the flame from a butane lighter or gas stove, steadying the hand holding the pliers with the opposite hand.

**3.** When the tip is very hot, touch it to the nail, and it will melt its way through the fingernail, leaving a clean, small, painless hole. There is no need to press down hard. Take your time,

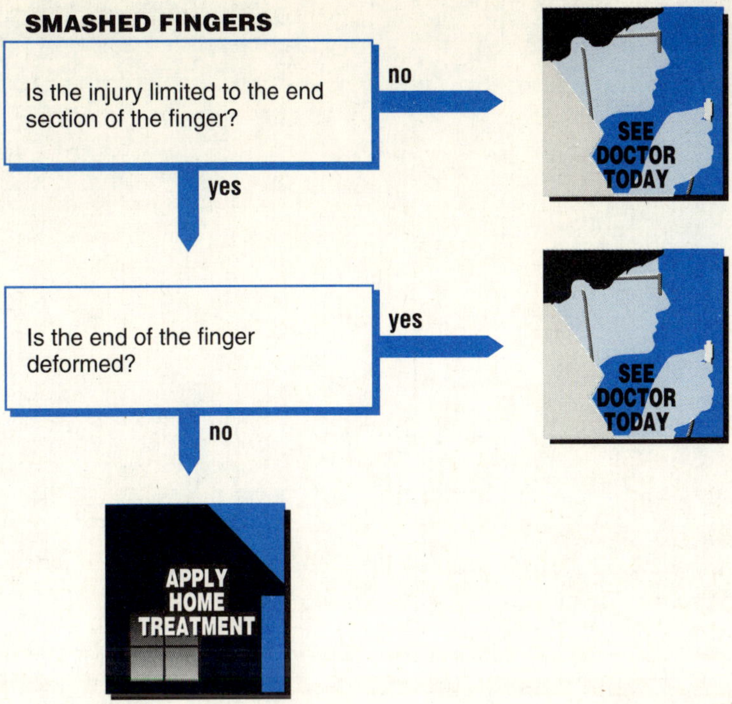

making a hole in a fingernail

lifting the paper clip to see if you are through the nail; usually the blood will spurt a little when you are through. Reheat the paper clip if necessary.

The blood trapped beneath the nail can now escape through the small hole, and the pain will be relieved as the pressure is released. If the hole closes and the blood reaccumulates, the procedure can be repeated using the same hole once again.

## WHAT TO EXPECT AT THE DOCTOR'S OFFICE

The doctor will examine the finger. An X-ray is likely if it appears that more than the end segment is involved. If there is a fracture involving the last joint on the finger, you should expect a discussion of the advantages and disadvantages of splinting the finger. The splinting of one finger is often accomplished by bandaging it together with the adjacent finger. If the finger is splinted, exercise it periodically to preserve mobility. Severe injuries of fingers may occasionally require surgery in order to preserve function.

## CHAPTER E

# *Fever, Headache, and Other Common Problems*

# Fever

Many people, including doctors, speak of fever and illness as if they were one and the same. Surprisingly, an elevated temperature is not necessarily a sign of illness. Normal body temperature varies from individual to individual. If we measured the body temperatures of a large number of healthy people while they were resting, we would find a difference of 1.5°F between the lowest and highest temperatures. We are all individuals, and there is nothing absolute about a 98.6°F (37°C) temperature.

Normal body temperature varies greatly during the day. Temperature is generally lowest in the morning upon awakening. Food, excess clothing, excitement, and anxiety can all elevate body temperature. Vigorous exercise can raise body temperature to as much as 103°F. Severe exercise, without water, can result in a condition known as **heat stroke,** with temperatures around 106°F. Other mechanisms also influence body temperature. Hormones, for example, account for a monthly variation of body temperature in ovulating women. Normal temperature is 1 to 1.5°F higher in the second half of the menstrual cycle. In general, children have higher body temperatures than adults and seem to have greater daily variation because of their greater levels of excitement and activity.

Having said all this, we know you would like a rule to follow:

- If the oral temperature is 99 to 100°F, start thinking about the possibility of fever.
- If it is 100°F or above, it's a fever.

## CAUSES OF FEVER

The most common causes for persistent fevers are viral and bacterial infections, such as colds, sore throats, earaches, diarrhea, urinary infections, roseola, chicken pox, mumps, measles, and occasionally pneumonia, appendicitis, and meningitis.

A viral infection can result in a normal temperature or a temperature of 105°F. The height of the temperature is *not* a reliable indicator of the seriousness of the underlying infection.

## TAKING A TEMPERATURE

Both Fahrenheit and Celsius thermometers are acceptable. Rectal temperatures are usually more accurate and are about 0.5°F higher than oral temperatures. Oral temperature can be affected by hot or cold foods, routine breathing, and smoking. Generally, oral thermometers can be recognized by the longer bulb at the business end of the thermometer. The longer length of the bulb provides a greater surface area and a faster, more accurate reading. Rectal thermometers have a shorter, rounder bulb to facilitate entry into the rectum.

Rectal thermometers can be used to take oral temperatures but require a longer period in the mouth to achieve the same degree of accuracy as the oral thermometer. Oral thermometers can be used to take rectal temperatures, but we do not recommend their use in children, because their shape is not ideal for younger children. Electronic thermometers have the advantage of quicker readings, which is useful for younger children, but are more expensive than traditional types.

Rectal thermometers are best for young children. Lubricants can make insertion of rectal thermometers easier. Place the child on his or her stomach and hold one hand on the buttocks to prevent movement. Insert the thermometer only an inch or so inside the rectum. On a rectal thermometer, the mercury will rise within seconds because the rectum closely contacts the thermometer. Remove the thermometer when the mercury is no longer rising, after a minute or two.

### FEBRILE SEIZURES (FEVER FITS)

The danger of an extremely high temperature is the possibility that the fever will cause a seizure (convulsion). All of us are capable of "seizing" if our body temperatures become too high. Febrile seizures are relatively common in normal, healthy children; about 3 to 5% will experience a febrile seizure. However, although common, they must be given due consideration.

Febrile seizures occur most often in children between the ages of six months and four years. Illnesses that cause rapid elevations to high temperatures, such as roseola, have been frequently associated with febrile seizure. Rarely, a seizure is the first sign of a serious underlying problem such as meningitis.

The brain, which is normally transmitting electrical impulses at a fairly regular rhythm, begins misfiring during a seizure because of overheating and causes involuntary muscular responses, termed a seizure, convulsion, fit, or "falling out spell." The first sign may be a stiffening of the entire body. Children may have rhythmic beating of a single hand or foot, or any combination of the hands and feet. The eyes may roll back and the head may jerk. Urine and feces may pass involuntarily.

Most seizures last only from 1 to 5 minutes. There is very little evidence that such a short seizure is of any long-term consequence. On the other hand, prolonged seizures of more than 30 minutes are often a sign of a more serious underlying problem. Less than half of all children who have a short febrile seizure will ever experience a second, and less than half who experience a second will ever have a third.

Although a "seizing" child is a terrifying sight to a parent, the dangers to the child during a seizure are small. The following commonsense rules should be followed during a seizure.

- Protect your child's head from hitting anything hard. Place the child on a bed.
- Considerable damage can be done by forcing objects into the child's mouth to prevent biting of the tongue. Surprisingly, cut tongues are uncommon and they usually heal quickly.
- Make sure the child's breathing passage is open. Forcing a stick in your child's mouth does not ensure an open airway.

To facilitate breathing, (1) clear the nose and mouth of vomitus or other material, and (2) pull the head backward slightly to hyperextend the neck. Artificial respiration is almost never necessary. These techniques are best learned in demonstrations. In a true emergency, hyperextend the neck and breathe ten times each minute through the child's nose while keeping the mouth covered (or through the child's mouth while keeping the nose pinched closed with your fingers). Only blow air in; the child will blow the air out naturally.

- Begin fever reduction (discussed below) and seek medical attention immediately. Do *not* give medicine by mouth to a seizing or unconscious patient. Fortunately, once the seizure has stopped, the child is usually temporarily resistant to a second seizure. However, because there are exceptions to this rule, medical attention is important.

After the seizure has subsided, the child may be very groggy and have no recollection of what has occurred. Others may show signs of extreme weakness and even paralysis of an arm or leg. This paralysis is almost always temporary but must be carefully evaluated.

The doctor will do a careful study to determine the cause of a febrile seizure. For the first febrile seizure, this will usually include a spinal tap (lumbar puncture) and fluid analysis to make certain that the seizure was not caused by meningitis. Following the termination of the fever, the doctor will stress the importance of fever control for the next few days and will often place the child on anticonvulsant medications.

## THE MEANING OF A CHILL

A chill is another symptom of a fever. The feeling of being hot or cold is maintained by a complex system of nerve receptors in our skin and in a part of our brain known as the hypothalmus. This system is sensitive to the difference between the body temperature and the temperature outside the body. Cold can be sensed in two different ways, either by lowering the environmental temperature or by raising the body temperature.

The body responds in a similar manner to a chill as it would if the outside temperature dropped. All of the normal systems that increase heat production, such as shivering, become active.

Because eating is a means of increasing heat production, hunger may be experienced. The body tries to conserve heat by causing constriction of the blood vessels near the skin. Children will sometimes curl up in a ball to conserve heat. Goose bumps are intended to raise the hairs on our body to form a layer of insulation. Don't bundle up the patient in blankets if he or she shivers or becomes chilled; this will only cause the fever to go higher. Use home treatment as described below.

## HOME TREATMENT

There are two ways to reduce a fever: sponging and medication. If fever remains above 103°F after an hour or so of home treatment, call the doctor.

### Sponging

Evaporation has a cooling effect on the skin and hence on the body temperature. Evaporation can be enhanced by sponging the skin with water. Although alcohol evaporates more rapidly, it is somewhat uncomfortable and the vapors can be dangerous. Generally, sponging with tepid water (water that is comfortable to the touch) will be sufficient. Heat is also lost by conduction when a patient is sponged or sitting in a tub. Conduction is the process in which heat is lost to a cooler environment (the bathwater or air) from the warmer environment of the body. A comfortable tub of water (70°F) is sufficiently lower than the body temperature to encourage conduction. Although cold water will work somewhat faster, the discomfort makes this less desirable. A child will tolerate cold bathing and sponging for a much shorter period.

### Medication

Temperature can be controlled in the conscious, alert patient with aspirin, ibuprofen (Motrin, Rufen, Advil, Nuprin, etc.), or acetaminophen (Tylenol, Tempra, Liquiprin, Valadol, Datril, Tenlap, etc.).

Remember that fever is the body's way of naturally responding to a variety of conditions, including infection. A fever may signify the response of a body's immune system to an infection and thus be the visible manifestation of a beneficial effect. Nonetheless, fevers are uncomfortable. Controlling a fever that is sufficiently high to interfere with eating, drinking, sleeping, or other important activities will make the patient feel better. In short, if the patient is suffering from the fever, treat it. If the fever is mild and the patient shows no effects, it may be unnecessary to treat.

### Dangers of Fever Medications

Children and teenagers who take aspirin when they have chicken pox or the flu stand a higher chance of later developing **Reye's syndrome,** a rare but serious problem of the brain and liver. Because it is hard to recognize chicken pox and flu in their early stages, we recommend that parents always give children and teenagers acetaminophen instead of aspirin. It does not carry the risk of Reye's syndrome and is slightly safer on the stomach than ibuprofen.

No medication should be given by mouth to a child who is seizing or unconscious. A child who has just had a febrile seizure can be given an aspirin suppository instead; to give the proper dose, the suppository can be cut lengthwise with a warm knife. See Table E on page 197 for the dosage—it can be slightly higher than the dose of aspirin taken by mouth.

In addition to the types of acetaminophen and ibuprofen sold over the counter, there are higher doses of these drugs available by doctor's prescription—potentially more than twice the strength of the non-prescription formulas. If you have both types of one drug in your house, do not mix up the two. Medication prescribed for one person should never be given to another, especially a child.

All drugs kept at home should be in childproof bottles. Because there are no totally childproof bottles, drugs should also be kept out of small children's reach. Aspirin in excessive doses has been responsible for more childhood deaths than any other medication. Acetaminophen and ibuprofen carry reputations for being safer than aspirin, but they, too, can cause damage in overdoses. There are no "safe" drugs.

### Aspirin

Aspirin is universally familiar, effective, and reliable. However, it is not the best drug for everyone on all occasions; we do not recommend giving it to children and teenagers with fever. A few individuals are allergic to aspirin and may experience severe skin rashes or gastrointestinal bleeding. All people will suffer if they take too much aspirin. Early signs of excess aspirin include rapid breathing and ringing in the ears. An excessive dose of aspirin can be fatal.

"Baby aspirin" contains 1¼ grains (81 mg) per tablet, one-quarter the amount of aspirin in an adult tablet. By the time a child is five, an adult aspirin or four baby aspirin (5 grains) can be given. See Table E on page 197 for the standard dosages for children at different ages. Toxic effects may begin to develop at less than twice the recommended dosage, so you must handle this medication carefully.

**The additional amount of aspirin or acetaminophen in "extra-strength" tablets is medically trivial. You can take more tablets of the cheaper aspirin and still save money. When you read that a product "contains more of the ingredient that doctors recommend most," you may be sure that the product contains a bit more aspirin per tablet.**

In adults, the standard dose for pain or fever relief is two tablets taken every three to four hours as required. The maximum effect occurs in about two hours. Each standard tablet is five grains (325 mg). If you use a non-standard concoction, you will have to do the arithmetic to calculate equivalent doses. The terms "extra-strength," "arthritis pain formula," and the like indicate a greater amount of aspirin per tablet: perhaps 400 to 500 mg. Aspirin does not come in liquid form.

### Ibuprofen

Ibuprofen is the most recently released over-the-counter drug for fever control. It is available in tablet form under different brand names (Advil, Nuprin, etc.) and appears in some other medications (Midol, etc.). Allergic reactions to ibuprofen are rare, as are gastrointestinal side effects. If you have problems with stomach irritation, you can take ibuprofen after a meal without badly affecting its absorption. Ibuprofen is safer for children than aspirin, but it is not available in as many forms as acetaminophen.

### Acetaminophen

Acetaminophen has sometimes been called "liquid aspirin," but it is a completely different medication. The advantage of acetaminophen is that it can be given in either liquid or tablet form. Acetaminophen is as effective as aspirin in fever reduction. It is not as effective as aspirin for other purposes, such as reducing inflammation. Fewer people are allergic to acetaminophen, and it does not cause as many gastrointestinal disturbances. However, if the patient has never had nausea, abdominal pain, or other gastrointestinal problems with aspirin, this is probably not an important consideration. Overdoses can cause liver damage and consequently can cause death.

Acetaminophen is available in drops, suspension, tablets, or capsules. See Table E for recommended dosages. The concentration of the drops is much higher than the suspension and therefore must be administered cautiously. An unsuspecting person used to a different preparation of acetaminophen can create a problem by using the wrong dosage on your child.

## WHAT TO EXPECT AT THE DOCTOR'S OFFICE

Treatment depends on how long you have had a fever and how sick you appear. To determine whether an infection is present, the doctor will examine the skin, eyes, ears, nose, throat, neck, chest, and belly. If no other symptoms are present

**TABLE E** *Dosages for Pain and Fever Relief*

| *Drug and Its Form* | *Amount* | *Dosages* |
|---|---|---|
| **Aspirin** | | |
| "baby aspirin" tablets | 81 mg per tablet | For children under 10: 65 mg per year of age every 4–6 hours |
| tablets | 325 mg per tablet ("extra-strength" tablets contain more aspirin: 400-500 mg) | For children over 10: 650 mg every 4–6 hours<br>For adults: 650 mg every 3–4 hours |
| suppositories | 325 mg per suppository | For children under 10: 81 mg (1/4 suppository) per year of age every 4–6 hours |
| **Ibuprofen** | | |
| tablets | 200 mg per tablet | For adults: 400 mg every 4–6 hours |
| **Acetaminophen** | | |
| tablets and capsules | 325 mg per tablet ("extra-strength" tablets contain more acetaminophen: 500 mg) | For children under 10: 65 mg per year of age every 4–6 hours<br>For children over 10 and adults: 650 mg every 4 hours |
| suspension or drops | varies by form (drops are more concentrated than suspension) | For children under 10: 65 mg per year of age every 4–6 hours |

**NOTE:** *We recommend that children and teenagers be given acetaminophen for fever instead of aspirin, so as to avoid the risk of Reye's syndrome.*

and the exam does not reveal an infection, watchful waiting may be advised. If the fever has been prolonged or the patient appears ill, tests of the blood and urine may be done. A chest X-ray or spinal tap may be needed. Specific infections will be treated appropriately; fever will be treated as discussed in "Home Treatment," page 194.

## FEVER

Is this a temperature of 101°F or more in a child less than three months of age?

yes →

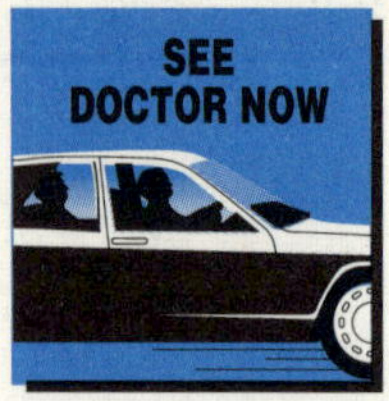


no ↓

Is there stiffness of the neck, confusion, marked irritability, or lethargy? Has there been a seizure or is breathing rapid?

yes →

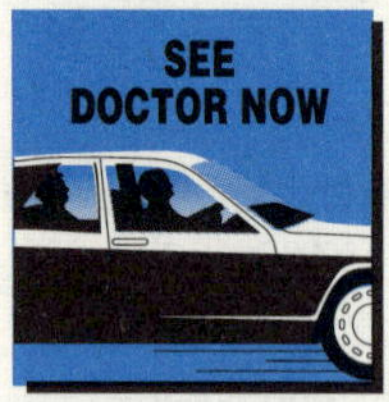


no ↓

In a child between three months and one year of age, has fever lasted more than 24 hours?

yes →

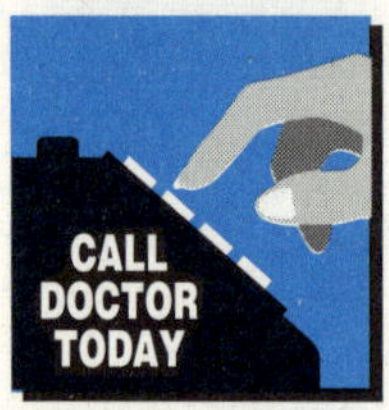


no ↓

Has fever shown no improvement in 72 hours or has it lasted more than five days?

yes →

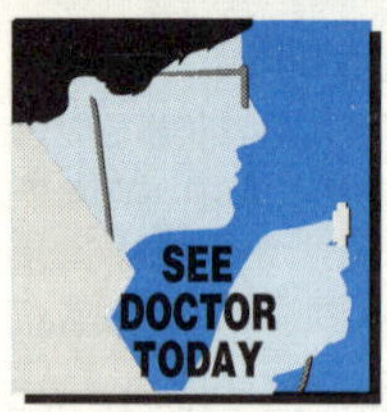


no ↓

Is there sore throat, ear pain, cough, abdominal pains, skin rash, diarrhea, urinary frequency, or other symptoms?

yes →

*See:* Discussions of these problems.

no ↓

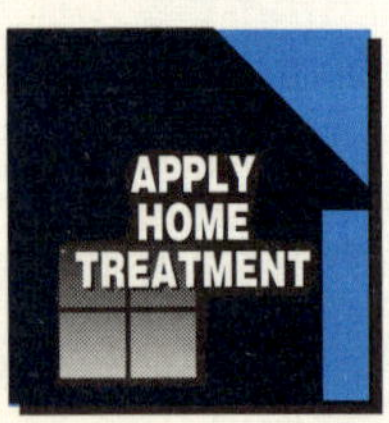


**Starve a fever? This folk remedy probably originated from people who noticed the relationship between food and temperature elevation. However, there are many reasons why patients should eat during a fever. The increased body heat increases caloric requirements because calories are being consumed rapidly. More important, there is an increased demand for fluid. Liquids should *never* be withheld from a feverish patient. If a patient will not eat because of the discomfort caused by fever, it is still essential that he or she drink fluids.**

# Headache

Headache is the most frequent single complaint of modern times. Most commonly, the causes are tension and muscle spasms in the neck, scalp, and jaw. Headache *without any other associated symptoms* is almost always caused by tension. Fever and a neck so stiff that the chin cannot be touched to the chest suggest the possibility of meningitis rather than an ordinary tension headache. But even with these symptoms, meningitis is rare. Flu is much more likely. Muscle aches and pains are seldom seen in meningitis.

### Migraines

Most so-called migraine headaches are really tension headaches. True migraine headaches are often associated with nausea or vomiting and preceded by visual phenomena such as seeing stars. They are caused by constriction and then relaxation of blood vessels in the head. True migraine headaches occur *only* on one side of the head during any particular attack.

Increased internal pressure due to head injury can cause headache and may also cause vomiting and difficulties with vision (see **Head Injuries**, page 176).

### Sign of Trouble?

Although headaches are *not* a reliable indicator of high blood pressure, if they are worse in the morning, check the blood pressure.

Headache patients frequently worry about brain tumors. In the absence of paralysis or personality change, the possibility that an intermittent headache is caused by a brain tumor is exceedingly remote. Although constant and slowly increasing headaches are frequently noted in patients with brain tumors, it is usually some other symptom that leads the doctor to begin an investigation for tumor. Headache patients should not be routinely investigated for possible brain tumor because the tests are costly and/or hazardous.

## HOME TREATMENT

All of the usual over-the-counter drugs (aspirin, ibuprofen, and acetaminophen) are quite effective in relieving headache. Aspirin and ibuprofen may be taken with milk or food to prevent stomach irritation. Because of a serious problem known as Reye's syndrome, aspirin should not be used for children and teenagers.

Headache may frequently be relieved by massage or heat applied to the back of the upper neck or by simply resting with eyes closed and the head supported. Relaxation techniques such as meditation may work also.

Persistent headaches that do not respond to such measures should be brought to the attention of a doctor. Headaches that are associated with difficulty in using the arms or legs or

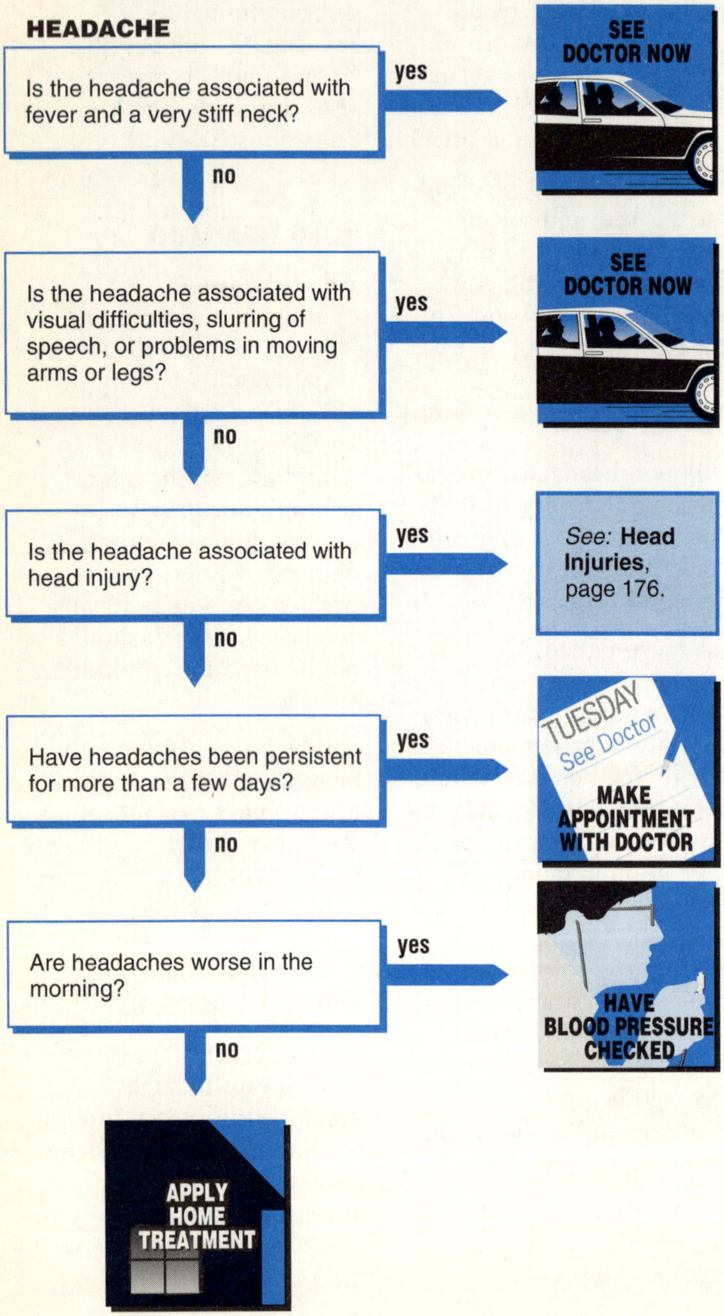


with slurring of speech as well as those that are rapidly increasing in frequency and severity also require a visit to the doctor.

## WHAT TO EXPECT AT THE DOCTOR'S OFFICE

The doctor will examine the head, eyes, ears, nose, throat, and neck, and will also test nerve function. The temperature will be taken. Abnormalities are rarely found. The diagnosis of a headache is usually based on the history given by the patient. If the doctor feels that the headache may be migraine, an ergot preparation (Cafergot, etc.) may be prescribed. Other uncommon types of headaches, such as cluster headaches, may also be treated with this medicine. However, most headaches are caused by tension, and the basic approach will be that outlined under "Home Treatment," page 199.

# Insomnia

Insomnia is not a disease, but it is a continuing problem for some 15 to 20 million Americans and causes occasional problems for almost everyone else. It is a frequent cause of doctor visits, many of which could be avoided. Many of these visits are made specifically to obtain sleeping pills that are "better" than those available without a prescription. Yet most doctors believe that sleeping pills should be avoided whenever possible.

The nonprescription sleep aids seem to depend mostly on what doctors call the "placebo effect"—they work only if you think they are going to. The antihistamines that they contain can increase daytime drowsiness and actually create the impression that the sleep problem is getting worse rather than better. The stronger drugs available by prescription are more likely to really knock you out, but they do not produce a natural, restful sleep. As a result, you feel more fatigued than ever and may conclude that you need more of the drug. The more of it you use, the more disturbed your sleep. This vicious cycle is called drug-dependent insomnia, is well recognized, and has become an unnecessary national health problem.

For most people, occasional insomnia is a response to excitement. Both good and bad events in your life can keep you awake and thinking at night. Other people develop poor sleeping schedules—sleeping late or napping during the day makes sleep at night more difficult. Finally, some people don't realize that they actually need less sleep as they get older. When they can't sleep the usual number of hours, they believe they have a sleeping problem.

A disease is rarely the cause of insomnia. Problems that wake you up at night are not insomnia; you should consult the sections of this book that deal with your particular complaints. Problems such as chest pain or shortness of breath require the prompt attention of a doctor.

## HOME TREATMENT

Here are some suggestions for developing a successful approach to your insomnia:

**1.** Avoid using alcohol in the evening.

**2.** Avoid caffeine for at least two hours before bedtime.

**3.** Establish a regular bedtime, but don't go to bed if you feel wide awake.

**4.** Use the bedroom for bedroom activities only. If the bedroom is used for activities such as paying bills, studying, and so on, entering the bedroom can be a signal to become active rather than to go to sleep.

**5.** Break your chain of thought before retiring. Relax by reading, watching television, taking a bath, or listening to soothing music—something that helps to keep your mind from working overtime on life's more serious activities.

**INSOMNIA**

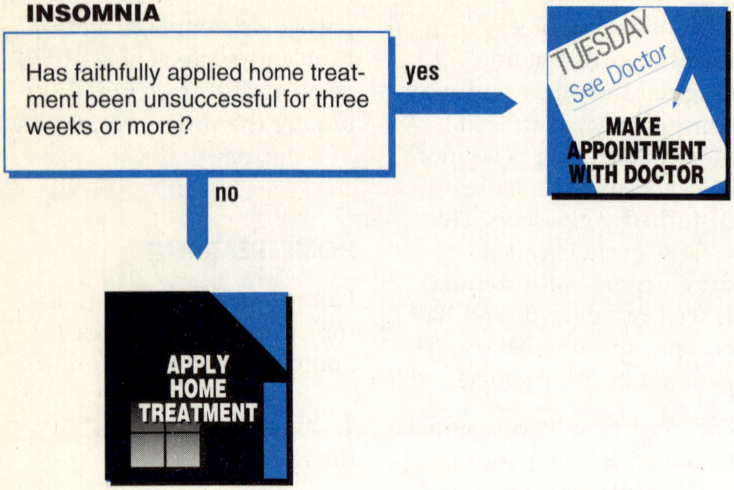


## WHAT TO EXPECT AT THE DOCTOR'S OFFICE

The doctor will focus on your sleeping schedule, factors that could be causing stress and anxiety, and other factors related to sleep such as the use of drugs. The physical examination is less important than the history and may be brief. In some instances, the doctor may want to obtain further studies such as an electroencephalogram (EEG) during sleep. On rare occasions, it may be necessary to refer you to a center for the study of sleep disturbances where complex studies of your sleep pattern may be conducted.

**6.** A snack seems to help many people as does the traditional glass of warm milk. However, don't eat a big meal before going to bed because this seems to cause problems with sleep.

**7.** Exercise regularly, but not in the last two hours before going to bed.

**8.** Give up smoking. Smokers have more difficulty getting to sleep than non-smokers.

**9.** Once you get into bed, use creative imagery and relaxation techniques to keep your mind off unrestful thoughts. Counting sheep is the oldest kind of creative imagery. Another image technique is to concentrate on a pleasant scene that relaxes you, such as walking along a beach and hearing the sounds of the ocean.

**10.** Finally, many researchers believe that the most effective natural sleep inducer is—you guessed it—sex.

It may take several weeks or more to establish a new, natural sleeping routine. If you are unable to make progress after giving these methods an honest try, a visit to the doctor may be necessary.

# Weakness and Fatigue

Weakness and fatigue are often considered to be similar, but in medicine they have distinct and separate meanings. Weakness refers to lack of strength. Fatigue is tiredness, lack of energy, or lethargy.

Weakness is usually the more serious condition and is particularly important when it is confined to one area of the body. Such weakness in one area is often due to a problem in the muscular or nervous system, such as a stroke.

Lack of energy, on the other hand, is typically associated with a viral infection or with feelings of anxiety, depression, or tension. It is caused by a large variety of illnesses.

Hypoglycemia means "low blood sugar," and many patients fear that this problem is the cause of their tiredness. A few individuals do in fact feel shaky and tremulous several hours after a meal because their blood-sugar level drops at that point. However, they do *not* feel fatigued. Low blood sugar throughout the day can cause fatigue, but this is a rare condition.

## HOME TREATMENT

There is time and need for careful reflection on the causes of fatigue. The most common situation was once termed "the tired housewife syndrome." Many young and middle-aged women come to the doctor's office complaining of fatigue and requesting tests for anemia or thyroid problems. Many adult women are mildly iron deficient, and thyroid problems may cause fatigue, but it is very unusual for one of these conditions to be the cause of fatigue. In most cases, fatigue is more closely related to boredom, unhappiness, some disappointment, or just plain hard work. The patient should consider these possibilities before consulting the doctor.

Vitamins are rarely helpful, but in moderation they do not hurt.

## WHAT TO EXPECT AT THE DOCTOR'S OFFICE

If the problem is weakness of only part of the body, the doctor will concentrate the examination on the nerve and muscle functions. A typical stroke will be identified by such an examination, whereas more uncommon ailments may require further testing and special procedures.

If the problem is fatigue, the medical history is the most important part of the encounter. Physical examination of heart, lungs, and the thyroid gland can be expected. The doctor

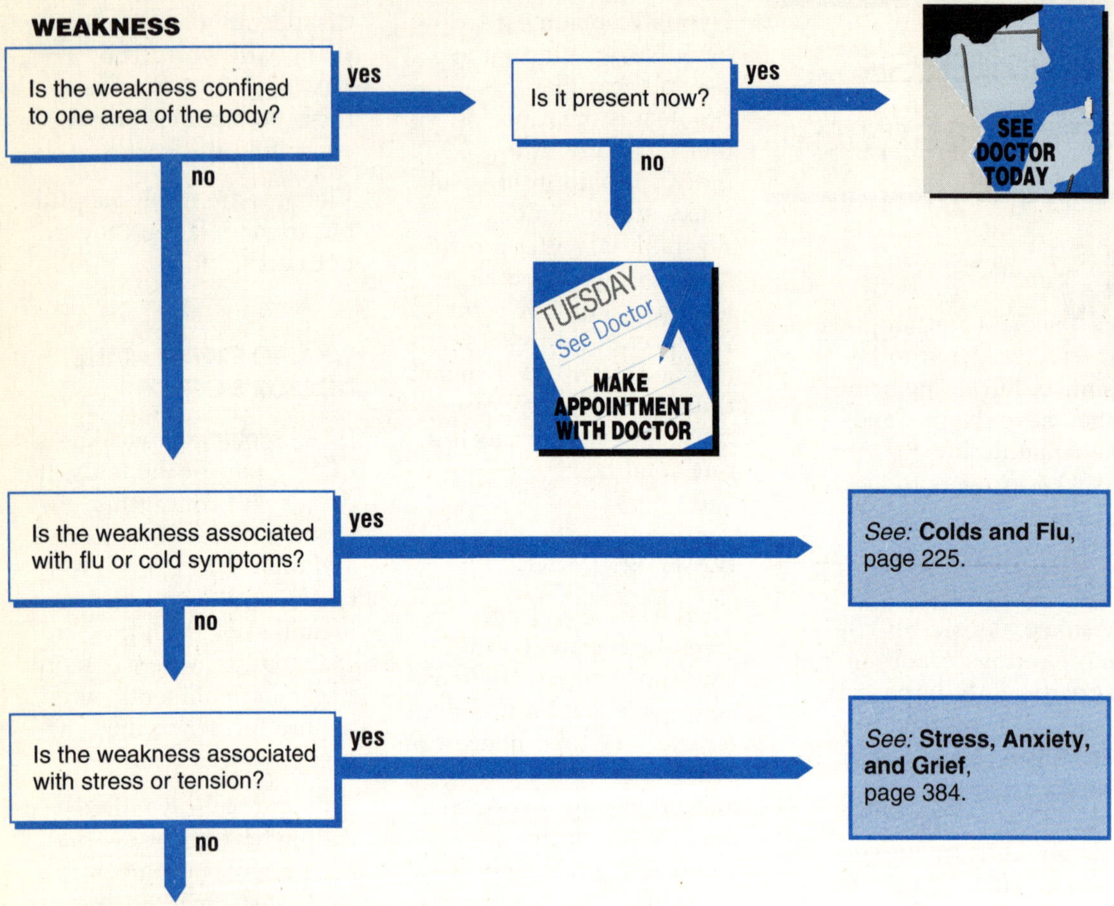


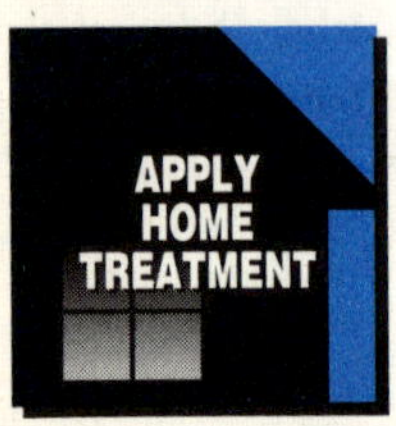


may test for anemia and thyroid dysfunction, as well as other problems. Inquiry into the patient's lifestyle and feelings is important.

There are no direct cures for the most common fatigue syndromes. Pep pills do not work, and the rebound usually makes the problem worse. Tranquilizers generally intensify fatigue. Vacations, job changes, undertaking new activities, and making marital adjustments are far more helpful.

# Dizziness and Fainting

Three different problems are frequently introduced by the complaint of dizziness or fainting: loss of consciousness, vertigo, and lightheadedness.

### Unconsciousness

True unconsciousness includes a period in which the patient has no control over the body and of which there is no recollection. Therefore, if consciousness is lost while standing, the patient will fall and may sustain injury in doing so. The common symptom of "blackout" in which the patient finds it difficult to see and needs to sit or lie down but can still hear is not true loss of consciousness. Such blackouts may be related to changes in posture or to emotional experiences. True loss of consciousness needs to be investigated promptly by a doctor.

### Vertigo

Vertigo is caused by a problem in the balance mechanism of the inner ear. Because this balance mechanism also helps control eye movements, there is loss of balance and the room seems to be spinning around. Walls and floors may seem to lurch in crazy motions. Most vertigo has no definite cause and is thought to be due to a viral infection of the inner ear. A doctor should be seen.

### Feeling Lightheaded

"Lightheadedness" is by far the most common of these problems. It is that woozy feeling that is such a common part of flu or cold syndromes. If such a feeling is associated with other flu or cold symptoms, refer to page 225.

Lightheadedness that is not associated with other symptoms is usually not serious either. Many such patients are tense or anxious. Others have low blood pressure and regularly feel lightheaded when standing up suddenly. This is called "postural hypotension" and does not require treatment. If lightheadedness is associated with the use of drugs, the doctor should be contacted to determine if the drug should be discontinued. Alcohol is a frequent cause.

## HOME TREATMENT

Postural hypotension is probably the most common cause of momentary blackout or lightheadedness. This problem becomes more frequent with increasing age. Typically, the patient notices a transient loss of vision or a lightheaded feeling when going suddenly from a reclining or sitting position to upright posture. The symptoms are caused by a momentary lack of blood flow to the brain. Most people will experience this phenomenon at one time or another. The therapy is to avoid sudden changes in posture. Unless postural hypotension suddenly becomes worse, a visit to the doctor is not needed. It may be reported on the next routine visit.

A persistent lightheaded feeling without any other symptoms is not an indication of brain tumor or

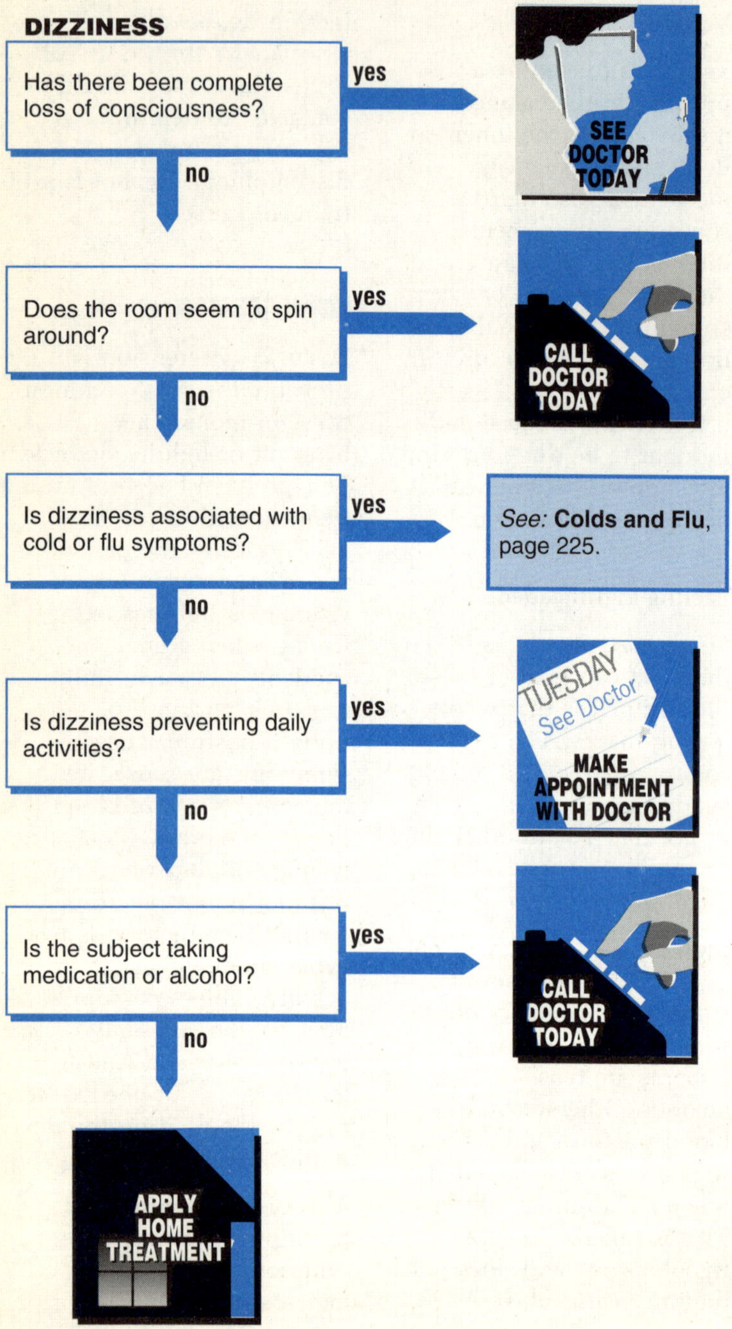


other hidden disease. This type of lightheadedness often disappears when anxiety is resolved. Not infrequently it is a problem with which the patient must learn to live.

If the problem persists for more than three weeks, call the doctor.

## WHAT TO EXPECT AT THE DOCTOR'S OFFICE

The doctor will obtain a history with emphasis on making the distinctions outlined above. If loss of consciousness is the problem, the heart and lungs will be examined, and nerve function will be tested. Special testing for irregular heartbeat or sudden drop in blood pressure may be necessary. If vertigo is the problem, the head, ears, eyes, and throat will be examined, along with neurological testing. Sometimes further tests of hearing or balance may be required. A search for predisposing factors, such as anxiety, will be made. Often a period of "watchful waiting" will be advised.

# High Blood Pressure

Discussion of the major chronic diseases—heart disease, diabetes, arthritis, cancer, and so on—is beyond the scope of this book, but we think that it is important to make an exception in the case of high blood pressure (hypertension). This is the most common of significant chronic problems and is the most treatable. It has been estimated that 30 to 40 million Americans have high blood pressure, more than 1 out of every 10.

Many of those who have high blood pressure do not know it. This is a uniquely silent disease. There are no symptoms until it is too late; the catastrophe of a heart attack or stroke is all too often the first indication of a problem. Do not wait for headaches or nosebleeds to give you fair warning; these are not reliable indicators of high blood pressure. Even if you have these symptoms, it is quite unlikely that they are due to high blood pressure.

## HAVE YOUR BLOOD PRESSURE CHECKED

Because high blood pressure is silent and can be treated effectively, early detection (screening) is important. Hypertension is unique in this regard. It is much more difficult to make the argument for routine screening of any other major diseases.

Once a year have your blood pressure checked. This is a reliable, cheap, and painless test. Often the doctor's office is not the best place to have this done because just being in the doctor's office can raise the blood pressure. Blood pressure checks are available without charge through corporations, public health departments, and voluntary health agencies; a visit to the doctor's office is almost never necessary. The blood pressure machines available in many stores are reasonably accurate.

Don't be panicked by any one reading. Because your blood pressure varies up and down, you will need to have several readings if the first reading is elevated. At least one-third of the people whose first reading is high will be found to have normal readings on subsequent checks.

The blood pressure reading has two numbers. The higher one is the **systolic pressure**, and the lower is the **diastolic pressure**. Blood pressure is considered to be high if the higher number exceeds 140 or the lower number exceeds 90. Traditionally, "normal" is said to be 120/80, but this has been overemphasized. Generally, the lower the blood pressure, the better (unless the low reading is due to disease). A low reading due to disease is unusual. Low readings are usually found in youngsters and in older people who are in excellent physical condition.

## IF YOU HAVE HIGH BLOOD PRESSURE

The most important thing to realize is that *you* must manage this problem yourself. It will be up to you to control your weight, your exercise, your salt intake, and to take your medicines. We think that it should be up to you to take your own blood pressure. Your doctor should be your trusted advisor but cannot assume your responsibility. No matter how much the doctor would like to take care of this for you, he or she cannot. You are in control, and good doctors will emphasize this point.

After the initial investigation and once the blood pressure is controlled, you should be able to handle the management of this problem with relatively few visits to the doctor.

### Blood Pressure Kit

If you have high blood pressure, you should buy a blood pressure kit. Blood pressure readings tell pretty much the whole story. If you are going to manage this problem, you need the blood pressure readings so that you can report changes or difficulties to the doctor.

### Keeping in Shape

Make exercise, weight control, and diet a part of your program. It is true that you can have high blood pressure even though you are slim and exercising regularly. But it is also true that being overweight and out of shape increases the risk of high blood pressure. Most important, recent studies have confirmed that people with high blood pressure who are overweight and not exercising can lower their blood pressure by losing weight and exercising regularly. Many can control their blood pressure entirely without the use of drugs. Most others can reduce the amount of medication that they require. That means less expense and fewer risks and side effects.

**Do not buy a blood pressure cuff unless you actually have high blood pressure or you plan to perform many blood pressure readings as a public service or for some other reason. While taking blood pressure is not difficult or mysterious, you do need some practice and doing it once or even several times a year is not enough.**

Aerobic exercise conditions the cardiovascular system so that blood pressure is reduced. Too high a weight means too high a blood pressure, and reducing your weight is a reliable method for reducing blood pressure. Exercise and diet are, of course, the keys to weight control (see pages 34–45). Decreasing the salt, fat, and cholesterol in your diet and increasing the potassium and calcium in your diet helps to lower blood pressure and decrease the risk of heart disease.

### Managing Any Drugs

If you do take drugs, understand how to manage them. Each drug has its own side effects and warning signs of which you should be aware. Chart the use of your drugs along with your blood pressure readings. This is essential. It is the only way that you and your doctor can make rational decisions about your program.

Drug treatment of high blood pressure is effective but is expensive and has risks and side effects. Getting off drugs is very desirable and is only surpassed by never needing the drug in the first place. In both cases, exercise and weight control can be the keys for most hypertensive people. Relaxation techniques and reduction of salt intake can also help greatly. Recent studies suggest that adequate potassium and calcium intake may lower blood pressure.

### Stick With It

The management of high blood pressure is a lifelong undertaking. You cannot stop your program because you feel good or wait for signs or symptoms to tell you what you need to do. This is a silent disease. If you take care of your blood pressure, the odds are overwhelmingly against it causing you a major problem. If you ignore high blood pressure or hope that someone else will take care of it, you are needlessly endangering your life and well-being.

## CHAPTER F

# *Eye Problems*

# Foreign Body in Eye

Eye injuries must be taken seriously. If there is any question, a visit to the doctor is indicated.

A foreign body must be removed to avoid the threat of infection and loss of sight in the eye. Be particularly careful if the foreign body was caused by the striking of metal on metal; this can cause a small metal particle to strike the eye with great force and penetrate the eyeball.

Under certain circumstances, you may treat at home. If the foreign body was minor, such as sand, and did not strike the eye with great velocity, it may feel as if it is still in the eye even when it is not. Small round particles like sand rarely stick behind the upper lid for long.

If it feels as if a foreign body is present but it is not, then the cornea has been scraped or cut. A minor corneal injury will usually heal quickly without problems; a major one requires medical attention.

Even if you think the injury is minor, run through the decision chart daily. If any symptoms at all are present after 48 hours and are not clearly resolving, see a doctor. Minor problems will heal within 48 hours—the eye repairs injury quickly.

## HOME TREATMENT

Be gentle. Wash the eye out. Water is good; a weak solution of boric acid is better if readily available.

Inspect the eye yourself and have someone else check it as well. Use a good light and shine it from both the front and the side. Pay particular attention to the cornea—the clear membrane that covers the colored portion of the eye.

Do not rub the eye; if a foreign body is present, you will abrade or scratch the cornea.

An eye patch will relieve pain. Take it off each day for recheck—it is usually needed for 24 hours or less. Make the patch with several layers of gauze and tape firmly in place—you want some gentle pressure on the eye.

Check vision each day; compare the two eyes, one at a time, by reading different sizes of newspaper type from across the room. If you are not sure that all is going well, see a doctor.

### FOREIGN BODY IN EYE

Are any of the following present:

- Can the foreign body be seen and does it remain after gentle washing?
- Could the injury have penetrated the globe of the eye?
- Can you see blood in the eye?

yes →

no ↓

Is there any problem with vision, or does it feel as if a foreign body might be trapped behind the upper lid?

yes →

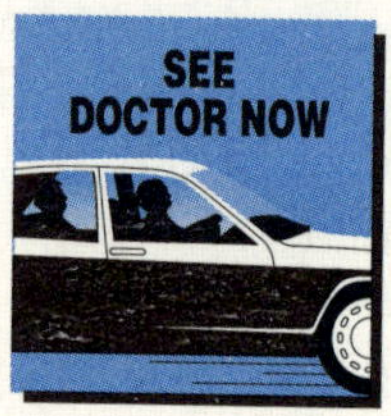


no ↓

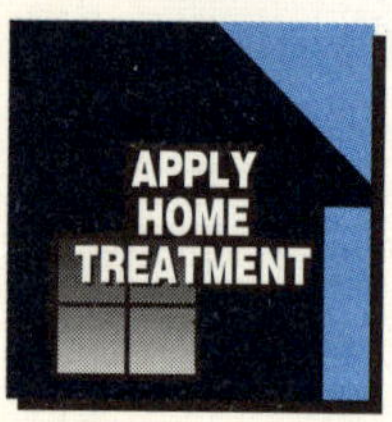


## WHAT TO EXPECT AT THE DOCTOR'S OFFICE

The doctor will check your vision and inspect the eye, including under the upper lid—this is not painful. Usually, a fluorescent stain will be dropped into the eye and the eye will then be examined under ultraviolet light—this is not painful or hazardous. The ophthalmologist (surgeon specializing in diseases of the eye) will examine the eye with a slit lamp.

A foreign body, if found, will be removed. In the office, this may be done with a cotton swab, an eyewash solution, or a small needle or "eye spud." An antibiotic ointment is sometimes applied, and an eye patch may be provided. Eye drops that dilate the pupil may be employed. X-rays may be taken if it is possible that a foreign body is inside the eye globe.

# Eye Pain

Pain in the eye can be an important symptom and cannot be safely ignored for long. Fortunately, it is an unusual complaint. Itching and burning (see page 217) are more common. Eye pain may be due to injury, to infection, or to an underlying disease.

An important disease that can cause eye pain is **glaucoma**. Glaucoma may slowly lead to blindness if not treated. In glaucoma, the fluid inside the eye is under abnormally high pressure, and the globe is tense, causing discomfort. Lateral vision is the first to be lost. Gradually and almost imperceptibly, the field of vision is constricted until the patient has "tunnel vision." In addition, a patient often will see "halos" around lights. Unfortunately, this sequence can occur even when there is no associated pain.

Eye pain is a nonspecific complaint, and questions relating to the pain are often better answered under the more specific headings in this chapter.

A feeling of tiredness in the eyes, or some discomfort after a long period of fine work (eye strain) is generally a minor problem and does not really qualify as eye pain. Severe pain behind the eye may result from migraine headaches, and pain either over or below the eye may suggest sinus problems.

Pain in both eyes, particularly upon exposure to bright light—photophobia—is common with many viral infections such as flu and will go away as the infection improves. More severe photophobia, particularly when only one eye is involved, may indicate inflammation of the deeper layers of the eye and requires a doctor.

## HOME TREATMENT

Except for eye pain associated with a viral illness or eyestrain, or minor discomfort that is more tiredness than pain, we do not recommend home treatment. In these instances, resting the eyes, taking a few aspirin, and avoiding bright light may help. Follow the chart to the discussion of other problems where appropriate. When symptoms persist, check them out in a routine appointment with your doctor.

## EYE PAIN

**Is the pain related to a significant injury, or is a foreign body present?**

- **yes** → *See:* **Foreign Body in Eye**, page 211.
- **no** ↓

**Is the pain an itching or burning sensation, or are the eyes runny?**

- **yes** → *See:* **Eye Burning, Itching, and Discharge**, page 217.
- **no** ↓

**Is there any decrease in vision?**

- **yes** → *See:* **Decreased Vision**, page 215.
- **no** ↓

**Is the pain severe or prolonged beyond 48 hours?**

- **yes** →

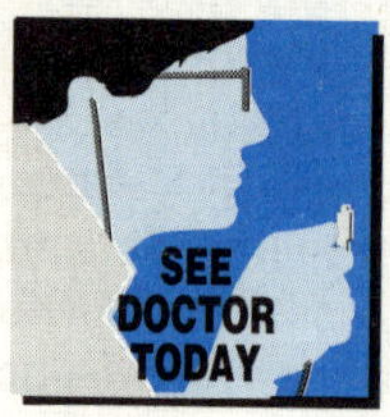


- **no** ↓

**Is the pain more of a feeling of tiredness in the eyes or are flu-like symptoms present?**

- **no** →

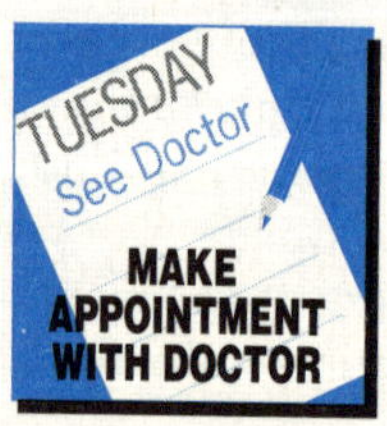


- **yes** ↓

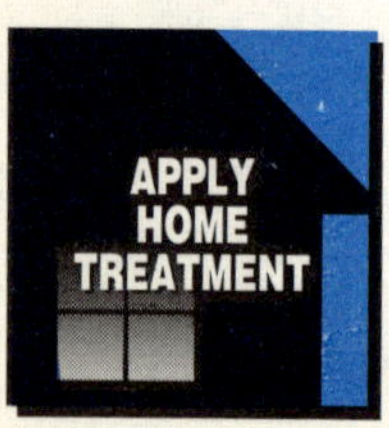


### WHAT TO EXPECT AT THE DOCTOR'S OFFICE

The doctor will check vision, eye movements, and the back of the eye with an ophthalmoscope. An ophthalmologist (surgeon specializing in diseases of the eye) may perform a slit-lamp examination. If glaucoma is possible, the doctor may check the pressure of the globe. This is simple, quick, and painless. (Many doctors feel uncomfortable with eye symptoms, and referral to an ophthalmologist is common. You may wish to go directly to an ophthalmologist if you have major concern.)

# Decreased Vision

Few people need urging to protect their sight. Decreased vision is a major threat to the quality of life. Usually, professional help is needed.

A few syndromes do not require a visit to a health professional. When small, single "floaters" drift across the eye from time to time and do not affect vision, they are not a matter for concern. Slight, reversible blurring of vision may occur after outdoor exposure or with overall fatigue. In young people, sudden blindness in both eyes is commonly a hysterical reaction and is not a permanent threat to sight; such patients need a doctor but not an eye doctor.

Usually, the question is not whether to see a health professional but, rather, which one to see. An **optician** dispenses glasses and does not diagnose eye problems.

The **optometrist** is not a medical doctor but is capable of evaluating the need for glasses, including screening for eye diseases, and determining what prescription lens gives the best vision. Conditions usually treated by an optometrist are myopia (near-sightedness), hyperopia (far-sightedness), and astigmatism (crooked-sightedness). In some states, optometrists can prescribe medicine.

If another problem is suspected, the optometrist may refer you to an **ophthalmologist**, who is a surgical specialist. The ophthalmologist is the final authority on eye diseases. Sometimes an eye problem is part of a general health problem; in these cases, the primary physician may be appropriate.

Try to find the right health professional on the first attempt; this will save you time and money. The following are some examples that usually help:

- **School nurse detects decreased vision in child:** visit ophthalmologist or optometrist —possible myopia (near-sightedness)
- **Sudden blindness in one eye in an elderly person:** visit ophthalmologist or internist—possible stroke or temporal arteritis
- **Halos around lights and eye pain:** visit ophthalmologist —possible acute glaucoma (increased pressure in the eye)
- **Gradual visual decrease in an adult who wears glasses:** visit ophthalmologist or optometrist—change in refraction of the eye
- **Sudden blindness in both eyes in a healthy young person:** visit internist or ophthalmologist—possible hysterical reaction
- **Gradual blurring of vision in an older person,** with no improvement by moving closer or farther away: visit ophthalmologist—possible cataract (scar tissue forming in the lens of the eye)

## DECREASED VISION

Did blindness (partial or complete) occur suddenly in one or both eyes, or has the visual loss been severe?

yes →

no ↓

Do you have trouble seeing objects to either side, or do you see halos around lights?

yes →

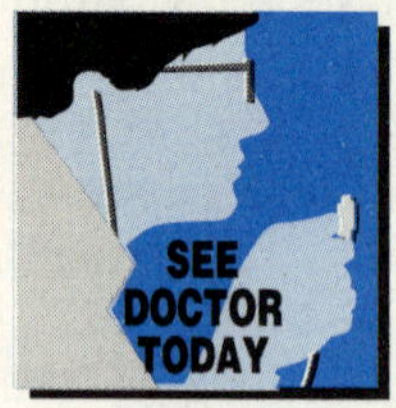


no ↓

Has the visual loss occurred very slowly over a long period?

yes →

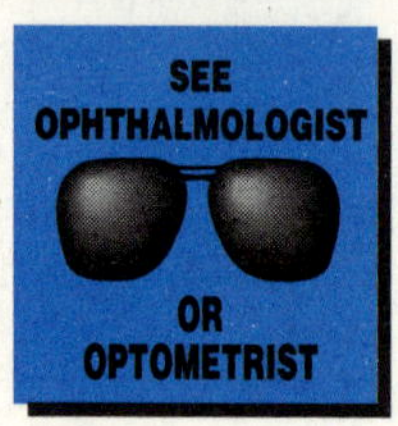


no ↓

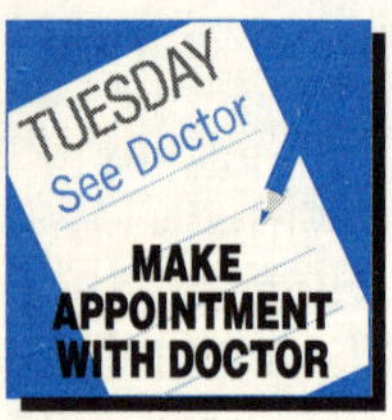


- **Older person who sees far objects best:** visit optometrist or ophthalmologist—possible presbyopia
- **Visual change while taking a medicine:** call the prescribing doctor—the drug may be responsible
- **Decreased vision, one eye,** with a "shadow" or "flap" in the visual field: visit ophthalmologist—possible retinal detachment

### WHAT TO EXPECT AT THE DOCTOR'S OFFICE

The doctor will check vision, eye movements, pupils, back of eye, and eye pressure when indicated; slit-lamp examination may be done. A general medical evaluation will be done as required. Refraction to determine a proper corrective lens may be needed; busy ophthalmologists will sometimes refer this procedure to an optometrist. Surgery will be recommended for some conditions.

# Eye Burning, Itching, and Discharge

These symptoms usually mean **conjunctivitis** or "pink eye," with inflammation of the membrane that lines the eye and the inner surface of the eyelids. The inflammation may be due to an irritant in the air, an allergy to something in the air, a viral infection, or a bacterial infection. The bacterial infections and some of the viral infections (particularly herpes) are potentially serious but are least common.

Environmental pollutants in smog can produce burning and itching that sometimes seem as severe as the symptoms experienced in a tear-gas attack. These symptoms represent a chemical conjunctivitis and affect anyone exposed to enough of the chemical. The smoke-filled room, the chlorinated swimming pool, the desert sandstorm, sun glare on a ski slope, or exposure to a welder's arc can provoke similar physical or chemical irritation.

In contrast, **allergic conjunctivitis** affects only those people who are allergic. Almost always the allergen is in the air, and grass pollens are probably the most frequent offender. Depending on the season for the offending pollen, this problem may occur in spring, summer, or fall and usually lasts two to three weeks.

A minor conjunctivitis frequently accompanies a viral cold, triggering the well-known symptoms and lasting only a few days. Some **viruses**, such as herpes, cause deep ulcers in the cornea and interfere with vision.

**Bacterial infections** cause pus to form, and a thick, plentiful discharge runs from the eye. Often the eyelids are crusted over and "glued" shut upon wakening. These infections can cause ulceration of the cornea and are serious.

Some major diseases affect the deeper layers of the eye—those layers that control the operation of the lens and the size of the pupillary opening. This condition is termed **iritis** or "uveitis" and may cause irregularity of the pupil or pain when the pupil reacts to light. Medical attention is required. For **Eye Pain**, see page 213.

## HOME TREATMENT

If a physical, chemical, or allergic exposure is the cause of the symptoms, the most important thing is avoiding exposure. Dark glasses, goggles at work, closed houses and cars with air-conditioning to filter the air, avoidance of chlorinated swimming pools, and other such measures are appropriate.

Antihistamines, either over the counter or by prescription, may help slightly if the problem is an allergy—but don't expect total relief without a good deal of drowsiness from the medication. Similarly, a viral infection related to a cold or flu will run its course in a few days, and it is best to be patient.

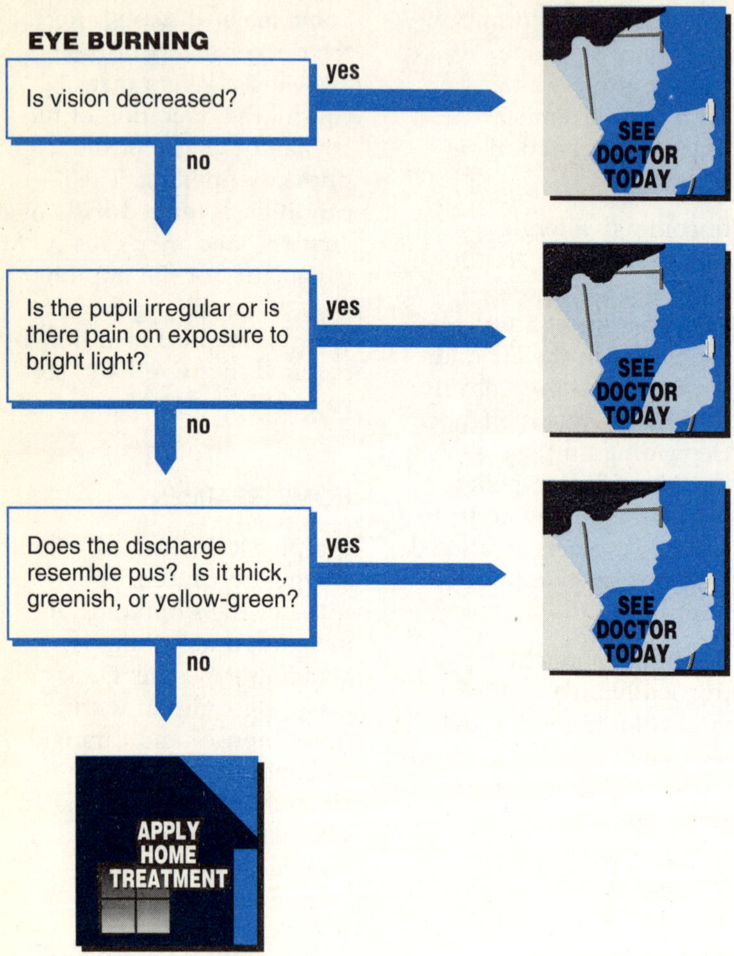


If it doesn't clear up, if the discharge gets thicker, or if you have eye pain or a problem with vision, see your doctor. Do not expect a fever with a bacterial infection of the eye; it may be absent. Because the infection is superficial, washing the eye gently with a boric acid solution will help remove some of the bacteria, but you should still see a doctor. Eyedrops (Murine, Visine, etc.) may soothe minor conjunctivitis but do not cure it.

Burning eyes may be a call to social action. If the smoking of others around you is annoying, say so. If an industrial plant in your area is polluting, get them to clean up their act.

## WHAT TO EXPECT AT THE DOCTOR'S OFFICE

The doctor will check vision, eye motion, eyelids, and the reaction of the pupil to light. An ophthalmologist (surgeon specializing in eye diseases) may perform a slit-lamp examination. Antihistamines may be prescribed, and general advice may be given. Antibiotic eyedrops or ointments are frequently given. Cortisone-like eye ointments should be prescribed infrequently; certain infections (herpes) may get worse with these medicines. If herpes is diagnosed—usually by an ophthalmologist—special eyedrops and other medicines will be needed.

# Styes and Blocked Tear Ducts

We might have called this problem "bumps around the eyes" because that is how they appear.

**Styes** are infections (usually with staphylococcal bacteria) of the tiny glands in the eyelids. They are really small abscesses, and the bumps are red and tender. They grow to full size over a day or so.

Another type of bump in the eyelid, called a **chalazion**, appears over many days or even weeks and is not red or tender. A chalazion often requires drainage by a doctor, whereas most styes will respond to home treatment. However, there is no urgency in the treatment of a chalazion.

### Tear Ducts

Tears are the lubricating system of the eye. They are continually produced by the tear glands and then drained away into the nose by the tear ducts. These tear ducts are often incompletely developed at birth so that the drainage of tears is blocked. When this happens, the tears may collect in the tear duct and cause it to swell, appearing as a bump along the side of the nose just below the inner corner of the eye (see page 220). This bump is not red or tender unless it has become infected. Most blocked tear ducts will open by themselves in the first month of life, and most of the remainder will respond to home treatment. Tears running down the cheek are seldom noted in the first month of life because the infant produces only a small volume of tears.

The eyeball itself is *not* involved in a stye or a blocked tear duct. Problems with the eyeball, and especially with vision, should not be attributed to these two relatively minor problems.

## HOME TREATMENT

### Stye

Apply warm, moist compresses for 10 to 15 minutes at least 3 times a day. As with all abscesses, the objective is to drain the abscess. The compresses help the abscess to "point." This means that the tissue over the abscess becomes quite thin and the pus in the abscess is very close to the surface. After an abscess points, it often will drain spontaneously. If this does not happen, the abscess may need to be lanced by the doctor. Most styes will drain spontaneously. They may drain inward toward the eye or outward onto the skin. Sometimes the stye goes away without coming to a point and draining.

Chalazions usually do not respond to warm compresses, but they will not be harmed by them. If no improvement is noted with home treatment after 48 hours, see the doctor.

### STYES, ETC.

**Is the problem confined to the eyelids or the area of the tear duct (see drawing)?**

- **no** → Suspect problem other than stye or tear-duct blockage. Refer to **Foreign Body in Eye** (page 211) and **Eye Burning, Itching, and Discharge** (page 217).
- **yes** ↓

**Is there difficulty with vision?**

- **yes** →

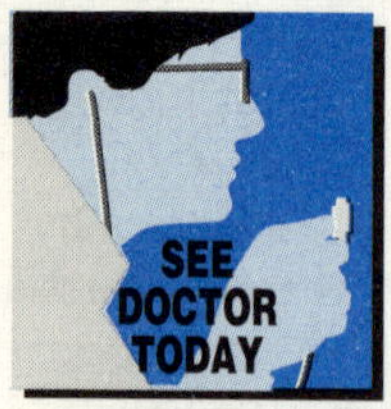


- **no** ↓

**Is there swelling or redness over the tear duct?**

- **yes** →

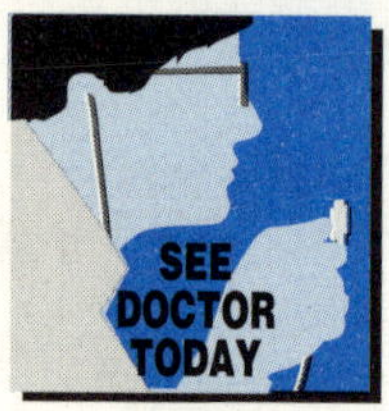


- **no** ↓

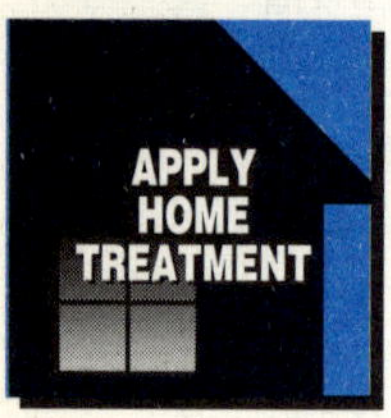

areas where blocked tear ducts may occur

**Blockage of the Tear Ducts**

Simply massage the bump downward with warm, moist compresses several times a day. If the bump is not red and tender (indicating infection), this may be continued for up to several months. If the problem exists for this long, discuss it with your doctor. If the bump becomes red and swollen, antibiotic drops will be needed.

## WHAT TO EXPECT AT THE DOCTOR'S OFFICE

If the stye is pointing and ready to be drained, the doctor will open it with a small needle. If it is not pointing, compresses will usually be advised, and antibiotic eyedrops sometimes will be added. Attempting to drain a stye that is not pointing is usually not very satisfactory.

A chalazion may be removed with minor surgery. Whether to have the surgery will be up to you. Chalazions are not dangerous and usually do not require removal.

If a child is over six months of age and is still having problems with blocked tear ducts, they can be opened in almost all cases with a very fine probe. This probing is successful on the first try in about 75% of all cases and on subsequent attempts in the remainder. Only rarely is a surgical procedure necessary to establish an open tear duct. For red and swollen ducts, antibiotic drops as well as warm compresses will usually be recommended.

## CHAPTER G

# *Ears, Nose, and Throat Problems*

## IS IT A VIRUS, BACTERIA, OR AN ALLERGY?

The following sections discuss upper respiratory problems, including colds and flu, sore throats, ear pain or stuffiness, runny nose, cough, hoarseness, swollen glands, and nosebleeds. A central question is important to each of these complaints: Is it caused by a virus, bacteria, or an allergic reaction? In general, the doctor has more effective treatment than is available at home only for bacterial infections. Remember that viral infections and allergies do *not* improve with treatment by penicillin or other antibiotics. To demand a "penicillin shot" for a cold or allergy is to ask for a drug reaction, risk a more serious "super-infection," and waste time and money. Among common problems well treated at home are:

- The common cold—often termed "viral URI (Upper Respiratory Infection)" by doctors
- The flu, when uncomplicated
- Hay fever
- Mononucleosis—infectious mononucleosis or "mono"

Medical treatment *is* commonly required for:

- Strep throat
- Ear infection

**TABLE F** *Is It a Virus, Bacteria, or an Allergy?*

| | *Virus* | *Bacteria* | *Allergy* |
|---|---|---|---|
| Runny nose? | Often | Rare | Often |
| Aching muscles? | Usual | Rare | Never |
| Headache (non-sinus)? | Often | Rare | Never |
| Dizzy? | Often | Rare | Rare |
| Fever? | Often | Often | Never |
| Cough? | Often | Sometimes | Rare |
| Dry cough? | Often | Rare | Sometimes |
| Raising sputum? | Rare | Often | Rare |
| Hoarseness? | Often | Rare | Sometimes |
| Recurs at a particular season? | No | No | Often |
| Only a single complaint (sore throat, earache, sinus pain, or cough)? | Unusual | Usual | Unusual |
| Do antibiotics help? | No | Yes | No |
| Can the doctor help? | Seldom | Yes | Sometimes |

*Remember, viral infections and allergies* do not *improve with treatment by penicillin or other antibiotics.*

How can you tell these conditions apart? Table F and the charts for the following problems will usually suffice. Here are some brief descriptions that may also help.

### Viral Syndromes

Viruses usually involve several portions of the body and cause many different symptoms. Three basic patterns (or syndromes) are common in viral illnesses; however, overlap between these three syndromes is not unusual. Your illness may have features of each.

**Viral URI.** This is the "common cold." It includes some combination of the following: sore throat, runny nose, stuffy or congested ears, hoarseness, swollen glands, and fever. One symptom usually precedes the others, and another symptom (usually hoarseness or cough) may remain after the others have disappeared.

**The Flu.** Fever may be quite high. Headache can be excruciating, muscle aches and pain (especially in the lower back and eye muscles) are equally troublesome.

**Viral Gastroenteritis.** This is "stomach flu" with nausea, vomiting, diarrhea, and crampy abdominal pain. It may be incapacitating and can mimic a variety of other more serious conditions including appendicitis.

### Hay Fever

Seasonal runny nose and itchy eyes are well known. Patients usually diagnose this condition accurately themselves. As with viruses, this disorder is treated simply to relieve symptoms. Given enough time, the condition runs its course without doing any permanent harm. Allergies tend to recur whenever the pollen or other allergic substance is encountered.

### Sinusitis

Inflammation of the sinuses is often associated with hay fever and asthma. Symptoms include a sense of heaviness behind the nose and eyes, often resulting in a "sinus headache." If the sinuses are infected, there may be fever and nasal discharge. Antihistamines and decongestants (see page 108) may be helpful in cases of sinusitis that accompany colds or hay fever. Do not use nasal sprays for more than three days. For recurring sinusitis, a doctor should be consulted to determine the precise cause and treatment; a course of antibiotics is frequently prescribed.

### Strep Throat

Bacterial infections tend to localize at a single point. Involvement of the respiratory tract by strep is usually limited to the throat. However, symptoms outside the respiratory tract can occur, most commonly fever and swollen lymph glands (from draining the infection) in the neck. A rash of scarlet fever sometimes may help to distinguish a streptococcal (strep) from a viral infection. In children, abdominal pain may be associated with a strep throat. This disorder must be diagnosed and treated because serious heart and kidney complications can follow if adequate antibiotic therapy is not given.

### Other Conditions

Factors other than diseases may cause or contribute to upper respiratory symptoms. Smoking is probably the largest single cause of coughs and sore throats. Pollution (smog) can produce the same problems. Tumors and other frightening conditions account for only a very small number. Complaints lasting beyond two weeks without one of the common diseases as the obvious cause are not alarming but should be investigated on a routine basis by the doctor.

# Colds and Flu

Most doctors believe that colds and the flu account for more unnecessary visits than any other group of problems. Because these are viral illnesses, they cannot be cured by antibiotics or any other drugs. However, there are non-prescription drugs—pain relievers, decongestants, antihistamines—that may decrease symptoms while these problems cure themselves.

There seem to be three main reasons why these unnecessary visits are made.

- Some patients are not sure that their illness is a cold or the flu, although this seems to be a relatively small part of the problem. Most patients state clearly that they know they have a cold or the flu.
- Many come seeking a cure. There are still large numbers of people who believe that penicillin or other antibiotics are necessary to recover from these problems.
- There are many patients who feel so sick that they feel that the doctor *must* be able to do something. Faced with this expectation, doctors sometimes try too hard to satisfy the patient. A doctor may give an antibiotic or fail to fully inform the patient as to the limitations of the drugs prescribed. This is understandable. Who wants to tell sick patients that they have wasted their time and money by coming to the doctor?

Of course, colds and flu do lead to necessary visits as well. These result from the complications of colds and the flu, primarily bacterial ear infections and bacterial pneumonia. In very young children, viral infections of the lung may lead to complications. The questions in the chart will help you look for the complications of colds and the flu.

### HOME TREATMENT

**Take two aspirin and call me in the morning.** This familiar phrase does *not* indicate neglect or lack of sympathy for your problem. Aspirin is an effective medicine for the fever and muscular aches of the common cold. For adults, two 5-grain aspirin tablets every four hours is standard treatment. The fever, aches, and prostration are most pronounced in the afternoon and evening: take the aspirin regularly over this period.

If you have trouble tolerating aspirin, use acetaminophen or ibuprofen in the same dose. You may buy a patent cold formula, but remember that the important ingredient that "doctors recommend most" is aspirin and that the formulas are simply combinations of drugs available singly without a prescription. This combination may or may not be right for your symptoms and costs more than the single generic drugs. Note also that they may contain significant amounts of alcohol.

Because recent information indicates an association with a rare but serious problem of the brain and liver known as Reye's syndrome, aspirin should not be used for children and teenagers. Use acetaminophen as directed on the label instead.

**Drink a lot of liquid.** This is insurance. The body requires more fluid when you have a fever. Be sure you get enough. Fluids help to keep the mucus more liquid and help prevent complications such as bronchitis and ear infection. A vaporizer (particularly in the winter if you have forced-air heat) will help liquefy secretions.

**Rest.** How you feel is an indication of your need to rest. If you feel like being up and about, go ahead. It won't prolong your illness, and your friends and family were exposed during the incubation period, the three days or so *before* you had symptoms.

**A word about chicken soup: Dizziness when standing up is common with colds and is helped by drinking salty liquids; bouillon and chicken soup are excellent.**

For relief of particular symptoms, see the appropriate section of this book: **Runny Nose**, page 237, **Ear Pain and Stuffiness**, page 231, **Sore Throat**, page 228, **Cough**, page 240, **Nausea and Vomiting**, page 407, **Diarrhea**, page 409, and so on.

If symptoms persist beyond two weeks, call the doctor.

## COLDS AND FLU

Any of the following in a child?
- Rapid or difficult breathing
- Wheezing
- Marked irritability or lethargy

yes →

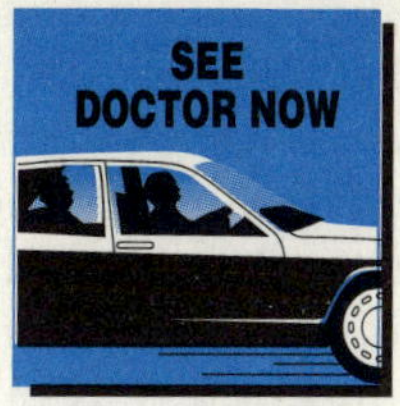


no ↓

Is ear discomfort more than mild?

yes →

no ↓

Has the cough produced thick, foul-smelling, rusty, or greenish sputum?

yes →

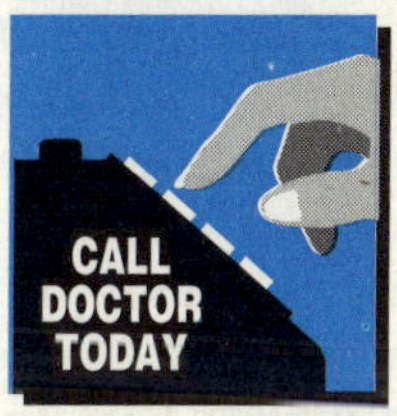


no ↓

Is the throat more than mildly sore?

yes →

*See:* **Sore Throat**, page 228.

no ↓

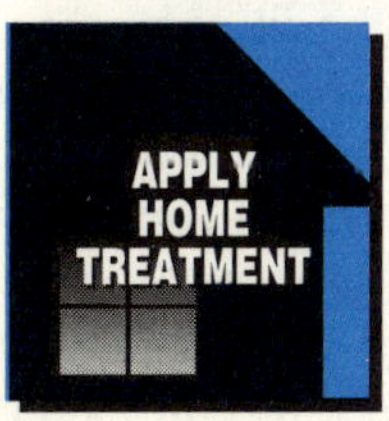


## WHAT TO EXPECT AT THE DOCTOR'S OFFICE

The ears, nose, throat, and chest will be examined routinely, and the abdomen may be examined. If a bacterial pneumonia is suspected, a chest X-ray may be done, but studies have indicated that X-rays rarely help. If a bacterial infection is present as a complication, antibiotics will be prescribed.

If the cold or flu is uncomplicated, the doctor should explain this and prescribe home treatment. Unnecessary use of antibiotics invites unnecessary complications, such as reaction to the antibiotics and super-infections by bacteria that are resistant to antibiotics.

# Sore Throat

Sore throats can be caused by either viruses or bacteria. Often, especially in the winter, breathing through the mouth can cause drying and irritation of the throat. This type of irritation always subsides quickly after the throat becomes moist again.

### Sore Throat Viruses

Viral sore throats, like other viral infections, cannot be treated successfully with antibiotics; they must run their course. Cold liquids for pain, and aspirin, ibuprofen, or acetaminophen for pain and fever, are often helpful.

Older children and adolescents may develop a viral sore throat known as infectious **mononucleosis** or "mono." Despite the formidable sounding name of this illness, complications seldom occur. The mono sore throat is often more severe and prolonged beyond a week, and the patient may feel particularly weak. Resting will be important. The spleen, one of the internal organs in the abdomen, may enlarge during mononucleosis. A viral sore throat that does not resolve within a week might be caused by the virus responsible for mononucleosis. Again, there is no antibiotic cure for mononucleosis.

### Strep Throat

The most important sore throats caused by bacteria are due to the streptococcal bacteria. These sore throats are commonly referred to as "strep throat." A strep throat should be treated with an antibiotic because of two types of complications. First, an abscess may form in the throat. This is an extremely rare complication but should be suspected if there is extreme difficulty in swallowing, difficulty opening the mouth, or excessive drooling in a child. The second and most significant type of complication occurs from one to four weeks after the pain in the throat has disappeared. One of these complications, called **acute glomerulonephritis**, causes an inflammation of the kidney.

It is not certain that antibiotics will prevent this complication, but they may prevent the strep from spreading to other family members or friends. Of greatest concern is the complication of **rheumatic fever**, which is much less common today than in the past but is still a significant problem in some parts of the country. Rheumatic fever is a complicated disease that causes painful, swollen joints, unusual skin rashes, and results in heart damage in half of its victims. Rheumatic fever can be prevented by antibiotic treatment of a strep throat.

**Frequent and recurrent sore throats are common in children between the ages of five and ten. There is no evidence that removing the tonsils decreases this frequency. Tonsillectomy is an operation that is very seldom needed.**

Strep throat is much less frequent in adults than in children, and rheumatic fever is very rare in adults. Strep throat is unlikely if the sore throat is a minor part of a typical cold (runny nose, stuffy ears, cough, and so on).

If you or someone in your family has had rheumatic fever or acute glomerulonephritis, make preventive use of antibiotics (prophylaxis) as prescribed by the doctor.

The choice of when to use antibiotics for sore throats is controversial. Many doctors believe that a test for strep (Q-Test, etc.) is the best way to determine the need for antibiotics. This is a reasonable approach, especially if the test is available without a full office visit. More recently, doctors have begun to rely on studies that indicate many patients do not need a test, either because the risk of rheumatic fever is almost nil or because this risk is high enough to justify the use of antibiotics regardless of the test results. (Remember that tests are not completely accurate—31 to 98% in various studies—and that many people are "strep carriers," i.e., they have strep in their throats but the strep is not causing illness.) In the decision chart, the symptoms that lead to "call doctor today" are those that make antibiotic use likely.

## HOME TREATMENT

Cold liquids, aspirin, ibuprofen, and acetaminophen are effective for pain and fever. Because recent information indicates an association with a rare but serious problem known as Reye's syndrome, aspirin should not be used for children or teenagers. Home remedies that may help include saltwater gargles and tea with honey or lemon. Time is the most important healer for pain. A vaporizer makes the waiting more comfortable for some.

## WHAT TO EXPECT AT THE DOCTOR'S OFFICE

A throat culture usually will be taken. Many doctors will delay treating a sore throat until the culture results are known; delaying treatment by one or two days does not seem to increase the risk of developing rheumatic fever. Further, antibiotic treatment has been shown to be effective in reducing only the complications and not the discomfort of a sore throat. Because the majority of sore throats are due to viruses, treating all sore throats with antibiotics would needlessly expose

## SORE THROAT

Is there severe difficulty in swallowing, difficulty in breathing, or excessive drooling in a young child?

yes →

no ↓

Are any of the following conditions present?

- A temperature of 101°F or greater
- Pus in the back of the throat
- A red rash that feels like "sandpaper," increased redness in the skin creases and a fever

yes →

no ↓

Is the patient's age less than 35?

no →

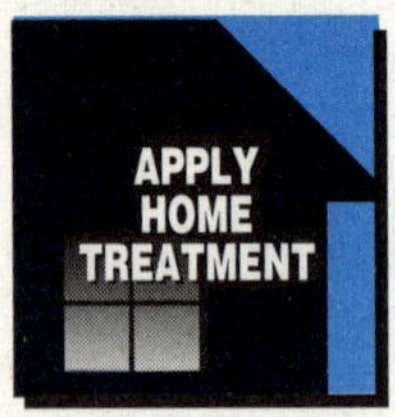


yes ↓

Are the patient's tonsils swollen?

no →

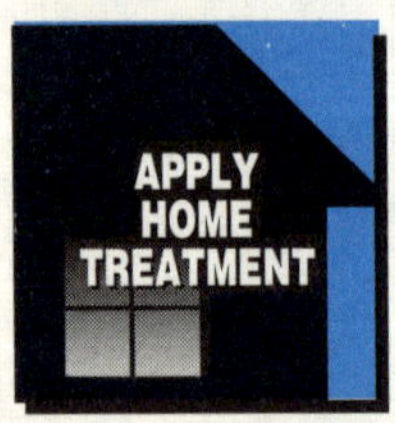


yes ↓

Test for strep throat.

patients to the risk of allergic reactions from the drugs. Doctors often will begin treatment with antibiotics immediately if there is a family history of rheumatic fever, or if the patient has scarlet fever (the rash described in the decision chart), or if rheumatic fever is commonly occurring in the community at the time.

If one child has a strep throat, the chances are very good that any other family members with a sore throat will also have strep. However, brothers and sisters without symptoms usually should not be tested for strep.

# Ear Pain and Stuffiness

Ear pain often is caused by a buildup of fluid and pressure in the middle ear (the portion of the ear behind the eardrum). Under normal circumstances, the middle ear is drained by a short narrow tube (the eustachian tube) into the nasal passages. Often during a cold or allergy, the eustachian tube will become swollen shut; this occurs most easily in small children in whom the tube is smaller. When the tube closes, the normal flow of fluid from the middle ear is prevented, and the fluid begins to accumulate. This causes stuffiness and decreased hearing.

The stagnant fluid provides a good place for the start of a bacterial infection. A bacterial infection usually results in pain and fever, often in one ear only.

Ear pain and ear stuffiness may occur when going from low to high altitudes, as when ascending in an airplane. Here again, the mechanism for the stuffiness or pain is obstruction of the eustachian tube. Swallowing will frequently relieve this pressure. Closing the mouth and holding the nose closed while pretending to blow one's nose is another method of opening the eustachian tube. Using a decongestant may help prevent this problem.

### Ear Infection in Children

The symptoms of an ear infection in children may include fever, ear pain, fussiness, increased crying, irritability, or pulling at the ears. Because infants cannot tell you that their ears hurt, increased irritability or ear pulling should make a parent suspicious of ear infection.

Parents are often concerned about hearing impairment after ear infections. Most children will have a temporary and minor hearing loss during and immediately following an ear infection, but there is seldom any permanent hearing loss with adequate treatment.

## HOME TREATMENT

Antihistamines, decongestants, and nose drops are used to decrease the amount of nasal secretion and shrink the mucus membranes in order to open the eustachian tube. Fluid in the ear will often respond to home treatment alone. See Chapter 9, "The Home Pharmacy," for information on these drugs.

Aspirin, ibuprofen, or acetaminophen will provide partial pain relief. Although ear pain is not usually a part of chicken pox or the flu, avoid the use of aspirin in teenagers or children because of the association with Reye's syndrome, a serious problem of the brain and liver.

### EAR PAIN

Is there an ear discharge?

yes → *See:* **Ear Discharges**, page 233.

no ↓

Is an infant rubbing, pulling or tugging at the ears, or does the patient feel more than mild ear discomfort?

yes →

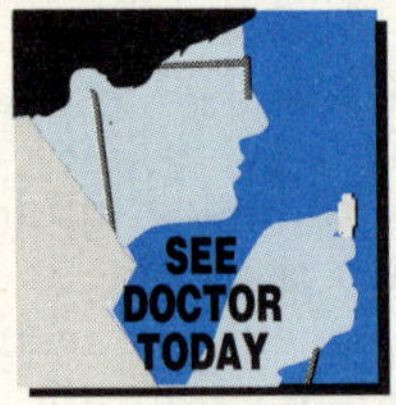


no ↓

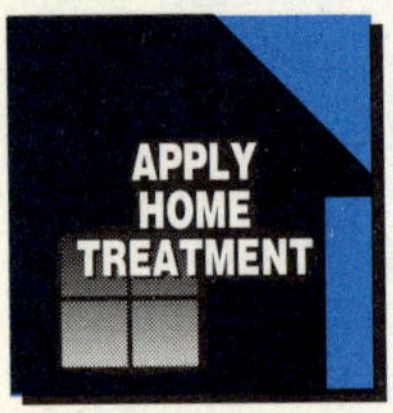


Moisture and humidity are important in keeping the mucus thin. Use a vaporizer if you have one. Curious maneuvers (such as hopping up and down in a steamy shower while shaking the head and swallowing) are sometimes dramatically successful in clearing out mucus.

If symptoms continue beyond two weeks, see the doctor.

## WHAT TO EXPECT AT THE DOCTOR'S OFFICE

An examination of the ear, nose, and throat as well as the bony portion of the skull behind the ears, known as the mastoid, will be performed. Pain, tenderness, or redness of the mastoid signifies a serious infection.

Therapy will generally consist of an antibiotic as well as an attempt to open the eustachian tube by medication. Nose drops, decongestants, and antihistamines can be used for this purpose. Antibiotic therapy generally will be prescribed for at least a week, while other treatments will usually be given for a shorter period. Be sure to give all of the antibiotic prescribed, and on schedule.

Occasionally fluid in the middle ear will persist for a long period without infection. In this case, there may be a slight decrease in hearing. This condition, known as **serous otitis media**, is usually treated by attempting to open the eustachian tube and allow drainage; it is not treated with antibiotics. If this condition persists, the doctor may resort to insertion of ear tubes in order to reestablish proper functioning of the middle ear. Placing ear tubes sounds frightening, but this is actually a simple and very effective procedure.

# Ear Discharges

Ear discharges are usually just wax but may be caused by minor irritation or infection. Ear wax is almost never a problem unless attempts are made to "clean" the ear canals. Ear wax functions as a protective lining for the ear canal. Taking warm showers or washing the external ears with a washcloth dipped in warm water usually provides enough vapor to prevent the buildup of wax. Children often like to push things in their ear canal, and they may pack the wax tightly. Adults armed with a cotton swab on a stick (for example, a Q-tip) often accomplish the same awkward result.

### Swimmer's Ear

In the summertime, ear discharges are commonly caused by **swimmer's ear**, an irritation of the ear canal and not a problem of the inner ear or eardrum. Children will often complain that their ears are itchy. In addition, tugging on the ear will often cause pain. This can be a helpful clue to an inflammation of the outer ear and canal, such as swimmer's ear. The urge to scratch inside the ear is very tempting but must be resisted. We especially caution against the use of hairpins or other instruments because injury to the eardrum can result.

### Ruptured Eardrum

In a child who has been complaining of ear pain, relief of pain accompanied by a white or yellow discharge—sometimes bloody—may be the sign of a ruptured eardrum. Sometimes parents will find dry crusted material on the child's pillow; here again, a ruptured eardrum should be suspected. The child should be taken to a doctor for antibiotic therapy. Do not be unduly alarmed. A ruptured eardrum is actually the first stage of a natural healing process that the antibiotics will help. Children have remarkable healing powers, and most eardrums will heal completely within a matter of weeks.

## HOME TREATMENT

Packed-down ear wax can be removed by using warm water flushed in gently with a syringe available at drugstores. A water jet (Water Pik, etc.) that is set *at the very lowest setting* can also be useful, but it can be frightening to young children and is dangerous at higher settings. We do not advise that parents attempt to remove impacted ear wax unless they are dealing with an older child and can see the impacted, blackened ear wax.

Wax softeners such as ordinary olive oil, Debrox, or Cerumenex are useful; however, all commercial products may be irritating, especially if not used properly. Cerumenex, for example, must be flushed out of the ear within 30 minutes using warm water.

## EAR DISCHARGES

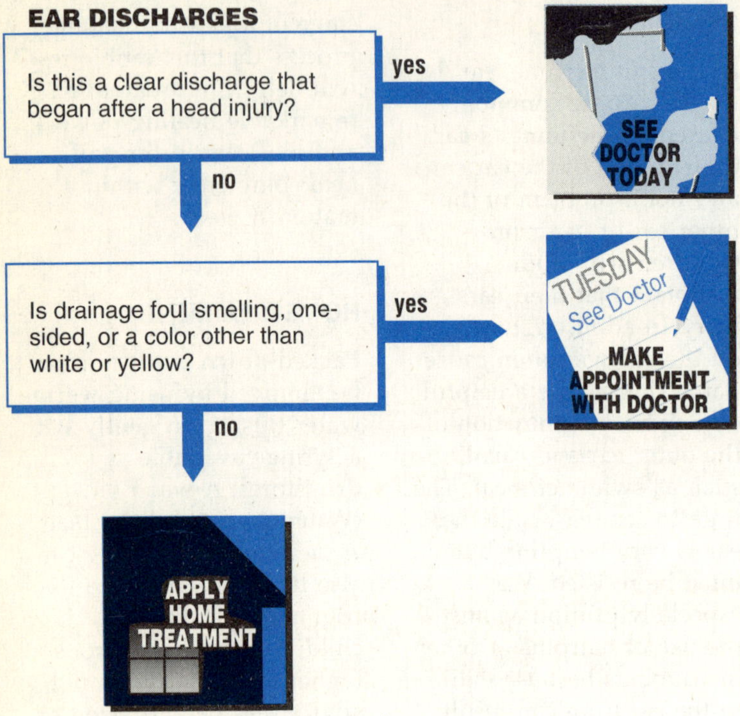


Two warnings:

- The water must be as close to body temperature as possible; the use of cold water may result in dizziness and vomiting.
- Washing should never be attempted if there is any question about the condition of the eardrum; it must be intact and undamaged.

Although swimmer's ear (or other causes of similar "otitis externa") is often caused by a bacterial infection, the infection is very shallow and does not often require antibiotic treatment. The infection can be effectively treated by placing a cotton wick soaked in Burow's solution in the ear canal overnight, followed by a brief irrigation with 3% hydrogen peroxide and then warm water. Success has also been reported with Merthiolate mixed with mineral oil (enough to make it pink), followed by the hydrogen peroxide and warm water rinse. For particularly severe or itching cases or persistence beyond five days, a doctor's visit is advisable.

### WHAT TO EXPECT AT THE DOCTOR'S OFFICE

A thorough examination of the ear will be performed. In severe cases, a culture for bacteria may be taken. Corticosteroid and antibiotic preparations that are placed in the ear canal may be prescribed, or one of the regimens described above under "Home Treatment" may be advised. Oral antibiotics will usually be given if a perforated eardrum is causing the discharge.

# Hearing Loss

Problems with hearing may be divided into two broad categories: sudden and slow. When a child of age five or older complains of a difficulty in hearing that has developed over a short period of time, the problem is usually a blockage in the ear of one type or another. On the outside of the eardrum, such blockage may be due to the accumulation of wax, a foreign object that the child has put in the ear canal, or an infection of the ear canal. On the inside of the eardrum, fluid may accumulate and cause blockage because of an ear infection or allergy.

Hearing problems in children may be present from birth. Hearing can now be tested in a child of any age through the use of computers that analyze changes in brain waves in response to sounds. More simply, an infant with normal hearing will react to a noise such as a hand clap, horn, or whistle. Normal speech development relies on hearing. A child whose speech is developing slowly or not at all may, in fact, have difficulty in hearing.

Some decrease in hearing, especially of the higher frequencies, is normal after the age of 20. If this decrease becomes a problem in later life, it is time to visit the doctor. Occasionally, hearing problems will mimic problems with thinking or understanding so that senility, Alzheimer's disease, or other neurological problems will be suspected erroneously.

## HOME TREATMENT

The need for an accurate ear examination usually necessitates a trip to the doctor. However, a problem that is known with certainty to be due to wax accumulation may be effectively treated at home. (See "Home Treatment," page 233.)

Be cautious about removing foreign bodies from ears. Do not try to remove the object unless it is easily accessible and removing it clearly poses no threat of damage to ear structures. Sharp instruments should never be used in an attempt to remove foreign bodies. Many times, efforts to remove an object push it further into the ear or damage the eardrum.

## HEARING LOSS

Is loss of hearing associated with the ear pain?

yes →

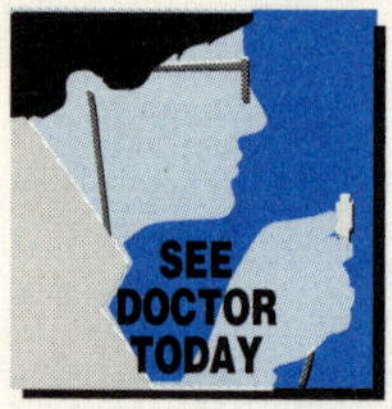


no ↓

Is ear wax known to be causing the hearing loss?

no →

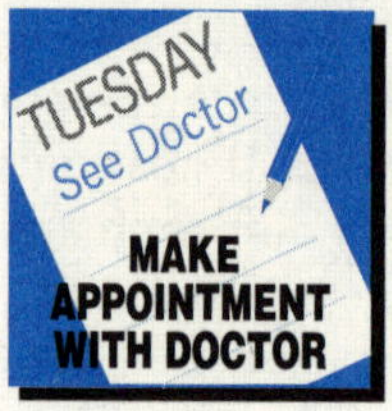


yes ↓

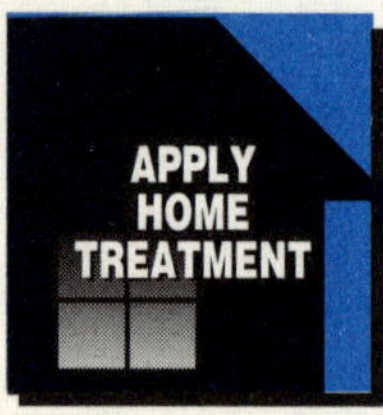


→ *See:* **Ear Discharges**, page 233.

### WHAT TO EXPECT AT THE DOCTOR'S OFFICE

A thorough examination of both ears often reveals the cause of the hearing loss. If it does not, the doctor may recommend audiometry (an electronic hearing test) or other tests. Hearing can often be improved by a variety of methods, including hearing aids.

# Runny Nose

The hallmark of the common cold is the runny nose. It is intended by nature to help the body fight the virus infection. Nasal secretions contain antibodies, which act against the viruses. The profuse outpouring of fluid carries the virus outside the body.

### Hay Fever

Allergy is a common cause of runny noses. People whose runny noses are due to an allergy are deemed to have **allergic rhinitis**, better known as hay fever. The nasal secretions in this instance are often clear and very thin. People with allergic rhinitis will often have other symptoms simultaneously, including sneezing, and itching, watery eyes. They will rub their noses so often that a crease in the nose may appear. This problem lasts longer than a viral infection, often for weeks or months, and occurs most commonly during the spring and fall when pollen particles or other allergens are in the air. A great many other substances may aggravate allergic rhinitis, including house dust, mold, and animal dander.

### Nose Drops

Another common cause of runny noses as well as stuffy noses is prolonged use of nose drops. This problem of excess medication is known as **rhinitis medicamentosum**. Nose drops containing substances like ephedrine should never be used for longer than three days. This problem can be avoided by switching to saline nose drops (made by placing a teaspoon of salt in a pint of water) for a few days.

### Uncommon Causes

Once in a very great while, a head injury causes the fluid around the brain to leak down into the nose. This results in a clear, watery discharge, often from one nostril, and requires a doctor's attention.

Bacterial infections may cause a foul-smelling discharge that is often rusty or green in color. Antibiotics may help in this case.

A runny nose may also be due to a small object that a young child has pushed into the nose. Usually, but not always, this will produce a discharge from only one nostril. Often the discharge will be foul-smelling and yellow or green.

**Post-nasal Drip**

Complications from a runny nose are due to the excess mucus. The mucus may cause a post-nasal drip and a cough that is most prominent at night. The mucus drip may plug the eustachian tube between the nasal passages and the ear, resulting in ear infection and pain. It may plug the sinus passages, resulting in secondary sinus infection and sinus pain. Finally, a post-nasal drip may make the throat sore.

## HOME TREATMENT

Using handkerchiefs or tissues has the great advantage of safely moving mucus, virus particles, and allergens outside the body. A facial tissue has no side effects and costs less than drugs.

If drugs must be used, there are two basic types:

- Decongestants such as pseudoephedrine and ephedrine act to shrink the mucous membranes and open the nasal passages.
- Antihistamines act to block allergic reactions and decrease the amount of secretion.

Decongestants make some children overly active. Antihistamines may cause drowsiness as well as interfere with sleep. Because of the complications of the medications, runny noses should be treated only when they are severely impairing comfort.

**Sneezes are healthy, removing germs, allergens, or dust from the nose. The only danger is infecting other people with the germ or virus that makes you sneeze. Cover your nose and mouth with a tissue or handkerchief. Wash your hands frequently. And let people say, "Bless you."**

If you choose to treat a runny nose with medication, nose drops are suitable. Saline nose drops are fine for young infants. Older children and adults may use drops containing decongestants. See Chapter 9, "The Home Pharmacy," for information on decongestants, antihistamines, and nose drops.

**RUNNY NOSE**

Is this a clear discharge that began after a head injury?

yes →

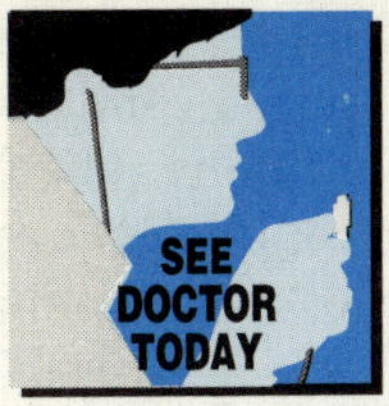


no ↓

Is drainage foul-smelling, one-sided, or a color other than white or yellow?

yes →

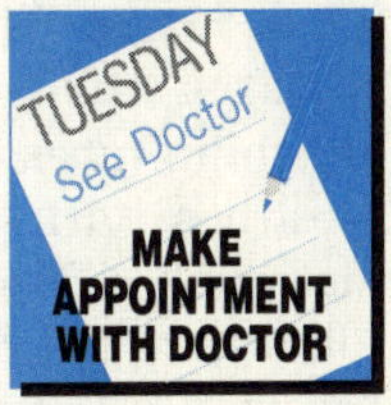


no ↓

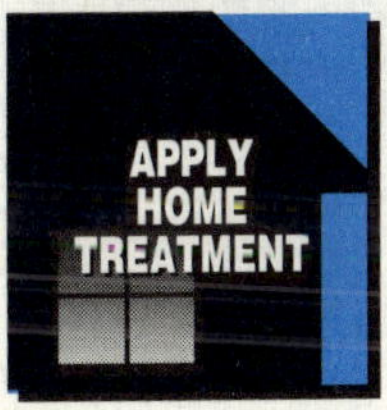


## WHAT TO EXPECT AT THE DOCTOR'S OFFICE

The doctor will thoroughly examine the ears, nose, and throat and will check for tenderness over the sinuses. Often, a swab of the nasal secretions will be taken and examined under a microscope. The presence of certain types of cells, known as eosinophils, will indicate the presence of hay fever (allergic rhinitis). If allergic rhinitis is found, antihistamines may be prescribed, and an avoidance program of dust, mold, dander, and pollen will be explained, similar to that described in Chapter H, **Allergies**.

Complications such as ear and sinus infection may be prevented by ensuring that the mucus is thin rather than thick and sticky. This helps prevent plugging of the nasal passages. Increasing the humidity in the air with a vaporizer or humidifier helps liquefy the mucus. Heated air inside a house is often very dry; cooler air contains more moisture and is preferable. Drinking a large amount of liquid will also help liquefy the secretions.

If symptoms persist beyond three weeks, your doctor should be contacted.

# Cough

The cough reflex is one of the body's best "defense mechanisms." Irritation or obstruction in the breathing tubes triggers this reflex, and the violent rush of air helps clear material from the breathing tubes. If abnormal material, such as pus, is being expelled from the body by coughing, the cough is desirable. Such a cough is termed "productive" and usually should not be suppressed by drugs.

Often, a minor irritation or a healing area in a breathing tube will start the cough reflex even though there is no material to be expelled, other than the normal mucus. At other times, mucus from the nasal passages will drain into breathing tubes at night (post-nasal drip) and initiate the cough reflex. Such coughs are not beneficial and may be decreased with cough suppressants.

**Hiccups, which are caused by an irregularity in contractions of the diaphragm, may occasionally prove troublesome. Although there have been many home remedies recommended over the years, including drinking large amounts of water and startling the sufferer, research suggests that ½ teaspoon of dry sugar placed on the back of the tongue is the most effective treatment.**

### Smoker's Cough

The smoker's cough bears testimony to the continual irritation of the breathing tubes. Smoke also poisons the cells lining these tubes so mucus cannot be expelled normally. Smoker's cough is a sign of deadly diseases yet to come.

### Viruses and Bacteria

Next to smoking, viral infections are the most common causes of coughs. These coughs usually bring up only yellow or white mucus. In contrast, coughs producing mucus that is rusty or green and looks like it contains pus are most likely to be caused by a bacterial infection. Bacterial infections require the doctor's help and antibiotics.

The term "pneumonia" is most often used to refer to a bacterial infection of the lung but can be used for viral infection and other problems as well. In fact, a "chest cold" is a viral pneumonia, as are "double pneumonia" and "walking pneumonia." So don't panic when you hear "pneumonia"—it is not a very precise term.

### COUGH

Did violent cough begin suddenly, without signs of a cold, in a child who might have inhaled a small object?

yes →

no ↓

Are any of the following present in a child?

- Rapid breathing
- Difficulty in breathing
- Wheezing

yes →

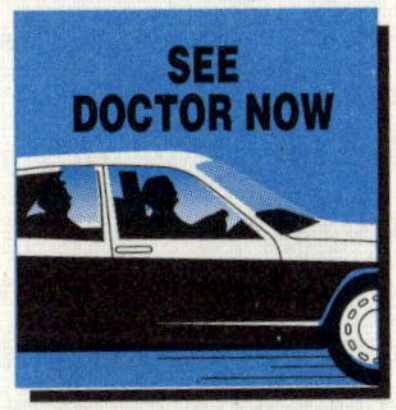


no ↓

Is the patient less than three months of age?

yes →

no ↓

Is the cough producing thick, foul-smelling, rusty or greenish mucus?

yes →

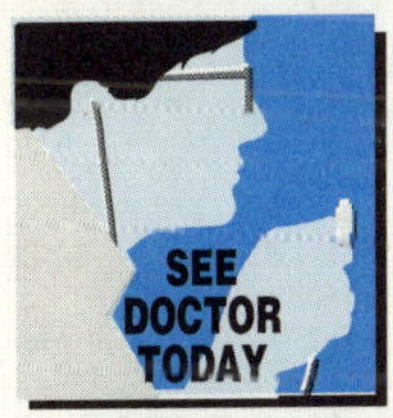


no ↓

Has fever lasted for more than four days or has cough persisted for more than ten days?

yes →

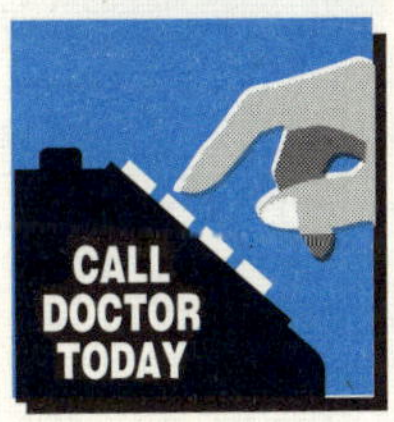


no ↓

**Children's Coughs**

In very young infants, coughing is unusual and may indicate a serious lung problem. In older infants, who are prone to swallowing foreign objects, an object may become lodged in the windpipe and cause coughing. Young children also tend to inhale bits of peanut and popcorn, which can produce coughing and serious problems in the lung. If the child's cough sounds like a seal's bark, refer also to **Croup**, page 243.

## HOME TREATMENT

The mucus in the breathing tubes may be made thinner and less sticky by several means. Increased humidity in the air will help. A vaporizer and a steamy shower are two ways to increase the humidity. In the severe croup cough of small children, high humidity is absolutely essential. Drinking large quantities of fluids is helpful for the cough, particularly if a fever has dehydrated the body.

Guaifenesin (Robitussin or Naldecon CX, for example) is available without prescription and may help liquefy the secretions. Liberal use of such common home substances as pepper and garlic also liquefies the secretions and may help relieve the cough.

Decongestants and/or antihistamines may help if a post-nasal drip is causing the cough. Otherwise, avoid drugs that contain antihistamines because they dry the secretions and make them thicker.

Various over-the-counter cough preparations will give relief from a bothersome cough. Dry, tickling coughs are often relieved by cough lozenges or sucking on hard candy. Dextromethorphan (Romilar, Vick's Formula 44, Robitussin-DM, etc.) is an effective cough suppressant available without prescription. Adults may require up to twice the dosage recommended in the package instructions. Do not exceed this amount; neither dextromethorphan nor codeine will completely eliminate coughs at any dosage, and side effects of drowsiness or constipation can occur. See Chapter 9, "The Home Pharmacy," for more information.

## WHAT TO EXPECT AT THE DOCTOR'S OFFICE

The doctor will examine the ears, nose, throat, and chest; a chest X-ray may be taken in some instances. Do not expect antibiotics to be prescribed for a routine viral or allergic cough; they do not help.

# Croup

Croup may be the most frightening of the common illnesses that parents encounter. It generally occurs in children under the age of three or four. In the middle of the night, a child may sit up in bed gasping for air. Often there will be an accompanying cough that sounds like the barking of a seal. The child's symptoms are so frightening that panic is often the response. However, the most severe problems with croup usually can be relieved safely, simply, and efficiently at home.

Croup is caused by one of several different viruses. The viral infection causes a swelling and outpouring of secretions in the larynx (voice box), trachea (windpipe), and the larger airways (bronchi) going to the lungs. The air passages of the young child are made narrower because of the swelling. This is further aggravated by the secretions, which may become dry and caked. This combination of swelling and thickened, dried secretions makes it difficult to breathe. There may also be a considerable amount of spasm of the airway passages, further complicating the problem. Treatment is aimed at dissolving the dried secretions.

In some children, croup is a recurring problem. These children may have three or four bouts of croup. This seldom represents a serious underlying problem, but a doctor's advice should be sought. Croup will be outgrown as the airway passages grow larger; it is unusual after the age of seven.

**Epiglottitis**

Occasionally, a more serious obstruction caused by a bacterial infection and known as **epiglottitis** can be confused with croup. Epiglottitis is more common in children over the age of three, but there is considerable overlap in the ages of children affected by these two conditions. Children with epiglottitis often have more serious difficulty in breathing. They may have an extremely difficult time swallowing all of their saliva and may drool. Often they assume a characteristic position with their head tilted forward and their jaw pointed out and will gasp for air.

Epiglottitis will *not* be relieved by the simple measures that bring prompt relief of croup. It must be brought to medical attention immediately.

## HOME TREATMENT

Mist is the backbone of therapy for croup and can be supplied efficiently by a cold-steam vaporizer. Cold-steam vaporizers are preferable to hot-steam ones because the possibility of scalding from hot water is eliminated.

If breathing is very difficult, you can obtain faster results by taking the child to the bathroom and turning on the hot shower to make thick clouds of steam. *(Do not put the child in the hot shower!)* Steam can be created more efficiently if there is some cold air in the room. Remember that steam rises, so the child will not benefit from the steam by sitting on the floor.

Relief usually occurs promptly and should be noticeable within the first 15 minutes. It is important to keep the child calm and not become alarmed; holding the child may comfort him or her and may help relieve some of the airway spasm. If the child is not showing significant improvement within 15 minutes, you should contact your doctor or the local emergency room immediately. They will want to see the child and will make arrangements in advance while you are in transit. Unfortunately, few emergency rooms can provide steam as easily as the home shower.

If improvement is significant but the problem persists for more than an hour, call the doctor.

## WHAT TO EXPECT AT THE DOCTOR'S OFFICE

If the doctor feels confident that this is croup, further use of mist will be tried. In difficult cases, X-rays of the neck are a reliable way of differentiating croup from epiglottitis. A swollen epiglottis often can be seen in the back of the throat, but this examination has its risks and should not be tried at home. If epiglottitis is diagnosed, the child will be admitted to the hospital; an airway will be placed in the child's trachea to enable the child to breathe, and intravenous antibiotics directed at curing the bacterial infection will be started. In the case of croup, the trip to the doctor often cures the problem that was resistant to steam at home; keep the car windows open a bit and let the cool night air in.

## CROUP

Are any of the following present?

- Drooling
- Breathing with chin jutting out and mouth open
- Severe difficulty in breathing

yes →

no ↓

Are the following present?

- Cough sounding like seal's bark
- Difficulty inhaling

no →

Suspect problem other than croup. *See:* **Cough**, page 240.

yes ↓

Does breathing improve with steam after 15 minutes?

no →

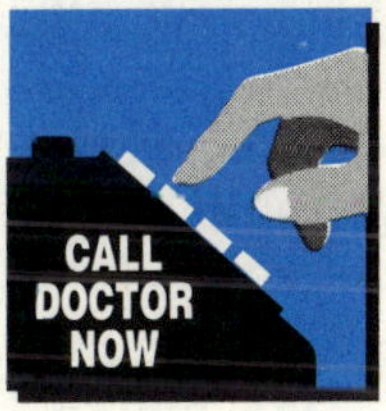


yes ↓

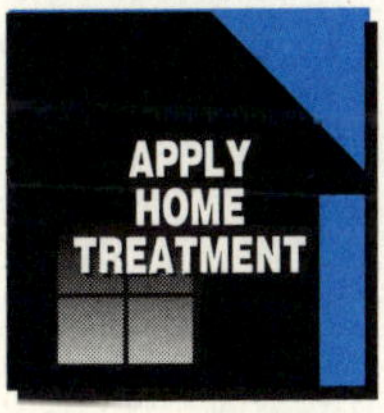

# Wheezing

Wheezing is the high-pitched whistling sound produced by air flowing through narrowed breathing tubes (bronchi and bronchioles). It is most obvious when the patient breathes out but may be present when breathing both in and out. Wheezing comes from the breathing tubes deep in the chest, in contrast to the croupy, crowing, or whooping sounds that come from the area of the voice box in the neck (see **Croup,** page 243).

Most often, a narrowing of the breathing tubes is due to a viral infection or to an allergic reaction as in asthma. In infants younger than age two, bronchiolitis or narrowing of the smallest air passages can occur because of a viral infection. Pneumonia can also produce wheezing. Occasionally, a foreign body may be lodged in a breathing tube, causing a localized wheezing that is difficult to hear without a stethoscope.

### Emphysema

Often there is an asthmatic component to emphysema (chronic obstructic pulmonary disease or COPD), and wheezing is commonly associated with exacerbations of this problem. The irritation of smoking by itself is sufficient to cause wheezing although almost all smokers have some degree of emphysema and bronchitis as well.

### Allergic Reaction

Wheezing can follow an insect sting or the use of a medicine. These allergic reactions require that the patient see a doctor. Any medication can cause the problem; some individuals even wheeze after taking aspirin.

### Alongside Fever

The importance of wheezing lies in its being an indicator of difficult breathing. In a child with a respiratory infection, wheezing may occur before shortness of breath is marked. Therefore when wheezing appears in the presence of a fever, early consultation with a doctor is advisable, even though the illness seldom turns out to be serious.

Treatment of wheezing is symptomatic. There are no drugs that cure viral illnesses or asthma. Home treatment is an important part of this approach. However, the doctor's help is needed so that drugs that widen the breathing passages can be used. Intravenous fluids may be required on some occasions.

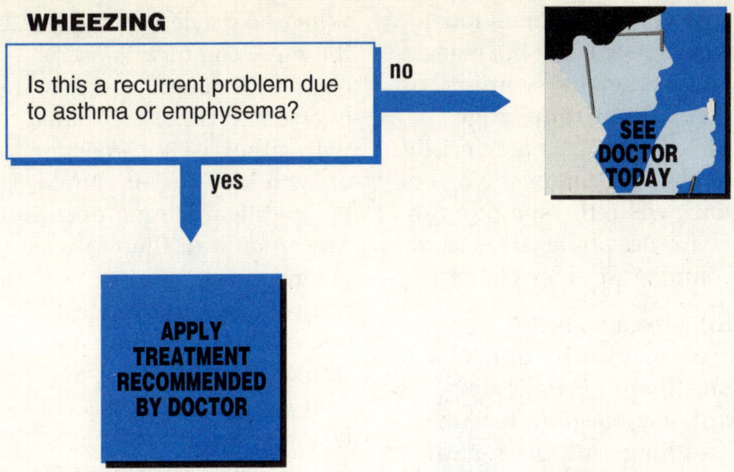


## HOME TREATMENT

Hydration by drinking fluids is very important. It is best to drink water, but fruit juices or soft drinks may be used if this will increase the amount taken. The use of a vaporizer, preferably one that produces a cold mist, may sometimes help. If a vaporizer is not available, the shower may be used to produce a mist.

Unfortunately, it is difficult to get much vapor down to the small breathing tubes. These measures will be part of the therapy that the doctor recommends and may be begun immediately, even though a visit to the doctor will be necessary.

## WHAT TO EXPECT AT THE DOCTOR'S OFFICE

Physical examination will focus on the chest and neck. Questions will be asked not only about the current illness but also about a past history of allergies either in the patient or the family. The possibility that a foreign body has been swallowed may also be investigated in small children.

Drugs to open up the breathing tube, such as epinephrine or theophylline, may be given by injection, by mouth, or by rectal suppository (See **Asthma,** page 265). Occasionally, hospitalization will be necessary to permit fluids to be given through a vein and for effective humidification of the air to be achieved. Most important, in this setting the patient can be closely watched. The hospital is used as a precautionary measure to prevent the condition from getting worse before it gets better.

# Hoarseness

Hoarseness is usually caused by a problem in the vocal cords.

### Children

In infants under three months of age, this can be due to a serious problem such as a birth defect or thyroid disorder. In young children, hoarseness is more often due to prolonged or excessive crying, which puts a strain on the vocal cords.

In older children, viral infections are the most common cause of hoarseness. If the hoarseness is accompanied by difficulty in breathing or a cough that sounds like a barking seal, the hoarseness is considered a symptom of croup (see **Croup,** page 243). Croup is characteristic in children under the age of four, while the symptom of hoarseness by itself is more common in older children.

If hoarseness is accompanied by difficulty in breathing or swallowing, drooling, gasping for air, or breathing with the mouth wide open and the chin jutting forward, a doctor must be seen immediately —this is a medical emergency. This problem is known as **epiglottitis** and is a bacterial infection that affects the entrance to the airway.

### Adults

In adults, a virus is most often responsible for the development of hoarseness or laryngitis when no other symptoms are present. As with any symptom of an upper respiratory tract infection, hoarseness may linger after other symptoms disappear.

When hoarseness is mild, the most common cause is cigarette smoke. If persistent hoarseness is *not* associated with either a viral infection or with smoking, it should be investigated by a doctor. The amount of time to wait before seeing a doctor is controversial; we suggest one month. If you are a smoker, stop smoking and wait one month. Persistent hoarseness has many causes. The most common are cysts or polyps on the vocal chords. Cancer is also a cause but is relatively rare. Naturally, overuse of the voice may result in hoarseness.

### HOME TREATMENT

Hoarseness, unassociated with other symptoms, is very resistant to medical therapy. Nature must heal the inflamed area. Humidifying the air with a vaporizer or taking in fluids can offer some relief. However, healing may not occur for several days. Resting the vocal cords is sensible; crying or shouting makes the situation worse. For the treatment of hoarseness associated with coughs, see **Cough**, page 240.

## HOARSENESS

Are any of the following present in a small child?

- Difficulty in breathing
- Difficulty in swallowing
- Drooling

yes →

no ↓

Is this child less than three months of age?

yes →

no ↓

Has hoarseness persisted for more than a week in a child or a month in an adult?

yes →

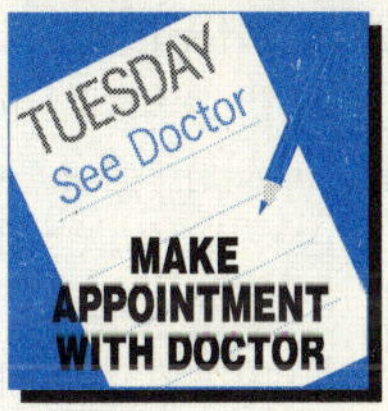


no ↓

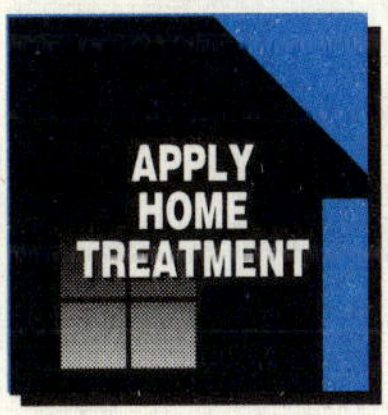


## WHAT TO EXPECT AT THE DOCTOR'S OFFICE

If a child has severe difficulty in breathing, the first priority is to ensure that the air passage is adequate. This may require the placement of a breathing tube at the emergency room, hospital, or doctor's office. If X-rays of the neck are taken, a doctor should accompany the child at all times in case emergency care,is needed.

In uncomplicated hoarseness that has persisted for a long period of time, a doctor will look at the vocal cords with the aid of a small mirror. Occasionally, a more extensive physical examination and blood tests will be performed.

# Swollen Glands

The most common types of swollen glands are lymph glands and salivary glands. The biggest salivary glands are located below and in front of the ears. When they swell, the characteristic swollen jaw appearance of mumps is the result (see **Mumps,** page 322).

Lymph glands play a part in the body's defense against infection. They may become swollen even if the infection is trivial or not apparent, although you can usually identify the infection that is causing the swelling.

- Swollen neck glands frequently accompany sore throats or ear infections. The swelling of a gland simply indicates that it is taking part in the fight against infection.
- Lymph glands in the groin are enlarged when there is infection in the feet, legs, or genital region. These glands are often swollen when no obvious infection can be found. Sometimes the basic problem may be so minor as to be overlooked (as with athlete's foot).
- Swollen glands behind the ears are often the result of an infection in the scalp. If there is no scalp infection, it is possible that the patient currently has or recently had **German measles** (see page 329). Infectious **mononucleosis** (mono) can also cause swelling of the glands behind the ears.

If a swollen gland is red and tender, there may be a bacterial infection within the gland itself that requires antibiotic treatment. Swollen glands otherwise require no treatment because they are merely fighting infections elsewhere. If there is an accompanying sore throat or earache, these should be treated as described on pages 229 and 231, respectively. However, the swollen glands are usually the result of viral infections that require no treatment.

If you have noticed one or several glands progressively enlarging over a period of three weeks, a doctor should be consulted. On very rare occasions, swollen glands can signal serious underlying problems.

## HOME TREATMENT

Observe the glands over several weeks to see if they are continuing to enlarge or if other glands become swollen. The vast majority of swollen glands that persist beyond three weeks

## SWOLLEN GLANDS

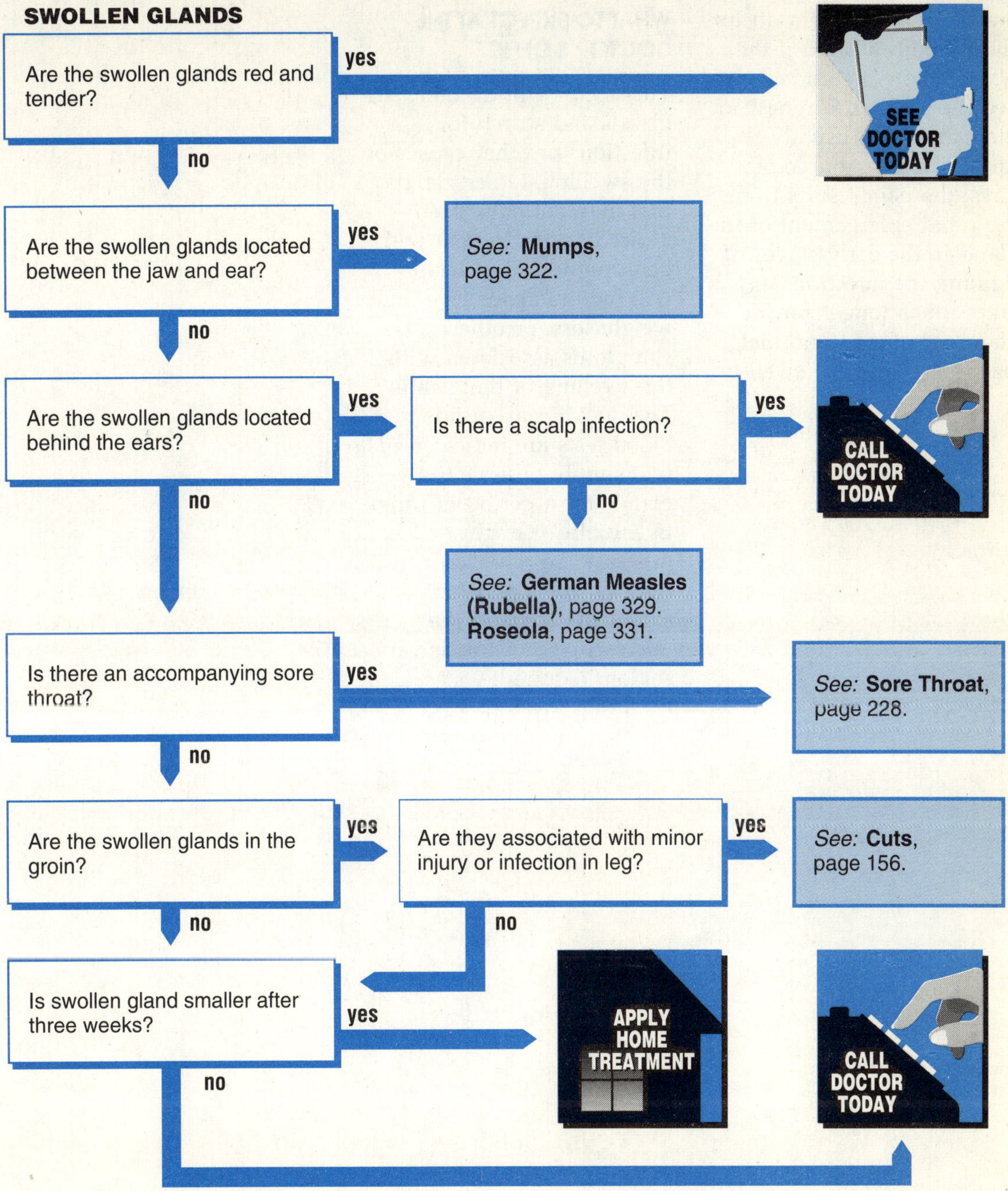

are not serious, but a doctor should be consulted if the glands show no tendency to become smaller. Soreness in the glands will usually disappear in a couple of days; the pain results from the rapid enlargement of the gland in the early stages of fighting the infection. It takes much longer for the gland to return to normal size than it does to swell up.

## WHAT TO EXPECT AT THE DOCTOR'S OFFICE

The doctor will examine the glands and search for infections or other causes of the swelling. Other glands that may not have been noticed by the patient will be examined. The doctor will inquire about fever, weight loss, or other symptoms associated with the swelling of the glands. The doctor may decide that blood tests are indicated or will simply observe the glands for a period of time. Eventually, it might be necessary to remove (biopsy) the gland for examination under the microscope, but this is very seldom required.

# Nosebleeds

The blood vessels within the nose lie very near the surface, and bleeding may occur with the slightest injury. In children, picking the nose is a common cause. Keeping their fingernails cut and discouraging the habit are good preventive medicine.

Nosebleeds are frequently due to irritation by a virus or to vigorous nose blowing. The main problem in this case is the cold, and treatment of cold symptoms will reduce the probability of the nosebleed. If the mucous membrane of the nose is dry, cracking and bleeding are more likely.

These key points should be remembered:

- You can almost always stop the bleeding yourself.
- The majority of nosebleeds are associated with colds or minor injury to the nose.
- Treatment such as packing the nose with gauze has significant drawbacks and should be avoided if possible.
- Investigation into the cause of recurrent nosebleeds is not urgent and is best accomplished when the nose is *not* bleeding.

**Medical opinion is divided about whether high blood pressure causes nosebleeds, but most doctors believe that the two conditions are seldom related. As a precaution, an individual with high blood pressure who experiences a nosebleed may want to have his or her blood pressure taken within a few days.**

## HOME TREATMENT

The nose consists of a bony part and a cartilaginous part: a "hard" portion and a "soft" portion. The area of the nose that usually bleeds lies within the soft portion, and compression will control the nosebleed. Simply squeeze the nose between thumb and forefinger just below the hard portion of the nose. Pressure should be applied for at least five minutes. The patient should be seated. Holding the head back is not necessary. It merely directs the blood flow backward rather than forward. Cold compresses or ice applied across the bridge of the nose may help. Almost all nosebleeds can be controlled in this manner if *sufficient time* is allowed for the bleeding to stop. If it just won't stop and bleeding is major, of course you should go to the emergency room.

Nosebleeds are more common in the winter when viruses and dry, heated interiors are common. A cooler house and a vaporizer to return humidity to the air help many people.

**NOSEBLEEDS**

Is the bleeding major, and does it continue after home treatment?

**yes** →

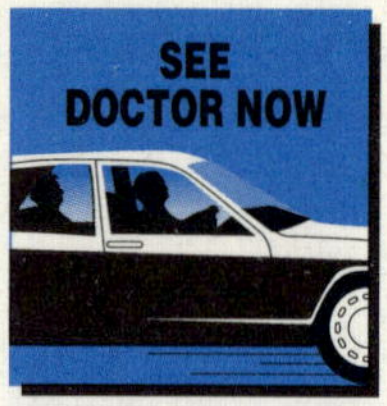


**no** ↓

Are nosebleeds recurrent and becoming more frequent?

**yes** →

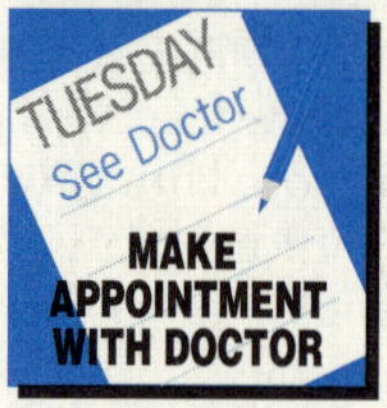


**no** ↓

Is the nosebleed associated with symptoms of a cold?

**yes** → Apply home treatment and see **Colds and Flu**, page 225.

**no** ↓

If nosebleeds are a recurrent problem, are becoming more frequent, and are not associated with a cold or other minor irritation, a doctor should be consulted. A doctor need not be seen immediately after the nosebleed because examination at that time may simply restart the nosebleed.

## WHAT TO EXPECT AT THE DOCTOR'S OFFICE

To stop the bleeding, the doctor will seat the patient and compress the nostrils. This will be done even if the patient has tried this at home, and it will usually work. Packing the nose or attempting to cauterize a bleeding point is less desirable. If the nosebleed cannot be stopped, the nose will be examined to see if a bleeding point can be identified. If a bleeding point is seen, coagulation by either electrical or chemical cauterization may be attempted. If this is not successful, packing of the nose may be unavoidable. Such packing is uncomfortable and may lead to infection; thus, the patient must be carefully observed.

If a doctor is visited because of recurrent nosebleeds, questions about events preceding the nosebleeds and a careful examination of the nose itself should be expected. Depending on the history and the physical examination, blood-clotting tests may be ordered on rare occasions.

# Bad Breath

Poor dental hygiene and smoking cause most cases of bad breath in adults. Infections of the mouth, including sore throats, may also be a cause of bad breath. Recently, it has been suggested that bad breath is occasionally due to gases absorbed from the intestine and released through the lungs. Unfortunately, even if this is correct, it is not clear what can be done about it.

### Smoker's Breath

The bad breath of smoking comes from the lungs as well as the mouth. Thus, mouthwashes and breath fresheners do little to help smoker's breath. Getting rid of this problem is another benefit of giving up cigarettes.

### Morning Breath

Bad breath in the morning is very common in adults. Flossing and regular tooth brushing should eliminate this problem.

### In Children

A rare cause of prolonged bad breath in a child is a foreign body in the nose. This is especially common in toddlers, who have inserted some small object that remains unnoticed. Often, but not always, there is a white, yellowish, or bloody discharge from one nostril.

Finally, unusual problems such as abscesses of the lung or heavy worm infestations have been reported to cause bad breath, although we have not seen these in our practices.

## HOME TREATMENT

Proper dental hygiene, especially flossing, and avoiding smoking will prevent most cases of bad breath. If this does not eliminate the odor, a visit to the doctor or dentist may be helpful.

Mouthwashes are of questionable value. Do not use mouthwashes that simply perfume the breath. These cover up but do not treat the underlying problem. If you smoke, bad breath is another good reason to quit.

## WHAT TO EXPECT AT THE DOCTOR'S OFFICE

The doctor will thoroughly examine the mouth and the nose. A culture may be taken if the patient has a sore throat or mouth sores. Antibiotics may be prescribed. If there is an object in the nose, the doctor will use a special instrument to remove it.

**BAD BREATH**

Does the patient have mouth sores or a sore throat?

yes → *See:* **Mouth Sores**, page 257, or **Sore Throat**, page 228.

no ↓

Is there a white, yellow, or bloody discharge from one nostril?

yes →

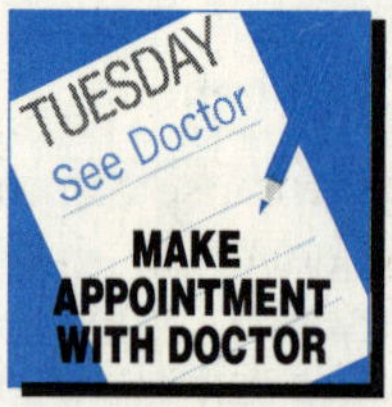


no ↓

Is there a decaying tooth?

yes →

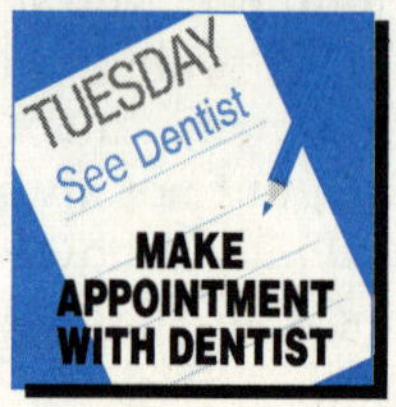


no ↓

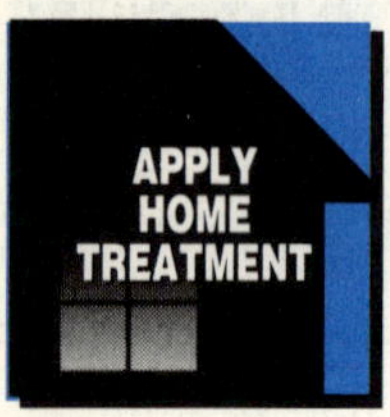

# Mouth Sores

Fever blisters or cold sores are a familiar problem caused by the **herpes virus**. They are usually found on the lips, although they can sometimes appear inside the mouth. Often the blisters have ruptured and only the remaining sore is seen. Fever is usually but not always present. The herpes virus often lives in the body for years, causing trouble only when another illness causes a rise in body temperature. Generally, fever blisters heal by themselves several days after the fever diminishes.

A **canker sore** is a painful ulcer that often follows an injury, such as accidently biting the inside of the lip or the tongue, or it may appear without obvious cause. Eventually, it heals by itself.

### In Children

Large white spots on the roof of the mouth are a sign of **thrush**, a monolial yeast infection. It often disappears without treatment.

A virus that can cause mouth lesions in children is the **Coxsackie virus**. These lesions are often accompanied by spots on the hands and feet; hence the name "hand-foot-mouth syndrome." The child feels well, and there is no fever. Again, this problem will go away by itself.

### Other Causes

Drugs sometimes cause mouth ulcers. In such cases, a skin rash may be present on other parts of the body as well, and a doctor must be contacted.

A cancer of the lip or gum is rare. It does not need to be treated in the first few days. Syphilis transmitted by oral sexual contact may produce a mouth sore. Both of these problems are usually painless. There are other conditions that may also cause mouth ulcers, but they also cause problems with eyes, joints, or other organs.

## HOME TREATMENT

Mouth sores caused by viruses heal by themselves. The goal of treatment is to reduce fever, relieve pain, and maintain adequate fluid intake.

Children will seldom want to eat when they have painful mouth lesions. Although children can go several days without taking solid foods, it is imperative that they maintain an adequate liquid diet. Cold liquids are the most soothing, and Popsicles or iced frozen juices are often helpful.

For sores inside the lip and on the gums, a non-prescription preparation called Orabase may be applied for protection. For canker sores and fever blisters, one of the phenol and camphor preparations (Blistex, Campho-Phenique, etc.) may provide relief, especially if applied early. If one of these preparations appears to cause further irritation, discontinue its use.

If the external sores have crusted over, cool compresses may be applied to remove the crusts. Mouth sores usually resolve in one to two weeks. Any sore that persists beyond three weeks should be examined by the doctor.

### WHAT TO EXPECT AT THE DOCTOR'S OFFICE

A thorough examination of the mouth will be carried out. A prescription will usually be given for thrush. For viral infections, doctors have no more to offer than home remedies. We caution against the use of oral anesthetics, such as viscous Xylocaine, for children. This anesthetic can interfere with proper swallowing and can lead to inhalation of food into the lungs.

## MOUTH SORES

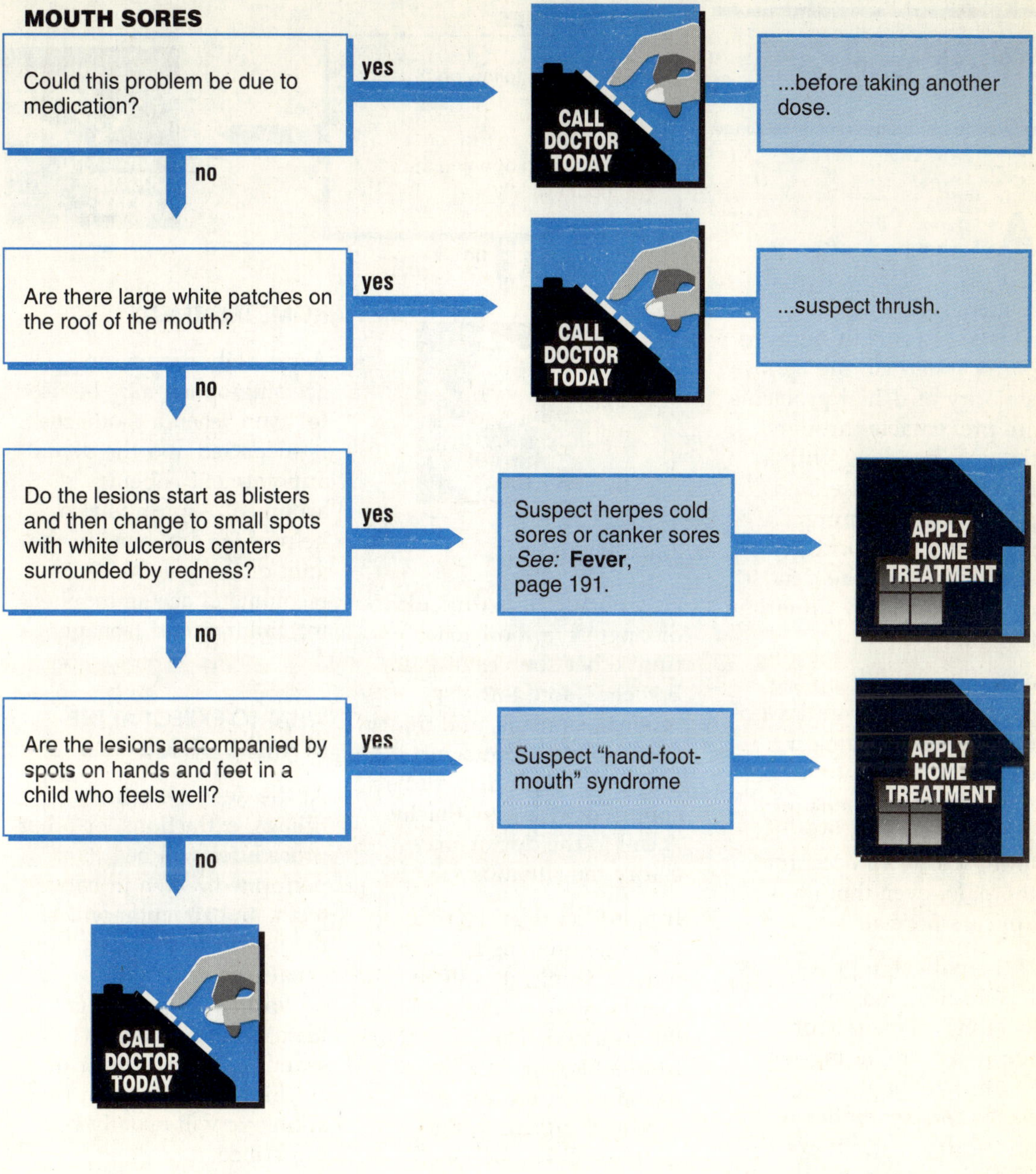
Could this problem be due to medication?
yes
CALL DOCTOR TODAY
...before taking another dose.
no
Are there large white patches on the roof of the mouth?
yes
CALL DOCTOR TODAY
...suspect thrush.
no
Do the lesions start as blisters and then change to small spots with white ulcerous centers surrounded by redness?
yes
Suspect herpes cold sores or canker sores *See:* **Fever**, page 191.
APPLY HOME TREATMENT
no
Are the lesions accompanied by spots on hands and feet in a child who feels well?
yes
Suspect "hand-foot-mouth" syndrome
APPLY HOME TREATMENT
no
CALL DOCTOR TODAY

# Toothaches

A toothache is often the sad result of poor dental hygiene. Although resistance to tooth decay is partly inherited, the majority of dental problems are preventable through flossing, brushing with a fluoride toothpaste, and professional cleaning. Sealants and fluoride applications by the dentist may be especially important for children.

Certainly, if you can see a decayed tooth or an area of redness surrounding a tooth, a diseased tooth is most likely the cause of pain. Tapping an infected tooth will often accentuate the pain, even though it appears normal.

If the patient appears ill, has a fever, and has swelling of the jaw or redness surrounding the tooth, a tooth abscess is likely and antibiotics will be necessary in addition to proper dental care.

**TOOTHACHES**

Are any of the following present?

- Fever
- Earache
- Pain upon opening the mouth widely

yes →

no ↓

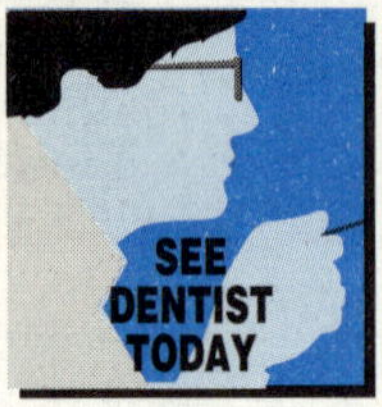


### Other Possibilities

Occasionally it is difficult to distinguish a toothache from other sources of pain. Earaches, sore throats, mumps, sinusitis, and injury to the joint that attaches the jaw to the skull may all be confused with a toothache. A call to the doctor may clarify the situation.

If pain occurs every time the patient opens his or her mouth widely, it is likely that the joint of the jaw has been injured. This can occur from a blow or just by trying to eat too big a sandwich. A call to the doctor will help decide what, if anything, should be done.

## HOME TREATMENT

Aspirin, ibuprofen, or acetaminophen may be used for pain when a toothache is suspected and the dental appointment is being arranged. Aspirin is also helpful for problems in the joint of the jaw. We recommend acetaminophen for children and teenagers.

## WHAT TO EXPECT AT THE DENTIST'S OFFICE

At the dentist's office, fillings, extractions, or other procedures will be performed. Often in baby teeth, an extraction will be the most likely course. Root canals are generally performed on permanent teeth if the problem is severe. If there is fever or swelling of the jaw, an antibiotic will usually be prescribed.

CHAPTER H

# *Allergies*

Allergy was first described at the turn of the century by a pediatrician named Clemens von Pirquet. The term "allergy" means "changed activity" and described changes that occurred after coming in contact with a foreign substance. Two types of change were noticed.

- One change was beneficial, developing protection against a foreign substance after having been exposed to it once. This response prevents us from developing many infectious diseases a second time and provides the scientific basis for most immunizations.
- The other type of response, generally not beneficial, was known as a hypersensitivity response. It is the response for which the term "allergy" is generally used.

Allergy is now known to be possible even without previous exposure to the substance. All people are capable of allergic responses. For example, anyone given a transfusion with the wrong type of blood will have an allergic reaction.

However, the term "allergy" is overused. When your eyes smart in Los Angeles, they are not allergic to the air but are experiencing a direct chemical irritation from the pollutants. Similarly, skin coming in contact with some plants or chemicals experiences direct damage and not an allergic response. A milk or food allergy is often blamed for vomiting, diarrhea, colic, crying, irritability, fretfulness, or sneezing in infants. Although allergy can cause these symptoms, countless other things can also.

Over the next few pages, we will discuss common allergies (involving food, insects, drugs, pets, pollen, and dust), the common allergic problems (such as asthma, hay fever, hives, and other skin problems), and the medical treatments available.

# Food Allergy

Food allergy occurs at all ages but is of most concern in children. Almost any food can produce an allergic response. Only breast milk appears to be an exception and a 1928 report did incriminate beans in a mother's diet, detected in the breast milk, as a cause of allergy in an infant.

Food allergy is not the only cause of digestive upsets but is blamed for much that it does not cause. For example, some children are born without an important digestive enzyme, known as **lactase**, which is necessary to digest the sugars present in milk. Other children lose the ability to make lactase after the age of three or four. Many adults have a relative deficiency of lactase. The absence of lactase can produce diarrhea, abdominal pain, and vomiting after drinking milk. This is only one example of a digestive problem that can be confused with food allergy; there are many others.

## SYMPTOMS OF FOOD ALLERGY

Food allergy may produce swelling of the mouth and lips, hives, skin rashes, vomiting, diarrhea, asthma, runny nose, and other problems. Of course, many other allergens besides food can cause these problems, making it difficult to prove that a particular food is the culprit. The best approach for detecting food allergy is to think like Sherlock Holmes. If your lips swell only after eating strawberries, you have the culprit!

## FOODS RESPONSIBLE FOR ALLERGY

Cow's milk is frequently blamed for food allergy in small children. Because almost any symptom can be blamed on allergy and because infants consume so much cow's milk, it is easy to see why milk is so quickly blamed. Infant intestines are capable of absorbing proteins that older children's digestive tracts would not absorb. These proteins may set up altered reactions or allergies.

Controversy exists about the relationship of early exposure to cow's milk and the later development of asthma. Some doctors maintain that avoidance of cow's milk will delay or eliminate the development of asthma. Others have found the opposite. The only agreement is that the children most likely to develop allergies, including asthma, come from families with allergic members. Cow's milk may have some effects on children who are likely to develop allergies but probably should not be of particular concern for children with no family history of allergy.

The rare allergic responses to cow's milk in infants involve vomiting, diarrhea, and even blood loss through the intestines. This situation is a clear indication for removal of cow's milk from the diet, if the cause of the severe diarrhea is documented by a doctor. The necessary tests are simple and require analysis of the stools (feces). Stool analysis should be repeated after the child has been taken off cow's milk.

Other foods that have been associated with allergic reactions in children include wheat, eggs, citrus fruits, beef and veal, fish, and nuts. Severe reactions are very rare in children. Parents need not be anxious about giving their children new foods. Families with a strong history of allergy can introduce one new food to an infant every few days so that if an allergy develops, the cause is obvious.

## SOYBEAN SUBSTITUTES FOR MILK

The amount of soybean formula produced in this country exceeds the amount needed for children with cow's milk allergy. Milk allergy consists of an altered response to the cow's milk protein, producing vomiting and/or diarrhea, and it is extremely rare. Intolerance to cow's milk because of lack of an enzyme (lactase) to digest milk sugar (lactose) will produce bloating, abdominal pain, vomiting, and/or diarrhea. This intolerance is also rare.

There are two possible explanations for the purchase of soybean preparations. First, parents may buy them because they like them. They are nutritious and children tolerate them well. However, they tend to be more expensive than cow's milk. The other reason for the high consumption of soybean formula is that parents have been instructed to substitute for cow's milk at the slightest suspicion of an allergy. Every childhood symptom known has been attributed to cow's milk allergy—yet the condition is rare.

Before you spend money on a soybean formula, make sure that your doctor has determined that the child really needs it. Many stories of children getting better on a soybean preparation result from the child spontaneously recovering from whatever was formerly producing the troublesome symptom.

# Asthma

Asthma is a severe allergic disorder that is most common in children and adolescents. It is discussed further in the description of its most prominent symptom—**Wheezing** (see page 244). The wheezing in asthma is caused by spasm of the muscles in the walls of the smaller air passages in the lungs. An excess amount of mucus production further narrows the air passages and can aggravate the difficulty in getting the air out. Infections and foreign bodies in the air passages can mimic asthma. All wheezing in children is potentially serious and should be evaluated by a medical professional, at least for the first few occurrences. Asthma tends to occur in families where other members have either asthma, hay fever, or eczema.

An attack can be triggered by an infection, by an emotionally upsetting event, or by exposure to an allergen. Common allergens include house dust, pollen, mold, food, and shed animal material or "animal dander." It is sometimes easy to identify airborne allergens to which a person is susceptible. Some people will wheeze only around cats, others only during a particular pollen season. (Pollens most often cause seasonal hay fever, or allergic rhinitis, rather than asthma.)

Most often, there is no clear reason for a particular asthmatic attack. If asthma is severe, it is desirable to identify the offending allergens if possible. However, usually no specific allergen(s) can be pinned down as the cause. Doctors call this "intrinsic asthma."

## TREATMENT OF ASTHMA

The treatment of asthma varies according to the severity of the problem. Some people have only one or two episodes of asthma and are never troubled again. We wonder if these episodes should even be called asthma attacks. Other people have daily attacks. These severely compromise their ability to function normally.

### Drug Treatments

Therapy provides relief of symptoms, often dramatically so, but must also work to remove the cause, whether it is allergic, infectious, or emotional. Symptomatic relief of asthma is provided through a variety of prescription medications, including epinephrine, isoproterenol, ephedrine, theophylline, prednisone, and others.

Several different prescription drugs are often combined, but we see no reason to begin treatment with such **combination drugs**. Many of these compounds have phenobarbital added to counteract some of the stimulating effects of the other medicines included. Medications to counteract the side effects of other drugs could be added endlessly. All these drugs are powerful, and all cause side effects. Minimal side effects may be acceptable to relieve major symptoms. If side effects are intolerable, a new treatment plan can be made. Try to avoid combination drugs.

**Corticosteroid drugs**, such as steroids and prednisone, are effective in severe asthmatic patients. They block the smooth muscle contractions that narrow the airway passages. They have many side effects, including growth retardation, and should be used only after full discussion with your doctor.

**Antihistamines** are not useful in the treatment of asthma. In fact, the drying of secretions by antihistamines may actually cause airways to plug up.

Inhaled sprays, **bronchodilators**, containing drugs to open airways may be abused and can even cause fatal reactions. They should be used sparingly in children, and only in those not responding to medication by mouth. Nebulizers containing freon should not be used.

**Cromolyn** is also taken by inhalation. Unlike other inhaled drugs, it is not useful during an attack but can prevent future attacks. Cromolyn is most useful in patients with severe asthma who require high doses of oral medications. Many patients on corticosteroid drugs have been able to reduce steroid dosage by using cromolyn. Cromolyn seems to work particularly well in patients sensitive to inhaled allergens and in patients who develop asthma after exercise.

Asthma is a complicated subject. If you or a family member is asthmatic, your doctor will need to thoroughly discuss management of the illness with you. You cannot manage this problem without medical help.

**Allergen Avoidance**

A relatively clean and dustfree house is healthy for all people but essential for the allergic person. Rugs, furniture, drapes, bedspreads, and other items that are particular dust-catchers should be vacuumed regularly. An asthmatic's bedroom should be especially allergen-free because eight to ten hours a night are spent sleeping. Except in very severe cases, we do not recommend changing the entire household furnishings to reduce potential allergen exposure. Even then, removal of items should progress on a rational basis after suspected allergens have been identified. Patients and pets may do fine together, although it is best not to allow pets to sleep in an allergic patient's room. Toy animals should be kept clean; washable ones are best. Avoid products that may be stuffed with animal hair. Finally, don't forget to change heating filters and air-conditioner filters regularly.

### Infection Control

Because infections can trigger asthma, a physical examination is important during the first or frequently recurring attacks. Antibiotics should not be given unless an infection is definitely present.

### Hydration Therapy

Water and other fluids taken by mouth are very important. Water can help loosen the mucus in the lungs and make breathing easier. Mist is not too helpful during asthmatic attacks because the affected airway passages are beyond the reach of the mist. Vaporizers are most useful for problems of the upper air passages of ears, nose, sinuses, mouth, and throat.

### Supportive Therapy

Severe asthma is strenuous for the asthmatic and his or her family. Assistance is often required to manage the emotional consequences of asthma for the whole family. Do not hesitate to seek help. Social workers and other counselors can be invaluable.

### Exercise and Asthma

Asthmatics can participate in athletics. Athletes with asthma have won numerous gold medals in Olympic swimming. Swimming appears to be far and away the best exercise and the best sport for the asthmatic. Exercise programs with long and steady energy requirements seem to work the best, and swimmers have the advantage of an environment that has very high humidity.

**Some doctors maintain that children never truly outgrow asthma, but the evidence is otherwise. More than half of the children diagnosed as having asthma never have an asthmatic attack as an adult. Another 10% will have only occasional attacks during adult life.**

# Hay Fever

Allergic rhinitis, commonly called hay fever, is the most common allergic problem. A stuffy, runny nose, watering itchy eyes, headache, and sneezing are all common symptoms. The cause in infants is often dust or food; in adults, it is dust or pollens. Most individuals are troubled only in pollen season; ragweed is particularly troublesome. Hay fever seems to run in families.

Treatment is directed toward both symptomatic relief and avoidance of the offending allergen. The use of tissues or handkerchiefs for symptomatic relief is often not enough. Drugs that will reduce symptoms may be prescribed or purchased over the counter, but all have some side effects.

Antihistamines block the action of histamine, a substance released during allergic reactions. They also have a drying effect and alleviate nasal stuffiness. They also may be useful in reducing itching, helping motion sickness, or decreasing vomiting. The antihistamines available over the counter and most often used for allergic rhinitis are diphenhydramine (Benadryl, etc.), chlorpheniramine maleate (ChlorTrimeton, etc.), tripelennamine (PBZ, etc.), and brompheniramine (Dimetane, etc.). These four drugs are from three different classes of antihistamine compounds. Individuals respond differently to different drugs, and a trial of the different types of antihistamines may be necessary to determine the most effective type.

The most common side effect of antihistamines is drowsiness, and this may interfere with work or school. Terfenadine (Seldane) is a prescription antihistamine that causes less drowsiness, but it may be less effective, too. Antihistamines should not be used as sleeping pills because the drowsiness they produce *decreases* the amount of deep sleep, which is necessary for normal rest.

Decongestants (pseudoephedrine, etc.) can be added to antihistamine medication. They may help with the runny nose as well as combat the sleepiness caused by antihistamines.

# Eczema

Atopic dermatitis, known commonly as eczema, is an allergic skin condition characterized by dry, itching skin. This itching often leads to scratching. The scratching then produces weeping, infected skin. Dried weepings lead to crusting. Sufficient scratching will produce a thickened, rough skin, which is characteristic of long-standing atopic dermatitis.

Atopic dermatitis runs in families along with asthma and allergic rhinitis. Like asthma, a variety of conditions can aggravate it. These conditions include infection, emotional stress, food allergy, and sweating.

Infants seldom exhibit any signs of this problem at birth. The first signs may be red, chapped cheeks. Often infants may rub these itchy areas and cause secondary infections.

As the child grows older, the atopic dermatitis can spread. It may be found on the back of the legs and front of the arms. Adults often have problems with their hands. This is especially true of people whose hands are in frequent contact with water. Water tends to have a drying effect on the skin and so aggravate the dry skin-itch-scratch-weep-crust cycle.

Therapy is based on avoidance of allergens and maintenance of good skin care.

- Avoid wool, which tends to aggravate itching.
- Avoid excessively warm clothing, which will cause sweat retention and aggravate itching.
- Keep a child's fingernails clipped short.
- Avoid bathing with soap and water because these tend to dry the skin. Instead use non-lipid cleansers. Some cleansers with cetyl alcohol aid in preventing drying of the skin (Cetaphil, etc.).
- Avoid all oil or grease preparations. They occlude the skin and increase sweat retention and itching.
- Avoiding cow's milk is often suggested, particularly for children. Make sure this really works for your child before permanently changing to more expensive feedings. When trying any milk-avoidance diet, make *no* other changes in food or other care for a full two weeks unless absolutely necessary.
- Itching is often worse at bedtime. Acetaminophen, ibuprofen, and aspirin are effective and inexpensive medications for reducing itching. Antihistamines also reduce itching but should be used only if necessary.
- Steroid creams are useful in severe cases. When possible, steroids should be used only for a short period of time. Prolonged use of steroids on the skin can produce numerous side effects.
- Antibiotics are sometimes necessary to clear up badly infected skin.
- Emotional factors may need attention and they may be the key to successful therapy.
- There has been no benefit demonstrated from either skin testing or hyposensitization (allergy shots).

For more information on treating eczema, see page 296.

# Allergy Testing and Shots

The purpose of allergy testing is to help decide what is causing the allergy. It is not a treatment. As a test, it is not always accurate. Once an allergy test is positive, there are two ways to use the information: avoidance and hyposensitization (desensitization).

Avoidance is sometimes, though not usually, possible. Seldom is a person allergic to cats and nothing else. Usually such an isolated allergy is noted by an alert patient or family member. Avoiding dusts, pollens, trees, and flowers is next to impossible, so hyposensitization is sometimes reasonable if the problem is severe.

Hyposensitization involves injecting a tiny amount of the offending allergen. Gradually larger and larger amounts are injected until the patient is able to tolerate exposure to the allergen with only mild symptoms.

Hyposensitization works in many cases, but there are many problems. Local reactions at the site of the injection are common but can be minimized by injecting through a different needle from the one used to withdraw the material from the bottle. Hyposensitization requires weekly injections for months or years. It may be considered for patients with moderate or severe asthma or severe hay fever but appears unwarranted, as does the preliminary skin testing, for patients with mild asthma or mild allergic rhinitis.

## CHAPTER I

# Skin Problems

Skin problems must be approached somewhat differently from other medical problems. Decision charts that proceed from complaints such as "red bumps" have been developed, but the charts are complicated and somewhat unsatisfactory. This is because most people, including doctors, identify skin diseases by recognizing a particular pattern. This pattern is composed of not only what the skin problem looks like at a particular time but also how it began, where it spread, and whether it is associated with other symptoms such as itching or fever. Also important are elements of the medical history that may suggest an illness to which the patient has been exposed. Fortunately, many times the patient already has a good idea how the problem developed, and it is possible to proceed immediately with the question of whether this is poison ivy, ringworm, or something else.

Each decision chart in this section begins with the question of whether the problem is compatible with the pattern for that skin disease. (Note that a more complete description of the pattern is given in the text that accompanies each decision chart.) If it is not, you are directed to reconsider the problem and consult the table on pages 274–275.

Most cases of a particular skin disease do not look exactly as a textbook says they should. We have tried to allow for a reasonable amount of variation in the descriptions. Don't be afraid to ask for other opinions. Grandparents and others have seen a lot of skin problems over the years and know what they look like. We have listed some of the more common problems, but by no means all. If your problem doesn't seem to fit any of the descriptions and you think the problem could be serious, call the doctor.

Finally, because every case is at least a little bit different, even the best doctors will not be able to identify all skin problems immediately. Simple office laboratory methods can help sort out the possibilities. Fortunately, the vast majority of skin problems are minor, self-limiting, and pose no major threat to health. Usually, it is reasonable for you to wait quite some time to see if the problem goes away by itself.

If you are confused about where to start, we have provided a decision chart to help point you in the right direction, and a table that allows you to quickly review the major symptoms of common skin problems.

**SKIN PROBLEMS**

Is there fever?

yes → Does the rash consist of raised bumps?

- yes → *See:* **Chicken Pox**, page 324 **Mouth Sores**, page 257 **Impetigo**, page 283 **Boils**, page 298 **Insect Bites or Stings**, page 183 **Hives**, page 287. If none of these, suspect drug reaction.
- no → *See:* **Measles**, page 327 **German Measles (Rubella)**, page 329 **Roseola**, page 331 **Scarlet Fever**, page 333.

no ↓

Is there itching?

yes → *See:* **Poison Ivy and Poison Oak**, page 289 **Lice and Bedbugs**, page 308 **Eczema**, page 296 **Jock Itch**, page 304 **Athlete's Foot**, page 302 **Chicken Pox**, page 324 **Insect Bites or Stings**, page 183 **Ringworm**, page 285.

no ↓

Are there hardly any symptoms?

yes → *See:* **Hair Loss**, page 281 **Dandruff and Cradle Cap**, page 315 **Skin Cancer**, page 293 **Patchy Loss of Skin Color**, page 317.

**TABLE H** *Skin Symptom Table*

| | *Fever* | *Itching* | *Elevation* | *Color* |
|---|---|---|---|---|
| **Baby rashes** (p.276) | No | Sometimes | Slightly raised dots | White or red dots; surrounding skin may be red |
| **Diaper rash** (p.279) | No | No | Only if infected | Red |
| **Impetigo** (p.283) | Sometimes | Occasionally | Crusts on sores | Golden crusts on red sores |
| **Ringworm** (p.285) | No | Occasionally | Slightly raised rings | Red |
| **Hives** (p.287) | No | Intense | Raised with flat tops | Pale raised lesions surrounded by red |
| **Poison ivy** (p.289) | No | Intense | Blisters are elevated | Red |
| **Rashes caused by chemicals** (p.291) | No | Moderate to intense | Sometimes blisters | Red |
| **Eczema** (p.296) | No | Moderate to intense | Occasional blisters when infected | Red |
| **Acne** (p.300) | No | No | Pimples, cysts | Red |
| **Athlete's foot** (p.302) | No | Mild to intense | No | Colorless to red |
| **Dandruff and cradle cap** (p.315) | No | Occasionally | Some crusting | White to yellow to red |
| **Chicken pox** (p.324) | Yes | Intense during pustular stage | Flat, then raised, then blisters, then crusts | Red |
| **Measles** (p.327) | Yes | None to mild | Flat | Pink,then red |
| **German measles (rubella)** (p.329) | Yes | No | Flat or slightly raised | Red |
| **Roseola** (p.331) | Yes | No | Flat, occasionally with a few bumps | Pink |
| **Scarlet fever** (p.333) | Yes | No | Flat; feels like sandpaper | Red |
| **Fifth disease** (p.335) | No | No | Flat; lacy appearance | Red |

| *Location* | *Duration of Problem* | *Other Symptoms* |
|---|---|---|
| Trunk, neck, skin folds on arms and legs | Until controlled | |
| Under diaper | Until controlled | |
| Arms, legs, face first, then most of body | Until controlled | |
| Anywhere, including scalp and nails | Until controlled | Flaking or scaling |
| Anywhere | Minutes to days | |
| Exposed areas | 7 to 14 days | Oozing; some swelling |
| Areas exposed to chemicals | Until exposure to chemical stopped | Some oozing and/or swelling |
| Elbows, wrists, knees, cheeks | Until controlled | Moist; oozing |
| Face, back, chest | Until controlled | Blackheads |
| Between toes | Until controlled | Cracks; scaling; oozing blisters |
| Scalp, eyebrows, behind ears, groin | Until controlled | Fine, oily scales |
| May start anywhere; most prominent on trunk and face | 4 to 10 days | Lesions progress from flat to tiny blisters, then become crusted |
| First face, then chest and abdomen, then arms and legs | 4 to 7 days | Preceded by fever, cough, red eyes |
| First face, then trunk, then extremities | 2 to 4 days | Swollen glands behind ears; occasional joint pains in older children and adults |
| First trunk, then arms and neck; very little on face and legs | 1 to 2 days | High fever for 3 days that disappears with rash |
| First face, then elbows, spreads rapidly to entire body in 24 hours | 5 to 7 days | Sore throat; skin peeling afterwards, especially palms |
| First face, then arms and legs, then rest of body | 3 to 7 days | "Slapped-cheek" appearance, rash comes and goes |

# Baby Rashes

The skin of the newborn child may exhibit a wide variety of bumps and blotches. Fortunately, almost all of these are harmless and clear up by themselves. The most common of these conditions are addressed in this section; only one, heat rash, requires any treatment. If the baby was delivered in a hospital, many of these conditions may occur before discharge so that advice will be readily available from nurses or doctors.

**Heat Rash**

Heat rash is caused by blockage of the pores that lead to the sweat glands. It actually can occur at any age but is most common in the very young child whose sweat glands are still developing. When heat and humidity rise, these glands attempt to secrete sweat as they would normally. But because of the blockage, sweat is held within the skin and forms little red bumps. It is also known as "prickly heat" or "miliaria."

**Milia**

On the other hand, the little white bumps of milia are composed of normal skin cells that have overaccumulated in some spots. As many as 40% of children have these bumps at birth. Eventually, the bumps break open, the trapped material escapes, and the bumps disappear without requiring any treatment.

**Erythema Toxicum**

Erythema toxicum is an unnecessarily long and frightening term for the flat red splotches that appear in up to 50% of all babies. These seldom appear after five days of age and usually disappear by seven days. The children who exhibit these splotches are perfectly normal, and whether or not any real toxin is involved is not clear.

**Acne**

Because the baby is exposed to the mother's adult hormones, a mild case of acne may develop. Acne may also occur when a child begins to produce adult hormones during adolescence. (The little white dots often seen on a newborn's nose represent an excess amount of normal skin oil, sebaceous gland hyperplasia, that has been produced by the hormones.) Acne usually becomes evident at between two and four weeks of age and clears up spontaneously within six months to a year. It virtually never requires treatment.

## BABY RASHES

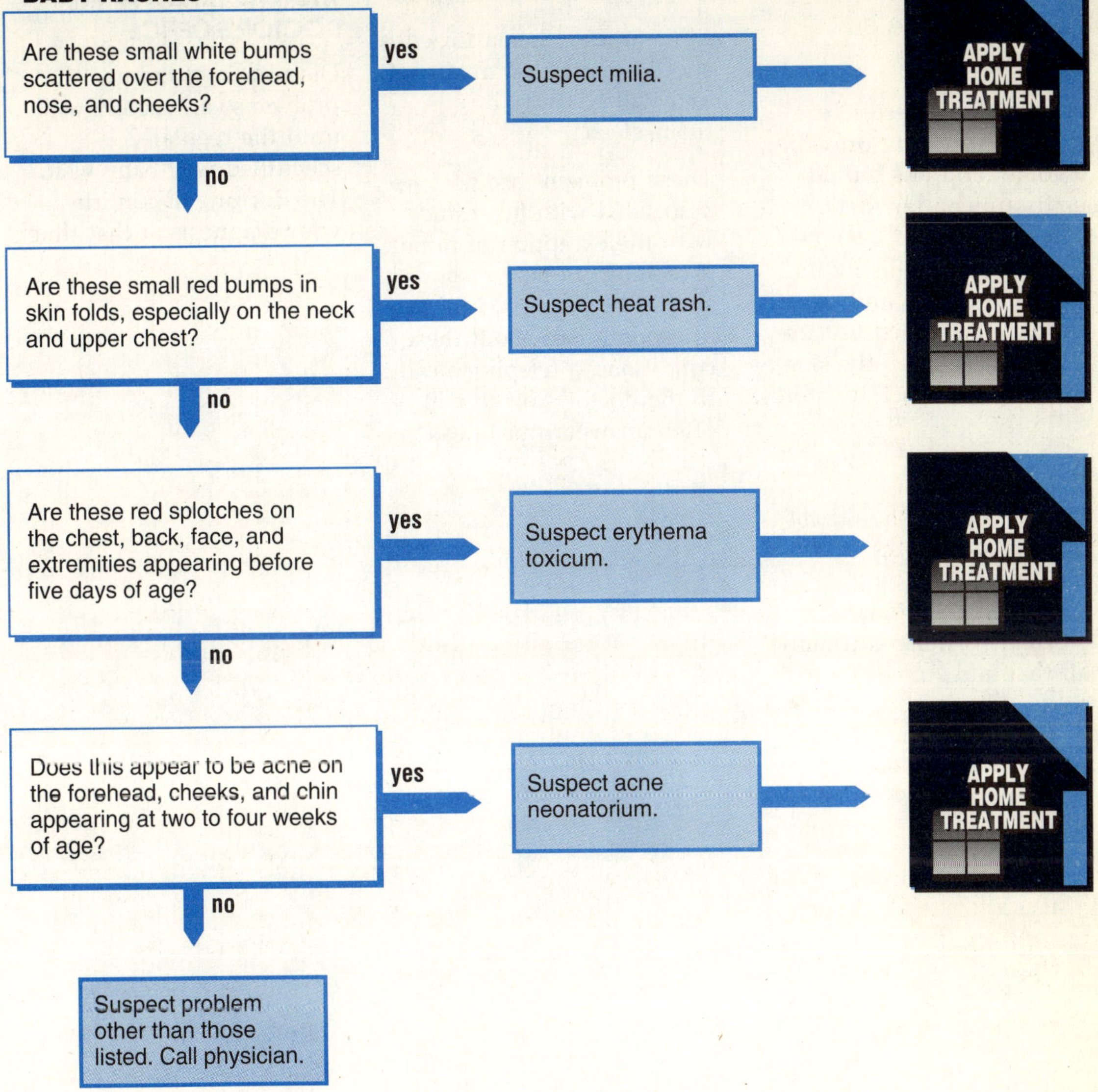
Are these small white bumps scattered over the forehead, nose, and cheeks?
yes
Suspect milia.
APPLY HOME TREATMENT
no
Are these small red bumps in skin folds, especially on the neck and upper chest?
yes
Suspect heat rash.
APPLY HOME TREATMENT
no
Are these red splotches on the chest, back, face, and extremities appearing before five days of age?
yes
Suspect erythema toxicum.
APPLY HOME TREATMENT
no
Does this appear to be acne on the forehead, cheeks, and chin appearing at two to four weeks of age?
yes
Suspect acne neonatorium.
APPLY HOME TREATMENT
no
Suspect problem other than those listed. Call physician.

## HOME TREATMENT

### Heat Rash

Heat rash is effectively treated simply by providing a cooler and less humid environment. Powders carefully applied do no harm but are unlikely to help. Ointments and creams should be avoided because they tend to keep the skin warmer and block the pores.

### Acne

Acne in babies should *not* be treated with the medicines used by adolescents and adults. Normal washing is usually all that is required.

### Milia and Erythema Toxicum

Milia and erythema toxicum should require no treatment and will go away by themselves.

These problems are not associated with fever and, with the exception of minor discomfort in heat rash, should be painless. If any question arises about these conditions, a telephone call to the doctor's office will often answer your questions.

## WHAT TO EXPECT AT THE DOCTOR'S OFFICE

Discussion of these problems can usually wait until the regularly scheduled well-baby visit. The doctor can confirm your diagnosis at that time.

# Diaper Rash

The only children who never have diaper rash are those who never wear diapers. An infant's skin is particularly sensitive and likely to develop diaper rash. Diaper rash is basically an irritation caused by dampness and the interaction of urine, feces, and skin. An additional factor is thought to be the ammonia produced from urine, and often its odor is unmistakably present. Factors that tend to keep the baby's skin wet and exposed to the irritant promote diaper rash:

- Constantly wet or infrequently changed diapers
- Using plastic pants

For the most part, treatment consists of reversing these factors.

The irritation of simple diaper rash may become complicated by an infection due to **yeast** (Candida) or bacteria. When yeast is the culprit, small red spots may be seen. Also, small patches of the rash may appear outside the area covered by the diaper, as far away as the chest. Infection with bacteria leads to development of large fluid-filled blisters. If the rash is worse in the skin creases, a mild underlying skin problem known as **seborrhea** may be present. This skin condition is also responsible for cradle cap and dandruff.

Occasionally, parents may notice blood or what appear to be blood spots when boys have diaper rash. This is due to a rash at the urinary opening at the end of the penis. This problem will clear up as the diaper rash clears up.

## HOME TREATMENT

Treatment of diaper rash is aimed at keeping the skin dry and exposed to air. As implied above, the first things to do are change the diapers frequently and stop using plastic pants. Leaving diapers off altogether for as long as possible will also help. Cloth diapers should be washed in a mild soap and rinsed thoroughly. Occasionally, the soap residues left in diapers will act as an irritant. Adding a half-cup of vinegar to the last rinse cycle may help counter the irritating ammonia.

While complete clearing of the rash will take several days at least, definite improvement should be noted within the first 48 to 72 hours. If the rash does not start clearing up by that time or if it is extraordinarily severe, the doctor should be consulted.

To prevent diaper rash, some parents use zinc oxide ointments, petroleum jelly or other protective ointments. Others use baby powders. (**Caution:** talc dust can injure lungs.) Always place powder in your hand first and then pat on the baby's bottom. Caldesene

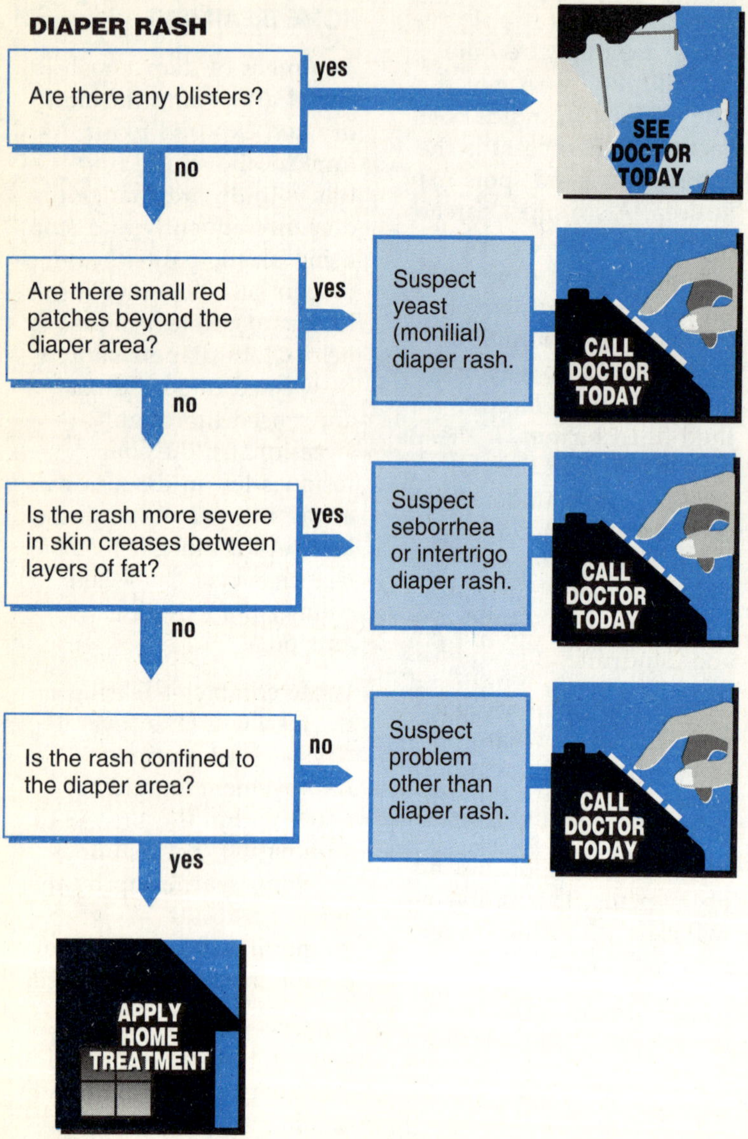


powder is helpful in preventing seborrhea and monilial rashes. We do not feel that all babies need powders and creams. If a rash has begun, avoid ointments and creams because they may delay healing.

## WHAT TO EXPECT AT THE DOCTOR'S OFFICE

All of the baby's skin should be inspected to determine the true extent of the rash. Occasionally, a scraping from the involved skin will be examined under the microscope. If a yeast (monilial) infection has complicated a simple diaper rash, the doctor will prescribe home treatment plus a medication to kill the yeast. If a bacterial infection has occurred, then an antibiotic to be taken orally will be recommended. If the rash is very severe or seborrhea is suspected, then a steroid cream (usually stronger than the 1% hydrocortisone available without prescription) may be advised. In any case, home therapy may be safely started before seeing the doctor.

# Hair Loss

This section is not about the normal hair loss that most men and many women experience as they get older. (See **Aging Spots, Wrinkles, and Baldness,** page 319.) Baldness isn't the only kind of hair loss.

Sometimes all the hair in one small area is completely lost, but the scalp is normal. This problem is called **alopecia areata**, and its cause is unknown. Usually, the hair will come back completely within 12 months, although about 40% of patients will have a similar loss within the next 4 to 5 years. This problem resolves by itself. Steroid (cortisone) creams will make the hair grow back faster, but the new hair falls out again when the treatment is stopped, so these creams are of little use.

Hair loss that may require a doctor's treatment are characterized by abnormalities in the scalp skin or the hairs themselves. The most frequent problem in this category is **ringworm** (see page 285). Ringworm may be red and scaly, or there may be pustules with oozing. The ringworm fungus infects the hairs so they become thickened and break easily. Whenever the scalp skin or hairs appear abnormal, the doctor may be able to help.

Hair pulling by children, or occasionally a friend, is often responsible for hair loss. Tight braids or ponytails may also cause some hair loss. If a child constantly pulls out his or her hair, you should discuss it with a doctor.

## HOME TREATMENT

In this instance, home treatment is reserved for presumed alopecia areata and consists of watchful waiting. The skin in the area involved must be completely normal for a diagnosis of alopecia areata. If the appearance of scalp or hairs becomes abnormal, the doctor should be consulted.

## WHAT TO EXPECT AT THE DOCTOR'S OFFICE

An examination of the hair and scalp is usually sufficient to determine the nature of the problem. Occasionally, the hairs may be examined under the microscope. Certain types of ringworm of the scalp can be identified because they fluoresce (glow) under an ultraviolet lamp. Ringworm of the scalp will require the

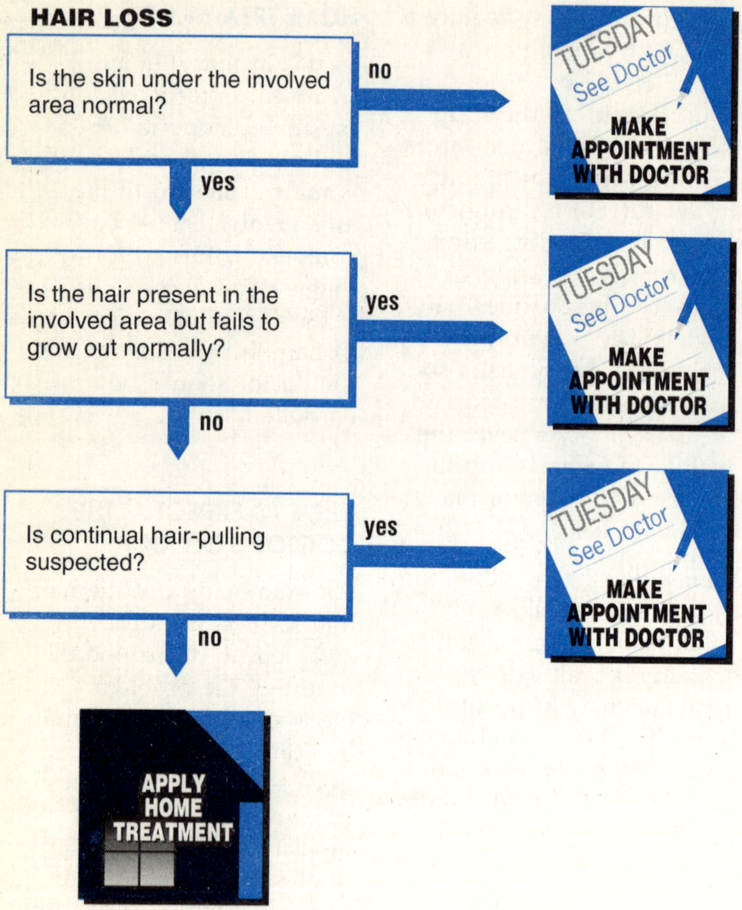


use of an oral drug, griseofulvin, because creams and lotions applied to the affected area will not penetrate into the hair follicles to kill the fungus.

We hope that no doctor would recommend the use of X-rays today as some did decades ago. If it is offered, you should flatly reject it and find another doctor.

There has been much discussion about medical treatments to prevent baldness. Hair transplants can help in some instances but are usually not fully satisfactory. The creams (minoxidil) only work a little and only early on; a lot of people are disappointed by this treatment.

# Impetigo

Impetigo is particularly troublesome in the summer, especially in warm, moist climates. It can be recognized by the characteristic lesions that begin as small red spots and progress to tiny blisters that eventually rupture, producing an oozing, sticky, honey-colored crust. These lesions usually spread very quickly with scratching.

Impetigo is a skin infection caused by streptococcal bacteria; occasionally, other bacteria may also be found. If it spreads, impetigo can be a very uncomfortable problem. There is usually a great deal of itching, and scratching hastens spreading of the lesions. After the sores heal, there may be a slight decrease in skin color at the site. Skin color usually returns to normal, so this need not concern you.

**Complication in the Kidneys**

Of greatest concern is a rare kidney problem known as **glomerulonephritis**. Glomerulonephritis will cause the urine to turn a dark brown (cola) color and is often accompanied by headache and elevated blood pressure. Although this complication has a formidable name, it is short-lived and heals completely in most people.

Unfortunately, antibiotics will not prevent glomerulonephritis but may help prevent the impetigo from spreading to other people, thus protecting them from both impetigo and glomerulonephritis. They are effective in healing the impetigo.

Although there is some debate on this matter, many doctors believe that if only one or two lesions are present and the lesions are not progressing, home treatment may be used for impetigo. The exception to this rule is if an epidemic of glomerulonephritis is occurring within your community.

## HOME TREATMENT

Crusts may be soaked off with either warm water or Burow's solution (Domeboro, Bluboro, etc.). Antibiotic ointments are no more effective than soap and water. The lesions should be scrubbed with soap and water after the crusts have been soaked off. If lesions do not show prompt improvement or if they seem to be spreading, the doctor should be seen without delay. Antibiotic ointments may be used but their value is debatable.

### IMPETIGO

Does the patient have small, crusted, yellow sores with or without a tiny surrounding area of redness?

**no** → Suspect problem other than impetigo. Check Skin Symptom Table on pages 274–275.

**yes** ↓

Has anyone in your family or neighborhood had glomerulonephritis recently?

**yes** →

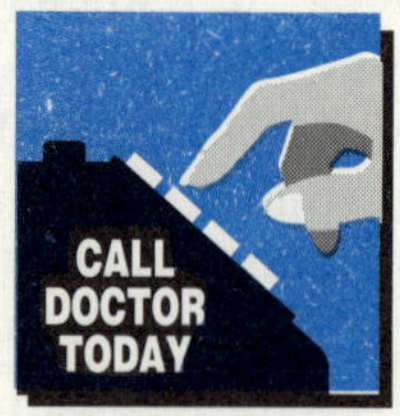


**no** ↓

Is there fever?

**yes** →

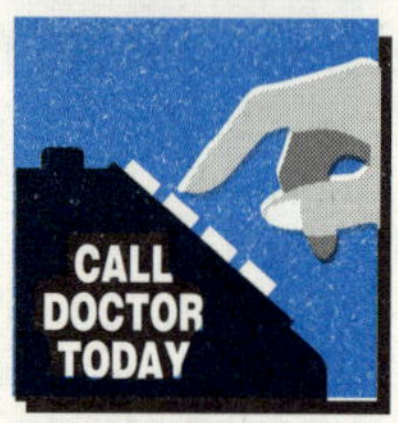


**no** ↓

Are there only one or two lesions?

**no** →

**yes** ↓

Are the lesions healing and not spreading to other family members?

**no** →

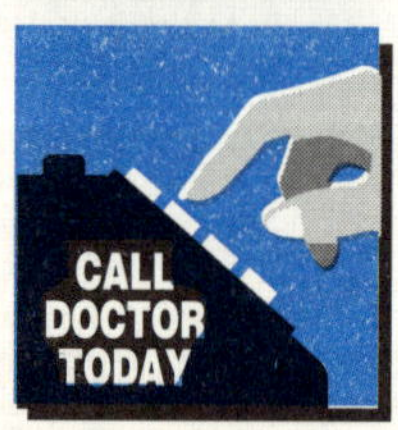


**yes** ↓

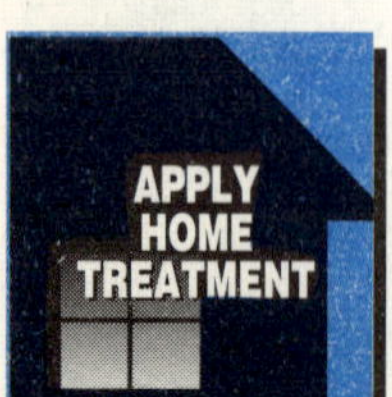


## WHAT TO EXPECT AT THE DOCTOR'S OFFICE

After examining the sores and taking an appropriate medical history, the doctor will usually prescribe an antibiotic to be taken by mouth. The drug of choice is penicillin unless there is penicillin allergy, in which case erythromycin is usually prescribed. Some doctors may check the blood pressure or urine in order to look for early signs of glomerulonephritis.

# Ringworm

Worms have nothing whatsoever to do with this condition. Ringworm is a shallow fungus infection of the skin. The designation "ringworm" is derived from the characteristic red ring that appears on the skin.

Ringworm can generally be recognized by its pattern of development. The lesions begin as small, round, red spots and get progressively larger. When they are about the size of a pea, the center begins to clear. When the lesions are about the size of a dime, they will have the appearance of a ring. The border will be red, elevated, and scaly. Often there are groups of infections so close to one another that it is difficult to recognize them as individual rings.

Ringworm may also affect the scalp or nails. These infections are more difficult to treat but fortunately are not seen very often. Ringworm epidemics of the scalp were common many years ago.

## HOME TREATMENT

Tolnaftate (Tinactin, etc.), miconazole (Micatin, etc.), and clotrimazole (Lotrimin, etc.) applied to the skin are effective treatments for ringworm. They are available in cream, solution, and powder and can be purchased over the counter. Either the cream or the solution should be applied two or three times a day. Only a small amount is required for each application. Resolution of the problem may require several weeks of therapy, but improvement should be noted within a week. Selsun Blue shampoo, applied as a cream several times a day, will often do the job and is less expensive. Ringworm that either shows no improvement after a week of therapy or continues to spread should be checked by a doctor.

## WHAT TO EXPECT AT THE DOCTOR'S OFFICE

The diagnosis of ringworm can be confirmed by scraping the scales, soaking them in a potassium hydroxide solution, and viewing them under the microscope. Some doctors may culture the scrapings. One of two agents usually will be prescribed if home treatment has failed: haloprogin (Halotex, etc.) or ciclopirox (Laprox, etc.).

**RINGWORM**

Are all of the following conditions present?

- Rash begins as a small red, colorless, or depigmented circle that becomes progressively larger.
- The circular border is elevated and perhaps scaly.
- The center of the circle begins healing as the circle becomes larger.

**no** → Suspect problem other than ringworm. Check Skin Symptom Table on pages 274–275.

**yes** ↓

Is the scalp infected?

**yes** → TUESDAY See Doctor **MAKE APPOINTMENT WITH DOCTOR**

**no** ↓

**APPLY HOME TREATMENT**

In infections involving the scalp, an ultraviolet light (called a Wood's lamp) will cause affected hairs to become fluorescent. The Wood's lamp is used to make the diagnosis; it does not treat ringworm. Ringworm of the scalp must be treated by griseofulvin, taken orally, usually for at least a month. This medication is also effective for fungal infections of the nails. Ringworm of the scalp should never be treated with X-rays.

# Hives

Hives are an allergic reaction. Unfortunately, the reaction can be to almost anything, including cold, heat, and even emotional tension. Unless you already have a good idea what is causing the hives or you have just taken a new drug, the doctor is unlikely to be able to determine the cause. Most often, searching for a cause is fruitless.

Here is a list of some of the things that are frequently mentioned as causes:

- drugs
- eggs
- milk
- wheat
- chocolate
- pork
- shellfish
- freshwater fish
- berries
- cheese
- nuts
- pollens
- insect bites

The only sure way to know whether one of these is the culprit is to expose the patient to it. The problem with this approach is that if an allergy does exist, the allergic reaction may include not only hives but also a systemic reaction causing difficulty with breathing or circulation.

As indicated by the decision chart, a systemic reaction is a potentially dangerous situation, and a doctor should be consulted immediately. Avoid exposure to a suspected cause to see if the attacks cease. Such a test is difficult to interpret because attacks of hives are often separated by long periods of time. Actually, most people suffer only one attack, lasting from a period of minutes to weeks.

Finally, an occasional single hive on the arm or trunk is so common that it is considered normal and of no significance. You may want to read about allergies in Chapter H.

## HOME TREATMENT

Determine whether there has been any pattern to the appearance of the hives. Do they appear after meals? After exposure to cold? During a particular season of the year? If there seem to be likely possibilities, eliminate them and see what happens.

If the reactions seem to be related to foods, an alternative is available. Lamb and rice virtually never cause allergic reactions. The patient may be placed on a diet consisting only of lamb and rice until completely free of

## HIVES

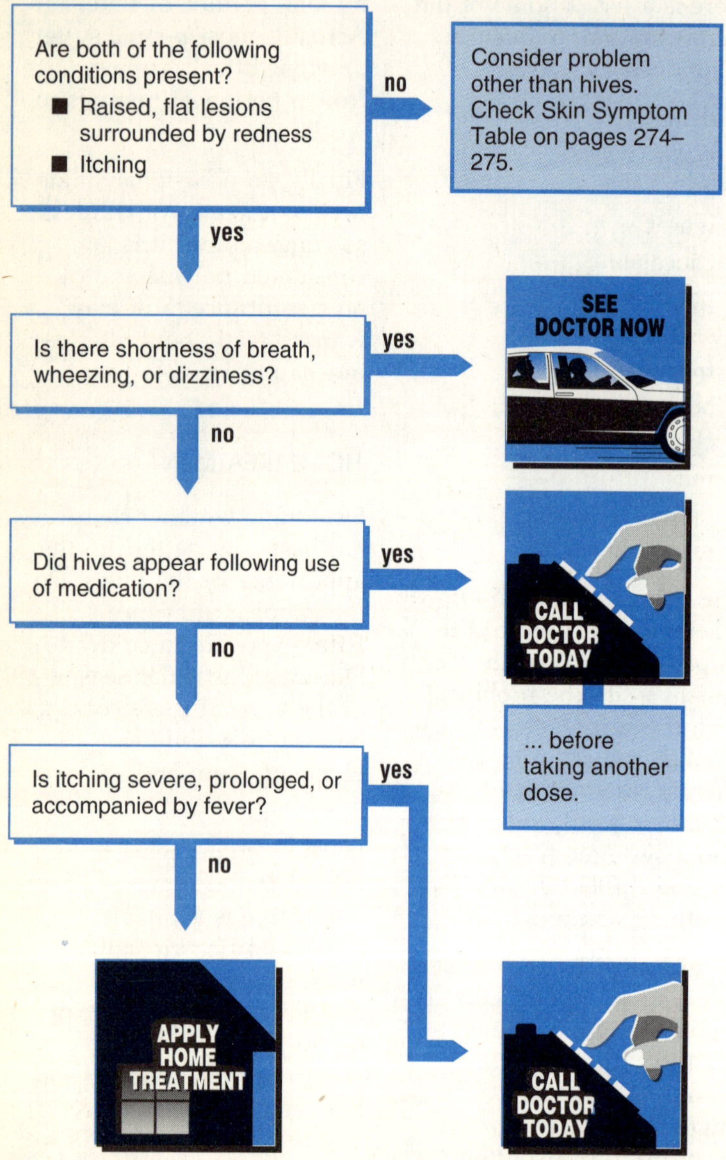


hives. Foods are then added back to the diet one at a time and the patient is observed for a recurrence of hives.

Itching may be relieved by applying cold compresses, taking aspirin, or trying antihistamines such as diphenhydramine or chlorpheniramine (see Chapter 9, "The Home Pharmacy").

### WHAT TO EXPECT AT THE DOCTOR'S OFFICE

If the patient is suffering a systemic reaction with difficulty breathing or dizziness, injections of adrenalin and other drugs may be given. In the more usual case of hives alone, the doctor may do two things. First, the doctor may prescribe an antihistamine or use adrenalin injections to relieve swelling and itching. Second, the doctor can review the history of the reaction to try to find an offending agent and advise you as to home treatment. Remember that most often the cause of hives goes undetected, and they stop occurring without any therapy.

# Poison Ivy and Poison Oak

Poison ivy and poison oak need little introduction. The itching skin lesions that follow contact with the plant oil of these and other members of the *Rhus* plant family are the most common example of a larger category of skin problems known as **contact dermatitis**. Contact dermatitis simply means that something that has been applied to the skin has caused the skin to react to it. An initial exposure is necessary to "sensitize" the patient; a subsequent exposure will result in an allergic reaction if the plant oil remains in contact with skin for several hours. The resulting rash begins after a delay of 12 to 48 hours and persists for about two weeks.

You do not have to come into direct contact with plants to get poison ivy. The plant oil may be spread by pets, contaminated clothing, or the smoke from burning *Rhus* plants. It can occur during any season.

## HOME TREATMENT

The best approach is to teach your children to recognize and avoid the plants, which are hazardous even in the winter when they have dropped their leaves.

Next best is to remove the plant oil from the skin as soon as possible. If the oil has been on the skin for less than six hours, thorough cleansing with ordinary soap, repeated three times, will often prevent a reaction. Alcohol-based cleansing tissues, available in pre-packaged form (such as Alco-wipe), are much more effective. Rubbing alcohol on a washcloth is even better, and is our favorite remedy. Recently a new solvent (Tecnu) has been shown to be effective in removing the oil and preventing the rash. Rubbing alcohol is a lot less expensive, however.

To relieve itching, many doctors recommend cool compresses of Burow's solution (Domeboro, BurVeen, Bluboro) or baths with Aveeno or oatmeal (one cup to a tub full of water). Aspirin is also effective in reducing itching. The old standby, calamine lotion, sometimes helps for early lesions but may spread the plant oil. (**Caution:** *Caladryl and Ziradryl are reported to cause allergic reactions in some people. Plain calamine lotion may be best.)* Be sure to cleanse the skin, as above, even if you are too late to prevent the rash entirely.

Another method of obtaining symptomatic relief is a hot bath or shower. Heat releases histamine, the substance in skin cells that causes the intense itching. Therefore, a hot shower or bath will cause intense itching as the histamine is released. The heat should be gradually increased to the maximum tolerable and continued until the itching has subsided. This process will deplete the cells of histamine and the patient will obtain up to eight hours of relief from the

**POISON IVY**

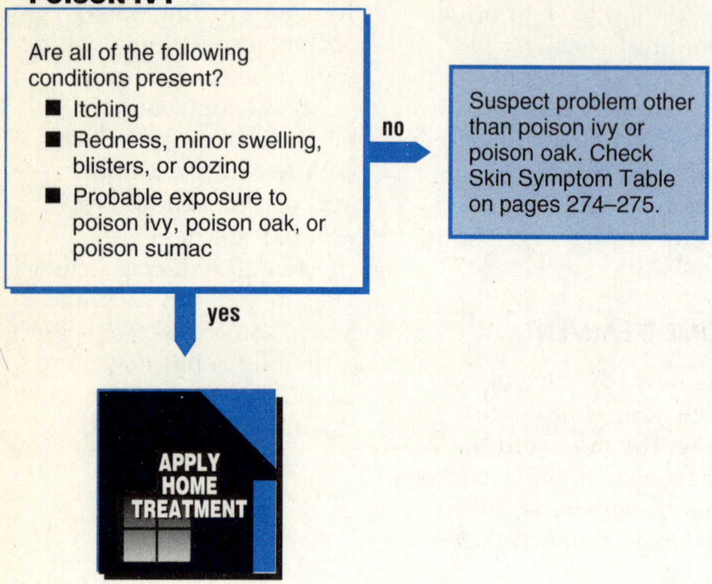


itching. This method has the advantage of not requiring frequent applications of ointments to the lesions and is a good way to get some sleep at night.

One-half percent hydrocortisone creams (Cortaid or Lanacort, for example) are available without prescription. They will decrease inflammation and itching, but relief is not immediate. The cream must be applied often (four to six times a day). Do not use these creams for prolonged periods (see Chapter 9, "The Home Pharmacy").

Poison ivy and poison oak will persist for the same length of time with or without medication. If secondary bacterial infection occurs, healing will be delayed; hence, scratching is not helpful. Cut nails to avoid damage to the skin.

Poison ivy is not contagious. It cannot be spread once the oil has been either absorbed by the skin or removed.

If the lesions are too extensive to be easily treated, if home treatment is ineffective, or if the itching is so severe that it can't be tolerated, a call to the doctor may be necessary.

## WHAT TO EXPECT AT THE DOCTOR'S OFFICE

After a history and physical examination, the doctor may prescribe a steroid cream stronger than 0.5% hydrocortisone to be applied to the lesions four to six times a day. This often helps only moderately. An alternative is to give a steroid (such as prednisone) by mouth for short periods of time. A rather large dose is given the first day, and the dose is then gradually reduced. We do not recommend oral steroids except when there have been either severe reactions to poison ivy or poison oak previously or extensive exposure. The itching may be treated symptomatically with either an antihistamine (Benadryl or Vistaril, for example) or aspirin. The antihistamines may cause drowsiness and interfere with sleep.

# Rashes Caused by Chemicals

Chemicals may cause a rash, **contact dermatitis**, in two ways. The chemical may have a direct caustic effect that irritates the skin—a minor "chemical burn." More often the rash is due to an allergic reaction of the skin to the chemical. The most common allergic dermatitis is **poison ivy** (see page 289). If you see a rash that looks like poison ivy, but contact with poison ivy or poison oak seems impossible, consider other chemicals that can cause an allergic contact dermatitis and produce an identical rash.

The chemicals most frequently found to cause contact dermatitis are dyes and other chemicals found in clothing, chemicals used in elastic and rubber products, cosmetics, and deodorants (including "feminine" deodorants.)

Usually the tip-off to the cause of the rash is its location and shape. Sometimes this is very striking as the rash leaves a perfect outline of a bra or the elastic bands of underwear or some other article of clothing. More often the rash is not so distinct, but its location suggests the possible cause.

## HOME TREATMENT

If you have had difficulty with particular types of clothing, cosmetics, deodorants, and so on, then avoiding contact is the best way to avoid a problem, of course. Changing brands may also help. For example, some cosmetics are manufactured so that they are less likely to cause an allergic reaction (hypoallergenic products). Rashes caused by deodorants are often the direct caustic type so that using a milder preparation less often may solve the problem.

Once the rash has occurred, eliminating contact with the chemical is essential. Washing thoroughly with soap and water may remove chemicals on the skin and is especially important with materials such as cement dust. Oily substances may best be removed with rubbing alcohol, or use paint thinner quickly followed by soap and water to prevent contact dermatitis from the cleaner itself.

### RASHES FROM CHEMICALS

Is this a red rash (sometimes with bumps or blisters and usually itchy or burning) that by its shape and location suggests contact with articles of clothing, cosmetics, deodorant, or other chemicals?

**no** → Suspect problem other than contact dermatitis. Check Skin Symptom Table on pages 274–275.

**yes** ↓

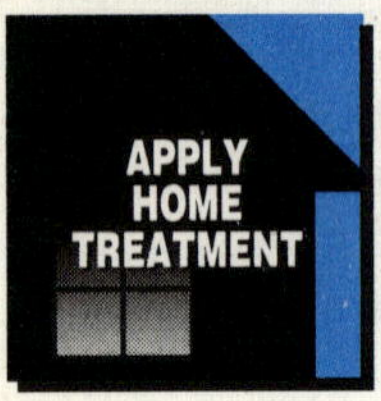


The rest of the home treatment is identical to that of poison ivy (see page 289) and consists of using Burow's solution, hot water, and 1.0% hydrocortisone cream to achieve relief from itching. If the lesions are too extensive to be treated easily, if home treatment is ineffective, or if the itching is so severe that it can't be tolerated, a call to the doctor may be necessary.

## WHAT TO EXPECT AT THE DOCTOR'S OFFICE

The doctor will examine the rash. A review of the patient's history will focus on possible exposure to substances such as those listed in the chart. A steroid cream stronger than 1.0% hydrocortisone may be prescribed. Another alternative is to give a steroid (such as prednisone) for a short period of time; a rather large dose is given the first day and the dose is then gradually reduced. Itching may be treated symptomatically with either an antihistamine (Benadryl, Vistaril, etc.) and/or pain relievers (aspirin, ibuprofen, or acetaminophen). Antihistamines may cause drowsiness or interfere with sleep. Preventing a reaction is better.

# Skin Cancer

There is no easy, sure way to identify skin cancer. The guidelines given here are those that doctors use in confronting this dilemma. When in doubt, they will remove or biopsy the lesion. You can do no better, so, when in doubt, see a doctor.

Decisions will be easier if you are familiar with common non-cancerous skin lesions. These include:

- Plain old freckles (flat, uniform, tan to dark brown color, regular border usually less than one-quarter inch in diameter)
- Warts (skin-colored, raised, rounded, rough or flat surface)
- Skin tags (wobbly tags of skin on a stalk)
- Seborrheic keratoses (greasy, dirty tan to brown, raised, flat lesions that first appear in mid-life on face, chest, and back and increase in number with the passing years)

### Types of Skin Cancer

The vast majority of skin cancers fall into three categories. **Malignant melanoma** is by far the most dangerous. Although often described as a mole that has undergone cancerous change, melanomas often do not look very much like moles. For example, they may be flat.

Doctors use two sets of criteria in judging the likelihood that the problem is a melanoma. First, there are changes in size, color, surface, shape or border that raise suspicion. The more rapid, unusual, and irregular these changes are, the higher suspicion is raised. Second, there are characteristics that are highly suspicious regardless of whether you are sure that these have changed recently. Variation in color (tans, browns, or blacks) is unusual for a benign lesion, but hues of red, white, and blue are almost never seen in such a lesion. A benign lesion usually has a regular border; an irregular border suggests the spread of abnormal cells.

**Squamous cell cancers** are raised, usually somewhat nodular lesions with rough, scaly surfaces on a reddish base. The border is usually irregular, and they often ulcerate and bleed. These lesions grow slowly and usually do not spread to other parts of the body. Most often they are recognized as sores that don't heal. **Solar** (actinic) **keratoses** have an appearance similar to squamous cell carcinoma except that they are not nodular and rarely ulcerate or bleed. Although solar keratoses are not malignant, they are considered to be a precursor of cancer and are often treated to avoid the development of cancer.

**Basal cell cancers** appear as pearly or waxy nodules with central depressions or ulcerations. As this cancer enlarges, the center usually becomes more ulcerated, giving it the appearance of having been gnawed. Hence, the term "rodent ulcer" is sometimes applied. This type of cancer grows slowly and only by direct extension so that it never spreads (metastasizes) to other organs of the body.

All these cancers are related to sun exposure. Squamous cell and basal cell cancers appear almost exclusively on the areas of skin most exposed to sun (head, neck, hands). Although melanoma is more common in these areas, it may also appear on covered areas such as the chest or back. Melanoma is most common in people who have had one or more severe blistering sunburns before the age of 18.

## HOME TREATMENT

This consists of watchful waiting and prevention. If the lesion has none of the characteristics that raise suspicion, then closely watching for change makes sense. But, if you are in doubt, see the doctor.

Let's face it, sun is no good for your skin. Sunscreens, hats with wide brims, long sleeves, and long pants will decrease the risk of skin cancer as well as keep your skin younger looking.

Non-cancerous lesions can be treated if they are troublesome. The doctor has a number of ways of removing these lesions that are not available to you at home.

Don't forget to mention any skin concerns when you make your next visit to the doctor for another reason. You can get the benefit of a medical opinion without the inconvenience or cost of a special trip.

## WHAT TO EXPECT AT THE DOCTOR'S OFFICE

Dermatologists (skin specialists) can usually offer the best advice about skin lesions because they have more experience with the diagnosis and treatment of these problems. Successful treatment can be accomplished on the initial visit and often doesn't require surgery.

A reminder: If you get one of these cancers, you are likely to get another. So, once you've had the first one cured, it is a good idea to have regular examinations to make sure that nothing new has developed. Avoiding further damage to the skin from the sun is a good way to make these checkups pleasant.

**SKIN CANCER**

Is there either of the following?

- Variation in color, especially the appearance of red, white, or blue
- Irregularity (notching, streaking) in the border

**yes** →

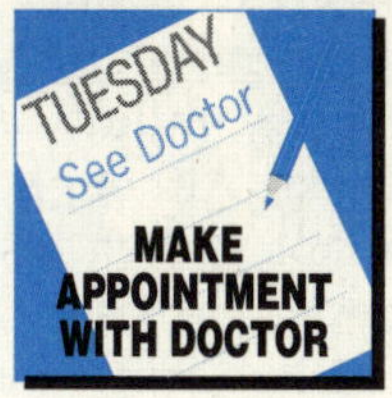


**no** ↓

Has there been a change in any of the following?

- Size (sudden increase in diameter)
- Color (streaking, mottled)
- Surface (irregular, ulcerated, bleeding)
- Shape (flat to raised, nodular)
- Border (notching, "leaking" of pigment)

**yes** →

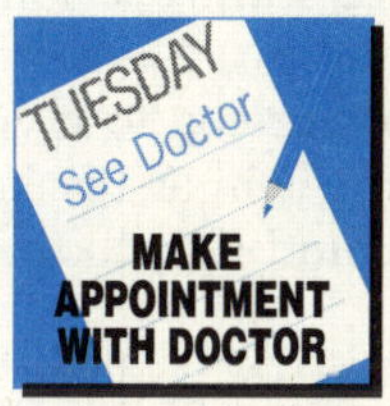


**no** ↓

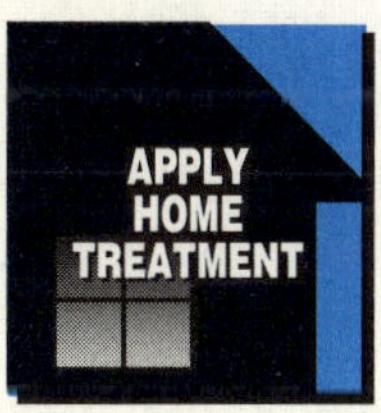


**Warts can be treated successfully at home using non-prescription preparations such as Compound W and Vergo. They usually go away by themselves anyway. You should see a doctor only for plantar warts appearing on the sole of the foot (see Foot Pain, page 380).**

# Eczema

Eczema is commonly found in people with a family history of either eczema, hay fever, or asthma. The underlying problem is the inability of the skin to retain adequate amounts of water. The skin of people with eczema is consequently very dry, which causes the skin to itch. Most of the manifestations of eczema are a result of scratching. For more information on allergy-related eczema, see page 269.

In young infants who are unable to scratch, the most common manifestation is red, dry, mildly scaling cheeks. Although the infant cannot scratch his or her cheeks, the cheeks can be rubbed against the sheets and thus become red. In infants, eczema may also be found in the area where plastic pants meet the skin. The tightness of the elastic produces the characteristic red, scaling lesion. In older children, it is very common for eczema to involve the area behind the knees and behind the elbows.

If there is a large amount of weeping or crusting, the eczema may be infected with bacteria, and a call to the doctor will most likely be required.

The course of eczema is quite variable. Some will have only a brief, mild problem; others have mild-to-severe manifestations throughout life.

### HOME TREATMENT

Attempts must be made to prevent the skin from becoming too dry, and frequent bathing makes the skin even drier. Although the person will feel comfortable in the bath, itching will become more intense after the bath because of its drying effect.

Sweating aggravates eczema. Avoid overdressing. Light night clothing is important. Contact with wool and silk seems to aggravate eczema and should be avoided.

Nails should be kept trimmed short to minimize the effects of scratching. Use rubber gloves to help prevent dryness of the hands when washing dishes or the car.

Washing is best accomplished with a cleansing and moisturizing agent (Cetaphil lotion, etc.).

Freshwater or pool swimming can aggravate eczema by causing loss of skin moisture, but ocean swimming does not do so and can be freely undertaken. (Also see Chapter H, "Allergies.")

**ECZEMA**

Are at least two of the following conditions present?

- Itching
- Flat red areas on cheeks, behind ears, on wrists, behind knees, or in front of elbows
- Family history of allergy

**no** → Suspect problem other than eczema. Check Skin Symptom Table on pages 274–275.

**yes** ↓

Is there any crusting of lesions?

**yes** →

**no** ↓

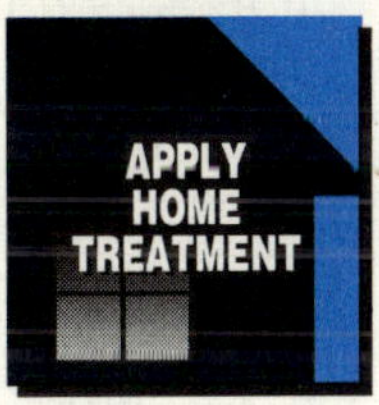


## WHAT TO EXPECT AT THE DOCTOR'S OFFICE

By history and examination of the lesions, the doctor can determine whether the problem is eczema. If home treatment has not improved the problem, steroid creams and lotions may be prescribed. While these are effective, they are not curative; eczema is characterized by repeated occurrences. If crusted or weeping lesions are present, bacterial infection is likely and an oral antibiotic will be prescribed.

# Boils

"Painful as a boil" is a familiar term and emphasizes the severe discomfort that can arise from this common skin problem. A boil is a localized infection usually due to the staphylococcus bacteria. Often a particularly savage strain of the bacteria is responsible. When this particular germ inhabits the skin, recurrent problems with boils may persist for months or years. Often several family members will be affected at about the same time.

Boils may be single or multiple, and they may occur anywhere on the body. They range from the size of a pea to the size of a walnut or larger. The surrounding red, thickened, and tender tissue increases the problem even further. The infection begins in the tissues beneath the skin and develops into an abscess pocket filled with pus. Eventually, the pus pocket "points" toward the skin surface and finally ruptures and drains. Then it heals.

Boils often begin as infections around hair follicles, hence the term **folliculitis** for minor infections. Areas under pressure (such as the buttocks) are often likely spots for boils to begin. A boil that extends into the deeper layers of the skin is called a **carbuncle**.

Special consideration should be given to boils on the face because they are more likely to lead to serious complicating infections.

## HOME TREATMENT

The goal of treatment is to let it all out—the pus, that is. Boils are handled gently, because rough treatment can force the infection deeper inside the body. Warm, moist compresses are applied gently several times each day to speed the development of a pocket of pus and to soften the skin for the eventual rupture and drainage. Once drainage begins, the compresses will help keep the opening in the skin clear. The more drainage, the better. Frequent, thorough soaping of the entire skin helps prevent reinfection. Ignore all temptation to squeeze the boil.

## WHAT TO EXPECT AT THE DOCTOR'S OFFICE

If there is fever or a facial boil, the doctor will usually prescribe an antibiotic. Otherwise, antibiotics may not be used. They are of limited help in abscess-like infections.

If the boil feels as if fluid is contained in a pocket but has not yet drained, the doctor may lance the boil. In this procedure, a small incision is made to allow the pus to drain. After drainage, the pain is reduced, and healing is quite prompt. While this is not a complicated procedure, it is tricky enough that you should not attempt it yourself.

## BOILS

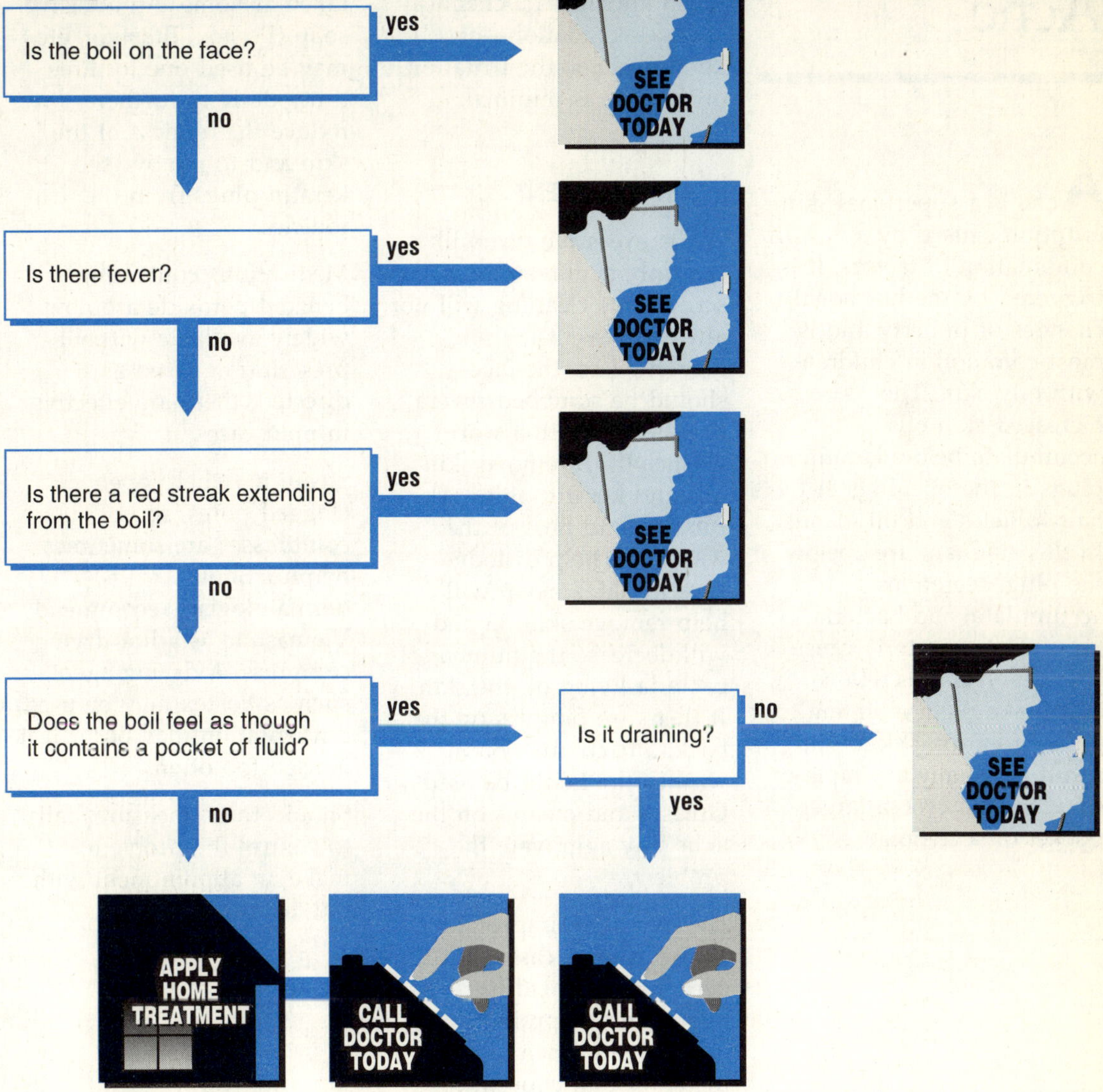

Is the boil on the face?
yes
SEE DOCTOR TODAY
no
Is there fever?
yes
SEE DOCTOR TODAY
no
Is there a red streak extending from the boil?
yes
SEE DOCTOR TODAY
no
Does the boil feel as though it contains a pocket of fluid?
yes
Is it draining?
no
SEE DOCTOR TODAY
yes
CALL DOCTOR TODAY
no
APPLY HOME TREATMENT
CALL DOCTOR TODAY

# Acne

Acne is a superficial skin eruption caused by a combination of factors. It is triggered by the hormonal changes of puberty and is most common in children with oily skin. The increased skin oils accumulate below keratin plugs in the openings of the hair follicles and oil glands. In this stagnant area below the plug, secretions accumulate, and bacteria grow. These bacteria cause changes in the secretions that make them irritating to the surrounding skin. The result is usually a pimple or sometimes a cyst, a larger pocket of secretions.

**Blackheads** are formed when air causes a chemical change—oxidation—of keratin plugs; the irritation of the skin is minimal.

## HOME TREATMENT

While excessive dirt will certainly aggravate acne, scrupulous cleaning will not always prevent it. Nevertheless, the face should be scrubbed several times daily with a warm washcloth to remove skin oils and keratin plugs. The rubbing and heat of the washcloth help dislodge keratin plugs. Soap will help remove skin oil and will decrease the number of bacteria living on the skin. If there are pimples on the back, a backbrush or washcloth should be used. Greases and creams on the skin may aggravate the problem.

Diet is not an important factor in most cases, but if certain foods tend to aggravate the problem, avoid them. There is scant evidence that chocolate aggravates acne, despite popular belief.

Several further steps may be taken at home. An abrasive soap (Pernox, Brasivol, etc.) may be used one to three times daily to further reduce the oiliness of the skin and to remove the keratin plugs from the follicles.

Medications containing benzoyl peroxide are now widely available without prescription. Used as directed, these are effective in mild cases.

Steam may help open clogged pores, so hot compresses are sometimes helpful. Some dermatologists recommend Vlemasque as a hot drying compress. A drying agent such as Fostex may be used, but irritation may occur if it is used too often.

Should these measures fail to control the problem, make an appointment with the doctor.

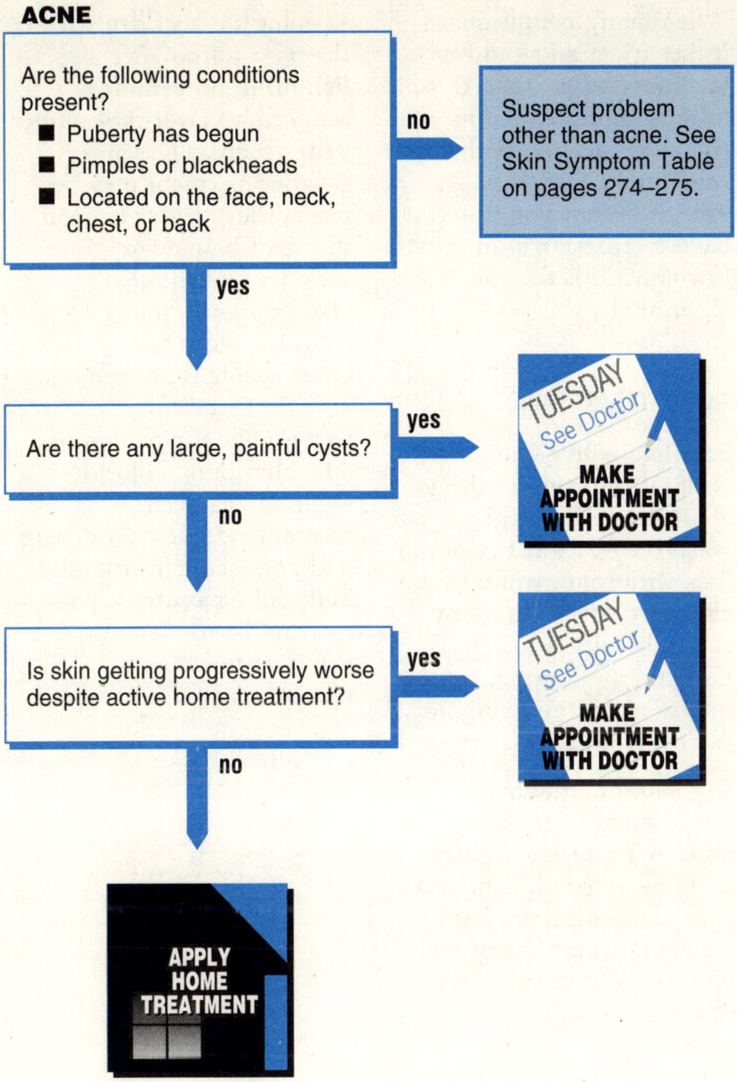


## WHAT TO EXPECT AT THE DOCTOR'S OFFICE

The doctor will advise about hygiene and the use of medications. Several new topical preparations such as retinoic acid (Retin-A) and benzoyl peroxide have been found helpful; they act by fostering skin peeling or eliminating bacteria. The peeling is not noticeable if the medication is used properly.

In resistant cases, an antibiotic (tetracycline or erythromycin) may be prescribed to be taken by mouth. Some doctors prescribe these antibiotics for application to the skin as well.

"Acne surgery" is a term generally applied to the doctor's removal of blackheads with a suction device and an eyedropper. Large developing cysts are sometimes arrested with the injection of steroids. Such procedures should be required only in severe cases and are more often performed on the back than on the face.

# Athlete's Foot

Athlete's foot is very common during and after adolescence, and relatively uncommon before. It is the most common of the fungal infections and is often persistent. When it involves toenails, it can be difficult to treat.

Moisture contributes significantly to the development of this problem. Some doctors believe bacteria and moisture cause most of this problem and that the fungus is only responsible for keeping things going.

When many people share locker room and shower facilities, exposure to this fungus is impossible to prevent; infection is the rule, rather than the exception. But you don't have to participate in sports to contact this fungus; it's all around.

## HOME TREATMENT

Scrupulous hygiene, without resorting to drugs, is often effective. *Twice a day* wash the space between the toes with soap, water, and a cloth. Dry the entire area carefully with a towel, particularly between the toes (despite the pain) and put on clean socks.

Use shoes that allow evaporation of moisture. Shoes with plastic linings must be avoided. Sandals or canvas sneakers are best. Changing shoes every other day to allow them to dry out is a good idea.

Keeping the feet dry with the use of a powder is helpful in preventing reinfection. Over-the-counter drugs such as Desenex powder or cream may be used. The powder has the virtue of helping keep the toes dry. Tolnaftate (Tinactin, etc.), miconazole (Micatin, etc.), and clotrimazole (Lotrimin, etc.) are effective. The twice-daily application of a 30% aluminum chloride solution has been recommended for its drying and antibacterial properties. You will have to ask your pharmacist to make up the solution, but it is inexpensive.

**ATHLETE'S FOOT**

Are both of the following conditions present?

- Redness and scaling between toes (may have cracks and small blisters)
- Itching

**no** → Suspect problem other than athlete's foot. Check Skin Symptom Table on pages 274–275.

**yes** → APPLY HOME TREATMENT

## WHAT TO EXPECT AT THE DOCTOR'S OFFICE

Through history, physical examination, and possibly microscopic examination of a skin scraping, the doctor will establish the diagnosis. Several other problems, notably a condition called **dyshydrosis**, may mimic athlete's foot. Haloprogin (Halotex) and ciclopirox (Loprox) are prescription creams and ointments that are effective against fungal infections of the skin, but not against fungal infections of nails (ciclopirox seems to work on nails occasionally). An oral drug, griseofulvin, may be used for the nails but is not recommended otherwise.

# Jock Itch

We might wish for a less picturesque name for this condition, but the medical term, *tinea cruris*, is understood by few. Jock itch is a fungus infection of the pubic region. It is aggravated by friction and moisture. It usually does not involve the scrotum or penis, nor does it spread beyond the groin area. (For the most part, this is a male disease.) Frequently, the fungus grows in an athletic supporter turned old and moldy in a locker room far from a washing machine. The preventive measure for such a problem is obvious.

## HOME TREATMENT

The problem should be treated by removing the contributing factors—friction and moisture. This is done by wearing boxer shorts rather than closer-fitting shorts or jockey briefs, by applying a powder to dry the area after bathing, and by frequently changing soiled or sweaty underclothes. It may take up to two weeks to completely clear the problem, and it may recur. The "powder-air-and-clean-shorts" treatment will usually be successful without any medication. Tolnaftate (Tinactin, etc.), miconazole (Micatin, etc.), or clotrimazole (Lotrimin, etc.) will usually eliminate the fungus if the problem persists.

## WHAT TO EXPECT AT THE DOCTOR'S OFFICE

Occasionally, a **yeast infection** will mimic jock itch. By examination and history, the doctor will attempt to establish the diagnosis and may also make a scraping in order to identify yeast. Medicines for this problem are virtually always applied to the affected skin; oral drugs or injections are rarely used. Haloprogin (Halotex) and ciclopirox (Loprox) are prescription creams and lotions that are effective against both fungi and certain yeast infections.

## JOCK ITCH

Are all of the following conditions present?

- Involves only the groin and thighs
- Redness, oozing, or some peripheral scaling
- Itching

**no** → Suspect problem other than jock itch. Check Skin Symptom Table on pages 274–275.

**yes** ↓

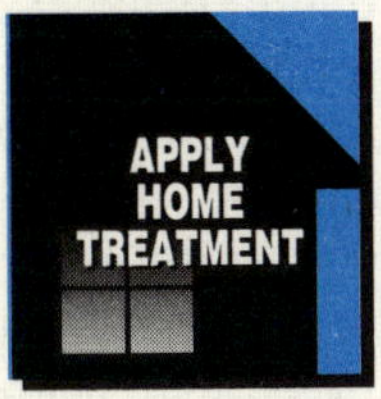

# Sunburn

Sunburn is common, painful, and avoidable. It is better prevented than treated. Effective sunscreens are available in a wide variety of strengths, as indicated by their sun protection factor or SPF. An SPF of 4 offers little protection, whereas 16 or above offers substantial protection.

Regardless of what you have heard, there are no sun rays that tan but don't burn. Tanning salons can fry you just as surely as the sun can.

The pain of sunburn is worst between 6 and 48 hours after sun exposure. Peeling of injured layers of skin occurs later—between 3 and 10 days after the burn.

Very rarely, people with sunburn have difficulty with vision. If so, they should see a doctor. Otherwise, a visit to the doctor is unnecessary unless the pain is extraordinarily severe or extensive blistering (not peeling) has occurred. Blistering indicates a second-degree burn and rarely follows sun exposure.

## HOME TREATMENT

Cool compresses or cool oatmeal baths (Aveeno, etc.) may be useful. Ordinary baking soda (one-half cup to a tub) is nearly as effective. Lubricants such as Vaseline feel good to some people, but they retain heat and should not be used the first day. Avoid products that contain benzocaine. These may give temporary relief but can irritate the skin and may actually delay healing. Aspirin by mouth may ease pain and thus help the patient sleep.

**SUNBURN**

Are any of these conditions present following prolonged exposure to sun?

- Fever
- Fluid-filled blisters
- Dizziness
- Visual difficulties

yes

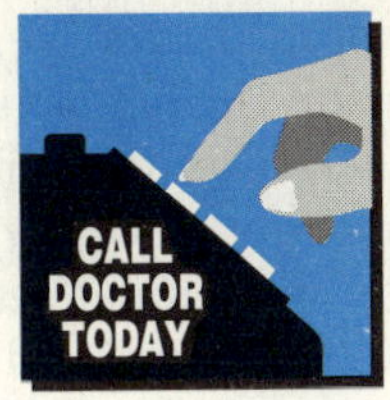


no

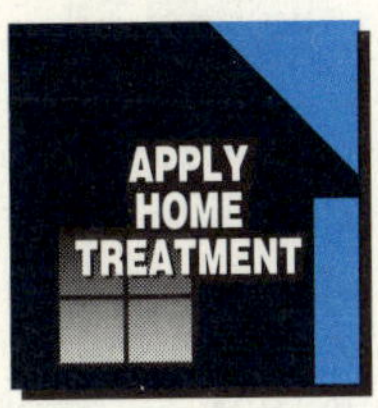


## WHAT TO EXPECT AT THE DOCTOR'S OFFICE

The doctor will direct the history and physical examination toward determining the extent of the burn and the possibility of other heat-related injuries like sunstroke. If only first-degree burns are found, a prescription steroid lotion may be prescribed. This is not particularly beneficial. The rare second-degree burns may be treated with antibiotics in addition to analgesics or sedation.

**Minor frostbite is surprisingly common among skiers and others indulging in winter recreational activities. Prevention is the key. Wear warm clothing. When your torso is warm, the blood flow to the fingers and toes is better. Don't forget a face mask. Use mittens instead of gloves when it is very cold. If there is wind, be sure that you have windproof outer garments.**

**If your fingers or nose or toes start to hurt despite these precautions, it's a warning to get out of the cold. If they begin to numb, you are starting to get frostbite. It used to be said that you should warm up a frostbitten limb slowly. Not so. Warm it up as quickly as possible with gentle rubbing. As the blood flow resumes, the frostbitten part will begin to hurt, sometimes a lot. This is a good sign, since the tissues are obviously still alive.**

**You may have leftover numbness for several months after minor frostbite, but this does not require medical attention. However, if tissues turn black, see a doctor so that the threatened tissues can be best preserved.**

# Lice and Bedbugs

Lice and bedbugs are found in the best of families. Lack of prejudice with respect to social class is as close as these insects come to having a virtue. At best they are a nuisance, and at worst they can cause real disability.

**Lice**

Lice themselves are very small and are seldom seen without the aid of a magnifying glass. Usually it is easier to find the "nits," which are clusters of louse eggs. Without magnification, nits will appear as tiny white lumps on hair strands.

The louse bite leaves only a pinpoint red spot, but scratching makes things worse. Itching and occasionally small, shallow sores at the base of hairs are clues to the disease.

Pubic lice are not a venereal disease, although they may be spread from person to person during sexual contact. Unlike syphilis and gonorrhea, lice may be spread by toilet seats, infected linen, and other sources. Pubic lice bear some resemblance to crabs. Hence, the term "crabs" is used to indicate a lice infestation of the pubic hair. A different species of lice may inhabit the scalp or other body hair.

Lice like to be close to a warm body all the time and will not stay for long periods of time in clothing that is not being worn, bedding, or other places.

**Bedbugs**

Although related to lice, bedbugs present a considerably different picture. The adult is flat, wingless, reddish in color, oval in shape, and about one-quarter inch in length. Like lice, they stay alive by sucking blood. Unlike lice, they feed for only 10 or 15 minutes at a time and spend the rest of the time hiding in crevices and crannies.

Bedbugs feed almost entirely at night, both because that is when bodies are in bed and also because they strongly dislike light. They have such a keen sense of the nearness of a warm body that the army has used them to detect the approach of an enemy at ranges of several hundred feet! Catching these pests out in the open is very difficult and may require some curious behavior. One technique is to dash into the bedroom at bedtime, flip on the lights and pull back the bedcovers in an effort to catch them anticipating their next meal.

The bite of the bedbug leaves a firm bump. Usually there are two or three bumps clustered together. Occasionally, sensitivity develops to these bites, in which case itching may be severe and blisters may form.

## HOME TREATMENT

Over-the-counter preparations are effective against lice; these include A200, Cuprex, and RID. RID has the advantage of supplying a fine-tooth comb, a rare item these

**LICE AND BEDBUGS**

Is either of the following conditions present?
- Lice seen on the skin or in clothing
- Nits seen on hair shafts

yes → **APPLY HOME TREATMENT**

no ↓

Have bedbugs been seen on or near bed?

yes → **APPLY HOME TREATMENT**

no ↓

Consider a problem other than lice or bedbugs. Check Skin Symptom Table on pages 274–275.

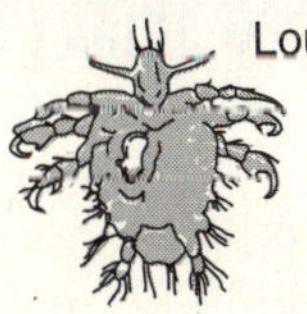

Louse X 10

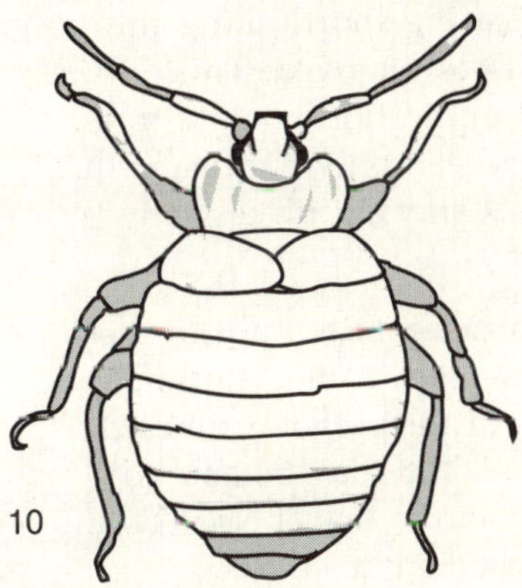

Bedbug X 10

days. Instructions that come with these drugs must be followed carefully. Linen and clothing must be changed simultaneously. Sexual partners should be treated at the same time.

Because bedbugs don't hide on the body or in clothes, it is the bed and the room that should be treated. Contact your local health department for information and help in doing this. Chemical sprays may be useful, but simply getting the infested bedding outdoors and exposed to sun and air for several days works, too.

## WHAT TO EXPECT AT THE DOCTOR'S OFFICE

If lice are the suspected problem, the doctor will make a careful inspection to find nits or the lice themselves. Doctors almost always use lindane (Kwell, Scabene) for lice. It may be somewhat more effective than the over-the-counter preparations. It is more expensive and has more side effects.

The doctor will be hard-pressed to make a certain diagnosis of bedbug bites without information from you that bedbugs have been seen in the house. However, the bumps may be suggestive, and initially it may be decided to assume that the problem is bedbugs. If this is the case, treatment with an insecticide as discussed under "Home Treatment" will be recommended.

# Ticks

Outdoor living has its dangers. While bears, mountain lions, and steep cliffs can usually be avoided, shrubs and tall grasses hide tiny insects eager for a blood meal from a passing animal or person. Ticks are the most common of these small hazards.

Ticks are about one-quarter inch long and easily seen. A tick bite usually has the creature who made it sticking out.

In some areas, ticks carry diseases, such as Rocky Mountain spotted fever and Lyme disease. If a fever, rash, joint pains, or headache follow a tick bite by a few days or weeks, a doctor should be consulted.

If a pregnant female tick is allowed to remain feeding for several days, under certain circumstances a peculiar condition called tick paralysis may develop. The female tick secretes a toxin that can cause temporary paralysis, clearing shortly after the tick is removed. This complication is quite rare and can only happen if the tick stays in place many days.

In tick-infested areas, check yourself, your children, and your pets several times a day. You may be able to catch the ticks before they become embedded.

### HOME TREATMENT

Ticks should be removed, although they will eventually "fester out"; complications are unusual. The trick is to get the tick to "let go" and not to squeeze the tick before getting it out. If the mouth parts and the pincers remain under the skin, healing may require several weeks. Rocky Mountain spotted fever and Lyme disease are somewhat more likely if mouth parts are left in or the tick is squeezed during removal. Make the tick uncomfortable. Grasp the tick with tweezers or with gloved fingers as close to the skin as possible, then pull straight up with slow, even pressure. If the head is

**TICKS**

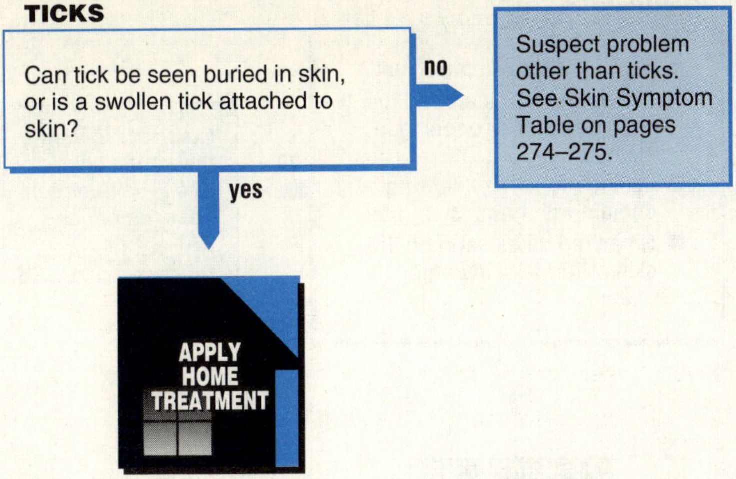


inadvertently left under the skin, soak gently with warm water twice daily until healing is complete. Call the doctor at once if the patient gets a fever, rash, or headache within three weeks.

Steroid creams (Cortaid, Lanacort, etc.) may be tried, but are usually not much help (see Chapter 9, "The Home Pharmacy").

## WHAT TO EXPECT AT THE DOCTOR'S OFFICE

The doctor can remove the tick but cannot prevent any illness that might have been transmitted. You can do just as well. Ticks are often removed from unusual places, such as armpits and belly buttons, but the scalp is the most common location. The technique is exactly the same no matter where the tick is.

# Chiggers

Chiggers are another small hazard of nature. Anyone who grew up in areas where they are common can testify to how excruciating the itch from chiggers' bites can be.

Chiggers are small red mites, sometimes called "redbugs," that live on grasses and shrubs. Their bite contains a chemical that eats away at the skin, causing a tremendous itch. Usually, the small red sores are around the belt line or other openings in clothes. Careful inspection may reveal the tiny red larvae in the center of the itching sore.

**CHIGGERS**

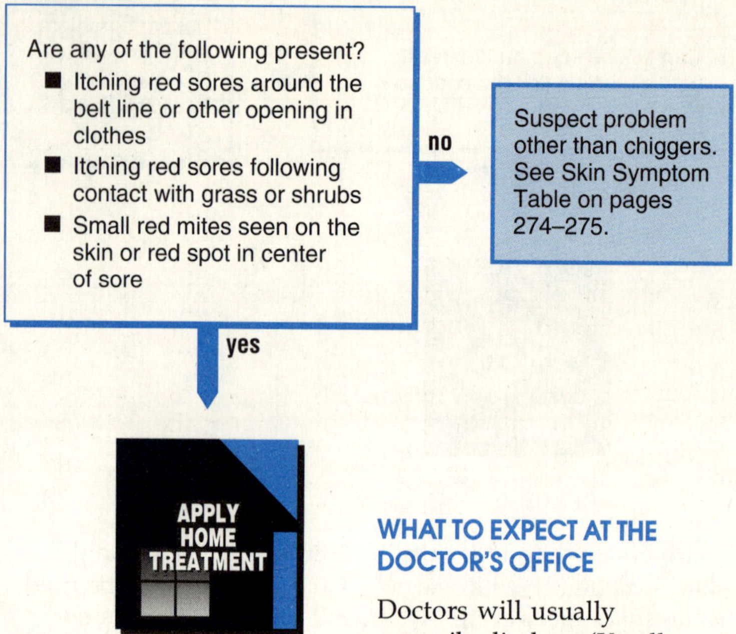


## HOME TREATMENT

Chiggers are better avoided than treated. Using insect repellents, wearing appropriate clothing, and bathing after exposure help to cut down on the frequency of bites. Once you get them, they itch, often for several weeks. Keep the sores clean, and soak them with warm water twice daily. Cuprex, RID, and A200 applied immediately may help kill the larvae, but the itch will persist.

Steroid creams (Cortaid, Lanacort, etc.) may be tried, but are usually not much help (see Chapter 9, "The Home Pharmacy").

Nail polish is said to give relief from itching, but we are not aware of scientific evaluations of its effect.

## WHAT TO EXPECT AT THE DOCTOR'S OFFICE

Doctors will usually prescribe lindane (Kwell, Scabene, etc.), which is perhaps somewhat more effective than A200, RID, or Cuprex but does not stop the itching either. Lindane is too strong to be used more than two times, a week apart.

Antihistamines make the patient drowsy and are not frequently used unless intense itching persists despite home treatment with aspirin, warm baths, oatmeal soaks (Aveeno, etc.), and calamine lotion.

# Scabies

Scabies is an irritation of the skin caused by a tiny mite related to the chigger. No one knows why, but scabies seems to be on the rise in this country. As with lice, it is no longer true that scabies is related to hygiene. It occurs in the best of families and in the best of neighborhoods. The mite easily spreads from person to person or by contact with items such as clothing and bedding that may harbor the mite. Epidemics often spread through schools despite strict precautions against contacts with known cases.

The mite burrows into the skin to lay eggs; its favorite locations are given in the decision chart. These burrows may be evident, especially at the beginning of the problem. However, the mite soon causes the skin to have a reaction so that redness, swelling, and blisters follow within a short period. Intense itching causes scratching so that there are plenty of scratch marks. These may become infected from the bacteria on the skin. Thus, the telltale burrows are often obscured by scratch marks, blisters, and secondary infection.

If you can locate something that looks like a burrow, you might be able to see the mite with the aid of a magnifying lens. This is the only way to be absolutely sure that the problem is scabies, but it is often not possible. The diagnosis is most often made based on symptoms and history that are consistent with scabies, as well as the fact that scabies is known to be in the community.

## HOME TREATMENT

Benzyl benzoate (25% solution) is effective against scabies and does not require a prescription. Unfortunately, it is not widely available. If you are able to find it, apply it once to the entire body *except for* the face and around the urinary opening of the penis and the vaginal opening. Wash it off 24 hours later. This medicine does have an odor that some find unpleasant. If you cannot find benzyl benzoate, you'll have to get a prescription for lindane from your doctor.

For itching, we recommend cool soaks, calamine lotion, and/or pain relievers (aspirin, ibuprofen, or acetaminophen). Antihistamines may help but often cause drowsiness. Follow the directions that come on the package. As in the case of poison ivy, warmth makes the itching worse by releasing

### SCABIES

Are all of the following conditions present?

- Intense itching
- Raised red skin in a line (represents a burrow) and possibly blisters or pustules
- Located on the hands, especially between the fingers, elbow crease, armpit, groin crease, or behind the knees
- Exposure to scabies

**no** → Consider a problem other than scabies. Check Skin Symptom Table on pages 274–275.

**yes** ↓

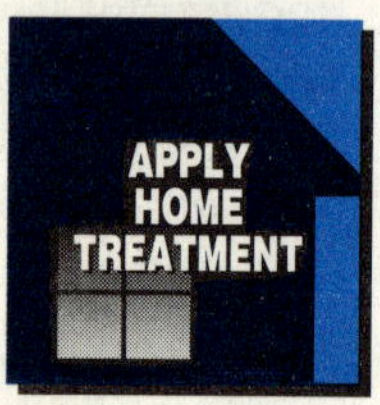


histamine, but if all the histamine is released, relief may be obtained for several hours (see **Poison Ivy and Poison Oak,** page 289).

It will take some time before the skin becomes normal, even with effective treatment, but at least some improvement should be noted within 72 hours. If this is not the case, visit the doctor.

## WHAT TO EXPECT AT THE DOCTOR'S OFFICE

The doctor should examine the entire skin surface for signs of the problem and may examine the area with a magnifying lens in an attempt to identify the mite. A scraping of the lesion may be taken for examination under the microscope. Most of the time the doctor will be forced to make a decision based on the probability of various kinds of diseases and then treat it much as you would at home. The proof will be whether or not the treatment is successful.

Lindane (Kwell, Scabene, etc.) will often be prescribed. Because of the potency of this medication it should not be used more than two times, a week apart.

# Dandruff and Cradle Cap

Although they look somewhat different, cradle cap and dandruff are really part of the same problem; its medical term is **seborrhea**. Oil glands in the skin become stimulated by adult hormones, leading to oiliness and flaking of the scalp. This occurs in infants because of exposure to the mother's hormones and in older children when they begin to make their own adult hormones. However, it does occur between these two ages, and once a child has the problem, it tends to recur.

Seborrhea itself is a somewhat ugly but relatively harmless condition. However, it may make the skin more susceptible to infection with yeast or bacteria. Children with seborrhea frequently have redness and scaling of the eyebrows and behind the ears as well.

### Lookalike Problems

Occasionally, this condition is mistaken for **ringworm** of the scalp. Careful attention to the conditions listed in the decision chart will usually avoid this confusion. Remember also that ringworm would be unusual in the newborn and very young child. See **Ringworm**, page 285.

Another potentially confusing problem is **psoriasis**. This condition often stops at the hairline. Furthermore, the scales of psoriasis are on top of raised lesions called "plaques," which is not the case in seborrhea. Home treatment is unlikely to be helpful for psoriasis, so the help of a doctor is needed.

## HOME TREATMENT

Many widely available anti-dandruff shampoos are helpful in mild to moderate cases of dandruff. For severe and more stubborn cases, there are some less well-known over-the-counter shampoos that are effective because they contain selenium sulfide. Selsun (available by prescription only) and Selsun Blue are examples of such shampoos. Over-the-counter preparations, while weaker, are just as good if you apply them more liberally and frequently. When using these shampoos, it is important that directions are followed carefully because oiliness and yellowish discoloration of the hair may occur. Sebulex, Sebucare, Ionil, and DHS are effective and must be used strictly according to directions also. Unfortunately, none of these shampoos is effective at making it easier to get a date.

**DANDRUFF**

In an infant, are all of the following conditions present?

- Thick, adherent, oily, yellowish scaling or crusting patches
- Located on the scalp, behind the ears, eyebrows, or (less frequently) in the skin creases of the groin
- Only mild redness in involved areas

**no** → Suspect problem other than cradle cap. Check Skin Symptom Table on pages 274–275.

In an older child (or adult), are all of the following conditions present?

- Fine, white, oily scales
- Confined to scalp and/or eyebrows
- Only mild redness in involved areas

**no** → Suspect problem other than dandruff. Check Skin Symptom Table on pages 274–275.

**yes** ↓

Cradle cap is best treated with a soft scrub brush. If it is thick, rub in warm baby oil, cover with a warm towel, and soak for 15 minutes. Use a fine tooth comb or scrub brush to help remove the scale. Then shampoo with Sebulex or other preparations listed above. Be careful to avoid getting shampoo in the eyes.

No matter what you do, the problem will often return, and you may have to repeat the treatment. If the problem gets worse despite home treatment over several weeks, see the doctor.

## WHAT TO EXPECT AT THE DOCTOR'S OFFICE

Severe cases of seborrhea may require more than the medications given above; a cortisone cream is most often prescribed. Usually, a trip made to the doctor clears up some confusion concerning the diagnosis. The doctor generally makes the diagnosis on the basis of the appearance of the rash. Occasionally, scrapings from the involved areas will be looked at under the microscope. Drugs by mouth or by injection are not indicated for seborrhea unless bacterial infection has complicated the problem.

# Patchy Loss of Skin Color

Seeing patches of paler skin on yourself or your child can be unnerving. Luckily, this condition is usually temporary and harmless.

Children are constantly getting minor cuts, scrapes, insect bites, and minor skin infections. During the healing process, it is common for the skin to lose some of its color. With time, the skin coloring generally returns.

Occasionally, **ringworm**, a fungal infection discussed on page 285, will begin as a small round area of scaling with associated loss of skin color.

In the summertime, many children have small round spots on their face in which there is little color. The white spots have probably been present for some time, but skin does not tan in these areas, thus making them visible. This condition is known as **pityriasis alba**. The cause is unknown, but it is a mild condition of cosmetic concern only. It may take many months to disappear and may recur, but there are virtually never any long-term effects.

If there are lightly scaled, tan, pink, or white patches on the neck or back, the problem is most likely due to a fungal infection known as **tinea versicolor**. This is a very minor and superficial fungal infection.

## HOME TREATMENT

Waiting is the most effective home treatment for loss of skin color. Tinea versicolor can be treated by applying Selsun Blue shampoo to the affected area, once every day or so until the lesions are gone.

Tolnaftate (Tinactin, etc.), miconazole (Micatin, etc.), and clotrimazole (Lotrimin, etc.) lotions or creams are also effective. Unfortunately, tinea versicolor almost always comes back no matter what type of treatment is used.

## WHAT TO EXPECT AT THE DOCTOR'S OFFICE

A history and careful examination of the skin will be performed. Scrapings of the lesions may be taken because tinea versicolor can be identified from them. Pityriasis alba should be distinguished from more severe fungal infections that may occur on the face. Again, scrapings will help to identify the fungus.

## PATCHY SKIN COLOR

Are the following conditions present?
- Scaling edges
- Circular enlarging area
- Clearing of center

**yes** → *See:* **Ringworm**, page 285.

**no** ↓

Are the following conditions present?
- Lightly scaled, tan, pink, or white confluent patches
- Confined to the neck and upper back

**yes** → Suspect tinea versicolor. →

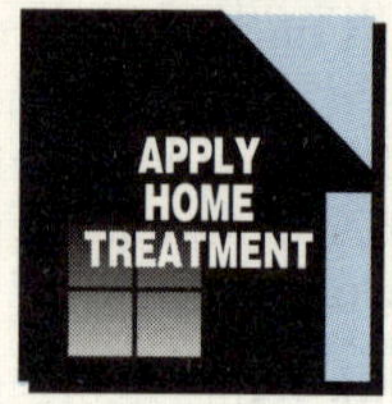


**no** ↓

Are the following conditions present?
- White, scaly patches on face
- More noticeable with suntan
- No signs of infection (crusting, redness, oozing, or fever)

**yes** → Suspect pityriasis alba. →

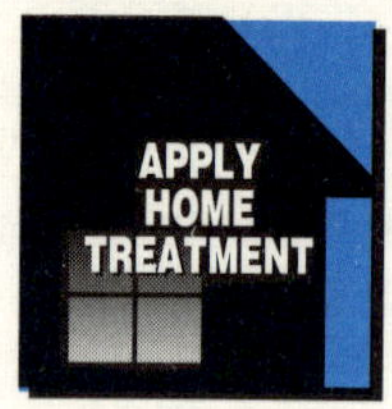


**no** ↓

Did loss of skin color follow cut or infection?

**yes** →

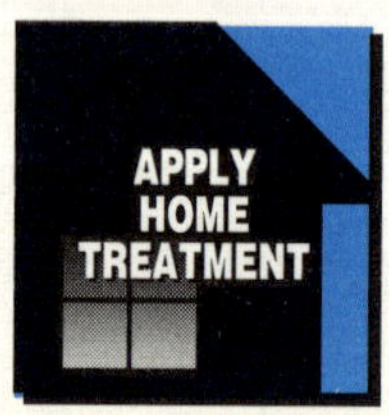


**no** ↓

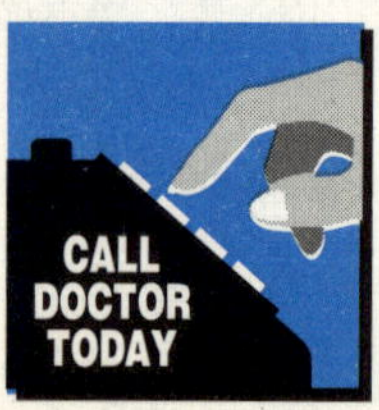

# Aging Spots, Wrinkles, and Baldness

Our aging skin presents a lot of superficial problems. The problems result from a combination of two factors:

- As we age the skin loses its elasticity. It develops more scar tissue and does not spring back as quickly into a smooth contour.
- Damage from the sun accumulates over our lifetime and causes additional problems in the sun-exposed areas of our body.

The aging skin lets air leak into the hair follicles so that the hair turns white. Some or all hair follicles lose the ability to produce hairs at all, and the hair thins or balds. The loss of elasticity means that skin tends to sag and crinkles in the face turn into deeper, fixed wrinkles.

In general, do not worry about these problems. The aging face is expressive of character as well as wrinkles. Thinning hair and baldness are not diseases, nor are aging spots.

Aging spots are pigmentary changes in the skin without any medical significance. Some cells lose the ability to produce the pigment melanin, whereas others produce a bit too much of it. These changes can be thought of as an adult form of freckles. As such they are flat, uniformly brown or tan in color, and have regular borders. If they are raised, irregular in outline, or have multiple colors in one spot (especially shades of red, white, and blue), then see **Skin Cancer,** page 293.

## HOME TREATMENT

Stay out of the sun and use a sunscreen. This is particularly important if you are fair-skinned because such skin is far more prone to sun damage. Outside of this, there is not really very much you can do at home for these problems except not to worry about them. And that is all that is really needed.

## WHAT TO EXPECT AT THE DOCTOR'S OFFICE

There are good medical approaches to these "problems," but they are entirely optional. Many people prefer their natural aging appearance to artificial cosmetic devices. Others, who can afford it, elect to fight the aging stereotype by a variety of measures that preserve a more youthful appearance. Alternatives currently available have low risk but high cost. The choices range all the way from wrinkle creams to an elaborate series of plastic surgical operations.

If you want to go the expensive route, you probably should see a dermatologist first, and then, perhaps, a plastic surgeon. The dermatologist is likely to be more familiar with the effective cosmetic interventions than a family physician or internist is. The dermatologist is also the key person to take care of any lumps and bumps about which you are concerned.

### AGING SPOTS

Is this a spot that is
- variable in color or
- irregular in outline or
- raised?

yes → *See:* **Skin Cancer**, page 293.

no ↓

Are you ready to try any of the following?
- Retin-A for wrinkles
- Minoxidil for baldness
- Plastic surgery

yes →

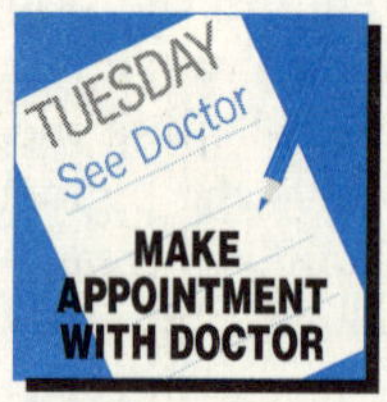


no ↓

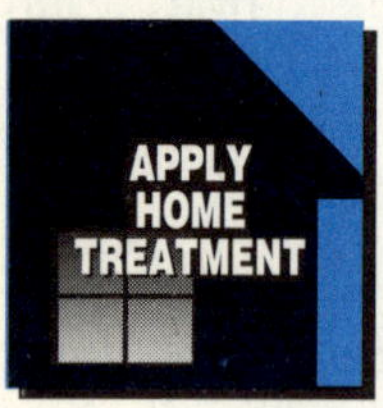


The most effective approaches to these conditions, among a huge variety of not-so-good treatments, are Retin-A for wrinkles and minoxidil (Rogain) for hair growth. Retin-A is the first wrinkle cream that actually works, and minoxidil does cause new hair to grow over previously bald spots. Unfortunately, Retin-A doesn't seem to work very well with old, fixed wrinkles; it may cause heat rashes in skin exposed to the sun, and it dries the skin out. The new minoxidil hair isn't usually everything that you would want; it is unusual that very much hair grows back, and the older you are, the less effective this treatment.

**Plastic Surgery**

The plastic surgeon can take out wrinkles by removing skin and stretching the remaining skin tighter. Many procedures are available. Wrinkles around the eyes can be taken out, as can bags under the eyes. A full face lift tightens the skin over the entire face. Sagging breasts can be reduced in size and lifted. Tucks can be taken in the tummy. Liposuction can remove fat, although the result usually is a little lumpy. Hair transplants can be partially effective in some people. Again, in good hands, done by a surgeon who performs the procedure often, these operations have low risk. However, they are expensive. There is pain and discomfort involved. There is an occasional serious complication. With some of the procedures, you won't want to be seen in public for a week or so after the operation.

CHAPTER J

# *Childhood Diseases*

# Mumps

Mumps is a viral infection of the salivary glands. The major salivary glands are located directly below and in front of the ear. Before any swelling is noticeable, there may be a low fever, headache, earache, or weakness. Fever is variable. It may be only slightly above normal or as high as 104°F. After several days of these symptoms, one or both salivary glands (parotid glands) may swell.

It is sometimes difficult to distinguish mumps from swollen lymph glands in the neck (see page 250). In mumps, you will not be able to feel the edge of the jaw that is located beneath the ear. Chewing and swallowing may produce pain behind the ear. Sour substances such as lemons and pickles may make the pain worse. When swelling occurs on both sides, people take on the appearance of chipmunks! Other salivary glands besides the parotid may be involved, including those under the jaw and tongue. The openings of these glands into the mouth may become red and puffy.

Approximately one-third of all patients who have mumps do not demonstrate any swelling of glands whatsoever. Therefore, many people concerned about exposure to mumps will already have had the disease without realizing it.

Mumps is quite contagious during the period from 2 days before the first symptoms to the complete disappearance of the parotid gland swelling (usually about a week after the swelling has begun). Mumps will develop in a susceptible exposed person approximately 16 to 18 days after exposure to the virus. In children, it is generally a mild illness.

The decision chart is directed toward detection of rare complications. These include encephalitis (viral infection of the brain), pancreatitis (viral infection of the pancreas), kidney disease, deafness, and involvement of the testicles or the ovaries. Complications are more frequent in adults than they are in children.

### HOME TREATMENT

The pain may be reduced with acetaminophen, aspirin, or ibuprofen. There may be difficulty in eating, but adequate fluid intake is important. Sour foods should be avoided, including orange juice. Adults who have not had mumps should avoid exposure to the patient until the swelling disappears completely.

Many adults who do not recall having mumps as a child may have had an extremely mild case and consequently are not at risk of developing mumps.

If swelling has not gone down within three weeks, call the doctor.

**MUMPS**

Is there lethargy, convulsions, or stiff neck?

**yes** →

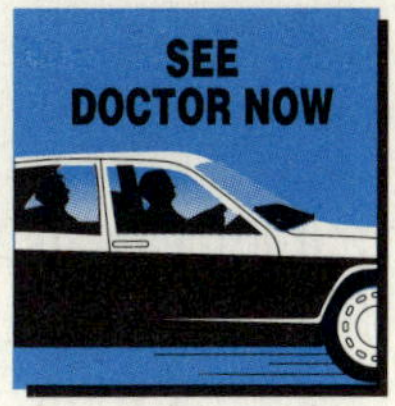


**no** ↓

Are any of the following present?

- Pain and swelling of one or both testicles
- Abdominal pain and vomiting
- Dizziness and difficulty in hearing

**yes** →

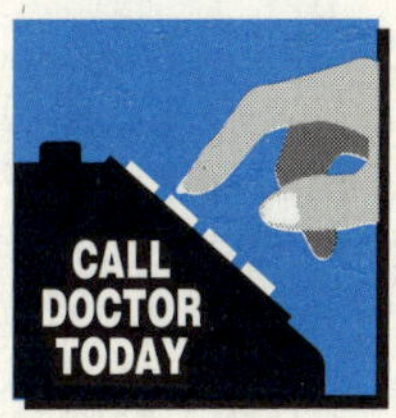


**no** ↓

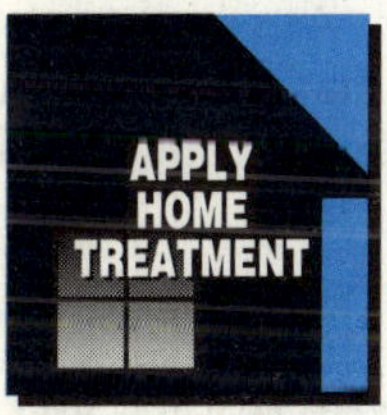


## WHAT TO EXPECT AT THE DOCTOR'S OFFICE

If a complication is suspected, a visit to the doctor's office may be necessary. The history and physical examination will be directed at confirming the diagnosis or the presence of a complication. The rare complication of an ovarian mumps infection on the right side may be confused with appendicitis and blood tests may be required. Because mumps is a viral disease, there is no medicine that will directly kill the virus. Supportive measures may be necessary for some of the complications. Fortunately, this is rare, and permanent damage to hearing or other functions is unusual. Mumps very rarely produces sterility in men or women even when the testes or ovaries are involved.

# Chicken Pox

Because chicken pox spreads quickly, and because taking aspirin during this disease is associated with Reye's syndrome, it is valuable to know its signs.

**How to Recognize Chicken Pox**

**Before the Rash.** Usually there are no symptoms, but occasionally there is fatigue and some fever in the 24 hours before the rash is noted.

**Rash.** The typical rash goes through the following stages.

**1.** It appears as flat red splotches.

**2.** They become raised and may resemble small pimples.

**3.** They develop into small blisters, called vesicles, which are very fragile. They may look like drops of water on a red base. The tops are easily scratched off.

**4.** As the vesicles break, the sores become pustular and form a crust. (The crust is made of dried serum, not true pus.) This stage may be reached within several hours of the first appearance of the rash. Itching is often severe in the pustular stage.

**5.** The crust falls away between the 9th and 13th day.

The vesicles tend to appear in crops with two to four crops appearing within two to six days. All stages may be present in the same area. The rashes often appear first on the scalp and in the mouth, and then spread to the rest of the body, but they may begin anywhere. They are most numerous over the shoulders, chest, and back. They are seldom found on the palms of the hands or the soles of the feet. There may be only a few sores, or there may be hundreds.

**Fever.** After most of the sores have formed crusts, the fever usually subsides.

**How Chicken Pox Spreads**

Chicken pox spreads very easily—over 90% of brothers and sisters catch it. It may be transmitted from 24 hours before the appearance of the rash up to about 6 days after. It is spread by droplets from the mouth or throat or by direct contact with contaminated articles of clothing. It is not spread by dry scabs. The incubation period is from 14 to 17 days. Chicken pox leads to lifelong immunity to recurrence with rare exceptions.

However, the same virus that causes chicken pox also causes **shingles**, and the individual who has had chicken pox may develop shingles (herpes zoster) later in life. Shingles is usually limited to one side of the body in a broad stripe, representing the skin area of a single nerve. Because it is limited to the nerve in which the virus is living, there is seldom fever although there may be pain. Follow the same treatment as you do for chicken pox. If you have any underlying medical problems, you should give your doctor a call.

Most of the time, chicken pox should be treated at home. Complications are rare and far less common than they are with measles. The specific questions on the chart deal with two severe complications that may require medical treatment: encephalitis (viral infection of the brain) and severe bacterial infection of the lesions. Encephalitis is rare.

## HOME TREATMENT

The major problems in dealing with chicken pox are control of the intense itching and reduction of the fever. Warm baths containing baking soda (one-half cup to a tubful of water) frequently help. Antihistamines may help; see Chapter 9, "The Home Pharmacy." Acetaminophen and ibuprofen are effective itch relievers. Because recent information indicates an association with a rare but serious problem of the liver and brain known as Reye's syndrome, aspirin should not be used for children or teenagers who may have chicken pox or influenza.

Cut the fingernails or use gloves to prevent skin damage from intense scratching. When lesions occur in the mouth, gargling with salt water (one-half teaspoon salt to an eight-ounce glass) may help give comfort. Hands should be washed three times a day, and all of the skin should be kept gently but scrupulously clean in order to prevent bacterial infection. Minor bacterial infection will respond to soap and time; if it becomes severe and results in return of fever, then call the doctor. Scratching and infection can result in permanent scars.

If itching is unable to be controlled or the problem persists beyond three weeks, call the doctor. Using the phone for questions to the doctor will avoid exposing others to the disease.

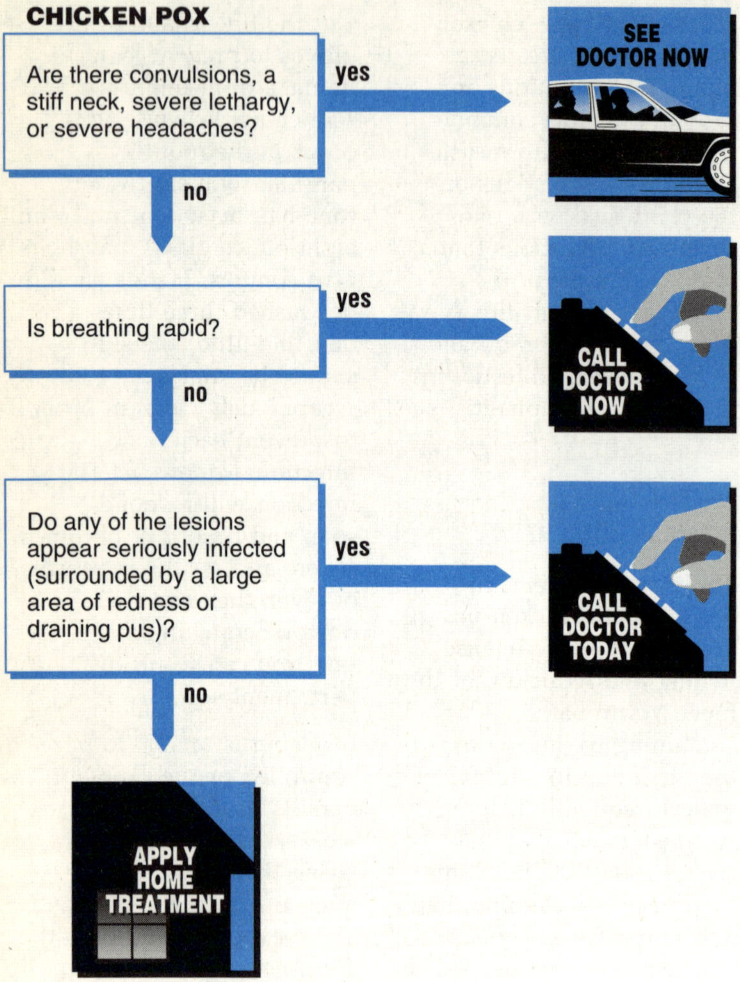


## WHAT TO EXPECT AT THE DOCTOR'S OFFICE

Do not be surprised if the doctor is willing and even anxious to treat the case over the phone. If it is necessary to go to the doctor's office, then attempts should be made to keep the patient separate from others. In healthy children, chicken pox has few lasting ill effects, but in people with other serious illnesses, it can be a devastating or even fatal disease. A visit to the doctor's office may not be necessary unless a complication seems possible.

# Measles

This type of measles is also called red measles, seven-day and ten-day measles, as opposed to German or three-day measles (see page 329). It is a preventable disease, but unlike some of the other childhood illnesses, can be quite severe. It is tragic that decades after the licensing of the measles vaccine, thousands of people still contract this disease annually, and some of them die. We would like to be able to eliminate this section in the next edition of this book. Only immunization of everyone can make this possible.

### How to Recognize Measles

**Early signs.** Measles is a viral illness that begins with fever, weakness, a dry "brassy" cough, and inflamed eyes that are itchy, red, and sensitive to the light. These symptoms begin three to five days before the appearance of the rash.

Another early sign of measles is the appearance of fine white spots on a red base inside the mouth opposite the molar teeth (Koplik's spots). These fade as the skin rash appears.

**Rash.** The rash begins on about the fifth day as a pink, blotchy, flat rash. The rash first appears around the hairline, on the face, on the neck, and behind the ears. The spots, which fade early in the illness when pressure is applied, become somewhat darker and tend to merge into larger red patches as they mature.

The rash spreads from head to chest to abdomen and finally to the arms and legs. It lasts from four to seven days and may be accompanied by mild itching. There may be some light brown coloring to the skin lesions as the illness progresses.

### How Measles Spread

Measles is a highly contagious viral disease. It is spread by droplets from the mouth or throat and by direct contact with articles freshly soiled by nose and throat secretions. It may be spread during the period from 3 to 6 days before the appearance of the rash to several days after. Symptoms begin in a susceptible person approximately 8 to 12 days after exposure to the virus.

There are a number of complications of measles: sore throats, ear infections, and pneumonia are all common. Many of these complicating infections are due to bacteria and will require antibiotic treatment. The pneumonias can be life-threatening. A very serious problem that can lead to permanent damage is **measles encephalitis** (infection of the brain); life-support measures and treatment of seizures may be necessary when this rare complication occurs.

## MEASLES

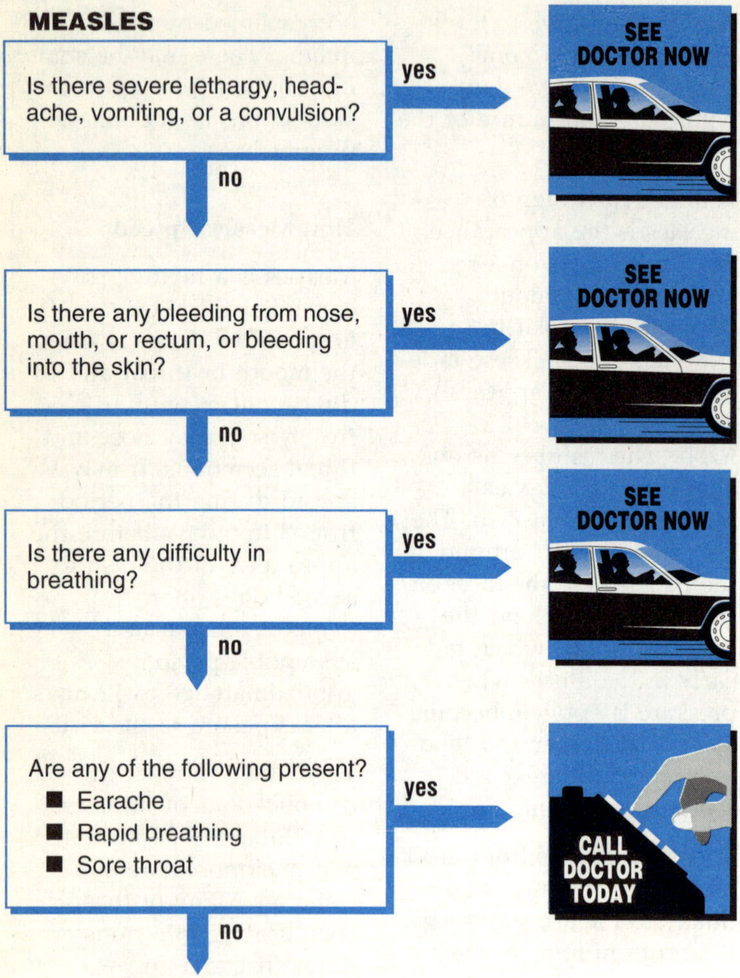


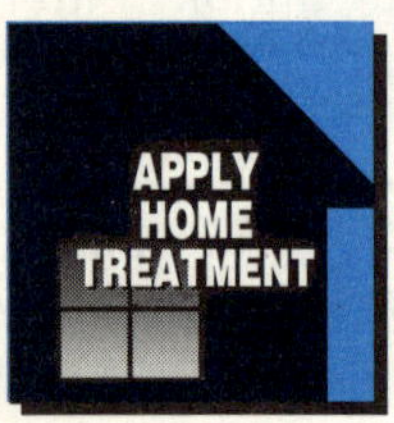


### HOME TREATMENT

Symptomatic measures are all that is needed for uncomplicated measles. Acetaminophen, aspirin, or ibuprofen should be used to keep the fever down, and a vaporizer can be used for the cough. Dim lighting in the room is often more comfortable because of the eyes' sensitivity to light. In general, the person feels "measley." The patient should be isolated until the end of the contagious period. All unimmunized people in contact with the patient should be immunized immediately. (People who have had the measles are considered to be immunized.)

### WHAT TO EXPECT AT THE DOCTOR'S OFFICE

The history and physical examination will be directed at determining the diagnosis of measles and the nature of any complications. Bacterial complications, such as ear infections and pneumonia, can usually be treated with antibiotics. The person with symptoms suggestive of encephalitis (lethargy, stiff neck, convulsions) will be hospitalized, and a spinal tap will be performed. Very rarely, there may be a problem with blood clotting so that bleeding occurs. Usually this is first apparent as dark purple splotches in the skin. It is best to avoid all of the problems through measles immunization.

# German Measles (Rubella)

German measles is also known as rubella and three-day measles. See page 327 for advice on measles.

### How to Recognize German Measles

**Before the Rash.** There may be a few days of mild fatigue. Lymph nodes at the back of the neck may be enlarged and tender.

**Rash.** The rash first appears on the face as flat or slightly raised red spots. It quickly spreads to the trunk and the extremities, and the discrete spots tend to merge into large patches. A rubella rash is highly variable and is difficult for even the most experienced parents and doctors to recognize. Often, there is *no* rash.

**Fever.** The fever rarely goes above 101°F and usually lasts less than two days.

**Pain.** Joint pain occurs in about 10 to 15% of older children and adults. The pains usually begin on the third day of illness.

### How German Measles Spread

German measles is a mild virus infection that is not as contagious as measles or chicken pox. It is usually spread by droplets from the mouth or throat. It can be spread from 7 days before the rash appears until 5 days afterwards.

The incubation period is from 12 to 21 days, with an average of 16 days.

The specific questions on the decision chart are addressed to possible complications, which are extremely rare. The main concern with German measles is an infection in an unborn child. If three-day measles occurs during the first month of pregnancy, there is a 50% chance that the fetus will develop an abnormality such as cataracts, heart disease, deafness, or mental deficiency. By the third month of pregnancy, this risk decreases to less than 10%, and it continues to decrease throughout the pregnancy. Because of the problem of congenital defects, a vaccine for German measles has been developed.

## HOME TREATMENT

Usually no therapy is required. Occasionally, fever will require the use of acetaminophen, aspirin, or ibuprofen. Isolation is usually not imposed.

Women who could possibly be pregnant should avoid any exposure to the patient. If a question of such exposure arises, the pregnant woman should discuss the risk with her doctor. Blood tests are available that will indicate whether a pregnant woman has had rubella in the past and is immune, or whether problems with the pregnancy might be encountered. In most states, these tests are required for a marriage license and there are now few pregnant women who are at risk.

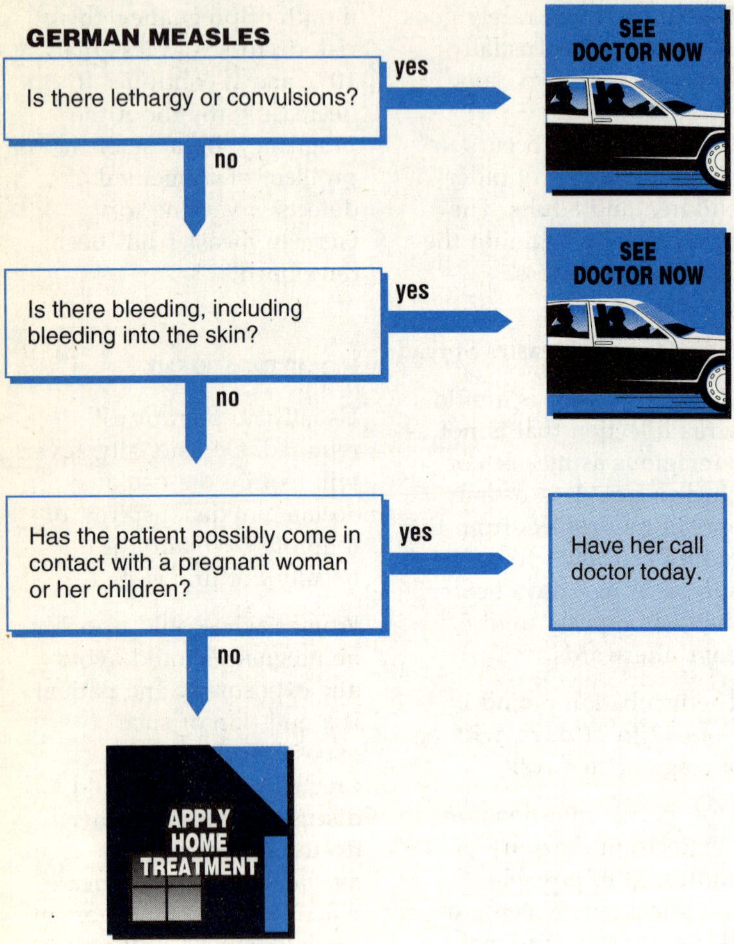


## WHAT TO EXPECT AT THE DOCTOR'S OFFICE

Visits to the doctor's office are seldom required for uncomplicated German measles. Questions about possible infection of pregnant women are more easily and economically discussed over the telephone. The question of immunization is complex, and we discuss it in detail in *Taking Care of Your Child*.

# Roseola

Roseola is most common in children under the age of three but may occur at any age. Its main significance lies in the sudden high fever, which may cause a convulsion. Such a convulsion is due to the high temperature and does not indicate that the child has epilepsy. Prompt treatment of the fever is essential (see **Fever,** page 191).

**How to Recognize Roseola**

**Fever.** There are usually several days of sustained high fever. Sometimes this fever can trigger a convulsion or seizure in a susceptible child. Otherwise, the patient appears well.

**Rash.** The rash appears as the fever is decreasing or shortly after it is gone. It consists of pink, well-defined patches that turn white on pressure and first appear on the trunk. It may be slightly bumpy. It spreads to involve the arms, legs, and neck but is seldom prominent on the face or legs. The rash usually lasts less than 24 hours.

**Other Symptoms.** Occasionally, there is a slight runny nose, red throat, or swollen glands at the back of the head, behind the ears, or in the neck. Most often, there are no other symptoms.

This disease is probably caused by a virus and is contagious. Contact with others should be avoided until the fever has passed. The incubation period is from 7 to 17 days.

**Encephalitis** (infection of the brain) is a very rare complication of roseola. Roseola is basically a mild disease.

## HOME TREATMENT

Home treatment is based on two principles. The first is effective treatment of the fever. The second is careful watching and waiting. The patient with roseola should appear well, and have no other significant symptoms once the fever is controlled. If symptoms of ear infection (a complaint of ear pain or tugging at the ear), cough (see page 240), or lethargy occur, then the appropriate sections of this book should be consulted. If the problem is still not clear, a phone call to the doctor should help.

Remember that roseola should not last more than four or five days. You should call your doctor if the symptoms persist.

**ROSEOLA**

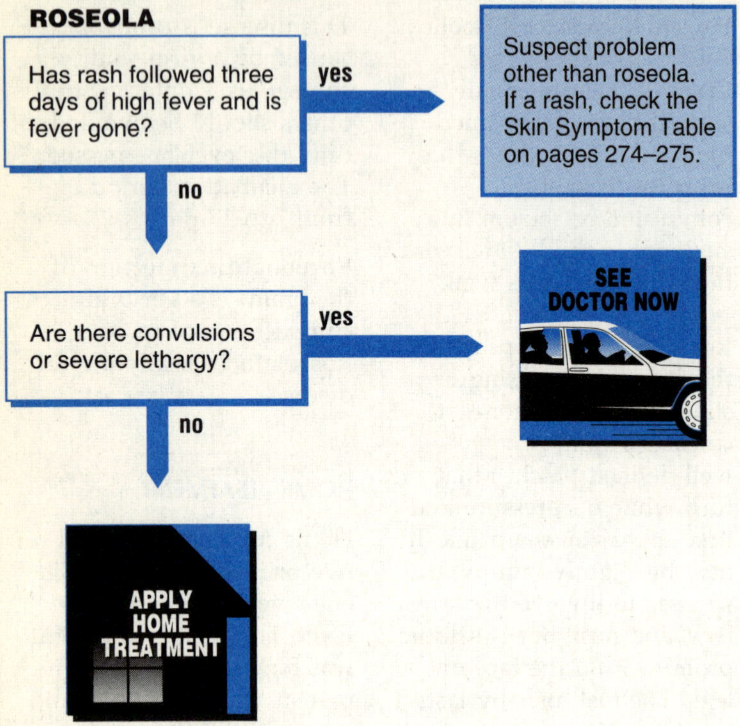


### WHAT TO EXPECT AT THE DOCTOR'S OFFICE

Patients are usually seen soon after the onset of the illness because of the high fever. As noted, at this stage there is little else to be found in roseola. The ears, nose, throat, and chest should be examined. If the fever remains the only finding, then the doctor will recommend home treatment (control of the fever with careful waiting and watching to see if a roseola rash appears). There is no medical treatment for roseola other than that available at home.

# Scarlet Fever

Scarlet fever derived its name over 300 years ago from its characteristic red rash. The illness is caused by a streptococcal infection, usually of the throat. Strep throats are discussed in **Sore Throat** (page 228).

You can recognize the illness by its characteristic features.

**1.** Fever and weakness are often accompanied by a headache, stomachache, and vomiting. A sore throat is usually but not always present.

**2.** The rash appears 12 to 48 hours after the illness begins. It begins on the face, trunk, and arms and generally covers the entire body by the end of 24 hours. It is red, very fine, and covers most of the skin surface. The area around the mouth is pale. It feels like fine sandpaper. Skin creases, such as in front of the elbow and the armpit, are more deeply red. Pressing on the rash will produce a white spot lasting several seconds.

**3.** The intense redness of the rash lasts for about five days, although peeling of skin can go on for weeks. It is not unusual for peeling, especially of the palms, to last for more than a month.

Examination often reveals a red throat, spots on the roof of the mouth (soft palate), and a fuzzy, white tongue that later becomes swollen and red. There may be swollen glands in the neck.

As with other streptococcal infections, the significance of scarlet fever is its connection with **rheumatic fever** (see **Sore Throat,** page 228).

### HOME TREATMENT

Because scarlet fever is due to a streptococcal infection, a medical visit is required for antibiotic treatment.

Streptococcal infections are quite contagious, and other members of the family should also be tested. In addition to antibiotics, you should reduce the fever with aspirin or acetaminophen, keep up with fluid requirements, and give plenty of cold liquids to help soothe the throat.

## SCARLET FEVER

Are both of the following present?

- Fever
- Fine, red rash on trunk and extremities that feels like sandpaper

**no** → Suspect problem other than scarlet fever. If there is a skin rash, check the Skin Symptom Table on pages 274–275.

**yes** ↓

### WHAT TO EXPECT AT THE DOCTOR'S OFFICE

There are several rashes that can be confused with scarlet fever, including those associated with measles and drug reactions. If the rash is sufficiently typical of scarlet fever, the doctor will probably begin antibiotics —usually penicillin (or erythromycin if the patient is allergic to penicillin)— and take throat cultures from the rest of the family. If the doctor is uncertain of the cause of the rash, a throat culture may be taken before beginning treatment. Treatment that is delayed by a day or two while waiting for culture results will still prevent the complication that causes the greatest concern: rheumatic fever.

# Fifth Disease

Consider the strange case of the fifth disease, whose only claim to fame is that it might be mistaken for another disease. It is so named because it is always listed last (and least) among the five very common contagious rashes of childhood. Its medical name, *erythema infectiosum*, is easily forgotten.

It comes very close to not being a disease at all. It has no symptoms other than rash, has no complications, and needs no treatment. It can be recognized because it causes a characteristic "slapped cheek" appearance in children. The rash often begins on the cheeks and is later found on the backs of the arms and legs. It often is very fine, lacy, and pink. It tends to come and go and may be present one moment and absent the next. It is prone to recur for days or even weeks, especially as a response to heat (such as warm bath or shower) or irritation. In general, however, the rash around the face will fade within four days of its appearance, and the rash on the rest of the body will fade within three to seven days of its appearance.

The only significance of fifth disease is that it could worry you or have you make an avoidable trip to the doctor's office.

Its recent resurgence makes this more likely. It is very contagious. Epidemics of fifth disease have resulted in unnecessary school closings. The agent responsible for this "non-disease" is not known; a virus is suspected. The incubation period is thought to be from 6 to 14 days.

**FIFTH DISEASE**

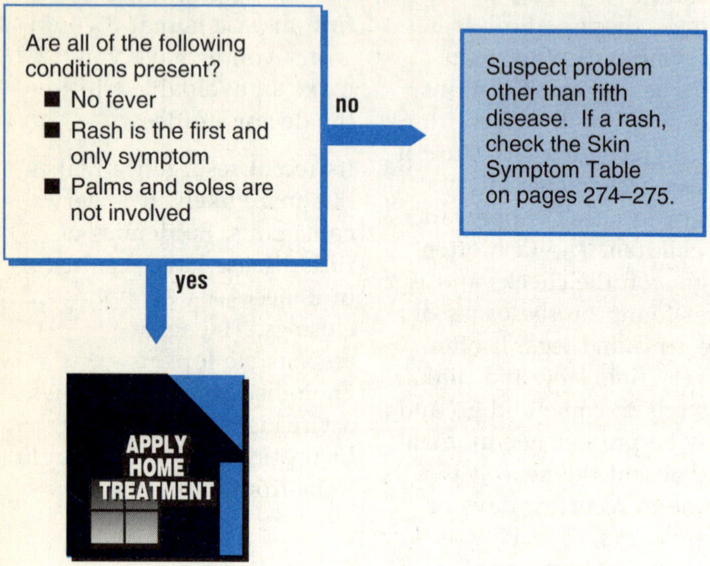


## HOME TREATMENT

There is no treatment. Just watch and wait to make sure you are dealing with fifth disease. Check that there is no fever. Fever is very unusual with fifth disease. No restrictions on activities are necessary.

## WHAT TO EXPECT AT THE DOCTOR'S OFFICE

The doctor may be able to distinguish fifth disease from other rashes. If the rash fits the description given in this section, the doctor is going to make the same diagnosis that you might have made. Checking the patient's temperature and looking at the rash can be expected. Because there are no tests currently available, laboratory tests are unlikely. Waiting and watching are the means of dealing with fifth disease.

CHAPTER K

# *Bones, Muscles, and Joints*

# Arthritis

Most so-called arthritis is not arthritis at all! Misunderstanding comes about because doctors and patients use the term differently. The "arth" part of the word means "joint"—*not* muscle, tendon, ligament, or bone. The "itis" means "inflamed." Thus, true arthritis affects the joints, so that they are red, warm, swollen, and painful to move. Pains in the muscles or ligaments are discussed on page 341.

### Types of Arthritis

There are over 100 types of arthritis. These are the four most common:

- **Osteoarthritis** is usually not serious, occurs in later life, and frequently causes knobby swelling at the most distant joints of the fingers.
- **Rheumatoid arthritis** usually starts in middle life and may cause you to feel sick and stiff all over, in addition to the joint problems.
- **Gout** occurs mostly in men, with sudden, severe attacks of pain and swelling in one joint at a time—frequently the big toe, the ankle, or the knee.
- **Ankylosing spondylitis** affects the back and joints of the lower back. It may be involved if your back is sore for a long time and particularly stiff in the morning, and if you are unable to touch your toes.

### Lyme Disease

Recently, Lyme disease has received much attention as a cause of arthritis. Lyme disease is the result of an infection spread by ticks, usually a small, fairly uncommon type called the deer tick. Three to 20 days following the bite of an infected tick, a distinctive oval rash develops along with fever, headache, stiff neck, and backaches. This is the end of the disease for most people, but others develop arthritis within 1 to 22 weeks. Less often, heart or neurological problems follow the rash.

## REASONS TO SEE A DOCTOR

Only rarely does a patient with arthritis need to see a doctor immediately. Urgent problems are:

- Infection
- Nerve damage
- Fractures near a joint
- Gout

In the first three, serious damage may result if the joint is neglected; in the fourth, the pain is so intense that immediate help is needed.

The complications of arthritis occur very slowly and are more easily prevented than corrected. Arthritis results in more lost workdays and sickness than any other disease category—it must be managed correctly and with care.

## ARTHRITIS

Are any of the following present?

- Swelling of a joint
- Redness or heat in a joint
- Pain upon motion of the joint

**no** → This is not arthritis—*see:* **Pain in the Muscles and Joints**, page 341.

**yes** ↓

Did the problem begin after an injury?

**yes** → *See* appropriate problem, such as:
**Broken Bone?**, page 167
**Ankle Injuries**, page 170
**Knee Injuries**, page 172
**Arm Injuries**, page 174.

**no** ↓

Are any of the following present?

- Fever
- Severe pain and swelling in one or two joints only
- Inability to use the joint
- Rash

**yes** →

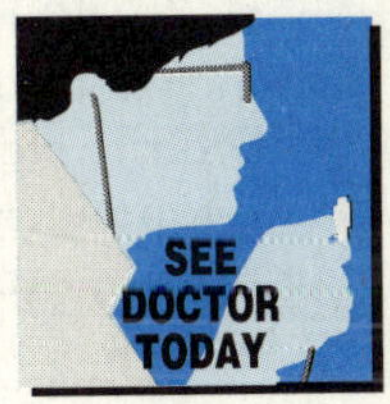


**no** ↓

Has the problem persisted for more than six weeks?

**yes** →

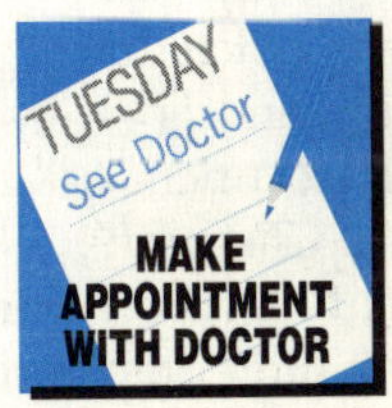


**no** ↓

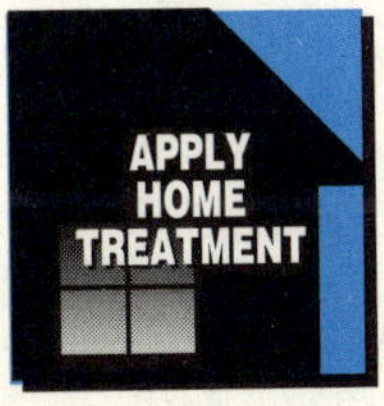

## HOME TREATMENT

Both aspirin and ibuprofen (Advil, Nuprin, etc.) can reduce the pain and swelling in the joints. The usual dosage for each is two tablets every four to six hours. The major concern with each medication is stomach irritation: both may contribute to bleeding and ulcers. Ibuprofen is somewhat less likely to cause stomach problems but is more expensive. The risk of upset stomach can be reduced by taking the tablets after meals, after an antacid, or by using coated aspirin tablets (Ecotrin, etc.). Warning signs of too much aspirin include ringing ears, dizziness, and hearing problems.

Although acetaminophen may provide some pain relief, it does not reduce inflammation and is rarely used in the treatment of arthritis. See Chapter 9, "The Home Pharmacy," for more information on aspirin and ibuprofen.

Resting an inflamed joint can speed healing. Heat may help. Usually, a painful joint should be worked through its entire range of motion twice daily to prevent stiffness or contracture.

If arthritis persists more than six weeks, see a doctor. For more information, consult James Fries, *Arthritis: A Comprehensive Guide;* and Kate Lorig and James Fries, *The Arthritis Helpbook.*

## WHAT TO EXPECT AT THE DOCTOR'S OFFICE

The doctor will examine the joints, obtain blood tests, and may take X-rays. If a single joint is the problem and it contains fluid, this fluid may also be removed and tested.

Most often one of the many non-steroidal anti-inflammatory drugs (NSAIDs) such as Naprosyn, Feldene, Voltaren, Tolectin, Meclomen, Ansaid, Relafen, or Indocin will be prescribed. Their effects, both good and bad, are essentially the same as those of aspirin or ibuprofen. The big problem is that they can cause stomach ulcers.

Steroid drugs such as prednisone are very effective in reducing inflammation, but their long-term use causes serious side effects. If they are to be continued for more than a few weeks, we recommend that a consultant concur in their use. Occasionally, a steroid drug will be injected into a particularly painful joint, but this usually should not be done more than three times.

# Pain in the Muscles and Joints

Here are two lesser-known medical terms: "arthralgia" means pain (without swelling, redness, etc.) in the joints, and "myalgia" means pain in the muscles. These pains are not arthritis but can be very bothersome. Usually they are not serious and will go away. They can be caused by tension, virus infections, unusual exertion, automobile or other accidents, or can have no obvious cause. Only seldom do they indicate a serious disease.

Rarely, thyroid disease, cancer, polymyositis (inflammation of the muscles), or, in older patients, polymyalgia rheumatica may cause arthralgias. If fever, weight loss, or severe fatigue is not present, give home treatment a trial of several weeks or even months before seeing a doctor. If pain is located at the upper neck and base of the skull, the problem is almost certainly minor.

Doctors often do not agree on diagnostic terms in this area and may identify your problem differently. Some terms frequently used are:

- Fibrositis
- Non-articular rheumatism
- Chronic muscle-contraction syndrome
- Psychogenic rheumatism
- Psychophysiological musculo-skeletal pain

These all mean about the same thing.

Medical treatment is often not very helpful. Tranquilizers, muscle relaxants, and pain relievers may be prescribed, but the side effects are often more spectacular than the relief provided. Antidepressants may be somewhat more helpful. The doctor is frequently unsure whether the problem is physical or emotional in origin. These problems are "diseases of civilization" and are rarely seen in underdeveloped societies.

## HOME TREATMENT

Both rest and exercise are important. A regular, adequate sleeping pattern seems essential for many people with these problems. Try to relax and gently stretch the involved areas. Warm baths, massage, and stretching exercises should be employed as frequently as possible.

### Heat or Cold?

Advice about the treatment of joint or muscle problems may seem contradictory. Some may suggest using cold, others using heat, and still others will advocate both! Actually, all this advice may be reasonable depending on the problem and when in the course of that problem the treatment is to be given. The best way to understand this is to learn about the stages of inflammation and how these stages are affected by heat and cold.

### Inflammation

Inflammation is the body's response to tissue damage and is a necessary part of healing. With joints and muscles, tissue damage is usually due to an injury such as a sprain, infection, or a cause still not completely understood, as with most arthritis. Inflammation starts with the widening of blood vessels that increases blood flow to the damaged tissue. These blood vessels also become leaky so that fluid and blood cells escape into the surrounding tissue. These events account for the four major signs of inflammation:

- Swelling
- Pain
- Warmth
- Redness

Injuries may also tear blood vessels so that frank bleeding occurs into the joint or muscle tissue. This is what causes very rapid swelling seen in ankle or knee sprains, for example.

When the damage to tissue stops, the changes to the blood vessels will eventually stop also. Decreases in redness and warmth usually follow rather quickly, but swelling and pain may continue because fluid and blood remain in the joint or muscle tissues. The fluid in blood cells will be removed gradually, mostly through the lymph channels and lymph nodes. This is the cause of the red streaks and swollen glands found near areas of inflammation. This final stage of healing may be aided by increased blood flow to the damaged tissue.

So what about heat vs. cold? Cold decreases blood flow. It is used in the first stage of inflammation to reduce the amount of fluid, blood cells, and blood that escapes into joints or muscle tissue from leaky or torn blood vessels. In this way, it may help to reduce the pain, swelling, warmth, and redness due to tissue damage.

Heat increases blood vessel size and blood flow so that its use in the first stages of inflammation would likely increase the amount of fluid and blood loss from blood vessels. Since this would increase the pain, swelling, warmth, and redness, the use of heat in these initial stages is usually not advised. However, heat helps in the final stages of healing when increased blood flow may be useful.

Heat has two other important affects on joints and muscles. The flexibility and elasticity of muscles, ligaments, and tendons is temperature dependent, i.e., they become stiffer when cold and more flexible when warm. The application of heat may immediately loosen up stiff muscles and joints. Unfortunately, this effect is lost when the heat is removed and the tissue returns to its previous temperature. Heat may also help relieve muscle spasms.

The use of cold and heat is fairly simple when the tissue damage occurs once and is over, as with a sprained ankle. Cold is applied immediately and for as long as the first stages of inflammation may be occurring (usually about 24 hours). After that time, heat may be applied to reduce discomfort by loosening up the joint and, perhaps, speed healing.

**Repeated Damage**

The situation is not so simple when the damage is repeated or constant. For example, some doctors believe that athletes with "bad" knees may damage them whenever they play their sport. These athletes may apply ice immediately before, during, and immediately after playing in an effort to reduce inflammation and then use heat at some later time in an effort to alleviate pain and swelling and to improve healing.

The situation is even more complex with respect to arthritis where damage may be continuous. Some doctors and patients believe that cold may work best by helping to decrease inflammation while others favor heat because it seems to increase flexibility and decrease discomfort in the joints. Both may be true, and the difference may largely depend on the fact that arthritis is not the same in every patient—or even in every joint of a single patient—and on what sort of benefit is being sought and when. So far there is no research that indicates a long-term advantage for the consistent use of either heat or cold, but this is an area that has been largely ignored by medical scientists.

In summary, use cold when you think that damage has just occurred and inflammation is developing. When you think that the initial stages of inflammation are over, use heat in order to improve flexibility and, perhaps, to speed healing.

**Preventing the Pain**

Sponge-soled shoes may help if you work on hard floors. Better light or a better chair may help if you work at a desk. Regular exercise (slowly increased from very gentle to more vigorous) may help restore proper muscle tone. We recommend walking, bicycling, and swimming. Aspirin or ibuprofen may help. A change in lifestyle or a move to a new location is frequently followed by improvement. If the problem goes away on vacation, you can be relatively certain that everyday stress accounts for the problem.

If the problem persists beyond three weeks, call your doctor.

## PAIN IN MUSCLES AND JOINTS

Are any of the following present?

- Swelling of a joint
- Redness or heat in a joint
- Pain upon motion of the joint

**yes** → *See:* **Arthritis**, page 338.

**no** ↓

Are any of the following present?

- Fever not associated with "flu" symptoms
- Weight loss of ten or more pounds

**yes** →

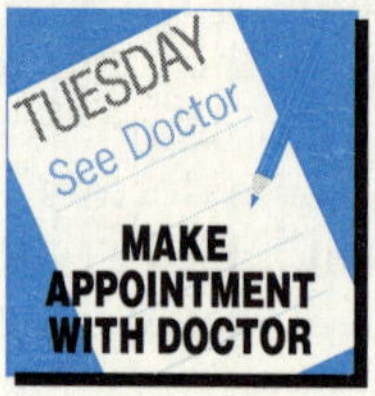


**no** ↓

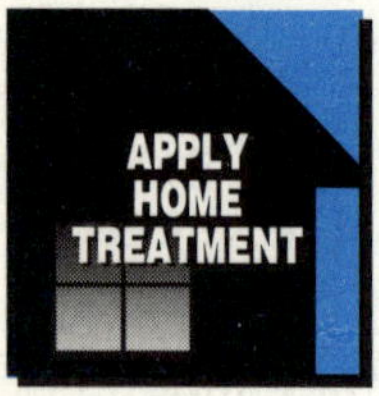


### WHAT TO EXPECT AT THE DOCTOR'S OFFICE

A physical examination, and often some blood tests, are carried out. X-rays are rarely useful for making a diagnosis. Advice similar to that above. In general, pain relievers containing narcotics or codeine are not useful. Oral corticosteroids such as prednisone should almost never be used unless a specific diagnosis can be made. If a particular spot in the body is causing the pain, a corticosteroid injection into that area may help greatly. Such injections should not be repeated if they do not help and they should only be repeated one or two times even if they do give prolonged relief.

# Neck Pain

Most neck pain is due to strain and spasm of the neck muscles. The common crick in the neck upon arising is one example of neck-muscle strain. This type of neck pain can be adequately treated at home. Neck pains that require the attention of a doctor include those due to meningitis or a pinched nerve.

**Meningitis**

With fever and headache, there is a possibility of meningitis. More commonly, though, neck pain is part of a flu syndrome with fever, muscle aches, and a headache. When generalized aching throughout the muscles is present, a visit to a doctor is seldom useful. Meningitis may cause intense spasms of the neck muscles and make the neck very stiff. When a stiff neck is due to one of the more common causes of muscle spasm, the patient can usually touch the chin to the chest, though perhaps with difficulty. If in doubt, it is better to see the doctor for an ordinary muscle spasm than to attempt to treat meningitis at home.

**Pinched Nerve**

Arthritis or injury to the neck can result in a pinched nerve. When this is the source of neck pain, the pain may extend down the arm, or there may be numbness or tingling sensations in the arm or hand. This pain is only on one side, and neck stiffness is not prominent.

## HOME TREATMENT

Neck pain in the morning may be due to poor sleeping habits. Sleep on a firm surface and stop using a pillow. A firm mattress is best. If this is not possible, a bed board will make a soft mattress firmer. If an ordinary bath towel is folded lengthwise into a long four-inch wide strip, wrapped around the neck at bedtime, and secured with tape or a safety pin, the relief obtained overnight is often striking.

Warmth may be of benefit in relieving spasms and pain. Heat may be applied with hot showers, hot compresses, or a heating pad. Heat may be used as often as practical, but don't burn the skin. Aspirin or ibuprofen (Advil, Nuprin, etc.) will help relieve pain and inflammation.

Neck pain, like back pain, is slow to improve and may take several weeks to completely resolve. If pain does not lessen in a week, call the doctor.

## NECK PAIN

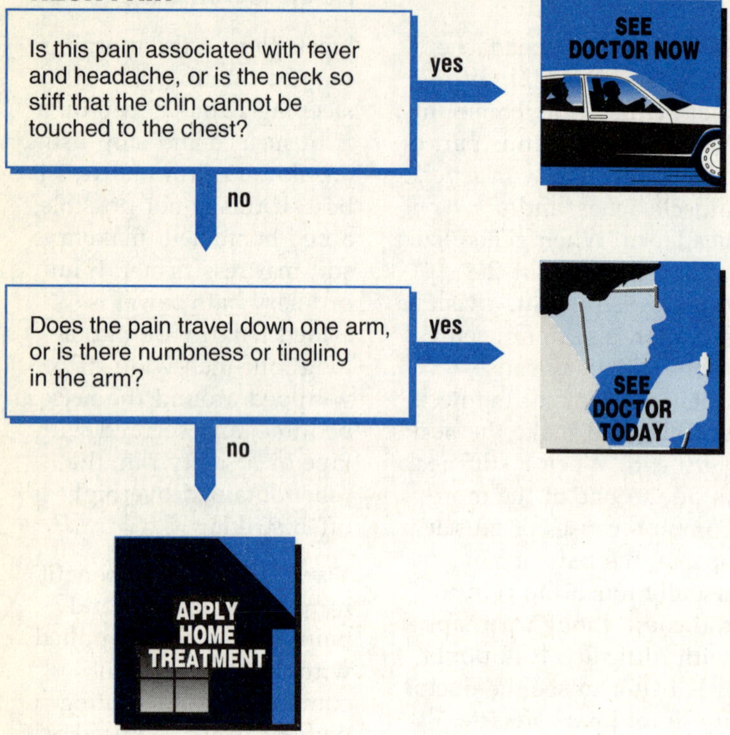


### WHAT TO EXPECT AT THE DOCTOR'S OFFICE

If meningitis is suspected, the doctor will perform a spinal tap as well as several blood tests. If a pinched nerve is likely, X-rays of the neck will be taken. A muscle relaxant may be prescribed and perhaps a more powerful pain reliever. Prescription drugs are not necessarily better than aspirin or ibuprofen. Usually, you are just as well off with home therapy if no infection or nerve damage is present.

The physician may prescribe a neck collar or, if there is nerve damage, refer you to a neurologist or neurosurgeon for consultation. Today the trend is away from drug treatment for this problem.

# Shoulder Pain

Pain located around the shoulder is common and almost never poses a serious threat to life. Nonetheless, it can persist for a long time and cause discomfort and disability. Most of the time the pain comes from the soft tissues near the joint and not from the bones or the joint itself. These soft tissues include the ligaments, tendons, and the bursae—little fluid-filled sacs at the joints.

**Bursitis.** This is an inflammation of the bursae that starts with an uneasy feeling in the shoulder and may progress to considerable pain within 6 to 12 hours. There may be swelling at the tip of the shoulder. It is often seen in persons who have been cutting hedges, painting the house, or playing sports.

**Rotator Cuff Tendinitis.** This is an irritation of the tendons and muscles around the shoulder and is most likely to be seen in baseball pitchers and racquet sport enthusiasts. Unlike bursitis, it is difficult to detect even a small amount of swelling, and the pain seems to occur in only a few positions.

**Bicep Tendinitis.** Much less common, this occurs in gymnasts and players of baseball and racquet sports. The tenderness and pain are located in the front of the shoulder.

Because these three common problems of the shoulder are treated the same initially, you need not worry about which condition you have. However, there are problems that should be differentiated from these:

- Injuries require a slightly different approach (see **Arm Injuries,** page 174).
- Infections are quite unusual in the shoulder, but fever, swelling, and redness of the shoulder suggest the need for a doctor's help.
- Complete inability to move the arm suggests pain severe enough that consulting with a doctor is reasonable.

If none of these problems seems to fit your situation, give your doctor a call for advice. Often a visit will not be necessary.

### HOME TREATMENT

For bursitis, rotator cuff tendinitis, and bicep tendinitis, the key word is RIMS:

- Rest
- Ice
- Maintenance of mobility
- Strengthening

At the first sign of trouble you should apply ice for 30 minutes, then let the shoulder rewarm for the next 15 minutes. Continue the cycle for the next 6 to 12 hours. Be careful not to freeze the skin.

Give the shoulder complete rest for the first 24 to 48 hours. After that time, gently put your arm through a full range of motion several times a day. Complete immobilization of the arm may result in stiffness and loss of motion in the shoulder (frozen shoulder). Thus, maintenance of the shoulder's range of motion is an important part of the treatment. Wait three to six weeks before returning to the activity that caused the problem, depending on the problem's severity. Returning too soon will increase the probability of reinjury.

After the initial rest period, exercises should be started to gradually strengthen the muscles around the shoulder. This is especially important in rotator cuff tendinitis. At first, the exercise need consist only of putting the arm through a full range of motion. Next a small amount of weight (1 to 1½ pounds) is held in the hand as the exercises are performed. Weight is gradually increased by a half pound every ten days. Heat may be applied before the exercise, but ice is recommended after exercise.

**Some of the problems related specifically to racquet sports, baseball pitching, or golf are due to poor technique. Coaching from a professional is well worth considering. It is less expensive than going to a doctor—and you will probably gain some help with your game.**

Aspirin or acetaminophen, two tablets every three to four hours, may be taken as needed. Aspirin and ibuprofen (Advil, Nuprin, etc.) may help decrease inflammation.

A doctor should be called if the condition persists beyond three weeks.

**SHOULDER PAIN**

Is this due to an injury?

yes → *See:* **Arm Injuries,** page 174.

no ↓

Are any of the following present?

- Fever
- Swelling and redness
- Inability to use the joint

yes →

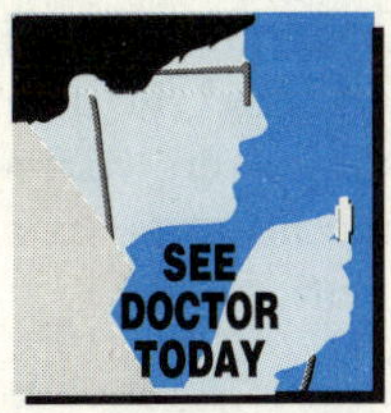


no ↓

Is this associated with sport or physical activity involving use of the shoulder?

no →

yes ↓

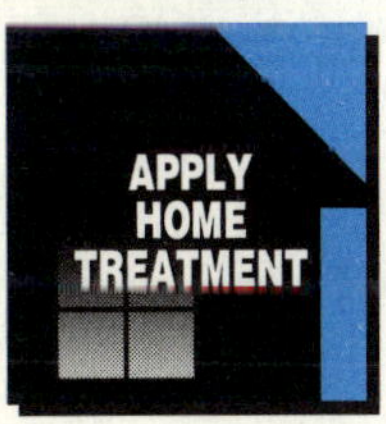


## WHAT TO EXPECT AT THE DOCTOR'S OFFICE

The doctor will examine the shoulder and prescribe a regimen similar to the one above, if one of the common causes of shoulder pain is diagnosed. If the problem is bursitis, a corticosteroid injection may be given on the first visit. Otherwise, such injections should be given only if home therapy does not work. There should be no more than two or three such injections. Non-steroidal anti-inflammatory drugs (NSAIDs) may be given. These are similar to aspirin and ibuprofen. They may decrease pain but do not speed the healing process. Expect instruction in rehabilitation exercises.

Surgery is the last resort and is a gamble. Satisfaction is not guaranteed.

# Elbow Pain

Aside from injuries, there are two main causes of elbow pain: bursitis and tennis elbow.

**Bursitis**

The elbow *bursa* is a fluid-filled sac located right at the tip of the elbow. When it is irritated, the amount of fluid increases, causing a swelling that looks very much like a small egg right at the end of the elbow. The swelling is the cause of discomfort. There should be no fever and only a little redness, if any.

**Tennis Elbow**

Of the cases of tennis elbow that reach the doctor's office, less than half are actually associated with playing tennis. The rest usually result from work that requires a twisting motion of the arm—such as using a screwdriver—or have no obvious associated event.

Regardless of cause, tennis elbow seldom means a visit to a doctor. The doctor's help is needed only for prolonged cases that don't get better; perhaps 1 person in 1000 needs such help.

The diagnosis of tennis elbow does not depend on tests or special examinations. Tennis elbow is simply defined as pain in the lateral (outer) portion of the elbow and upper forearm. The pain occurs after repeatedly rolling or twisting the forearm, wrist, and hand.

Professional tennis players and baseball pitchers get a tennis elbow that is different from the tennis elbow the rest of us get. They have more problems with the inside portion of the elbow and forearm than the outside portion, probably due to very hard serves or throws.

For amateurs, tennis elbow seems to be caused by the tremendous impact transmitted to the forearm when the tennis ball is hit with the backhand motion. The risk that this force will create tennis elbow is raised by:

**1.** Hitting the ball with the elbow bent rather than locked in a position of strength.

**2.** Attempting to put top spin on the ball by rolling the wrist on contact (this doesn't work, by the way).

**3.** Holding the thumb behind the racket.

**ELBOW PAIN**

Is this due to an injury?

yes → *See:* **Arm Injuries**, page 174.

no ↓

Are any of the following present?

- Fever
- Swelling and redness
- Inability to use the joint

yes → 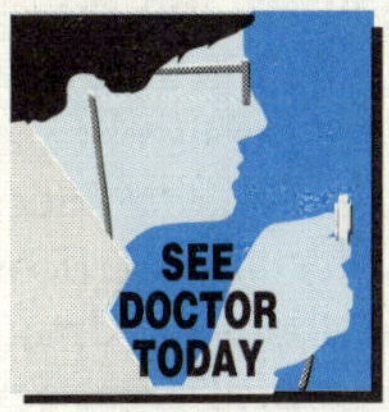


no ↓

Is this associated with sport or physical activity involving use of the shoulder?

no → 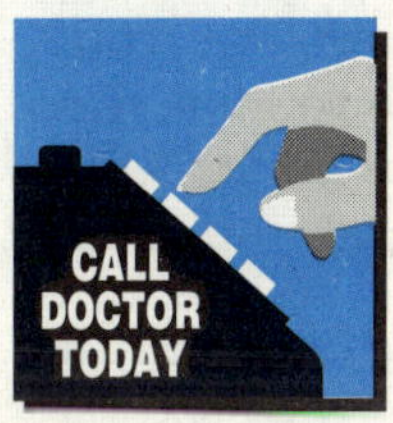


yes ↓

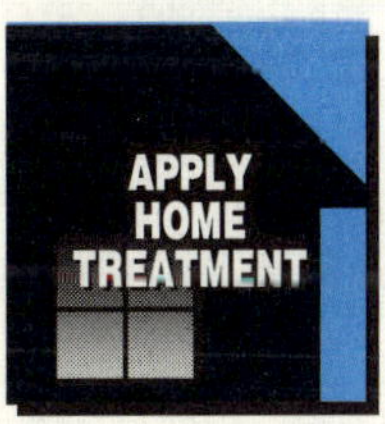


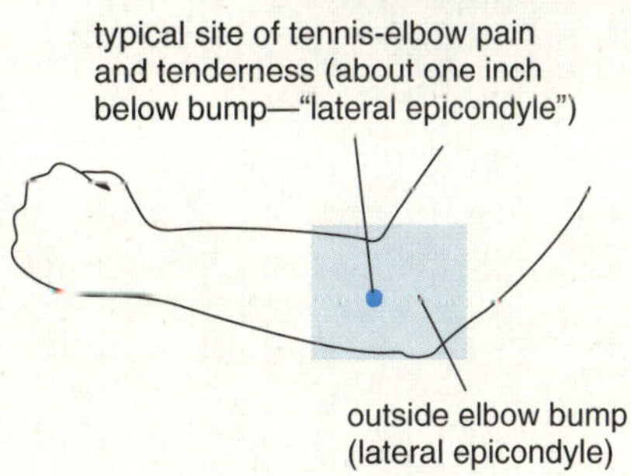


**4.** Using a racket that is head-heavy, especially a wood racket.

**5.** Switching from a slower to a faster court surface.

**6.** Using heavier balls, such as those of foreign manufacture or the pressureless type.

**7.** Using a very stiff racket.

According to the experts, the single most important preventive measure for tennis players is to use a two-handed backhand stroke.

## HOME TREATMENT

Bursitis of the elbow is treated very much like bursitis of the shoulder (see page 347).

At the first sign of tennis elbow you should, of course, take preventive measures. But suppose that you already use a two-handed backhand, have switched to a light and supple metal racket, and so on. Or suppose your job or favorite hobby requires repeated use of screwdrivers or other tools that aggravate the problem. What now? Resting the arm will surely make it hurt less, but most likely taking two weeks off will not cure it forever. Interestingly, most authorities now think that you can "play with pain" and not cause permanent injury.

We advocate a commonsense approach to tennis elbow: cut down on your playing time. When you do play, warm up slowly and do some stretching exercises of the wrist and elbow before you begin to hit the ball. Using a tennis elbow strap may help. Applying ice after playing may also help.

### WHAT TO EXPECT AT THE DOCTOR'S OFFICE

Bursitis of the elbow is treated by the doctor very much like bursitis of the shoulder (see page 347).

If you are the rare person with tennis elbow who has severe persistent pain, the next step is to inject a pain reliever and corticosteroid (cortisone-like drug) into the painful area. Three such injections is the limit. Surgery should be a last resort—an act of desperation. If you get to this point, perhaps it's time to take up another game.

# Wrist Pain

The wrist is an unusual joint because stiffness or even complete loss of motion causes relatively little difficulty. However, if it is wobbly and unstable, this can pose real problems. The wrist provides the platform from which the fine motions of the fingers operate. It is essential that this platform be stable. The eight wrist bones form a rather crude joint that is very limited in motion compared with, for example, the shoulder. But this joint is strong and stable. The wrist platform works best when it is bent upward just a little. Almost no normal human activities require the wrist to be bent all the way back or all the way forward, and the fingers don't operate as well when the wrist is fully flexed or fully extended.

## Causes of Pain

Fever and/or rapid swelling accompanying the onset of pain suggest the possibility of an infection. This requires prompt medical attention.

The wrist is very frequently involved in rheumatoid arthritis, and the side of the wrist by the thumb is very commonly involved in osteoarthritis.

**Carpal tunnel syndrome** can cause pain at the wrist. In addition, this syndrome can cause pains to shoot down into the fingers or up into the forearm. Usually, there is a numb feeling in the fingers as if they were asleep. In this syndrome, the median nerve is trapped and squeezed as it passes through the fibrous carpal tunnel in the front of the wrist. Generally, the squeezing results from too much inflammatory tissue. Some causes can be playing tennis, a blow to the front of the wrist, canoe paddling, rheumatoid arthritis, or a lot of other activities that repeatedly flex and extend the wrist.

You can diagnose carpal tunnel syndrome pretty well yourself. The numbness in the fingers does not involve the little finger and often does not involve the half of the ring finger nearest the little finger. If you tap with a finger on the front of the wrist, you may get a sudden tingling in the fingers similar to the feeling of hitting your funny bone. Tingling and pain in carpal tunnel syndrome may be worse at night or when the wrists are cocked down (flexed).

### HOME TREATMENT

The key to management of wrist pain is splinting. Because stability is essential and loss of motion is not as serious in the wrist as in other joints, the treatment strategy is a little different. Exercises to increase the motion of the joint are not very important. The strategy is to rest the joint in the position of best function.

Wrist splints are available at hospital supply stores and many drug stores. Any that fit you are probably all right. The splint will be made of plastic or aluminum, and the hand rest will cock your wrist back just a bit. You can put a cloth sleeve around the splint to make it more comfortable against your skin. Wrap the splint gently with an elastic bandage to keep it in place. That's all there is to it. Wear it all the time for a few days, then just at night for a few weeks. This simple treatment is all that is required for most wrist flare-ups. Even carpal tunnel syndrome is initially treated by splinting. But, because nerve damage is potentially serious, give your doctor a call if you seem to have carpal tunnel syndrome.

No major pain medication should be necessary. Aspirin and similar medications are all right but probably won't help too much. If you are taking a prescribed anti-inflammatory drug, be certain that you are taking it just as directed. Sometimes a flare-up is simply due to inadequate medication. If you know what triggered the pain, work out a way to avoid that activity. Common sense means listening to the pain message.

**As more people type on computers, there have been more worries about carpal tunnel syndrome. Research continues, but there seem to be two important factors: stress, especially from pressure to type quickly or without interruption, and poor hand positioning. Keep your wrists supported, take brief rests, and consider using a different keyboard to help avoid pain.**

If the problem persists after six weeks of home treatments, see the doctor.

## WRIST PAIN

Is this due to an injury?

yes → *See:* **Arm Injuries**, page 174.

no ↓

Is there either of the following?

- Fever
- Rapid swelling or severe pain at rest

yes →

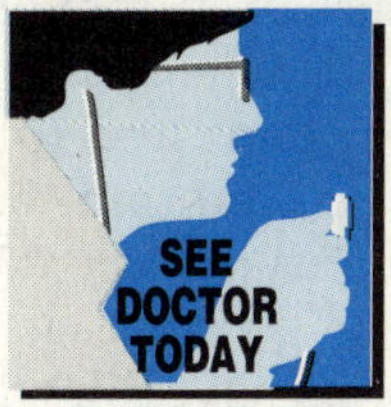


no ↓

Is there numbness or tingling in fingers?

yes →

no ↓

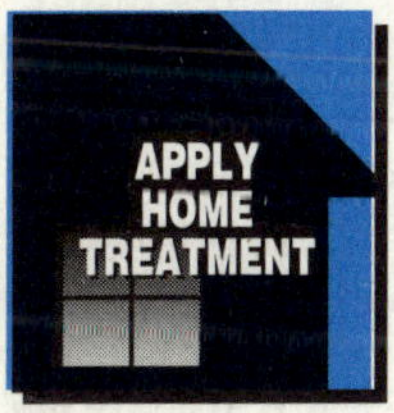


### WHAT TO EXPECT AT THE DOCTOR'S OFFICE

The wrist will be examined and advice similar to that above will be given. X-rays may be required, but only rarely. Anti-inflammatory drugs may be prescribed. Injection with a steroid medication may be performed on occasion and is likely to help if carpal tunnel syndrome has not responded to splinting.

Several different kinds of surgery are available, and one or another procedure may be recommended in difficult cases. Carpal tunnel nerve compression may be released surgically. In rheumatoid arthritis, the synovial tissue on the back of the hand may be removed to protect the tendons that run through the inflamed area. The wrist may be casted or the bones fused. Rarely, removal of the ends of the forearm bones will help prevent further damage.

# Finger Pain

Each hand has 14 finger joints, and each of these acts like a small hinge. These joints are operated by muscles in the forearm that control them via an intricate system of tendons that run through the wrist and hand. The small size and complex arrangement mean that any inflammation or damage to the joint is likely to result in some stiffness and lost motion. Even a small scar or adhesion will limit motion.

You shouldn't expect that a problem with a small finger joint will resolve completely. Even after healing is complete, some leftover stiffness and occasional twinges of discomfort are likely. Unrealistically high expectations lead to feelings that you did something wrong or that the doctor was no good. In fact, almost all of us have a few fingers that have been injured and remain a bit crooked or stiff. The hand functions very well despite these minor deformities. Fingers need not open fully or close completely to be perfectly functional.

**Osteoarthritis** frequently causes knobby swelling of the most distant joints of the fingers and also swelling of the middle joints. It can also cause problems at the base of the thumb. If we live long enough, all of us get these knobby swellings. They cause most of the changed appearance that we associate with the aging hand. As a rule, they cause relatively little pain or stiffness and don't need specific treatment other than exercise.

Numbness or tingling may indicate a problem with nerves or circulation. A call to the doctor will help you make a decision about what to do.

### HOME TREATMENT

Listen to the pain message and avoid activities that cause or aggravate pain. Rest the finger joints so that they can heal, but use gentle stretching exercises to keep them limber and maintain motion. The key to managing finger problems is to use common sense.

With a bit of ingenuity, you can find a less stressful way to do almost any activity that puts stress on the joints. Because everyone's activities are a bit different, you will have to invent some of these new methods yourself. Here are a few hints to get you going:

**FINGER PAIN**

Is this due to an injury?

yes → *See:* **Smashed Fingers**, page 188.

no ↓

Is there either of the following?

- Numbing or tingling in the fingers
- Severe pain at rest

yes →

no ↓

Is it impossible to straighten fingers?

yes →

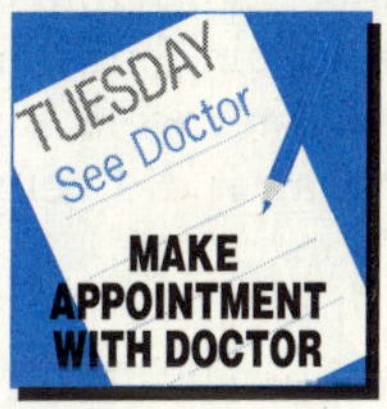


no ↓

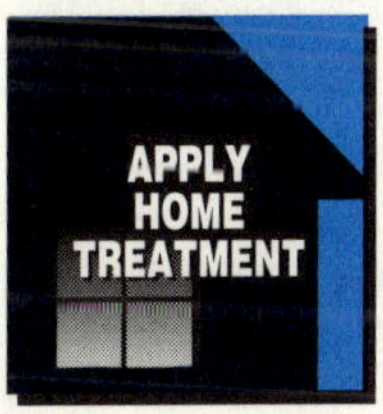


- A big handle can be gripped with less strain than a small handle. Wrapping pens, knives, and other similar objects with tape or putting a sponge-rubber handle over the original handle can protect the grip.
- Lift smaller loads. Make more trips. Plan ahead rather than blundering through an activity.
- Let others open a car door for you. Get power steering or a very light car.
- Use a gripper for opening tough jar lids or stop buying products that come in hard-to-open jars. When opening a tough lid, apply friction pressure on the top of the lid with your palm and twist with your whole hand, not your grip.
- Cultivate creative friends who are handy at making little gadgets to help you.
- Don't put heavy objects too high or too low. Organize your kitchen, workshop, study, and bedroom.

Stretch the joints gently twice a day to maintain motion.

**1.** Straighten the hand out against the table top.

**2.** Make a fist and then cock the wrist to increase the stretch.

**3.** Use one hand to move each finger of the other hand through from full flexion to straight out. Don't force, but stretch just to the edge of discomfort. If the motion of a joint is normal, one repetition is enough. If the motion is limited, do up to ten repetitions.

Putting the hands in warm water before stretching may help you get more motion.

Don't use strong pain medicines. They mask the pain so that you may overdo an activity or exercise. Be sure that you take prescribed medication for inflammation just as instructed. Good hand function is important, and you want to pay close attention to treatment.

If the problem persists after six weeks of home treatment, see the doctor.

### WHAT TO EXPECT AT THE DOCTOR'S OFFICE

The doctor will examine your hands and the finger motions. Sometimes an X-ray is taken, but usually not more often than every two years. Anti-inflammatory medications such as aspirin, acetaminophen, or ibuprofen can help, but doses should usually be low to moderate. Rarely, injection of steroids into a particularly bad finger joint is helpful, but this is less effective with small joints than with large ones.

Surgery is also less effective with small joints and is often not indicated. Operations such as replacement with plastic joints or removal of inflamed tissue usually succeed in making the hand look more normal and may decrease pain, but the hand often doesn't work much better than it did before the operation.

# Low Back Pain

Few problems can frustrate patient and doctor alike as much as low back pain. The pain is slow to resolve and apt to recur. Frustration then becomes a part of the problem and may also require treatment.

Low back pain usually involves spasm of the large supportive muscles alongside the spine. Any injury to the back may produce such spasms. Pain—often severe—and stiffness result. The onset of pain may be immediate or may occur some hours after exertion or injury. Often the cause is not clear.

Most muscular problems in the back are linked to some injury and must heal naturally. Give them time. Back pain that results from a severe blow or fall may require immediate attention. As a practical matter, if back pain is caused by an injury received at work, examination by a doctor is required by the workers' compensation laws.

Pain due to muscular strain is usually confined to the back. Occasionally, it may extend into the buttocks or upper leg. Pain that extends down the leg to below the knee suggests pressure on the nerves as they leave the spinal cord and requires help from a doctor. If backache occurs with other symptoms (such as difficult menstrual periods), refer to the appropriate decision chart for that symptom.

## HOME TREATMENT

The low-back-pain syndrome is a vicious cycle in which injury causes muscle spasm, the spasm induces pain, and the pain results in additional muscle spasm. Rest and pain relief are meant to interrupt this cycle.

The injury must heal by itself. To heal most rapidly, you must avoid reinjury. Either rest flat on your back for the first 24 hours or be very, very careful.

Severe muscle-spasm pain usually lasts for 48 to 72 hours and is followed by days or weeks of less severe pain. Strenuous activity during the next six weeks can bring the problem back and delay complete recovery. After healing, an exercise program will help prevent reinjury. *No* drug will hasten healing; drugs only reduce symptoms.

The patient should sleep, pillowless, either on a very firm mattress, with a bed board under the mattress, on a waterbed, or even on the floor. A folded towel beneath the low back and a pillow under the knees may increase comfort.

Heat applied to the affected area will provide some relief. Aspirin or ibuprofen should be continued as long as there is significant pain. To avoid upset stomach, take the medication with milk or food, or else use buffered aspirin (Ascriptin, Bufferin, etc.).

If there is no nerve damage, hospitalization and the doctor have little to offer. If significant pain persists beyond a week, call the doctor.

## WHAT TO EXPECT AT THE DOCTOR'S OFFICE

Expect questions similar to those on the decision chart. The examination will center on the back, the abdomen, and the extremities, with special attention to testing the nerve function of the legs. If the injury is the result of a fall or a blow to the back, X-rays are indicated; otherwise, they usually are not. X-rays reveal injury only to bones, not to muscles. If the history and the physical examination are consistent with lower-back strain, the doctor's advice will be similar to that described above.

A muscle relaxant may be prescribed. If the history and physical examination indicate damage to the nerves leaving the spinal cord, a special X-ray, such as a myelogram, CAT scan, or MRI, may be necessary. If there is pressure on nerves, hospitalization, traction, or surgery may be considered. Such treatments may be considered if pain is continuous over a long period, even if there is no pressure on any nerves. The chance that these treatments will help, however, is slim. For example, less than half of those who have surgery for chronic pain have substantial relief. Chronic pain may respond best to increasing flexibility and strength of the muscles, as well as learning to control pain through mental relaxation and thought-control techniques.

**LOW BACK PAIN**

Is pain associated with any of the following?

- Flu-like symptoms
- Nausea, vomiting, or diarrhea
- Abdominal pain
- Pain, bleeding, or frequent urination
- Menstrual period

**yes** →

*See* the following problems:
**Colds and Flu**, page 225
**Nausea and Vomiting**, page 407
**Diarrhea**, page 409
**Abdominal Pain**, page 413
**Painful, Frequent, or Bloody Urination**, page 430
**Difficult Periods**, page 437.

**no** ↓

Is there fever or does pain travel down the legs below the knee?

**yes** →

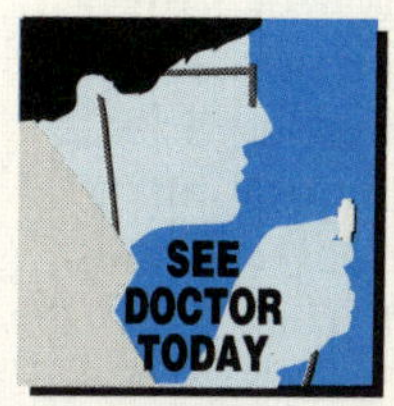


**no** ↓

Is this due to a blow or fall?

**yes** →

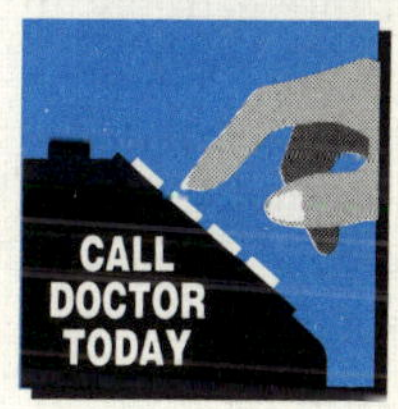


**no** ↓

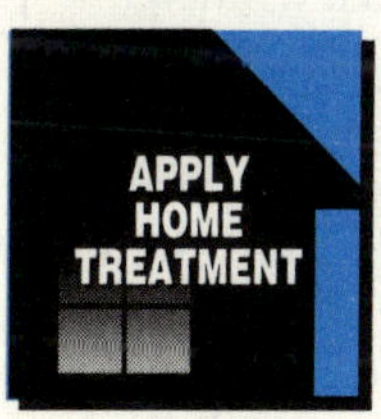

# Hip Pain

The hip is a "ball-and-socket" joint. The largest bone in the body, the femur, is in the thigh. The femur narrows to a "neck" that angles into the pelvis and ends in a ball-shaped knob. This ball fits into a curved socket in the pelvic bones (acetabulum). This arrangement provides a joint that can move freely in all directions. The joint itself is located rather deeply under some big muscles so that it is protected from dislocation—that is, from coming out of its socket.

Two special problems arise because of this anatomical arrangement. The narrow neck of the femur can break rather easily, and this is usually what happens when an older person breaks a hip after a slight fall. Also, the ball portion of the femur gets its blood through the narrow neck. The small artery that supplies the head of the femur can get clogged, leading to death of the bone and a kind of arthritis called **aseptic necrosis**.

The hip joint can also get infected. Rarely, it will be the site for an attack of gout. The bursae that lie over the joint can be inflamed with bursitis. Rheumatoid arthritis and osteoarthritis can also injure the joint. Conditions such as ankylosing spondylitis can cause stiffness or loss of motion of the hip.

### Related Problems

A **flexion contracture** is a common consequence of hip problems. This means that motion of the hip joint has been partly lost. The hip becomes partially fixed in a slightly bent position. When walking or standing, this causes the pelvis to tilt forward, so that when you stand straight, the back has to curve a little more. This throws extra strain on the lower back.

For poorly understood reasons, pain in the hip is often felt down the leg, often at or just above the knee. This is called **referred pain**. Nonreferred hip pain may be felt in the groin or the upper outer thigh. Pain that starts in the low back is often felt in the hip region. Because the hip joint is so deeply located, it can often be troublesome to locate the exact source of pain.

## HOME TREATMENT

Listen for the pain message and try to avoid activities that aggravate your hip. You should avoid pain medication as much as possible. Rest the joint after painful activities.

Use a cane or crutches if necessary. The cane is usually best held in the hand opposite to the painful hip because this allows greater relaxation in the large muscles around the sore hip joint. Move the cane and the affected side simultaneously, then move the good side, then repeat.

**HIP PAIN**

Is this due to an injury?

yes → *See:* **Broken Bone?**, page 167.

no ↓

Is there any of the following?

- Fever
- Severe pain when not bearing weight
- Inability to walk at all

yes →

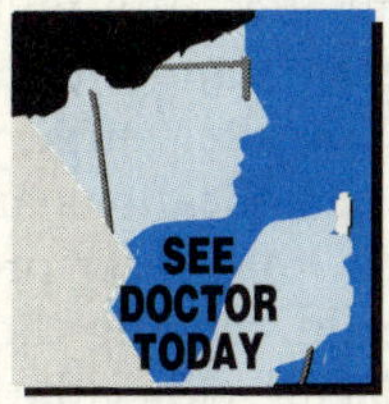


no ↓

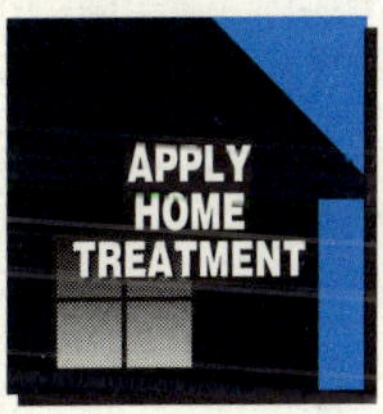


As the pain begins to resolve, exercise should be gradually introduced. First, use gentle motion exercises to free the hip and prevent stiffness.

- Stand with your good hip by a table and lean on the table with your hand. Let the bad hip swing to and fro and front and back.
- Lie on your back with your body half off the bed and the bad hip hanging. Let the leg stretch backward toward the floor. See how far apart you can straddle your legs and bend the upper body from side to side. Try to turn your feet apart like a duck so that the rotation ligaments get stretched.

Repeat these exercises gently two or three times a day.

Then, introduce more active exercises to strengthen the muscles around the hips.

- Lie on your back and raise your legs.
- Swimming stretches muscles and builds good muscle tone.
- Bicycle or walk. When walking, start with short strides and gradually lengthen them as you loosen up. Gradually increase your efforts and distance, but not by more than 10% each day.

A good firm bed will help. The best sleeping position is on your back. Avoid pillows beneath the knees or under the lower back. Make sure you are taking anti-inflammatory medication as prescribed, especially if you have rheumatoid arthritis or ankylosing spondylitis.

If pain persists after six weeks of home treatment, see the doctor.

### WHAT TO EXPECT AT THE DOCTOR'S OFFICE

The hip will be examined and taken through its range of motion. Your other leg joints and back will also be examined. X-rays may well be necessary. Anti-inflammatory medication may be prescribed or the dosage increased. Injection is only rarely needed.

One of several surgical procedures may be recommended if the pain is intense and persistent, if you are having real problems walking, or if time and home treatment have not solved the problem. Total hip replacement is a remarkable operation and has largely replaced many older techniques. This operation is almost always successful in stopping pain and may help mobility a great deal. An artificial hip should last at least 10 to 15 years with current techniques. You will be able to get up and around quite quickly after surgery, and the complications are rather rare. Other older procedures include: pinning the hip; replacing either the ball or the socket, but not both; or removing a wedge of bone to straighten out the angle of the joint.

# Knee Pain

The knee is a hinge. It is a large weight-bearing joint, but its motion is much more strictly limited than that of most other joints. It will straighten for stable support, and it will bend to more than a right angle, to approximately 120°. However, it will not move in any other direction. The limited motion of the knee gives it great strength, but it is not engineered to take side stresses.

There are two cartilage compartments in the knee—one inner and one outer. If the cartilage wears unevenly, the leg can bow in or bow out. If you were born with crooked legs, there can be strain that causes the cartilage to wear more rapidly. If you are overweight, you are far more likely to have knee problems.

The knee must be stable, and it must be able to extend fully so that the leg is straight. If it lacks full extension, the muscles have to support the body at all times and strain is continuous. Normally, our knee locks in the straight position and allows us to rest. (Horses are able to sleep standing up because they can rest with their knees locked.) If the knee wobbles from side to side, there is too much stress on the side ligaments, and the condition may gradually worsen.

### When to See a Doctor

If the knee is unstable and wobbles, or if it cannot be straightened out, you need a doctor. This is also true if there is a possibility of gout or an infection; the knee is the joint most frequently bothered by these serious problems.

Finally, if there is pain or swelling in the calf below the sore knee, you may have a blood clot. But more likely, you have a **Baker's cyst**. These cysts start as fluid-filled sacs in an inflamed knee but enlarge through the tissues of the calf and may cause swelling quite a distance below the knee. You should see your doctor for this condition.

These are the reasons to see the doctor about knee pain:

- Inability to walk at all
- Rapid development of swelling without injury
- Associated fever
- Associated recent injury with the knee wobbling from side to side or inability to straighten leg
- Severe pain when not bearing weight
- Pain and swelling of the calf below a swollen or painful knee
- Pain persisting after six weeks of home treatment

## HOME TREATMENT

Listen to the pain message and try not to do anything that aggravates the pain. If you have arthritis make sure that you are taking any medication as directed. Your painful knee could be caused by too little medication. Otherwise, aspirin, ibuprofen, or acetaminophen may be used to ease the pain.

Using a cane can help; usually, the cane is best carried in the hand on the same side as the painful knee, but some prefer to carry it on the opposite side.

Do not use a pillow under the knee at night or at any other time. This can make the knee stiffen so that it cannot be straightened out.

Exercises should be started slowly and performed several times daily if possible. Swimming is good because it is non-weight bearing.

**1.** From the beginning, pay close attention to flexing and straightening the leg. A friend can help because it may be more comfortable to move the leg passively. But work at getting it straight and keeping it straight.

**2.** Next, begin isometric exercises. Tense the muscles in your upper leg, front and back, at the same time, so that you are exerting force but your leg is not moving. Exert the force for two seconds, then rest two seconds. Do ten repetitions three times a day.

**3.** Begin gentle active exercises. A bicycle in low gear is a good place to start. Stationary bicycles are fine. Be sure that the seat is relatively high. Your knee should not bend to more than a right angle during the bicycle stroke.

**Many people have wondered if exercise such as walking or running can cause knee problems. No. If the knee is not injured, exercise and weight-bearing are good. They help nourish the cartilage, and they keep the side ligaments, the muscles, and the bones strong, which keeps the knee stable.**

**4.** Walking is probably the best overall exercise, and distances should be gradually increased.

Avoid exercises or activities that simulate deep knee bends because they place too much stress on the knee. Knee problems can develop from the feet so proper shoes can help.

## KNEE PAIN

Is this due to an injury?

yes → *See:* **Knee Injuries**, page 172.

no ↓

Are there any of the following?

- Fever
- Rapid swelling
- Severe pain when not bearing weight
- Inability to walk at all
- Swelling or pain in calf

yes →

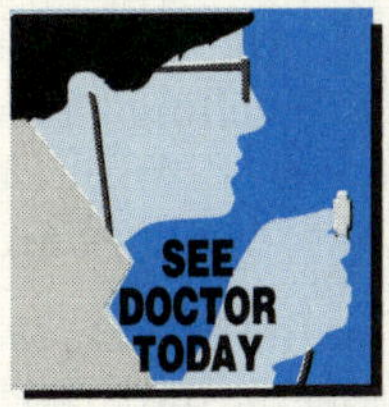


no ↓

Is the knee unstable or unable to be straightened?

yes →

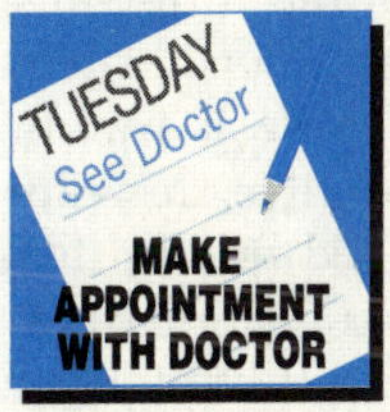


no ↓

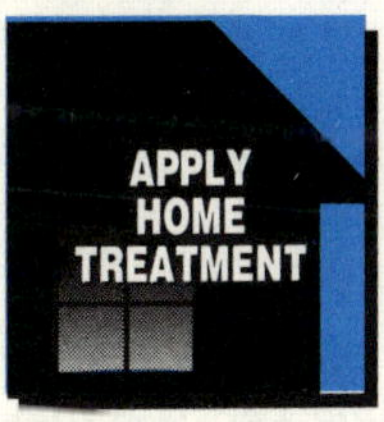


## WHAT TO EXPECT AT THE DOCTOR'S OFFICE

The knee and other joints will be examined and taken through their range of motion. An X-ray of the knee may be taken. Fluid may be drawn from the knee through a needle and tested if a Baker's cyst is suspected or for other diagnostic reasons. This procedure is easy, not too uncomfortable, and quite safe.

There are a number of operations that are quite helpful for knee problems. A torn meniscus may be removed, or cartilage may be shaved through arthroscopic surgery. Increasingly, doctors are using the arthroscope to view the condition and often to help cure it. This is a minor procedure. For severe and persistent problems, total knee replacement may be recommended. This is an excellent operation and usually gives total pain relief. Next to the hip, knee replacement is the most successful total joint-replacement surgery.

# Leg Pain

Three types of problems account for most leg pain not associated with injuries:

- Inflammation and clots in veins—thrombophlebitis
- Narrowing of arteries—intermittent claudication
- "Overuse" problems associated with vigorous exercise, referred to collectively as "**shin splints**" (see page 370).

**Thrombophlebitis** is most likely to occur after a prolonged period of inactivity, such as a long car or plane ride. The pain is aching and usually not localized, but sometimes a firm and tender vein can be felt in the middle of the calf. Swelling does not always occur or may be so slight that it's hard to detect.

In older people or heavy smokers, the arteries in the leg may become narrowed so that enough blood does not reach the muscles during even such mild exercise as walking. The pain that this causes is called **intermittent claudication** because the pain is brought on by exercise, but relief comes in a few minutes with rest.

Both thrombophlebitis and intermittent claudication will require the help of the doctor, but thrombophlebitis is more urgent. A decision on the method of treatment should be made as soon as possible.

Consult the physician by telephone for leg pain that does not fit the description of intermittent claudication, thrombophlebitis, or shin splints.

## WHAT TO EXPECT AT THE DOCTOR'S OFFICE

If thrombophlebitis is suspected, the crucial question is whether or not to prescribe anticoagulants (blood thinners). The purpose of anticoagulants is to minimize the risk of a clot going to the lungs—**pulmonary embolism**. However, the effectiveness of anticoagulants is far from complete and the therapy itself carries substantial risks.

## LEG PAIN

Is the leg swollen?

yes →

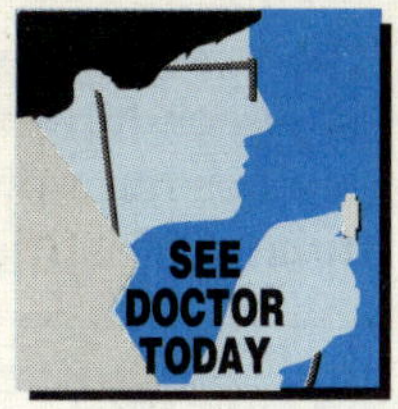


no ↓

Is this leg pain in an older person or heavy smoker that comes on with exercise and is relieved by rest?

yes →

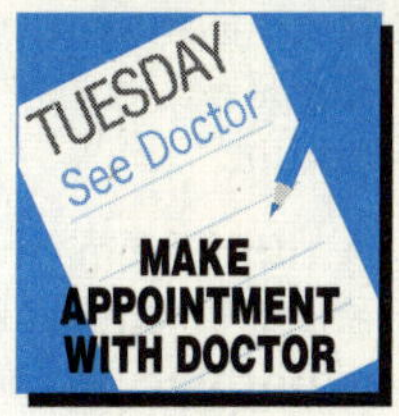


no ↓

Is this pain in the front or inner aspect of leg that is associated with vigorous exercise (running, basket-ball, etc.)?

no →

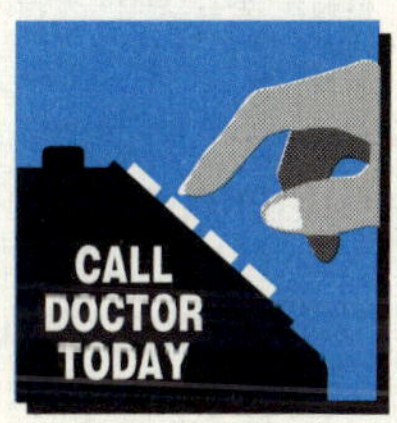


yes ↓

*See:* **Shin Splints,** page 370.

Current information suggests that a simple test called impedance plethysmography (IPG) is very useful in detecting the presence of thrombophlebitis in the thigh. Because thrombophlebitis in the calf alone is thought to produce little risk of pulmonary embolism, a negative IPG test indicates no need for anticoagulants. IPG is painless and requires no surgery or injections. Regardless of whether IPG is done, you and the doctor must come to an understanding about the risks and benefits of anticoagulant therapy before making a decision.

Intermittent claudication can usually be diagnosed from history and physical examination. However, if the problem is substantial, an arteriogram (a special X-ray of the arteries of the legs) will be required to determine where the problem lies before treatment can be considered. Therapy, if required, is one of several surgical procedures ranging from insertion of a special tube (balloon catheter) so that the artery is widened to bypassing the obstructed segment with a synthetic graft.

# Shin Splints

"Shin splints" is a catch-all term that may indicate any one of four conditions associated with strenuous exercise, usually after a period of relative inactivity.

**Posterior tibial shin splints** are the "original" shin splints and account for about 75% of the problems affecting athletes in the front portion of their legs. Overstressing the posterior tibial muscle causes pain where it attaches to the tibia, or shin bone, which is easily seen and felt in the front of your leg. Pain and tenderness are located in a three- to four-inch area on the inner edge of the tibia about midway between the knee and ankle. It is the muscle and the attachments to the bone that are painful; the front of the tibia itself, felt immediately beneath the skin, is not tender.

The front of the tibial bone is tender, however, in another form of shin splint, **tibial periostitis**. The pain and tenderness are similar to that in posterior tibial shin splints except that it is further toward the front of the leg and the bone itself is tender.

A third form of shin splint, **anterior compartment syndrome**, is located on the outer side of the front of the leg. You can readily feel the difference between the hard tibial bone and the muscles located in the anterior compartment. Pain arises when the muscles swell with blood during hard use. The compartment cannot increase in size so that the swelling squeezes the blood vessels and diminishes blood flow. The lack of adequate blood flow to the muscles causes the pain. After resting for 10 to 15 minutes, the pain goes away.

Sharply localized pain and tenderness in the tibia one or two inches below the knee is typical of a **stress fracture**. Just as with stress fractures of the foot, these are likely to occur two or three weeks into an increased training program after the legs have taken a real pounding. As with stress fractures of the foot, stress fractures of the tibia are not treated with casts, but with rest.

### HOME TREATMENT

**Posterior tibial shin splints** will usually respond to a week of rest during which the area of tenderness is iced twice a day for 20 minutes. Aspirin or ibuprofen with every meal may also help. When the pain is gone, stretch the posterior tibial muscle using the exercises described for Achilles tendinitis (see page 378). If you have flat feet, consider getting an arch support (orthotic) for your athletic shoe. Do not begin running again for another two to four weeks, and then only at half speed and with a gradual increase in speed and distance.

**SHIN SPLINTS**

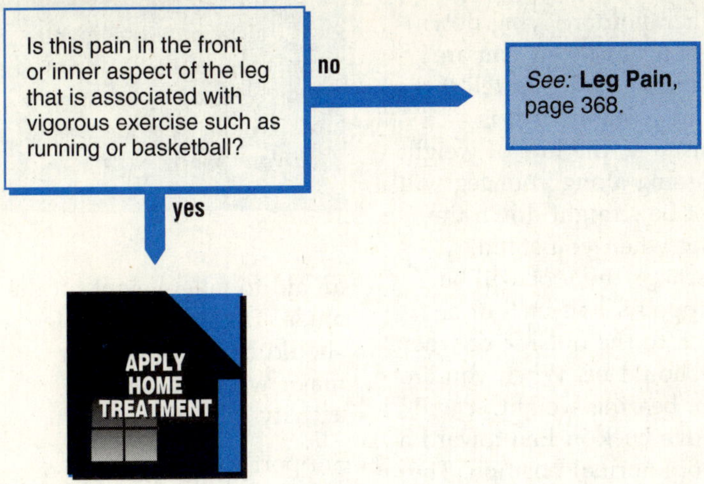


**Tibial periostitis** is treated in the same way as posterior tibial shin splints, except that your gradual return to sports can begin after a week of rest, aspirin or ibuprofen, and ice therapy. Athletic shoes with good shock absorption, especially in the heel, are very important.

**Anterior compartment syndrome** will almost always go away as the muscles gradually become accustomed to vigorous exercise. You can help by resting for 10 minutes when pain occurs before beginning to run slowly again. Cooling the leg with ice for 20 minutes after each workout may also help. Complete rest is not necessary. Shoes and aspirin are unimportant in the treatment of anterior compartment syndrome. If you are the 1 person in 1000 with anterior compartment syndrome for whom the problem does not go away with home treatment, surgery can be considered.

**Stress fractures** require rest from running, usually for a month before gradually starting to recondition your legs. Complete healing requires between four and six weeks. Crutches can be used, but usually are not necessary.

Note again that only the anterior compartment syndrome has any treatment other than home treatment and that this treatment (surgery) is used only as a last resort. However, if you are unsure as to the nature of the problem or you have made no progress with home treatment after several weeks, consult the doctor.

## WHAT TO EXPECT AT THE DOCTOR'S OFFICE

Home treatment will be prescribed for any of the four varieties of shin splints. In the very rare event that an anterior compartment syndrome does not go away over time, the pressure can be relieved by splitting the tough, fibrous tissue (fascia) that surrounds the muscles. This is a relatively simple surgical procedure and can be accomplished without requiring a stay in the hospital.

# Ankle Pain

The ankle is a large weight-bearing joint that is unavoidably stressed at each step. Several kinds of arthritis can involve the bones and cartilage of the ankle, but pain and instability are more frequently a result of problems in the ligaments.

The **sprained ankle** is a simple example of this. With an ankle sprain, the ligament attaching the bump on the outer side of the ankle to the outer surface of the foot is injured at one or both ends. The ankle itself is all right.

With **arthritis**, the ligaments may have been injured so that the joint slips and wobbles. This results in further stress on the ligaments, and pain and instability result. Walking on an unstable joint just increases the damage, but if you can stabilize the joint, walking is usually all right.

If you look at your leg when you are lying down and again when you are standing, you can tell if the joint is stable. If it is unstable, the line of weight passing along your leg will not be straight down the foot when you stand. Perhaps the foot will be slipped a half-inch or an inch to the outside of where it should be. When you are not bearing weight, it will move back in line toward a more normal position. The unstable joint may actually slip sideways if you try to move the foot with your hands. Instability is not just due to a swollen ankle (see page 374); the ankle must be displaced sideways or be crooked.

## HOME TREATMENT

Listen to the pain message. It is telling you to rest your ankle a bit more, to provide support for an unstable ankle, to back off of your exercise program, or to use an aid to take weight off the ankle. The unstable ankle should be supported for major weight-bearing activity.

**Crutches should be short enough so you don't injure the nerves in your armpits by leaning on the crutch. Take the weight on your hands or arms.**

Support is most simply obtained from high-lacing boots; but sometimes these will be too uncomfortable, and you will have to have specially made boots or an ankle brace. Professional help is required for adequate fitting of such devices, and they can be quite expensive.

Crutches and even a cane can help you take the weight off the sore ankle.

For the stable ankle, an elastic bandage and a shoe with a comfortable, thick heel pad will help. Jogging shoes are good. Very light hiking boots are available. They are just like running shoes but go above the ankle. These are often excellent.

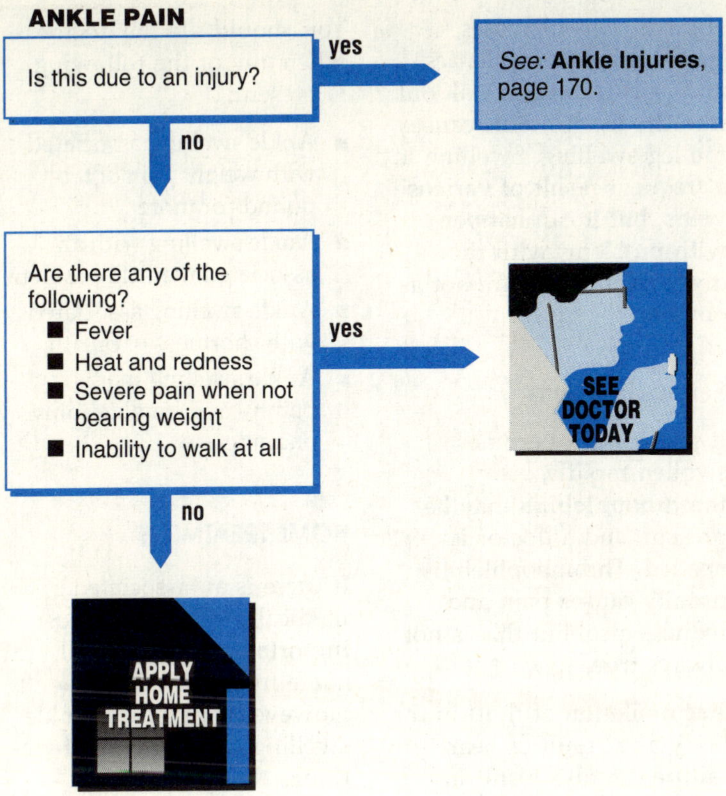


If you have arthritis, make particularly sure that you have been taking any prescribed medication exactly as ordered. Sometimes a patient gets a little bored and lax with the pill-taking routine and a few days later experiences difficulty walking because of pain or swelling.

As soon as the pain begins to decrease, you can gently begin to exercise the joint again. Swimming is good, because you don't have to bear weight. Start easy and slowly with your exercises.

**1.** Sit on a chair, let the leg hang free, and wiggle the foot up and down and in and out.

**2.** Later, walk carefully with an ankle bandage for support. Stretch the ankle by putting the forefoot on a step and lowering the heel.

**3.** As the ankle gains strength, you can walk on tiptoe and walk on your heels to stretch and strengthen the joint.

Do the exercises several times a day. The ankle shouldn't be a lot worse after exercising if you aren't overdoing it. Keep at it, take your time, and be patient.

## WHAT TO EXPECT AT THE DOCTOR'S OFFICE

The ankle and the area around it will be examined. X-rays may be necessary. Anti-inflammatory medications may be prescribed or the dosage increased. Special shoes or braces may be prescribed. Surgery is occasionally necessary. Fusion of the ankle is the most generally useful procedure. A fixed, pain-free ankle is far preferable to an unstable and painful one. The artificial ankle joint is not yet satisfactory for most people, but progress is rapid in this area.

# Ankle and Leg Swelling

Painless swelling of the ankles is a common problem, and the swelling usually affects both legs and may extend up the calves or even the thighs.

Usually, the problem is fluid accumulation. This is most pronounced in the lower legs because of the effects of gravity. If there is excess fluid and you press firmly with your thumb on the area that is swollen, it will squeeze the fluid out of that area and leave a deep impression. The depression will stay for a few moments.

Fortunately, most swelling is due to local causes. Often, breakdowns in the veins over time have made it difficult for blood to be returned to the heart fast enough. This increases pressure in the capillaries and causes fluid to leak out into the tissues. This causes the leg swelling. Swelling is a frequent result of **varicose veins**, but it can happen with problems with the deeper veins that are not as obvious.

### Serious Problems

If just one leg becomes swollen rapidly, **thrombophlebitis** may be present, and a doctor is needed. Thrombophlebitis usually causes pain and redness also, but this is not always true.

Accumulation of fluid in the body as a result of heart failure can also result in swollen ankles. With serious lung disease, such as emphysema, blood may "back up" through the heart and increase pressure in the veins and thus cause ankle swelling. More rarely, a problem with the kidneys can result in swelling of the ankles. With serious liver disease, retention of fluid is very common. This fluid tends to accumulate primarily in the abdomen but is also frequently present in the legs.

You should see the doctor when any of the following is present:

- Ankle swelling associated with weight gain of ten pounds or more
- Ankle swelling with an associated medical problem
- Ankle swelling associated with shortness of breath
- Ankle swelling that is painful and involves only one side

## HOME TREATMENT

If there is an associated medical problem, the most important treatment will come from your doctor. However, all kinds of ankle swelling can be helped by things that you can do yourself. First, you need to exercise your legs. As you work the muscles, the fluid tends to work back into the veins and lymphatic channels and the swelling tends to go down.

## ANKLE SWELLING

Is this due to an injury?

**yes** → *See:* **Ankle Injuries**, page 170, or **Broken Bone?**, page 167.

**no** ↓

Is there pain?

**yes** → *See:* **Ankle Pain**, page 372, or **Leg Pain**, page 368.

**no** ↓

Is this swelling
- on one side only

or
- associated with shortness of breath?

**yes** →

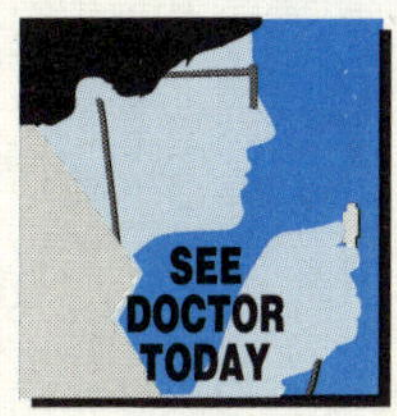


**no** ↓

Is this associated with a medical problem such as heart, kidney, or liver disease?

**yes** →

**no** ↓

Is this associated with a weight gain of ten pounds or more?

**yes** →

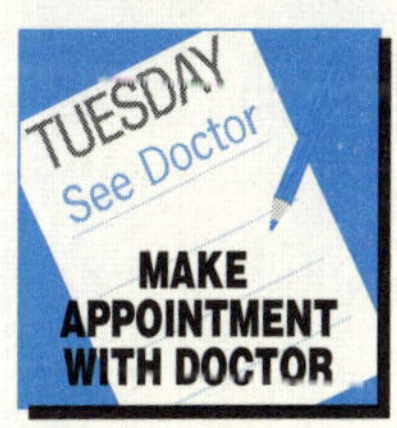


**no** ↓

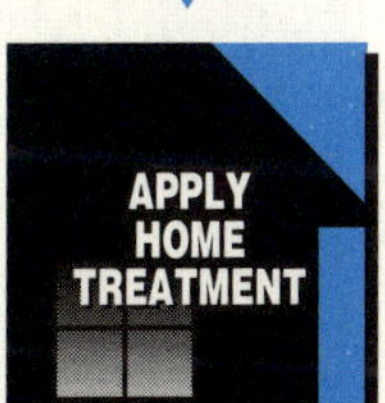


Ankle swelling is almost always a signal that your body has too much salt. A low-salt diet helps decrease the fluid retention and the ankle swelling.

Elevating your legs can help the fluid drain back into more proper parts of your circulatory system. Lie down and prop your legs up so they are higher than your heart as you rest. One or two pillows under the calves will help. Be sure not to place anything directly under the knees and don't wear any constricting clothing or garters on the upper legs. Avoid sitting or standing without moving for long periods of time. If you must be in these positions, work the muscles in your calves by wiggling your feet and toes frequently. Support stockings, by applying constant external pressure, help reduce ankle swelling.

## WHAT TO EXPECT AT THE DOCTOR'S OFFICE

The doctor will conduct a thorough examination including heart and lungs as well as the legs. Blood tests may be taken to check the function of your kidneys, your liver, and to measure the proteins in your blood. The specific treatment will be directed at whatever underlying cause is found. Diuretics (fluid pills) may be prescribed. These are effective, but, of course, they have some side effects. If home treatment is successful, it is generally better than using drugs.

# Heel Pain

The most frequent causes of heel pain are sometimes referred to as injuries, but they are not due to a single event, such as a fall or twist.

**Plantar fasciitis** is inflammation of the tendon that is attached to the front of the heel bone and runs forward along the bottom of the foot. There are four main causes of plantar fasciitis:

- Feet that flatten and roll inwardly (pronate) excessively when walking or running
- Shoes with inadequate arch support
- Shoes with soles that are too stiff
- Sudden turns that put great stress on the ligaments.

The retrocalcaneal bursa surrounds the back of the heel and may become inflamed (**bursitis**) due to pressure from shoes. For this reason, it is sometimes called a "pump bump." The inferior calcaneal bursa is located underneath the heel. Inflammation is usually caused by landing hard or awkwardly on the heel.

The Achilles tendon is the large tendon that connects the calf muscles to the back of the heel. **Achilles tendinitis** occurs when the calf muscles repeatedly contract hard or suddenly. There are four factors that contribute to Achilles tendinitis:

- The main cause, shortening and lack of flexibility in the calf muscle–Achilles tendon unit
- Shoes that do not provide good stability and shock absorption for the heel
- Sudden inward or outward turning of the heel when striking the ground (this is due to the shape of the foot, an inherited trait)
- Running on hard surfaces such as concrete or asphalt

With each of the problems the main symptom is pain, but tenderness and some swelling are usually present.

## HOME TREATMENT

**Plantar Fasciitis.** Give your feet as much rest as possible for a week or so. Aspirin or ibuprofen can be used for comfort. Use that time to get proper-fitting shoes—that is, shoes that have adequate arch supports and flexible soles. A one-quarter-inch heel pad is a good idea, and a heel cup may help as well. Some people need to wear only well-padded shoes, such as running shoes, for a time. An orthotic device (obtained through a podiatrist or orthopedic surgeon) should be tried if these remedies fail, especially if there is excessive pronation of the foot. Be very patient. This problem can take a year or more to go away.

**Bursitis.** Resting for seven to ten days and taking two aspirin or ibuprofen with each meal will help relieve the initial problem. For retrocalcaneal bursitis, getting a new shoe or stretching the old shoe so that there is no rubbing against the heel is recommended; moleskin may be used to relieve pressure from the "pump bump." Again, orthotics may be useful for people who have excessive pronation—that is, flat feet.

**Achilles Tendinitis.** No exercise, apply ice twice daily to the tendon, and two aspirin or ibuprofen with each meal for a week. After that, stretching is the most important treatment. Remember to stretch and hold the stretched position. Do not bounce.

One method is wall push-ups:

**1.** Stand four feet from a wall, hands outstretched and placed on the wall.

**2.** Bend elbows so that body moves closer to the wall. Keep heels on the ground.

**3.** Hold for a count of ten and push away from wall.

**4.** Repeat ten times per session, three sessions a day.

Another method is to stand with a board or book under the balls of your feet so that the Achilles tendon is stretched. A heel lift decreases the stretch pull on the tendon. If you run hills, stop for a while because this aggravates the stress.

Slow improvement is the rule in most cases. If things are getting worse despite home treatment or if there is little progress after a month, see your doctor.

## WHAT TO EXPECT AT THE DOCTOR'S OFFICE

**Plantar Fasciitis and Bursitis.** Cortisone injections, no more than three, may be tried if adjustments to the shoe and the use of orthotics have not been successful. Surgery is a last resort and is seldom necessary.

**Achilles Tendinitis.** A stronger oral anti-inflammatory medicine may be prescribed, but cortisone injections are *not* done because they may weaken the tendon and lead to rupture. In particularly resistant cases, a walking cast may be tried. Surgery is almost never recommended.

**HEEL PAIN**

Is this pain on the bottom of the foot about 1 to 2 inches from the back edge of the heel?

- **yes** → Suspect plantar fasciitis. → APPLY HOME TREATMENT
- **no** ↓

Is this pain and swelling just above the back of the heel or on the bottom of the heel near the back edge?

- **yes** → Suspect (retrocalcaneal or inferior calcaneal) bursitis. → APPLY HOME TREATMENT
- **no** ↓

Is this pain and tenderness in the Achilles tendon, usually about 2 to 3 inches above the bottom edge of the heel?

- **yes** → Suspect Achilles tendinitis. → APPLY HOME TREATMENT
- **no** ↓

Consider another problem.

# Foot Pain

There are a few foot problems that lead to unnecessary pain or an unnecessary visit to the doctor's office.

The nerves that supply sensation to the front portion of your foot and your toes run between the long bones of the foot, the metatarsals. (There is a metatarsal just behind each toe.) Tight-fitting shoes can squeeze the nerves between the bones, and this may cause swelling in a nerve, a **Morton's neuroma**. The swelling is very sensitive, and pressure can cause intense pain. If pressure is constant, some numbness between the toes may also occur. Morton's neuroma occurs most commonly between the third and fourth metatarsals.

If your big toe points outward toward the other four toes, the end of the metatarsal behind the big toe may rub against the shoe. The skin thickens over the end of the metatarsal, and the metatarsal itself may develop a bony spur at that point. This is a **bunion**, and if it becomes inflamed and sore, it can make life miserable.

Corns and calluses are the results of friction, and friction is usually caused by ill-fitting shoes. **Corns** appear as lumps of thickened skin that may be hard with a clear core or soft and moist. They are usually found on the tops of toes. **Calluses** also appear as thickened skin but are less lumpy and are most often found across the ball of the foot.

**Plantar warts** are caused by a virus, not friction, and are often found on the ball of the foot. They may be distinguished from calluses by small, black dots within the wart, the interruption of normal skin lines, and the inward growth of the wart.

Unaccustomed, heavy use of the feet as in beginning training for running or basketball may produce enough stress to produce a crack—**stress fracture**—in the metatarsals. The fourth metatarsal is most vulnerable to this. The first metatarsal (behind the big toe) is so strong that it almost never suffers a stress fracture. A stress fracture usually occurs several weeks into an increased training session or other activity involving strenuous use of the feet. Pain usually comes on gradually and can be ignored at first, but becomes worse with continued activity.

## HOME TREATMENT

**Morton's Neuroma.** Shoes with adequate room around the ball of the foot are necessary. Aspirin or ibuprofen (Advil, Nuprin, etc.) three times a day for two to three weeks may also help.

**Bunion.** Place a small sponge or pad between the big and second toe so that the big toe becomes aligned with the other four toes. Moleskin or padding around the bunion may help relieve pressure. Of course, shoes wide enough

## FOOT PAIN

Is this a bump on top of the toes or on the ball of the foot?

- **yes** → Suspect a corn, callus, or plantar wart. → **APPLY HOME TREATMENT**
- **no** ↓

Is this a sharp or burning pain in the ball of the foot (may go into toes)?

- **yes** → Suspect a Morton's neuroma. → **APPLY HOME TREATMENT**
- **no** ↓

Is this a painful bump at the base of the big toe?

- **yes** → Suspect a bunion. → **APPLY HOME TREATMENT**
- **no** ↓

Is this an aching pain, gradually increasing, just behind the base of the 2nd, 3rd, 4th, or 5th toe (usually the 4th and never the big [1st] toe) occurring 1 to 3 weeks after beginning strenuous activity involving the foot?

- **yes** → Suspect metatarsal stress fracture. → **APPLY HOME TREATMENT**
- **no** ↓

Consider another problem.

in the ball of the foot, so that pressure is not applied, will help. Aspirin or ibuprofen may be used as above for pain.

**Corns and Calluses.** The first step is to make sure your shoes fit properly. Sandals, if practical, and cushioning socks can be helpful. The "corn plasters" containing 40% salicylic acid available without prescription are effective. Be sure to follow their directions: cut the plaster so that it is smaller than the corn or callus, and be careful in removing the dead skin that the plaster produces. A doctor's visit is rarely needed.

**Plantar Warts.** Good shoes and corn plasters can be effective for plantar warts also, but the removal of dead skin may be more difficult and time-consuming. For this reason, plantar warts end up in the doctor's office more often than corns and calluses. See the doctor if you are making no progress in decreasing the size of the problem. Meanwhile, wear slippers or bath shoes to decrease the likelihood of passing the virus on to someone else.

**Metatarsal Stress Fracture.** You are going to have to give your foot a rest. Using crutches for a week or so may be helpful in getting pressure off the foot if it is particularly painful. Remember that it may take from six weeks to three months for the fracture to heal completely so that you can return to full activity. A cast does not reduce the healing time and may create other problems, so most doctors avoid any kind of cast if at all possible.

**Morton's Neuroma.** Cortisone injections, no more than three, may be tried if relief has not been obtained with oral medication and switching shoes. If these fail, the neuroma can be removed surgically. The operation usually leaves a region of skin on the foot permanently numb.

**Bunion.** If the bunion is particularly inflamed, a cortisone injection can provide temporary relief. If the big toe is so crooked that adjusting the shoes and using moleskin do not help, then surgery to realign the big toe may be needed.

**Plantar Warts.** The doctor may use cold (liquid nitrogen), heat (electrocoagulation), or surgery to remove a plantar wart. Unfortunately, plantar warts often recur.

**Metatarsal Stress Fracture.** The doctor has little to offer to relieve metatarsal stress fractures. You can get crutches at the drug store. Casts are to be avoided if at all possible, and surgery is virtually never done. A walking cast for an incredibly painful foot is about the only thing that the doctor can do for you that you can't.

## CHAPTER L

# *Stress, Mental Health, and Addiction*

# Stress, Anxiety, and Grief

Stress is a normal part of our lives. It is not necessarily good or bad. It is not a disease. But reactions to stress can vary enormously, and some of these reactions are undesirable.

### Anxiety

The most frequent undesirable reaction is anxiety. The degree of anxiety is much more a function of the individual than the degree of stress. A person who reacts with excessive anxiety to everyday stress has a personal rather than a medical problem. The person who does not recognize anxiety as the problem will have difficulty in solving the problem.

Some common symptoms of anxiety are insomnia and an inability to concentrate. These symptoms can lead to a vicious cycle that aggravates the situation. But the symptoms are effects, not causes. The person who focuses on the insomnia or the lack of concentration as the problem is far from a solution.

Most communities have several resources that can help with anxiety. Ministers, social workers, friends, neighbors, and family may all play a beneficial role. The doctor is an additional resource but is not necessarily the first or the best place to seek help for these problems.

### Grief

Grief is an appropriate reaction to certain situations, such as death of a loved one or loss of a job. In such cases, time is the healer, although significant help may be gained from various family and community resources. Working through grief is an important part of getting over a loss. If the reaction persists for several months, seek outside help.

The limitations of drugs, such as tranquilizers or alcohol, when a person is grieving must be understood. While they may provide short-term symptomatic relief, they are brain depressants that do not enhance mental processes or solve problems. They are a crutch. In this instance, the long-term use of a crutch ensures that the person using it will become a cripple. The underlying problem must be confronted.

## HOME TREATMENT

An honest attempt to identify the cause of the anxiety is a requisite first step in resolving the problem. When physical symptoms are due to job pressures, marital woes, wayward children, or domineering parents, the situation must be accurately identified, admitted, and confronted. When anxiety or depression is reactive, the cause is often obvious; simply talking about it with friends or counselors will help.

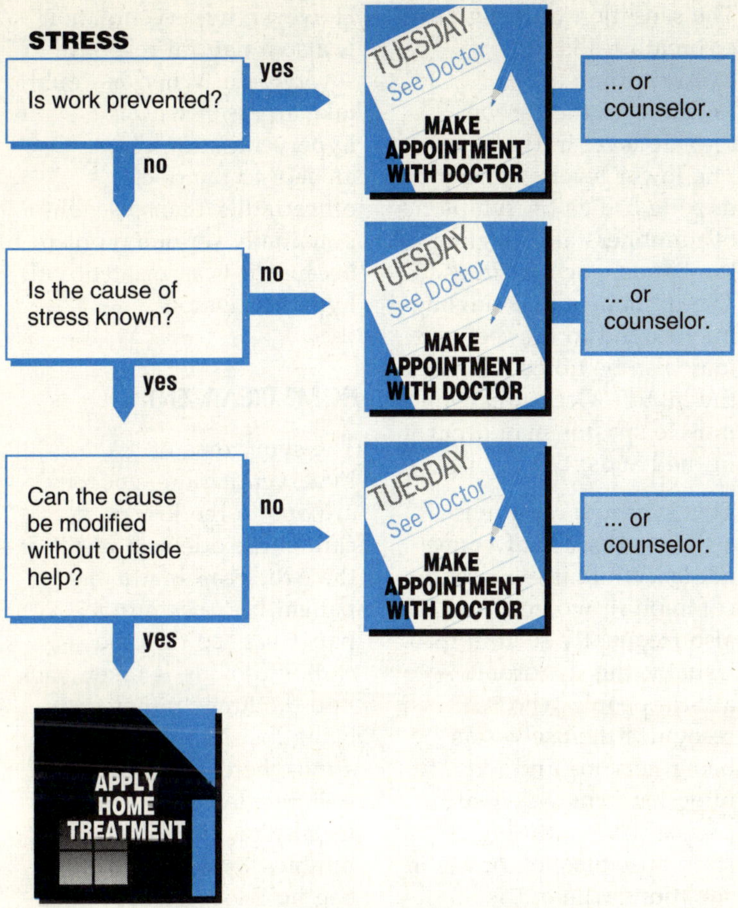


In other instances, identifying the source of the anxiety will be difficult, painful, time-consuming, and may eventually require the help of a professional counselor or psychiatrist.

Unfortunately, no scientific studies have been able to show which particular type of therapy produces the best results. So your choice should depend on what makes you feel that you are making progress.

In addition, sometimes the symptoms of anxiety are associated with too much caffeine. Try cutting down on your caffeine intake and see if you feel more relaxed. Remember that caffeine is found in coffee, colas, tea, a variety of cold and headache remedies, and even chocolate. Of course, caffeine is the active ingredient in non-prescription stimulants (No-Doz, Vivarin, etc.).

Relaxation techniques, such as those on page 388, can be helpful.

## WHAT TO EXPECT AT THE DOCTOR'S OFFICE

The family doctor will attempt to identify the problem and determine if the help of a psychiatrist or psychiatric social worker is required. Personal questions may be asked, and frank, honest answers must be given. Try to report the underlying problems and avoid emphasis on the effects, such as insomnia, muscle aches, headache, or inability to concentrate.

# Hyperventilation Syndrome

Anxiety, especially unrecognized anxiety, can lead to physical symptoms. The hyperventilation syndrome is such a problem. In this syndrome, a nervous or anxious person becomes concerned about his or her breathing and rapidly develops a feeling of inability to get enough air into the lungs. This is often associated with chest pain or constriction.

The sensation of being out of breath leads to overbreathing and a lowering of the carbon dioxide level in the blood. The lower level of carbon dioxide brings on symptoms of numbness and tingling of the hands, and dizziness. The numbness and tingling may extend to the feet and may also be noted around the mouth. Occasionally, muscle spasms may occur in the hands.

This syndrome is almost always a disease of young adults. While it is more common in women, it is also frequently seen in men. Usually, this syndrome afflicts people who recognize themselves as being nervous and tense. It often happens when such people have additional stress, use alcohol, or are in situations where it is advantageous to the patient to have a sudden, dramatic illness. A classical example is the occurrence of the hyperventilation syndrome during separation or divorce proceedings, so that a call for help is sent out to the estranged spouse.

However, hyperventilation is also a natural response to severe pain. When in doubt, take a person who is hyperventilating due to anxiety to the doctor's office rather than discount a potentially serious problem because it is associated with hyperventilation.

## HOME TREATMENT

The symptoms of hyperventilation syndrome are due to the loss of carbon dioxide as a result of the overbreathing. If the patient breathes into a paper bag, so that the carbon dioxide is taken back into the lungs rather than being lost into the atmosphere, the symptoms will be alleviated. This usually requires 5 to 15 minutes with a small paper bag held loosely over both the nose and the mouth. This is not always as easy as it sounds because a major feature of the hyperventilation syndrome is panic and a feeling of impending suffocation. Approaching such a person with a paper bag for the mouth and nose may prove to be difficult, so be sure to reassure the patient first.

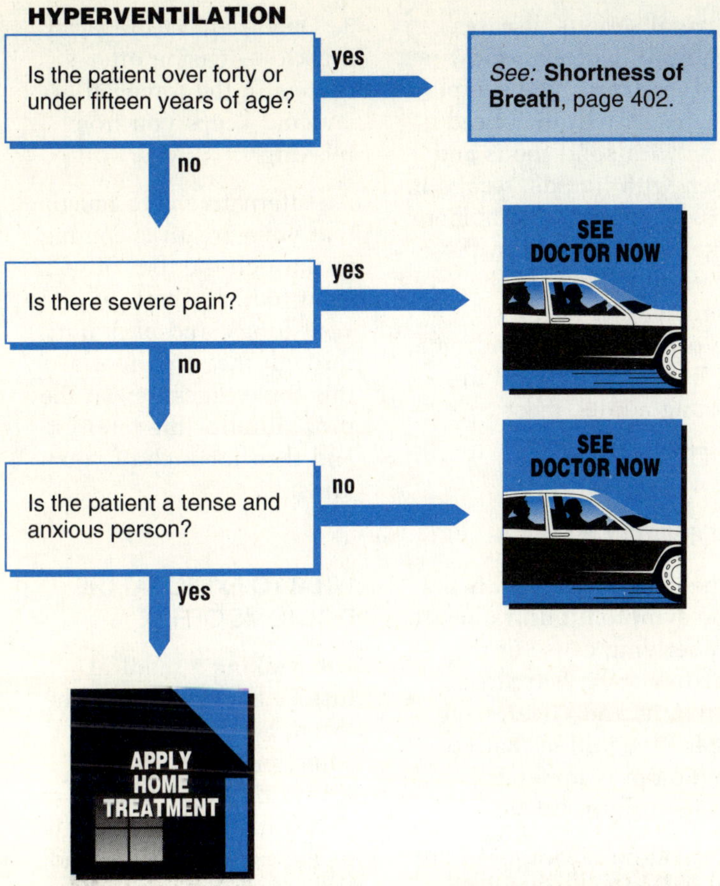


Repeated attacks may occur. Once the patient has honestly recognized that the problem is anxiety rather than an organic disease, the attacks will stop because the panic component will not come into play. Convincing the patient is the main obstacle. Having the patient voluntarily hyperventilate (50 deep breaths while lying on a couch) to demonstrate that this reproduces the symptoms of the previous episode is frequently helpful. Patients are usually afraid that they are having a heart attack or are on the verge of a nervous breakdown. Neither is true, and when the fear has dissipated, hyperventilation usually ceases.

## WHAT TO EXPECT AT THE DOCTOR'S OFFICE

The doctor will obtain a history and direct attention primarily to the examination of the heart and lungs. In the young person with a typical syndrome, with a normal physical examination and no abdominal pain, the diagnosis of hyperventilation is easily made. Electrocardiograms (EKGs) and chest X-rays are seldom needed. These procedures may occasionally be necessary in less clear-cut cases.

If hyperventilation syndrome is diagnosed, the doctor will usually provide a paper bag and the instructions given above. A tranquilizer may be administered; we prefer merely to reassure the patient. It is seldom possible to deal effectively with the cause of the anxiety during the hyperventilation episode. The patient should not assume that the underlying problem is solved simply because the hyperventilation has been controlled.

# Lump in the Throat

The feeling of a "lump in the throat" is the best known of all anxiety symptoms. There may even be some difficulty swallowing, although eating is possible if an effort is made. The sensation is intermittent and is made worse by tension and anxiety.

The difficulty in swallowing is worst when the patient concentrates on swallowing and on the sensations within the throat. As an experiment, try to swallow rapidly several times without any food or liquid, and concentrate on the resulting sensation. You will then understand this symptom.

Several serious diseases can cause difficulty swallowing. In these cases, the symptom begins slowly, is noticed first with solid foods and then with liquids, results in loss of weight, and is more likely to be found in those over 40. "Lump in the throat," like the hyperventilation syndrome, is likely to be found in young adults, most frequently women.

## HOME TREATMENT

The central problem is not the symptom but, rather, the underlying cause of the anxiety state. See **Stress, Anxiety, and Grief,** page 384. Recognition that the symptom is minor is crucial to its disappearance.

Relaxation techniques may be helpful. One such technique is called progressive relaxation:

**1.** Imagine that your toes weigh 1000 pounds and you couldn't move if you wanted them to. Let them go completely limp.

**2.** Work your way up to the top of your head by relaxing the muscles in each part of your body.

**3.** Don't neglect the facial muscles—tension often centers in the forehead or jaw and keeps you from relaxing.

An alternative is to imagine that your breath is coming in through the toes of your right foot, all the way up to your lungs, and back out through the same foot. Do this three times; repeat the procedure for the left foot and then for each of your arms.

## WHAT TO EXPECT AT THE DOCTOR'S OFFICE

After taking a medical history and examining the throat and chest, a doctor sometimes may feel that X-rays of the esophagus are necessary. If an abnormality of the esophagus is found, further studies may be performed. Reassurance will probably be the treatment given.

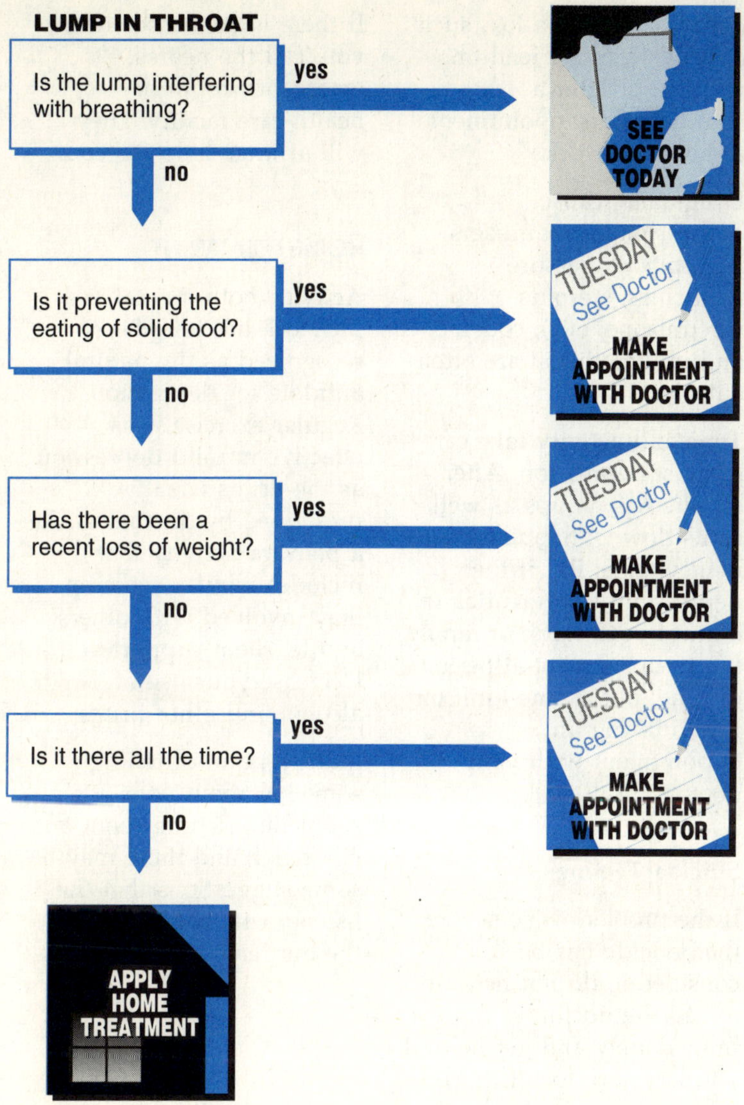
LUMP IN THROAT
Is the lump interfering with breathing?
yes
SEE DOCTOR TODAY
no
Is it preventing the eating of solid food?
yes
TUESDAY See Doctor
MAKE APPOINTMENT WITH DOCTOR
no
Has there been a recent loss of weight?
yes
TUESDAY See Doctor
MAKE APPOINTMENT WITH DOCTOR
no
Is it there all the time?
yes
TUESDAY See Doctor
MAKE APPOINTMENT WITH DOCTOR
no
APPLY HOME TREATMENT

# Depression

The blues and the blahs —everybody gets them sometime. There is no more common problem. It can range from a feeling of no energy all the way to such an overwhelming sense of unhappiness and defeat that ending it all seems the only way out.

Depression may appear to be simple fatigue or a general feeling of ill health. You just don't feel good, and you may not know the reason why. The future may seem to hold no promise. There is a sense of loss: a feeling of defeat or of having lost something—or someone—important.

In medical terms, most depression is "reactive," meaning that it is a reaction to an unhappy event. It is natural to have some depression after a loss such as a death of a friend or relative, or after a significant disappointment at home or work.

Drugs may cause depression. Tranquilizers, high blood pressure medicines, steroids (prednisone, etc.), codeine, and indomethacin are often culprits.

Time and activity take care of most depression. After all, life has its ups as well as its downs; happiness also is inevitable. But if the depression is so great as to disrupt your work or family life for a substantial period of time, put a time limit on it by making an appointment with your doctor.

### Suicidal Feelings

If the problem is so severe that suicide has been considered, do not hesitate to call the doctor immediately and get help. If you have no doctor or you prefer to find help elsewhere, many communities have telephone hotlines for such situations. If there is no service near you, call the nearest emergency room or health-care facility. They will arrange help for you.

## HOME TREATMENT

Activity, both mental and physical, has long been recognized as the natural antidote for depression. Regular exercise is as effective in mild depression as the drugs usually prescribed by doctors. Make a plan for activity that includes regular exercise. Stay involved with others and let them support you. Decrease your use of alcohol and other drugs.

Make a point of telling someone about your problems. Getting them out is a relief, and there may be some suggestions that the listener can make to ease the burden.

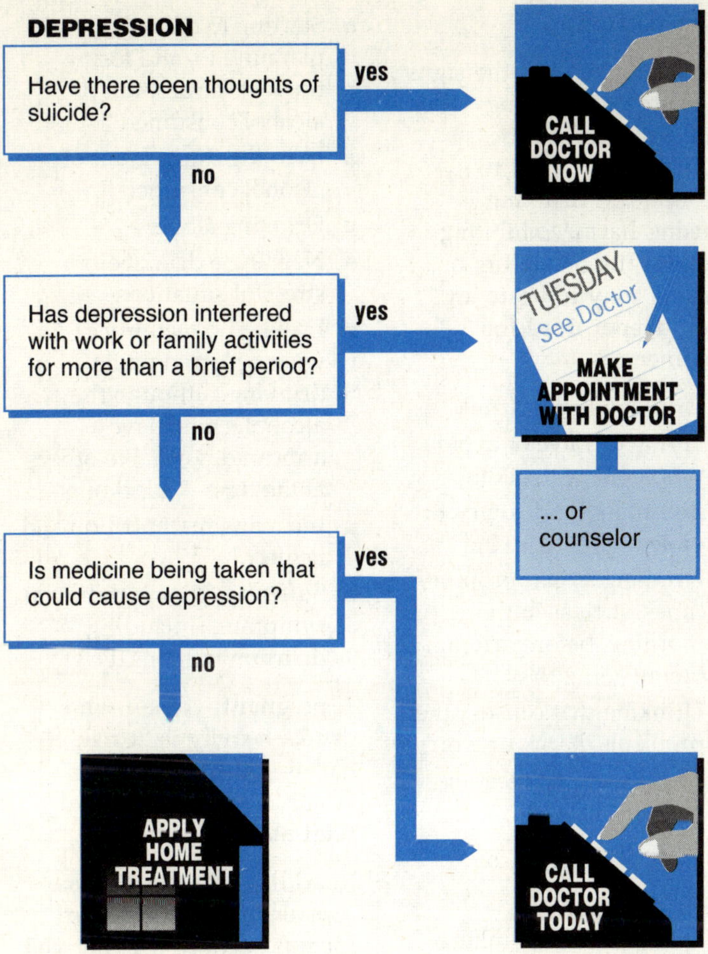


## WHAT TO EXPECT AT THE DOCTOR'S OFFICE

The doctor will explore the issues and events associated with depression. Listening and responding are the most important things. The doctor will make some suggestions about activities and exercise. Using drugs is to be avoided if possible. Hospitalization is best if the patient might commit suicide. If drugs that could cause depression are being used, these will be changed.

# Alcoholism

Addiction to alcohol is not hopeless, but a person with a drinking problem seldom changes this harmful behavior alone. Although recovery must come from within, the decisive nudge often comes from without. The drinker needs input, feedback, and support from a relative, friend, or coworker. If, like most Americans, you know someone who drinks too much, you can provide that help.

If in reading this section you recognize *yourself* as a person who drinks too much, be your own best friend and get help now.

**Warning Signs**

These are some of the signs of **problem drinking**, when a person may not be medically addicted to alcohol, but drinking is causing harm. Exhibiting *many* of the behaviors on this list may indicate an even deeper need for treatment:

- Drinking to get drunk
- Trying to solve or avoid problems by drinking
- Becoming loud, angry, or violent after drinking
- Drinking at inappropriate times, such as in the morning, before driving, or before going to work
- Drinking that causes other problems, harm, or worry
- Developing an ulcer or gastritis

These are the signs of **alcoholism**:

- Spending time thinking about drinking, planning where and when to get the next drink
- Hiding bottles for quick pick-me-ups
- Receiving citations for driving while intoxicated
- Having an automobile accident after any alcohol intake
- Starting to drink without planning to, and losing track of the amount of alcohol consumed
- Denying the amount of alcohol consumed
- Drinking alone
- Needing a drink before stressful situations
- Having no memory of what occurred while drinking, although the alcoholic may have appeared normal to others at the time—"blackouts"
- Incurring malnutrition and neglect
- Suffering from withdrawal symptoms, including delirium tremens (DTs)

A **pregnant** woman who drinks heavily is at risk of harming the fetus in her womb, a condition called **fetal alcohol syndrome**.

In addition to these signs, consult the decision chart for this section. It is derived from a questionnaire created to help physicians decide if their patients have drinking problems.

**Barriers to Helping**

There are many reasons why people hesitate to suggest that someone has a drinking problem. You might feel that you are butting into a painful and private area. Remember that you wouldn't be concerned in the first place unless the problem has already affected you. It is best to think of the alcohol abuser as someone with a problem that harms *your* ability to enjoy each other's company. That means that you are responsible for helping the alcoholic own up to problem behavior toward you.

Don't wait for a person to hit rock bottom. Alcoholism is a progressive disease, and early intervention can halt the person's decline. It can also save you and the person from the grief that usually accompanies problem drinking.

It is easy, but harmful to let yourself be drawn into the "alcoholic's game." The alcoholic creates a crisis by drinking (passes out at a party, smashes up the car, loses a job); you condemn the alcoholic; this person then seeks and obtains your forgiveness—until the cycle begins again. The drinker needs this periodic forgiveness and sympathy to sustain this destructive cycle. As long as you play this game, the alcoholic's behavior is reinforced.

Alcoholism can be a frightening subject. It helps to know as much as possible. Seek information from self-help groups, counselors, and your doctor. Then put that information to use when you talk to your friend.

**What to Say**

Pick a good time: not when the person is drunk but not long after a crisis, so that it's fresh. Tell the person what you have observed and how it causes problems. Describe your feelings, and ask how the person feels about the situation. Suggest a way out.

Try not to sound like you are charging the person with a crime. Don't try to punish, bribe, or emotionally blackmail the person, but remain calm, detached, and factual. Use your leverage, but use it fairly. For instance, if you are a drinker's supervisor, give fair warning before threatening him or her with loss of a job. Make sure you leave the responsibility for the negative behavior and for changing it with the drinker; set limits on what you will tolerate and be sure the drinker understands these limits.

The person may deny having a problem. Indeed, denial is one of the alcoholic's biggest fallbacks. Stating your concern and pointing out examples of trouble may be all you can do this time. Let the person know that you are learning about alcoholism. If the problem recurs, talk to the drinker again. People with drinking problems need to help themselves, but it is unlikely they can do so without a push from friends like you.

## HOME TREATMENT

Alcoholism is not a problem that is easily solved at home, but a doctor cannot cure it, either. The focus of any treatment must be on the patient changing his or her behavior. There are many worthwhile methods, some involving physicians or professional counselors and some not. Certain techniques insist on abstinence and others aim to reduce drinking to within acceptable limits.

The route to recovery pioneered by Alcoholics Anonymous (AA) has been as successful as any and more so than most. AA is based in local communities. It uses a self-help format to encourage the problem drinker to face up to his or her alcoholism and come to grips with the consequences. Almost all clinic- and hospital-based alcohol-treatment programs refer their patients to AA once they have gotten off to a good start. Successful recovery requires a long-term commitment, and AA provides such sustained support.

Allied with AA are Al-Anon—for people affected by a family member's alcoholism—and Alateen—for teenage alcoholics, who are also welcome at AA meetings. Other groups follow some, but not all, of the AA precepts. There is a group for just about every approach. The most important ingredient in every program is commitment on the part of the patient.

### Where to Find Help

Start by looking in your phonebook's white pages under "alcohol abuse"; there are many information hotlines that operate around the clock. Alcoholics Anonymous and its related groups are community-based, meaning that there is almost definitely a branch in your neighborhood. For more information, you can contact these central offices:

- Alcoholics Anonymous (AA)
  General Service Office
  P.O Box 459
  Grand Central Station
  New York, NY 10163
  (212) 686-1100
- Al-Anon and Alateen Family Group Headquarters
  P.O. Box 862
  Midtown Station
  New York, NY 10018-0862
  (212) 302-7240
- National Council on Alcoholism
  12 West 21st Street, 7th Floor
  New York, NY 10010
  (212) 206-6770
- National Clearinghouse for Alcohol and Drug Information
  P.O. Box 2345
  Rockville, MD 20852
  (301) 468-2600

**ALCOHOLISM**

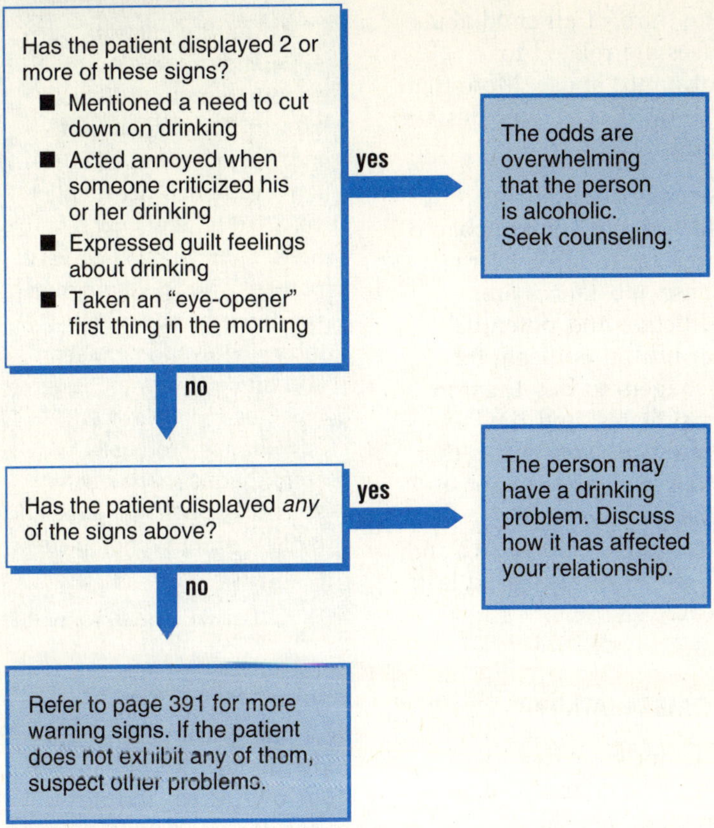


## WHAT TO EXPECT AT THE DOCTOR'S OFFICE

Tell your doctor if you are recovering from alcoholism or suspect you have a drinking problem. A history of drinking can affect many aspects of your medical care, from the possible causes of certain illnesses to how strongly you might react to anesthetics or pain-relievers.

If you ask your doctor for help with an alcoholic friend, you will probably be referred to counseling. Don't expect the doctor to suggest a clinic to "dry out." Many clinics do a fine job of starting people on the road to recovery, but an alcoholic's success rides on the ability to control drinking in the everyday world. Since the cost of outpatient treatment is less than one-tenth the cost of inpatient care, hospitals best serve:

- Patients whose bodies are so poisoned with alcohol that they require acute detoxification
- Patients who may go into severe withdrawal, requiring medical care
- The rare patients who suffer from profound psychological problems beyond alcoholism

# Drug Abuse

From 5 to 13% of adults in this country abuse or depend on some kind of psychoactive substance other than alcohol. This problem extends beyond illegal drugs, such as cocaine and some narcotics, to abuse of prescription drugs. People addicted to drugs need someone to push them towards getting help. You, as a loved one or colleague, can start that process and improve both your lives.

Drug dependency causes many medical problems because abusers need the substance so much they will harm themselves or others to have it. Overdoses and withdrawal symptoms are just two of the dangers. The craving for a drug may cause people to steal, share needles, engage in risky sex, neglect their health, and take other risks. Addictions also make abusers more emotionally volatile, and thus more prone to violence. At least one-half of all spouse-abuse cases and one-third of all child-abuse cases are related to substance abuse. More than one-third of all suicides are drug-related.

Teenagers who drink alcohol and smoke tobacco are a cause for concern. These substances are addictive and potentially harmful, it is illegal for teenagers to buy them in most states, and they are "gateway" substances that often lead to drug abuse. One quarter of all youngsters between 12 and 17 used an illicit drug last year.

**Steroids are drugs that target the muscles instead of the brain, encouraging muscle cell growth. They have positive medical uses, but taking them without a prescription can lead to dependency. Steroids have become very popular among young men and teenage boys, both those involved in athletics and those who want larger muscles to improve their appearance. Ironically, steroid abusers risk acne, stunted growth, impaired fertility, and psychological problems.**

## HOME TREATMENT

It is not your role to diagnose or treat a drug problem. Let the professionals do that. Your first task is to acknowledge the situation, which is difficult. The decision chart lists some of the signs of substance abuse. Unfortunately, they aren't all as easy to spot as the chronic runny nose of a cocaine abuser.

If you suspect that a person is abusing drugs, find out more about the problem for your own sake. Talk to counselors, self-help groups, and your doctor. Phone hotlines are available locally and nationwide. Groups like Al-Anon can provide support during this troubled period.

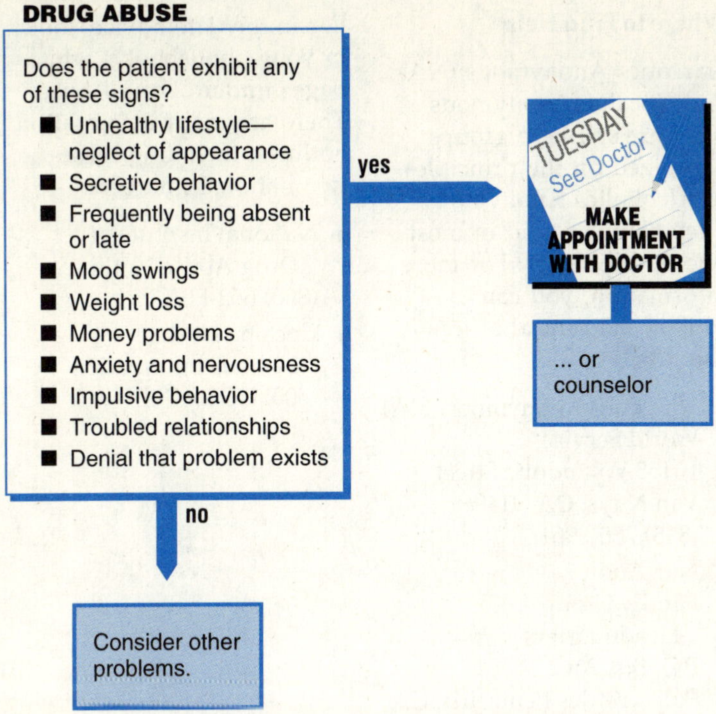


You may then be able to confront the drug abuser with your worry. There is nothing wrong in saying: "I'm concerned about your behavior. You seem troubled. Why not speak to someone about it?" See **Alcoholism**, page 392, for more advice on bringing up the subject. If the person agrees to seek help, share your knowledge about counseling services.

Many substance abusers resist such advice, however. Again, it is not your role to force them to stop their behavior, only to protect yourself from its consequences. Don't assist the drug abuser to continue abusing by:

- Covering up his or her behavior from others
- Hiding the full impact of the behavior from him or her
- Taking over the abuser's responsibilities in the home or at work
- Rationalizing the drug as a benefit for the abuser
- Cooperating in buying, selling, or using the drug

## WHAT TO EXPECT AT THE DOCTOR'S OFFICE

For the drug abuser who refuses your entreaty to get help, a doctor or other professional advisor might recommend a method called **intervention**. After meeting several times with an advisor, family members and friends confront the user. Led by the advisor, they express their concerns, citing specific examples. If the abuser agrees, he or she immediately enters a treatment program. If the abuser still refuses help, it is critical that family members receive counseling so that they do not inadvertently enable the abuser to continue his or her behavior.

After diagnosing substance abuse, most doctors will refer the patient to a treatment program run by specialists. There is no cure for substance dependence; the craving can persist for life. However, it can be controlled. Treatment programs are geared to the long haul. Successful rehabilitation or recovery can be expected for 50 to 70% of all substance abusers.

Sometimes a short stay in a hospital is necessary to prevent a patient from dying of an overdose or withdrawal. A hospital may also be used to hold an unstable person who is a threat. Some people may need to be hospitalized for complications of drug abuse, primarily infections. The average stay for drug abuse programs is 12 days. After the immediate danger has passed, the hospital should guide the patient to an outside treatment program.

**Where to Find Help**

Narcotics Anonymous (NA) and Cocaine Anonymous (CA) are self-help groups organized on the principles of Alcoholics Anonymous. They can be found in most phone directories. For more information, you can contact the central offices listed below:

- Narcotics Anonymous (NA)<br>World Service<br>16155 Wyandotte Street<br>Van Nuys, CA 91406<br>(818) 780-3951
- Nar-Anon<br>Family Group Headquarters<br>P.O. Box 2562<br>Palos Verdes Peninsula, CA 92704<br>(213) 547-5800

For immediate advice, look in your phonebook's white pages under "Drug Abuse." There are many information hotlines, including these two national numbers:

- National Institute of Drug Abuse Hotline<br>(800) 662-HELP
- Cocaine Hotline<br>24-hour information<br>(800) COCAINE

## CHAPTER M

# *Chest Pain, Shortness of Breath, and Palpitations*

# Chest Pain

Chest pain is a serious symptom meaning "heart attack" to most people. Serious chest discomfort should usually be evaluated by a doctor.

However, pain can *also* come from other sources:

- The chest wall—including muscles, ligaments, ribs, and rib cartilage
- The lungs and outside covering of the lungs—pleurisy
- The outside covering of the heart—pericarditis
- The gullet
- The diaphragm
- The spine
- The skin
- The organs in the upper part of the abdomen

Often it is difficult even for a doctor to determine the precise origin of the pain. Therefore, there are no absolute rules that enable you to determine which pains may be treated at home. The following guidelines usually work and are used by doctors, but there are occasional exceptions.

### Signs of Non-heart Pain

A shooting pain lasting a few seconds is common in healthy young people and means nothing. A sensation of a "catch" at the end of a deep breath is also trivial and does not need attention. Heart pain almost never occurs in previously healthy men under 30 years of age or women under 40 and is uncommon for the following ten years in each sex.

**Chest-wall pain** can be demonstrated by pressing a finger on the chest at the spot of discomfort and reproducing or aggravating the pain. Heart and chest-wall pain are rarely present at the same time.

The **hyperventilation syndrome** (see page 386) is a frequent cause of chest pain, particularly in young people. If you are dizzy or have tingling in your fingers, suspect this syndrome.

**Pleurisy** gets worse with a deep breath or cough. Heart pain does not. When inflammation of the outside covering of the heart—**pericarditis**—is present, the pain may throb with each heartbeat. **Ulcer pain** burns with an empty stomach and gets better with food. **Gallbladder pain** often becomes more intense after a meal. Each of these four conditions, when suspected, should be evaluated by a doctor.

### Signs of Heart Pain

While heart pain may be mild, it is usually intense. Sometimes a feeling of pressure or squeezing on the chest is more prominent than the actual pain. Almost always, the pain or discomfort will be beneath (inside) the breastbone. It may also be felt in the jaw or down the inner part of either arm. There may be nausea, sweating, dizziness, or shortness of breath.

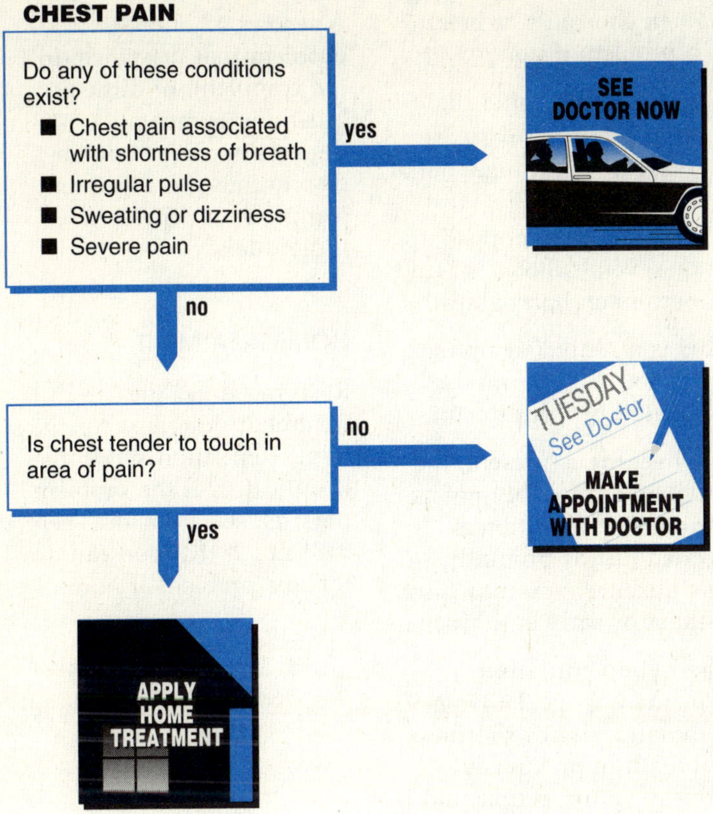


When shortness of breath or irregularity of pulse is present, it is particularly important that a doctor be seen immediately.

Heart pains may occur with exertion and go away with rest—in this case they are not an actual heart attack but are termed **angina pectoris** or "angina." Any new pains that might be angina should be brought to the attention of the doctor.

## HOME TREATMENT

You should be able to deal effectively with pain arising from the chest wall. Pain medicines (aspirin, ibuprofen, or acetaminophen), topical treatments (Ben-Gay, Vicks Vaporub, etc.), and general measures such as heat and rest should help. If symptoms persist for more than five days, see a doctor.

## WHAT TO EXPECT AT THE DOCTOR'S OFFICE

The doctor will thoroughly examine the chest wall, lungs, and heart and will frequently order an electrocardiogram (EKG) and blood tests. A chest X-ray is usually not helpful and may not be ordered. If the source of the pain remains mysterious, a whole battery of expensive and complex tests may be recommended or required. Pain relief, by injection or by mouth, will sometimes be needed. Hospitalization will be required in instances when the heart is involved or when the cause of the pain is not clear.

# Shortness of Breath

This symptom is normal under circumstances of strenuous activity. The medical use of "shortness of breath" does not include shortness of breath after heavy exertion, being "breathless" with excitement, or having clogged nasal passages. These instances are not cause for alarm.

Rather, shortness of breath is a problem if you:

- Get "winded" after slight exertion or at rest
- Wake up in the night out of breath
- Have to sleep propped up on several pillows to avoid becoming short of breath

This is a serious symptom that should be promptly evaluated by your doctor.

If **wheezing** is present, the problem is probably not as serious, but attention is needed just as promptly. In this instance, you may have asthma or early emphysema.

The **hyperventilation syndrome** (page 386) is a common cause of shortness of breath in previously healthy young people and is almost always the problem if the fingers are tingling. In this syndrome, the patient is actually overbreathing but has the sensation of shortness of breath.

A second emotional problem that may include the complaint of difficult breathing is mental **depression**. Deep, sighing respirations are a frequent symptom in depressed individuals.

## HOME TREATMENT

Rest, relax, use the treatment described for the hyperventilation syndrome if indicated. If the problem persists, see a doctor. There isn't much that you can do for this problem at home.

**SHORTNESS OF BREATH**

Is there shortness of breath at rest, or is shortness of breath associated with wheezing?

**yes** →

**no** ↓

Is there tingling in the fingers?

**yes** → *See:* **Hyperventilation Syndrome**, page 386.

**no** ↓

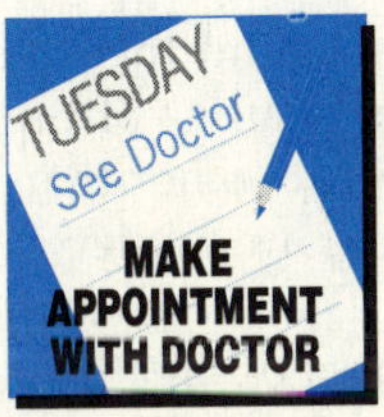


## WHAT TO EXPECT AT THE DOCTOR'S OFFICE

The doctor will thoroughly examine the lungs, heart, and upper airway passages. Electrocardiograms (EKGs), chest X-rays, and blood tests will sometimes be necessary. Depending on the cause and severity of the problem, hospitalization, fluid pills, heart pills, or asthma medicine may be prescribed. Oxygen is less frequently helpful than commonly imagined and can be hazardous for patients with emphysema.

# Palpitations

Everyone experiences palpitations. Pounding of the heart is brought on by strenuous exercise or intense emotion and is seldom associated with serious disease. Most people who complain of palpitations do not have heart disease but are overly concerned about the possibility of such disease and thus overly sensitive to normal heart actions. Often this anxiety is because of heart disease in parents, other relatives, or friends.

### Understanding the Pulse

The pulse can be felt on the inside of the wrist, in the neck, or over the heart itself. Ask the nurse to check your method of taking pulses on your next visit. Take your own pulse and those of your family, noting the variation with respiration. There is a normal variation in the pulse with respiration (faster when breathing in, slower when breathing out). Even though the pulse may speed up or slow down, the normal pulse has a regular rhythm.

Occasional extra heart beats, felt as "flip-flops" or thumps in the chest, occur in nearly everyone. The most common time to notice these extra beats is just before going to sleep. They are of no consequence unless they are frequent (more than five per minute) or if they occur in runs of three or more.

Rapid pulses may also mimic palpitations. In adults, a heart rate greater than 120 beats per minute (without exercise) is cause to check with your doctor. Young children may have normal heart rates in that range, but they rarely complain of the heart pounding. If one does, check the situation with your doctor.

### Causes

Keep in mind that the most frequent causes of rapid heart beat (other than exercise) are **anxiety** and **fever**. The presence of shortness of breath (page 402) or chest pain (page 400) increases the chances of a significant problem.

**Hyperventilation** may also cause pounding and chest discomfort, but the heart rate remains less than 120 beats per minute.

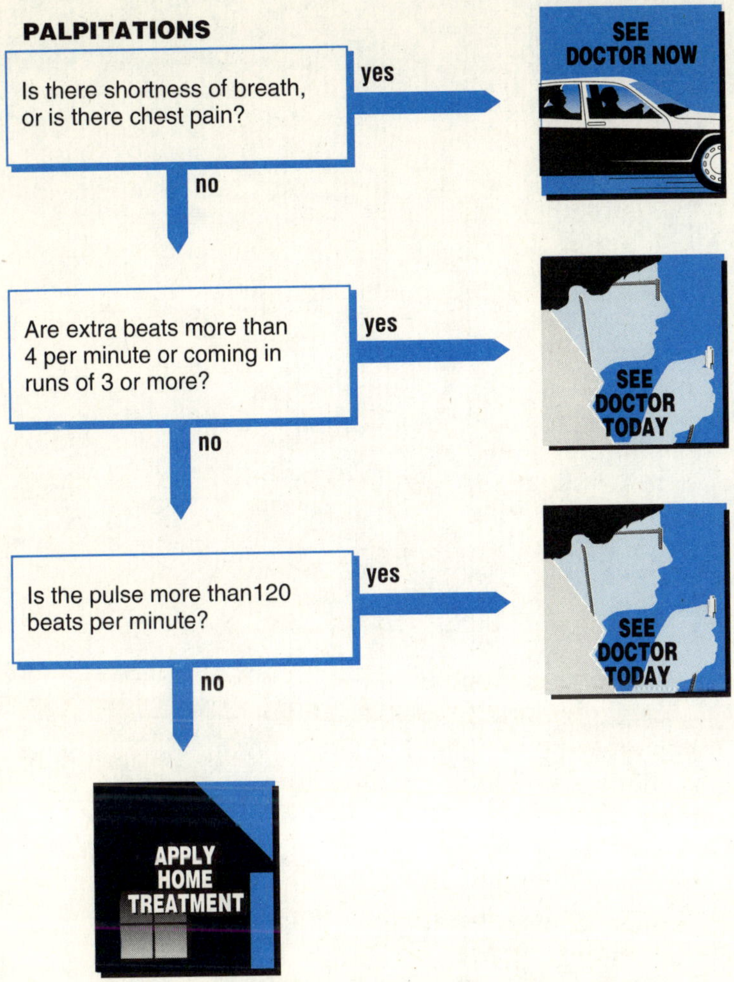


## WHAT TO EXPECT AT THE DOCTOR'S OFFICE

Tell the doctor the exact rate of the pulse and whether or not the rhythm was regular. Usually, the symptoms will disappear by the time you see the doctor, so the accuracy of your story becomes crucial. The doctor will examine your heart and lungs. An electrocardiogram (EKG) is unlikely to help if the problem is not present when it's being done. A chest X-ray is seldom needed.

Do not expect reassurance from a doctor that your heart will be sound for the next month, year, or decade. Your doctor has no crystal ball, nor can he or she perform an annual tune-up or oil change. You, not the doctor, are in charge of preventive maintenance of your heart (see Chapters 1 and 2).

## HOME TREATMENT

If a patient seems stressed or anxious, focus on this rather than on the possibilities of heart disease. If anxiety does not seem likely and the patient has none of the other symptoms on the chart, discuss it with the doctor by phone. If the problem persists, see the doctor.

CHAPTER N

# Digestive Tract Problems

# Nausea and Vomiting

Medications are the most common cause of nausea and vomiting in the elderly, whereas viral infections are the most common cause in children and young adults. When viruses are to blame, diarrhea is usually present as well.

Food poisoning is often blamed for stomach problems, but is actually one of the less frequent causes of nausea and vomiting.

### Dangers of Vomiting

**Dehydration** is the real threat with most vomiting. The speed with which dehydration develops depends on the size of the individual, the frequency of the vomiting, and the presence of diarrhea. Thus, infants with frequent vomiting and diarrhea are at the greatest risk. Signs of dehydration are:

- Marked thirst
- Infrequent urination or dark yellow urine
- Dry mouth or eyes that appear sunken
- Skin that has lost its normal elasticity. To determine this, gently pinch the skin on the stomach using all five fingers. When you release it, it should spring back immediately; compare with another person's skin if necessary. When the skin remains tented up and does not spring back normally, dehydration is indicated.

**Bleeding** (bloody or black vomitus) or severe abdominal pain also requires a doctor's attention immediately. Some abdominal discomfort accompanies almost every case of vomiting, but severe pain is unusual.

Head injuries may be associated with vomiting (see **Head Injuries,** page 176).

When pregnancy, diabetes, or medications cause nausea and vomiting, getting the doctor's advice by phone is usually sufficient to determine the approach you should take.

Headache and stiff neck along with vomiting are sometimes seen in **meningitis** so that an early visit to the doctor's office for further advice is wise. Lethargy or marked irritability in a young child has a similar implication.

Persistent nausea without vomiting is often due to medication, occasionally to ulcers or cancer.

## HOME TREATMENT

The objective of home treatment is to take in as much fluid as possible without upsetting the stomach any further. Sip clear fluids such as water or ginger ale. Suck on ice chips if nothing else will stay down. Don't drink much at any one time, and avoid solid foods. As your condition improves, try soups, bouillon, Jell-O, and applesauce. Milk products may help but sometimes aggravate the situation. Work up to a normal diet slowly. Popsicles or iced fruit bars often work well with children.

## NAUSEA

Are any of the following present?
- Black or bloody vomit
- Severe abdominal pain
- Marked irritability or lethargy in a small child
- Headache and stiff neck

yes →

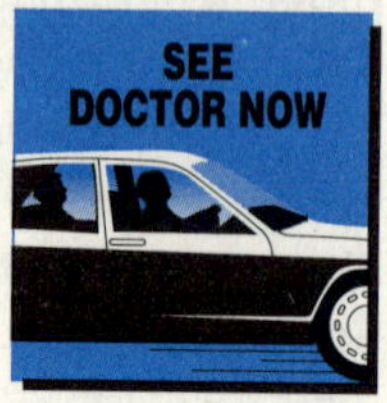


no ↓

Are any of the following present?
- Painful or frequent urination
- Signs of dehydration
- Child unable to retain any fluids for eight hours or more
- Adult unable to retain any fluids for twelve hours or more

yes →

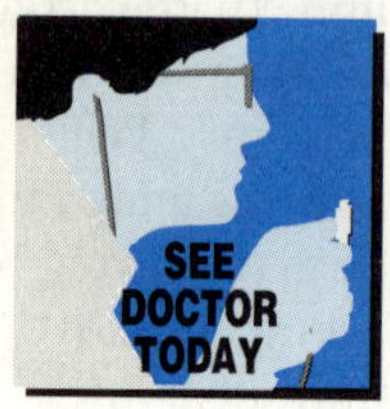


no ↓

Has there been a head injury recently?

yes → *See:* **Head Injuries,** page 176.

no ↓

Are any of the following present?
- Diabetes
- Pregnancy or possible pregnancy
- Patient is taking medication

yes →

no →

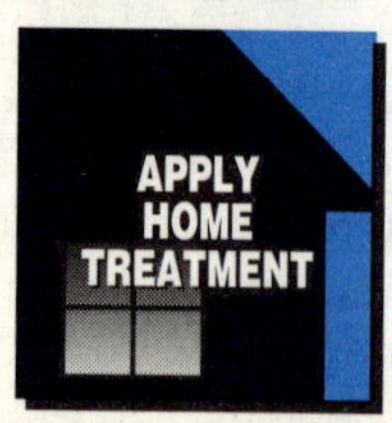


If vomiting persists for more than 72 hours, or if hydration is not adequate, check with your doctor.

If a medication might be responsible, call the doctor to see if it should be discontinued.

If nausea persists for four weeks, call the doctor.

### WHAT TO EXPECT AT THE DOCTOR'S OFFICE

The history and physical examination will be focused on determining the degree of dehydration as well as the possible causes. Blood tests and a urinalysis may be ordered but are not always necessary. Ordinary X-rays of the abdomen are usually not very helpful, but special X-ray procedures may be necessary in some cases. If dehydration is severe, intravenous fluids may be given. This may require hospitalization, although it can often be done in the doctor's office. The use of antivomiting drugs is controversial, and they should only be used in severe cases.

# Heartburn

Heartburn is irritation of the stomach or the esophagus, the tube that leads from the mouth to the stomach. The stomach lining is usually protected from the effects of its own acid. Certain factors, however, such as smoking, caffeine, aspirin, and stress, cause this protection to be impaired. The esophagus is not protected against acid, and a backflow of acid from the stomach into the esophagus causes irritation.

**Ulcers** of the stomach or the upper bowel (duodenum) may also cause pain. Treatment for ulcers is the same as for uncomplicated heartburn, provided that pain is not severe and there is no evidence of bleeding. Vomiting black, "coffee-ground" material or bright red blood means giving the doctor a call. Black stools, rather like tar, have the same significance; however, iron supplements and bismuth subsalicylate (Pepto-Bismol) will also cause black stools.

Heartburn pain ordinarily does not go through to the back, and such pain may signal involvement of the pancreas or a severe ulcer.

## HOME TREATMENT

Avoid substances that aggravate the problem. The most common irritants are coffee, tea, alcohol, aspirin, and ibuprofen. The contributing effect of smoking or stress must be considered in every patient.

Relief is often obtained with the frequent (every one to two hours) use of nonabsorbable antacids (Maalox, Mylanta, Gelusil, etc.); see Chapter 9, "The Home Pharmacy." Antacids should be used with caution by people with heart disease or high blood pressure because many have a high salt content. Sodium bicarbonate may provide quick relief but is not suitable for repeated use. Milk may be substituted for antacid but adds calories.

If the pain is worse when lying down, the esophagus is probably the problem. Measures that help prevent backflow of acid from the stomach into the esophagus should be employed:

- Avoid reclining after eating.
- Elevate the head of the bed with four inch to six-inch blocks.
- Don't wear tight-fitting clothes (girdles, tight jeans).
- Avoid eating or drinking for two hours prior to retiring.

If the problem lasts for more than three days, call your doctor.

## HEARTBURN

Is there vomiting of black or bloody material, or is the patient passing tar-like black stools?

yes →

no ↓

Does the pain go through to the back?

yes →

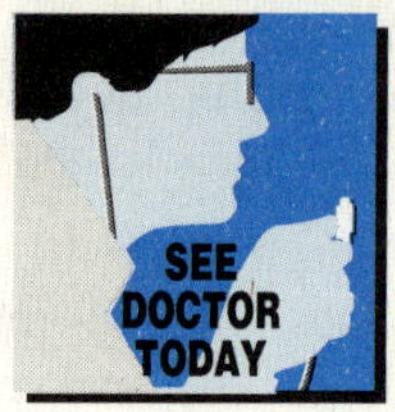


no ↓

Are all of these present?

- Burning pain just below breast bone or ribs
- Some relief obtained with milk or bland food
- Aggravated by coffee or tea, or alcohol

no →

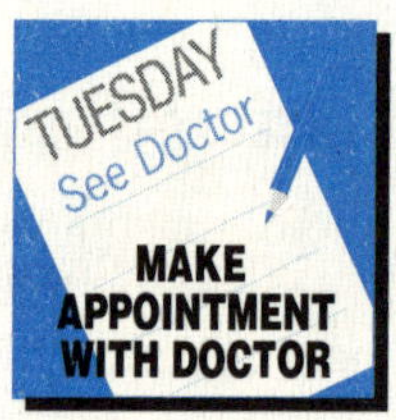


yes ↓

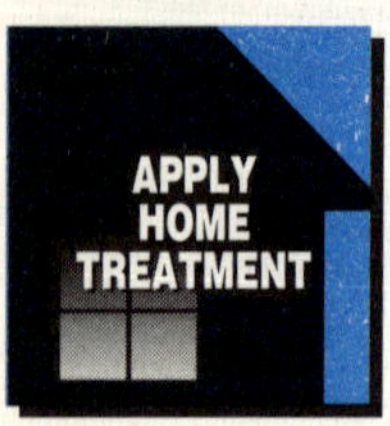


## WHAT TO EXPECT AT THE DOCTOR'S OFFICE

The doctor will determine if the problem is due to stomach acid, a peptic acid syndrome. If so, treatment will be similar to that outlined above. Medications to reduce secretion of acid may be prescribed. X-rays of the esophagus and stomach after swallowing barium (upper GI) may be done to determine the presence of ulcers and to note if backflow of acid from the stomach into the esophagus, or hiatal hernia, is present. Because the treatment for any acid syndrome is essentially the same, an X-ray is usually not done on the first visit. Any indication of bleeding will require a more vigorous approach to therapy.

# Abdominal Pain

Abdominal pain can be a sign of a serious condition. Fortunately, minor causes for these symptoms are much more frequent.

Location of the pain can be helpful in suggesting the cause.

- **Appendix pain** usually occurs in the right lower quarter of the abdomen
- **Diverticulitis** usually hurts in the left lower quarter of the abdomen
- **Kidney pain**, the back
- **Gallbladder**, the right upper quarter
- **Stomach**, the upper abdomen
- **Bladder** or female organs, the lower areas

Exceptions to these rules do occur.

Pain from hollow organs —such as the bowel or gallbladder—tends to be intermittent and resembles gas pains or colic. Pain from solid organs—kidneys, spleen, liver—tends to be more constant. There are exceptions to these rules as well.

### When to See a Doctor

If the pain is very severe or if bleeding from the bowel occurs, see a doctor. Similarly, if there has been a significant recent abdominal injury, see the doctor—a ruptured spleen or other major problem is possible.

Pain during **pregnancy** is potentially serious and must be evaluated. An "ectopic pregnancy"—in the fallopian tube rather than the uterus—can occur before the patient is even aware she is pregnant. Pain localized to one area is more suggestive of a serious problem than generalized pain; again, there are exceptions. Pain that recurs with the menstrual cycle, especially pre-menstrually, is typical of **endometriosis**.

### Appendicitis

The most constant signal of appendicitis is the *order* in which symptoms occur:

**1.** Pain—usually first around the belly button or just below the breast bone; only later in the right lower quarter of the abdomen

**2.** Nausea or vomiting, or at the very least, loss of appetite

**3.** Local tenderness in the right lower quarter of the abdomen

**4.** Fever ranging from 100°F to 102°F.

Appendicitis is unlikely if fever precedes or is present at the time of initial pain; if there is *no* fever or a *high* fever, greater than 102°F, in the first 24 hours; if vomiting accompanies or precedes the first bout of pain.

### Colic

In infants, "colic" is the term commonly used to mean a prolonged period of unexplained crying. Abdominal pain is not necessarily the cause, although the attack occasionally ends with a passage of gas or stool. Typically, colic begins after the second week of life and peaks at about three months. It generally occurs in the evening and can be extremely frustrating for parents. Cuddling, rocking, back rubs, and soothing talk are just some of the home treatments that may bring relief. For a thorough discussion of infant colic, refer to *Taking Care of Your Child* by Robert H. Pantell, James F. Fries, and Donald M. Vickery.

## HOME TREATMENT

Sip water or other clear fluids, but avoid solid foods. A bowel movement, passage of gas through the rectum, or a good belch may give relief—don't hold back. A warm bath helps some patients.

The key to some treatment is periodic reevaluation; any persistent pain should be evaluated at the emergency room or the doctor's office. Home treatment should be reserved for mild pains that resolve within 24 hours or are clearly identifiable as viral gastroenteritis, heartburn, or other minor problems.

## WHAT TO EXPECT AT THE DOCTOR'S OFFICE

The doctor will give a thorough examination, particularly of the abdomen. Usually, a white blood count and urinalysis and often other laboratory tests will be recommended. X-rays are generally not important for pain of short duration but are sometimes needed. Observation in the hospital may be required. If the initial evaluation was negative but pain persists, reevaluation is necessary.

### ABDOMINAL PAIN

Are any of the following present?
- Black or bloody stool
- Very severe abdominal pain
- Abdominal injury in the last forty-eight hours

**yes** →

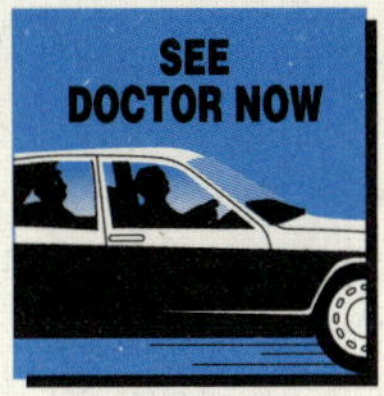


**no** ↓

Is pain localized to one area of the abdomen, or is the patient pregnant or possibly pregnant?

**yes** →

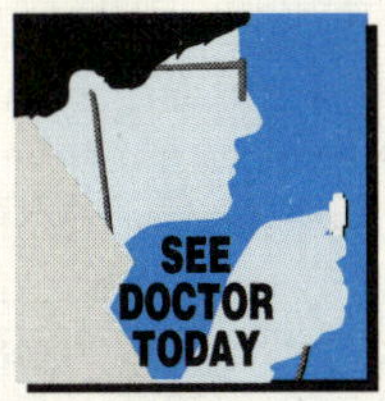


**no** ↓

Is there nausea, vomiting, or diarrhea?

**yes** →

*See:*
**Nausea and Vomiting**, page 407, or
**Diarrhea**, page 409.

**no** ↓

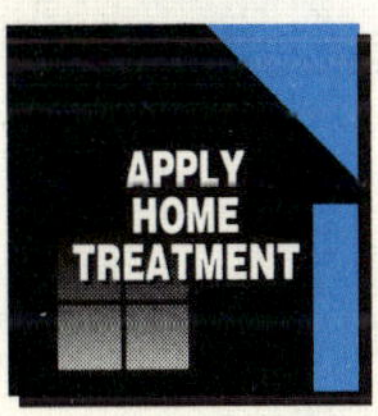

# Constipation

Many patients are preoccupied with constipation. Concern about the shape of the stool, its consistency, its color, and the frequency of bowel movements are often reported to doctors. Such complaints are medically trivial. Only rarely (and then usually in older patients) does a change in bowel habits signal a serious problem.

Weight loss and thin, pencil-like stools suggest a tumor of the lower bowel.

Abdominal pain and a swollen abdomen suggest a possible bowel obstruction.

## HOME TREATMENT

We like to encourage a healthy diet for the bowel, followed by a healthy disinterest in the details of the stool-elimination process. The diet should contain fresh fruits and vegetables for their natural laxative action and adequate fiber residue. Fiber is present in brans, celery, and whole-wheat breads and is absent in foods that have been overly processed. Fiber draws water into the stool and adds bulk; thus it decreases the transit time from mouth to bowel movement and softens the stool.

Bowel movements may occur three times daily or once every three days and still be normal. The stools may change in color, texture, consistency, or bulk without need for concern. They may be regular or irregular. Don't worry about them unless there is a major deviation.

**High-fiber diets not only prevent constipation but they also may prevent diverticulosis, hemorrhoids, intestinal polyps, even colon cancer. For more on fiber, see page 44.**

If laxatives are required, we prefer a fiber and bulk laxative (Metamucil, etc.). Milk of magnesia is satisfactory, but it and stronger traditional laxatives should not be used over a long period.

For an acute problem, an enema may help. Fleet's enemas are handy and disposable. If such remedies are needed more than occasionally, ask your doctor about the problem on your next routine visit.

**CONSTIPATION**

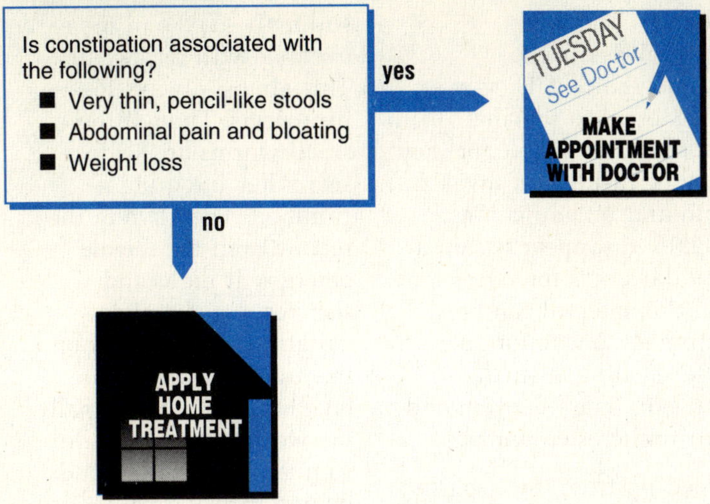


## WHAT TO EXPECT AT THE DOCTOR'S OFFICE

If you have had a major change in bowel habits, expect a rectal examination and, usually, inspection of the lower bowel through a long (sometimes cold) metal tube called a sigmoidoscope. An X-ray of the lower bowel (using a barium enema) is often needed. These procedures are generally safe and only mildly uncomfortable. If you have only a minor problem, you may receive advice similar to that under "Home Treatment," without examination or procedures.

# Rectal Pain, Itching, or Bleeding

Seldom is a rectal problem major, but the discomfort it can cause may materially interfere with the quality of life. Unlike most other medical problems, rectal pain does not yield the dividend of a good topic for social conversation.

**Hemorrhoids**, or "piles," are the most common cause of these symptoms. There is a network of veins around the anus, and they tend to enlarge with age, particularly in individuals who sit a great deal during the day. Straining to have a bowel movement and the passage of hard, compacted stools tend to irritate these veins, and they may become inflamed, tender, or clogged. The veins themselves are the "hemorrhoids." They may be external to the anal opening and visible, or they may be inside and invisible. Pain and inflammation usually disappear within a few days or a few weeks, but this interval can be extremely uncomfortable. After healing, a small flap—or "tag"—of vein and scar tissue often remains.

**Bleeding** from the digestive tract should be taken seriously. We are *not* talking here about the bright red, relatively light bleeding that originates from the hemorrhoids but about blood from higher in the digestive tract. This blood will be burgundy or black. Iron supplements or bismuth subsalicylate (Pepto-Bismol) may also turn the stool black. Blood from hemorrhoids may be on the outside of the stool but will not be mixed into the stool substance and frequently will be seen on the toilet paper after wiping. Such bleeding from hemorrhoids is not medically significant unless it persists for several weeks.

Sometimes a child will suddenly awake in the early evening with rectal pain. This almost always means **pinworms**. Though these small worms are seldom seen, they are quite common. They live in the rectum, and the female emerges at night and secretes a sticky and irritating substance around the anus into which she lays her eggs. Occasionally, the worms move into the vagina, causing pain and itching in that area. Although the Food and Drug Administration has approved the nonprescription sale of a drug effective against pinworms, the manufacturer refuses to sell it without a prescription. You will have to call a doctor for a prescription even if you are sure the problem is pinworms.

If rectal pain persists more than a week, the doctor should be consulted. In such cases, a fissure in the wall of the rectum may have developed, or an infection or other problem may be present.

## RECTAL PAIN

Are any of the following present?

- More than a small amount of blood
- Burgundy or black blood
- Blood mixed in the stool

yes →

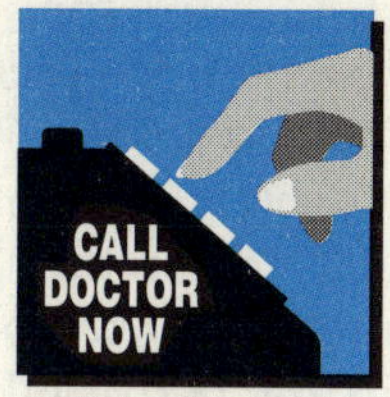


no ↓

Are hemorrhoids present?

yes →

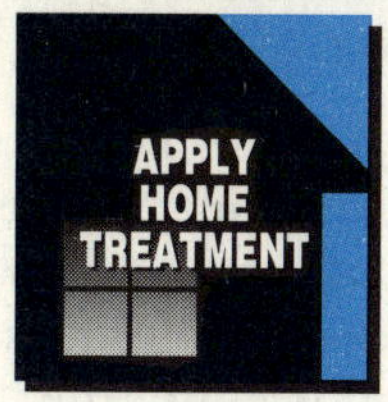


no ↓

## HOME TREATMENT

**Hemorrhoids.** Soften the stool by including more fresh fruits and fiber (bran, celery, whole-wheat bread) in the diet, or by using fiber bulk (Metamucil, etc.) or laxatives (milk of magnesia). Keep the area clean. Use the shower as an alternative to rubbing with toilet paper. After gently drying the painful area, apply zinc oxide paste or powder. This will protect against further irritation.

The various proprietary hemorrhoid preparations are less satisfactory. We prefer not to use compounds with a local anesthetic agent because these compounds may sensitize and irritate the area and may prolong healing. Such compounds have "caine" in the brand name or in the list of ingredients.

Internal hemorrhoids sometimes may be helped by using a soothing suppository in addition to stool-softening measures. If relief is not complete within a week, see the doctor. Even if the problem resolves quickly, mention it to your doctor on your next visit.

## WHAT TO EXPECT AT THE DOCTOR'S OFFICE

The doctor will examine the anus and rectum. If a clot has formed in a hemorrhoid, the vein may be lanced and the clot removed. Major hemorrhoid surgery is seldom required and should be reserved for the most persistent problems. Usually, advice such as that given in "Home Treatment" will be given.

# Incontinence

Incontinence is the inability to hold feces or urine. We are all born incontinent, and as we grow older there is a tendency for this problem to return. Incontinence is a complicated issue because there are many causes and many treatments. It is not a hopeless condition. The vast majority of people can be greatly helped, and many times the problems can be made to entirely disappear.

**Effects of Aging**

In women, the uterus and pelvic floor sag with aging. This changes the angle at which the urethra (the tube leading from the bladder) exits the body and predisposes it to leaking urine.

In men, benign (harmless) enlargement of the prostate gland tends to block passage of urine from the bladder until finally the bladder must overflow.

With age, there are sometimes uninhibited contractions of the bladder muscles. This results in increased pressures at unexpected times. There can be decreased sensitivity to the presence of a full bladder; once realized, it can be difficult to get to the toilet in time.

**Causes of Incontinence**

Drugs such as diuretics (water pills) can cause major surges in urine flow. Other drugs, such as tranquilizers, sedatives, anticholinergics, pain pills, antidepressants, and others can block the normal voiding mechanisms. This results in retention of urine and then incontinence.

Stones in the bladder can predispose a person to infection. Infections of the urinary tract can cause an urgency for which there is no time to react.

**Fecal Incontinence**

Fecal incontinence is usually due to the presence of impacted stool in the rectum. This results in diarrhea and incontinence around the impacted stool.

Problems with incontinence should be reported to your doctor. This is not a complaint to be shy about. If you let it persist, it will begin to affect every part of your life and even your self-image.

**INCONTINENCE**

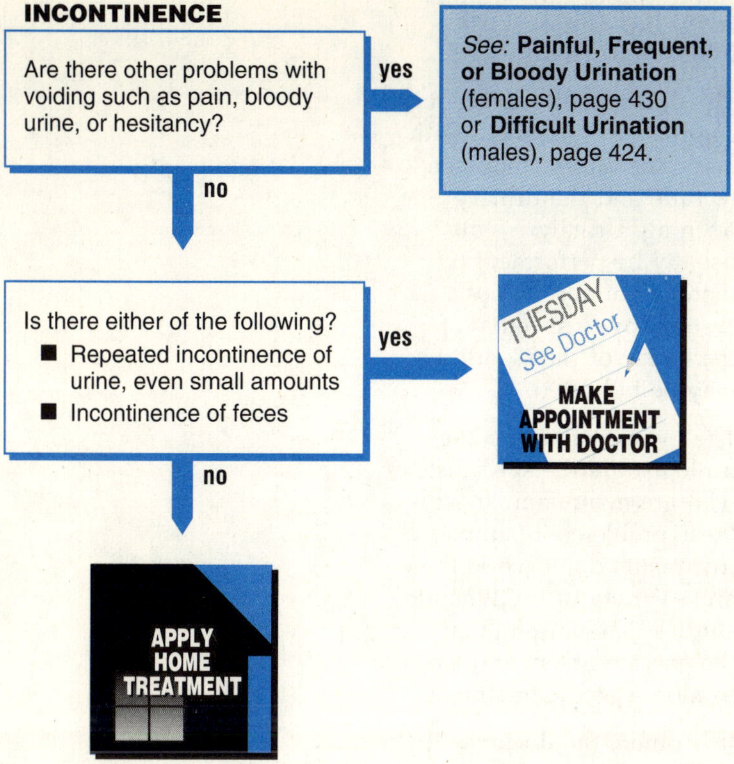


## HOME TREATMENT

There are many approaches at home that can be of great help, but you should talk with your doctor about the ones which are most appropriate for you.

### Fecal Incontinence

For fecal incontinence, it is important that your diet contain adequate fiber, water, and bulk. A soft stool passed twice a week is normal, but you should consider a hard, impacted stool (even if passed in small amounts twice daily) a problem to be addressed. Fiber—as in whole-wheat grains, bran, celery, fresh fruits, and vegetables—is helpful. Preparations (Metamucil, Fiberall, etc.) can be used to add bulk. Because the presence of impacted feces in the rectum can make you feel bad all over, it is important to get this taken care of immediately. The doctor will help.

### Bladder Incontinence

Performance of the bladder can often be improved by exercising the muscles that control the urinary outlet. Practice stopping urination in mid-stream and then starting again. This is often difficult, especially for women, but the exercise will build stronger sphincter muscles. Deliberately contracting the muscles around your anus and urinary tract for a second or two, then relaxing, then repeating will build strength in these muscles and help tighten the pelvic floor. Many doctors recommend that these exercises be done up to 100 times daily.

Double voiding techniques can be helpful. Here, you empty the bladder as much as you can, wait a minute or so and then empty it again. It is surprising how much additional urine will sometimes be present. "Bladder drill" consists of urinating at fixed intervals, perhaps each four hours, during the day, whether the sensation of urgency is present or not; this can help.

If you have trouble getting to the toilet on time, consider keeping a urine receptacle close at hand.

Always suspect that drugs that you are taking might be aggravating the problem; be sure to bring this possibility to the attention of your doctor.

### WHAT TO EXPECT AT THE DOCTOR'S OFFICE

The doctor will perform a complete examination, with emphasis on the abdomen, rectum, and the urinary opening. Urinalysis will usually be performed. If there are abnormalities, cystoscopy (inspection of the inside of the bladder) may be indicated.

The gynecologist and the urologist are the specialists who are most familiar with these problems. If simple treatments don't work, there are a variety of urodynamic studies that can pinpoint the exact problem and lead to more specific treatment.

In women, the doctor will sometimes prescribe a local estrogen cream, which can be surprisingly effective. Uterine or pelvic suspension operations are sometimes needed.

Men may choose prostatectomy, drugs, or simple "watchful waiting." Internal or external catheters are sometimes necessary.

CHAPTER O

# *Men's Health*

# Difficult Urination

Infections of the bladder may be signaled by:

- Pain or burning upon urination
- Frequent, urgent urination
- Blood in the urine

However, these symptoms are not always caused by infection due to bacteria. They can be due to a viral infection or excessive consumption of caffeine-containing beverages (coffee, tea, and some soft drinks), or they may have no known cause and may be blamed on "nerves."

Infection of the prostate gland—**prostatitis**—may cause symptoms similar to those of a bladder infection. Difficulty in starting urination, dribbling, or decreased force of the urinary stream—symptoms of prostatism—may also be present. However, prostatism is much more likely to be due to **benign prostatic hypertrophy** (BPH) than prostatitis. Some degree of BPH is universal in elderly men. **Prostatic cancer** may also cause prostatism.

Vomiting, back pain, or teeth-chattering, body-shaking chills are not typical of bladder or prostate infections and suggest **kidney infection**. This requires a more vigorous treatment and follow-up. A history of kidney disease (infections, inflammations, and kidney stones) also alters the treatment.

Most, if not all, bacterial bladder infections will respond to home treatment. Nevertheless, use of antibiotics has become standard medical practice. Given this and the difficulty of distinguishing between bladder infection and prostatitis, see a doctor unless the symptoms respond quickly and completely to home treatment. Prostatitis and prostatism require the doctor's help.

## HOME TREATMENT

For symptoms of a bladder infection:

- Drink a lot of fluids. Increase fluid intake to the maximum (up to several gallons of fluid in the first 24 hours). Bacteria are literally washed from the body during the resulting copious urination.
- Drink fruit juices. Putting more acid into the urine, while less important than the quantity of fluids, may help bring relief. Cranberry juice is the most effective because it contains a natural antibiotic.

Begin home treatment as soon as symptoms are noted. If symptoms persist for 24 hours or recur, see the doctor.

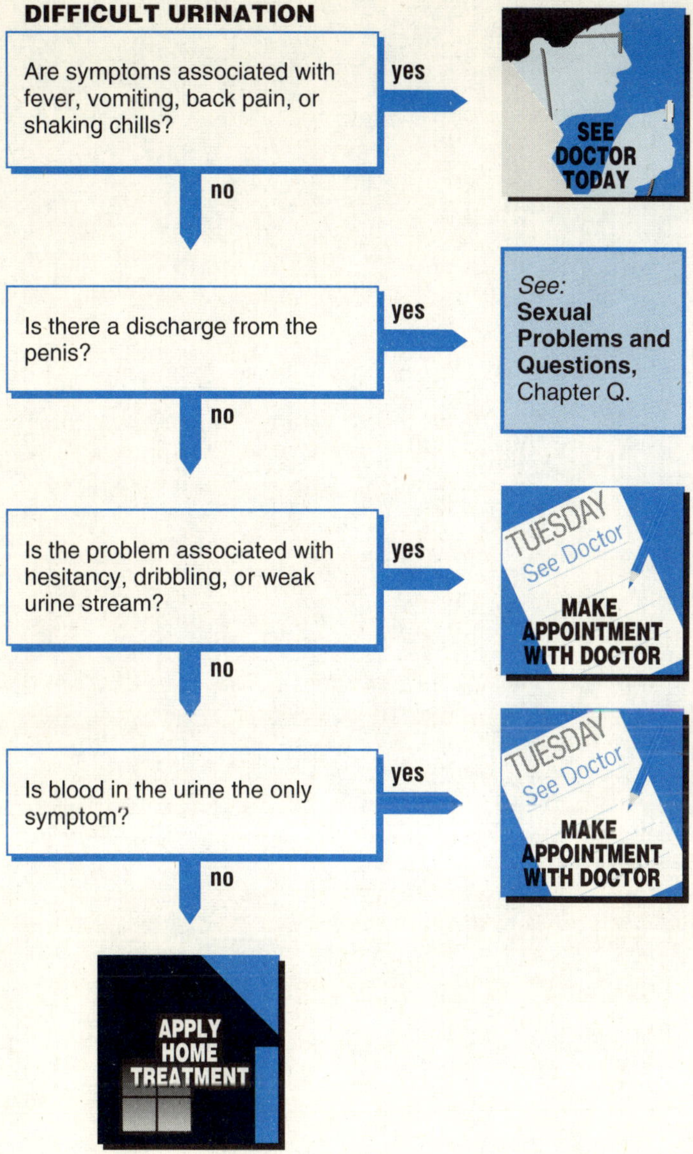


## WHAT TO EXPECT AT THE DOCTOR'S OFFICE

A urinalysis and culture should be performed. The back and abdomen are usually examined. With symptoms of prostatitis or prostatism, a rectal examination (so that the prostate can be felt) should be expected. With pre-existing kidney disease or symptoms of kidney infection, a more detailed history and physical as well as extra laboratory studies may be needed.

If bacterial infection is determined, an antibiotic will be prescribed. A surgical procedure—there are several—may be chosen to relieve prostatism, but drugs or simple "watchful waiting" may be best for you.

## CHAPTER P

# *Women's Health*

# How to Do a Breast Self-examination

Most lumps in the breast are not cancerous. Most women will have a lump in a breast at some time during their life. Many women's breasts are naturally lumpy (so-called benign fibrocystic disease). Obviously, every lump or possible lump cannot and should not be subjected to surgery.

Cancer of the breast does occur, however, and is best treated earlier than later. Regular self-examination of your breasts gives you the best chance of avoiding serious consequences. Self-examination should be done monthly, just after the menstrual period.

The technique is as follows:

**1.** Examine your breasts in the mirror, first with your arms at your side and then with both arms over your head. The breasts should look the same. Watch for any change in shape or size, or for dimpling of the skin. Occasionally, a lump that is difficult to feel will be quite obvious just by looking.

**2.** Next, while lying flat, examine the left breast using the inner finger tips of the right hand and pressing the breast tissue against the chest wall. Do not pinch the tissue between the fingers; all breast tissue feels a bit lumpy when you do this. The left hand should be behind your head while you examine the inner half of the left breast and down at your side when you examine the outer half. Do not neglect the part of the breast underneath the nipples or that which extends outward from the breast toward the underarm. A small pillow under the left shoulder may help.

**3.** Repeat this process on the opposite side.

Any lump detected should be brought to the attention of your doctor. Regular self-examination will tell you how long it has been present and whether it has changed in size. This information is very helpful in deciding what to do about the lump. Even the doctor often has difficulty with this decision. Self-examination is an absolute necessity for a woman with naturally lumpy breasts. She is the only one who can really know whether a lump is new, old, or has changed size. For all women, regular self-examination offers the best hope that surgery will be performed when, and only when, it is necessary.

# The Gynecological Examination

Examination of the female reproductive organs, usually called a "pelvic examination," may be expected for complaints related to these organs and along with the annual Pap smear. This examination yields a great deal of information and is often absolutely essential for diagnosis. By understanding the phases of the examination and your role in them, you can make it possible for an adequate examination to be done quickly and with a minimum of discomfort.

**Positioning.** Lying on your back, put your heels in the stirrups (the nurse may assist in this step). Move down to the very end of the examination table, with knees bent. Get as close to the edge as you can. Now let your knees fall out to the sides as far as they will go. Do not try to hold the knees closed with the inner muscles of the thigh. This will tire you and make the examination more difficult.

The key word during the examination is "relax"; you may hear it several times. The vagina is a muscular organ and if the muscles are tense, a difficult and uncomfortable examination is inevitable. You may be asked to take several deep breaths in an effort to promote relaxation.

**External Examination.** Inspection of the labia, the clitoris, and vaginal opening is the first step in the examination. The most common findings are cysts in the labia, rashes, and so-called venereal warts. These problems have effective treatments or may need no treatment at all.

**Speculum Examination.** The speculum is the "duck-billed" instrument used to spread the walls of the vagina, so that the inside may be seen. It is *not* a clamp. It may be constructed of metal or plastic. The plastic ones will click open and closed; don't be alarmed.

If a Pap smear or other test is to be made, the speculum examination usually will come before the finger (manual) examination, and the speculum will be lubricated with water only. A lubricant or a manual examination may spoil the test. If these tests are not needed, the manual examination may come first. The speculum also opens the vagina so that insertion of an intrauterine device (IUD) or other procedures can be accomplished.

**Manual Examination.** By inserting two lubricated, gloved fingers into the vagina and pressing on the lower abdomen with the other hand, the doctor can feel the shape of the ovaries and uterus as well as any lumps in the area. The accuracy of this examination depends on both the degree of relaxation of the patient and the skill of the doctor. Obese women cannot be examined as easily; this is another reason not to be overweight.

Usually, the best pelvic examinations are done by those who do them most often. You do not need a gynecologist, but be sure that your internist or family practitioner does "pelvics" on a regular basis before you request a yearly gynecological exam. A nurse practitioner who does pelvic examinations regularly is usually an expert also. The Pap smear alone does *not* require a great deal of experience.

Many doctors will also perform a rectal or recto-vaginal (one finger in rectum and one in vagina) examination. These examinations can provide additional information. Usually, during the examination there is a drape over your knees and the doctor sits on a stool out of your line of sight. Ask the doctor to explain what is going on.

## THE PAP SMEAR

You should be familiar with the basics of this test. As explained above, a scraping of the cervix and a sample of the vaginal secretions are obtained with the aid of a speculum. This provides cells for study under the microscope. A trained technician (a cytologist) can then classify the cells according to their microscopic characteristics. There are five classes:

- Classes I and II are negative for tumor cells.
- Classes III and IV are suspicious but not definite for tumors; your doctor will ask you to return for another Pap test or a biopsy of the cervix. This does *not* mean that cancer is definite.
- Class V is a definite indication of tumors.

Your doctor will explain the approach to confirming the diagnosis and starting treatment.

A single Pap smear detects up to 90% of the most common cancers of the womb and 70 to 80% of the second most common. Both of these common types of cancer grow slowly. Current evidence indicates that it may take ten years or more for a single focus of cancer of the cervix to spread. Thus, there is an excellent chance that regular Pap smears will detect the cancer before it spreads.

Cancer of the cervix is more frequent with moderate-to-heavy sexual activity, especially, and perhaps only, if you have multiple partners. Regular Pap testing probably should begin when regular sexual activity begins or at age 21, whichever is earlier. Testing is done annually for the first three years. If these first Pap smears are normal, then tests are done every three years. Some experts suggest that the tests can be discontinued at age 65 if all previous tests have been normal. While this recommendation probably carries little risk, we think that a Pap smear every three years is a small burden and prefer to continue the tests. There is almost no evidence that the use of birth control pills requires more frequent Pap smears.

# Painful, Frequent, or Bloody Urination

The best-known symptoms of bladder infection are:

- Pain or burning on urination
- Frequent urgent urination
- Blood in the urine

These symptoms are not always caused by infection due to bacteria. They can be due to a viral infection, excessive use of caffeine-containing beverages (coffee, tea, and cola drinks), bladder spasm, or they can have no known cause (i.e., "nerves").

**Bladder infection** is far more common in women than it is in men. The female urethra, the tube leading from the bladder to the outside of the body, is only about one-half inch long—a short distance for bacteria to travel to reach the bladder. Sometimes bladder infection is related to sexual activity; hence, "honeymoon cystitis" has become a well-known medical syndrome.

Bladder infections are common during pregnancy. Treatment may be more difficult and must, of course, take the pregnancy into account.

Vomiting, back pain, or teeth-chattering, body-shaking chills are not typical of bladder infections but suggest **kidney infection**. This requires more vigorous treatment and follow-up. A history of kidney disease (infections, inflammations, and kidney stones) also alters the treatment.

Most, if not all, bacterial bladder infections will respond to home treatment alone. Nevertheless, using antibiotics has become standard medical practice and it is possible that they shorten the illness. Antibiotics may be more important in recurrent bladder infections.

## HOME TREATMENT

- Drink a lot of fluids. Increase fluid intake to the maximum (up to several gallons of fluid in the first 24 hours). Bacteria are literally washed from the body during the resulting copious urination.
- Drink fruit juices. Putting more acid into the urine, although less important than the quantity of fluids, may help bring relief. Cranberry juice is the most effective, as it contains a natural antibiotic.

Begin home treatment as soon as symptoms are noted. If relief is not substantial in 24 hours and complete in 48, call the doctor.

### PAINFUL URINATION

Are symptoms associated with fever, vomiting, back pain, or shaking chills, or is pregnancy possible?

yes → SEE DOCTOR TODAY

no ↓

Is the problem associated with a new, irritating vaginal discharge?

yes → *See:* **Vaginal Discharge**, page 433.

no ↓

Is it possible to obtain a urinalysis without examination?

yes → SEE DOCTOR TODAY — Obtain urinalysis.

↓

Is infection present?

yes → SEE DOCTOR TODAY

no → APPLY HOME TREATMENT

no (urinalysis not possible without examination) → APPLY HOME TREATMENT — SEE DOCTOR TODAY

For women with recurrent problems, an important preventive measure is to wipe from front to back following urination. Most bacteria that cause bladder infections come from the rectum.

### WHAT TO EXPECT AT THE DOCTOR'S OFFICE

A urinalysis and culture will be performed. The back and abdomen are usually examined. In women with a vaginal discharge, an examination of both vagina and discharge is often necessary. With pre-existing kidney disease or symptoms of kidney infection, a more detailed history and physical are needed and extra laboratory studies may be necessary.

If urinary tract infection is proved, an antibiotic will be prescribed.

# Vaginal Discharge

Abnormal discharge from the vagina is common, but should not be confused with the normal vaginal secretions. Some of the many possible causes require the doctor.

The problem may be treated at home—for a time—if:

- The discharge is slight, doesn't hurt or itch, and is not cheesy, smelly, or bloody
- There is no possibility of a venereal disease
- The patient is past puberty

### Signs of Trouble

**Abdominal pain** suggests the possibility of serious disease, ranging from gonorrhea to an ectopic pregnancy in the fallopian tube. **Bloody discharge** between periods, if recurrent or significant in amounts, suggests much the same. Discharge in a girl before puberty is rare and should be evaluated.

If sexual contact in the past few weeks might possibly have resulted in a **venereal disease**, the doctor *must* be seen. Do not be afraid to take this problem to the doctor. Be frank in naming your sexual contacts, for their own benefit. Information will be kept confidential and the doctor will not embarrass you; doctors are commonly confronted with this situation.

**Monilia** is a yeast that may infect the walls of the vagina and cause a white, cheesy discharge.

**Trichomonas** is a common micro-organism that can cause a white, frothy discharge and intense itch. A mixture of bacteria may be responsible for a discharge, so-called nonspecific vaginitis. These infections are not serious and do not spread to the rest of the body, but they are bothersome. They will sometimes but not always go away by themselves. If discharge persists beyond a few weeks, make an appointment with the doctor.

In older women, lack of hormones can cause **atrophic vaginitis**. Prescription creams are sometimes needed if symptoms are bothersome. Foreign bodies, particularly forgotten tampons, are a surprisingly frequent cause of vaginitis and discharge.

## HOME TREATMENT

Hygiene and patience are the home remedies. If you have a discharge, douche daily and following intercourse with a Betadine solution (two tablespoons to a quart of water) or baking soda (one teaspoon to a quart).

## VAGINAL DISCHARGE

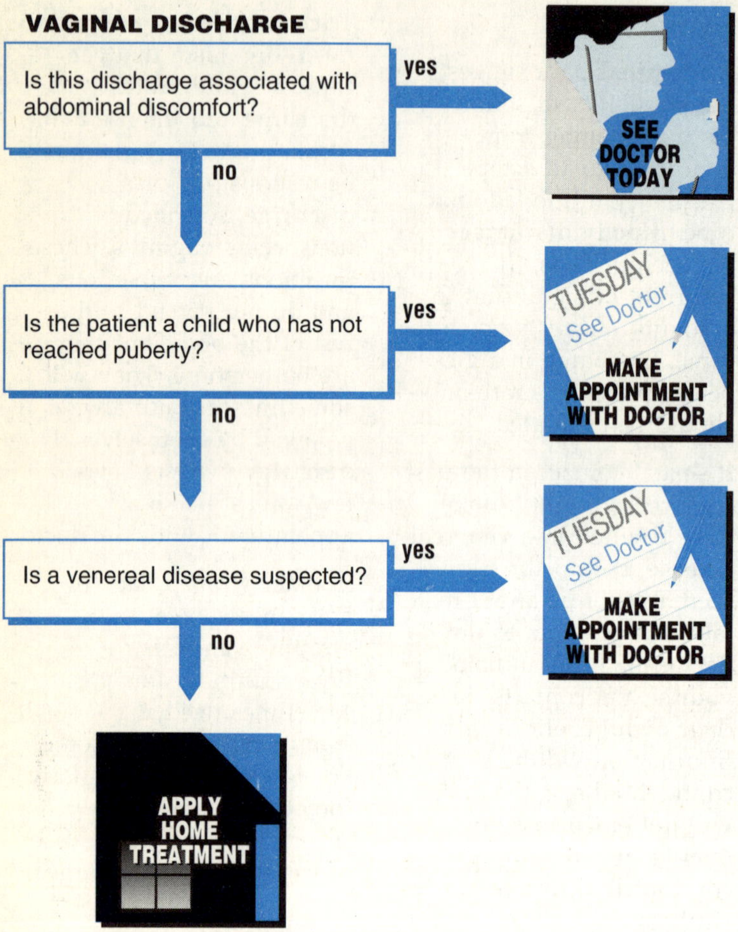


Medications active against yeast (Monistat, etc.) are now available without prescription.

### WHAT TO EXPECT AT THE DOCTOR'S OFFICE

You should anticipate a pelvic examination. If a venereal disease is suspected, a culture of the mouth of the womb—or cervix—is mandatory. If not, examination of the discharge under the microscope or a culture of the discharge is sometimes, but not always, needed. Suppositories or creams are the usual treatment. If venereal disease is at all likely, antibiotics, normally penicillin, will be prescribed. Oral medication for fungus or trichomonas may be used in severe cases. The sexual partner(s) may require treatment as well.

If you are taking an antibiotic such as tetracycline for some other condition, call your doctor for advice on changing medication.

If the discharge persists despite treatment for more than two weeks or becomes worse, see the doctor. Do not douche for 24 hours prior to seeing the doctor.

# Bleeding Between Periods

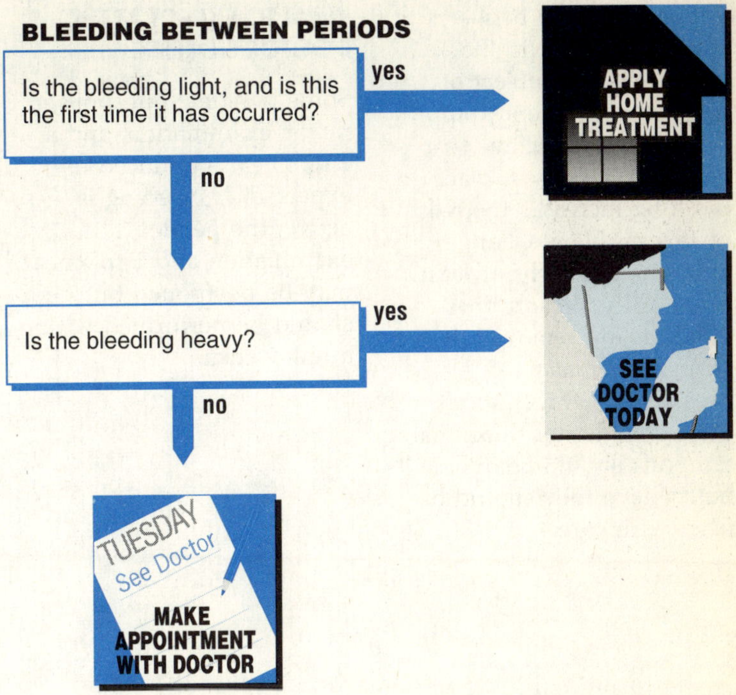


Most often, the interval between two menstrual periods is free of bleeding or spotting. Many women experience such bleeding, however, even though no serious condition is present. Women with an intrauterine birth control device (IUD) are particularly likely to have occasional spotting. If the bleeding is slight and occasional, it may be ignored.

Serious conditions such as cancer and abnormal pregnancy may be first suggested by bleeding between periods. If bleeding is severe or occurs three months in a row, a doctor must be seen. Often, a serious problem can be detected best when the bleeding is *not* active. The gynecologist or the family doctor is a better resource than the emergency room.

Any bleeding after the menopause should be evaluated by a doctor.

## HOME TREATMENT

Relax and use pads or tampons. Avoid taking aspirin if possible; it may prolong the bleeding. If in doubt about the effect of any medication, call your doctor.

The relationship between tampons and toxic shock syndrome is a subject of medical controversy, but many doctors believe that leaving tampons in place too long increases the risk of this problem. Change tampons regularly, at least twice daily. Be sure that tampons are removed: it is surprisingly easy to occasionally forget about them. We do not think that tampons should be avoided but believe they should be used with care.

### WHAT TO EXPECT AT THE DOCTOR'S OFFICE

Some personal questions, a pelvic examination, and a Pap smear should be expected. If bleeding is active, the pelvic examination and Pap smear may be postponed but should be performed within a few weeks.

# Difficult Periods

Adverse mood changes and fluid retention are very common in the days just prior to a menstrual period. Such problems are vexing and can be difficult to treat but are a result of normal hormonal variations during the menstrual cycle.

The menstrual cycle varies from woman to woman. Periods may be regular, irregular, light, heavy, painful, pain-free, long, or short, and yet still be normal. The rhythm of a menstrual cycle is medically less significant than bleeding, pain, or discharge between periods. Only when problems are severe or recur for several months is medical attention required. In this way, problems such as endometriosis can be found. Emergency treatment is seldom needed.

## HOME TREATMENT

We do not believe that diuretics, fluid pills, or hormones are frequently indicated. As we have said in other sections of this book, we prefer the simple and natural to the complex and artificial. Following hormone treatment, we have all too frequently seen mood changes that are worse than pre-menstrual tension, in addition to potassium loss, gouty arthritis, and psychological drug dependency on diuretics.

Salt tends to hold fluid in the tissues and to cause edema. The most natural diuretic is to cut down on salt intake. In the United States, the typical diet has ten times the required amount of salt. Many authorities feel that this is one cause of high blood pressure and arteriosclerosis. If you can eliminate some salt, you may have less edema and fluid retention. If food tastes flat without salt, try using lemon juice as a substitute. Commercial salt substitutes are also satisfactory. Products with the word "sodium" or the chemical symbol "Na" anywhere in the list of ingredients contain salt.

For menstrual cramps, use ibuprofen (Advil, Nuprin, Midol, etc.) or aspirin. Products claimed to be designed for menstrual cramps (such as Midol) now have ibuprofen as the main ingredient. Many patients swear by such compounds, and they are fine if you want to pay the premium. We don't understand why, on a scientific basis, they should be any better than plain ibuprofen. Ibuprofen is usually most effective, but sometimes aspirin or acetaminophen may be preferred.

## WHAT TO EXPECT AT THE DOCTOR'S OFFICE

The doctor will give you some advice. Frequently, a prescription for diuretics or hormones will be given. For menstrual cramps, ibuprofen (Motrin, etc.) or another prostaglandin

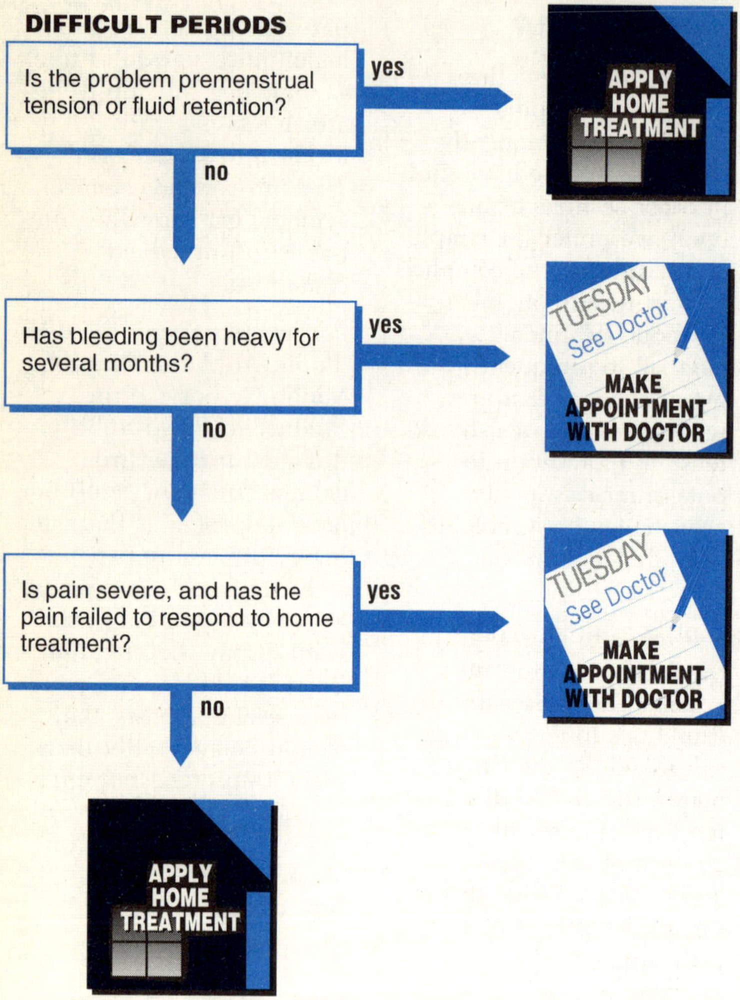


inhibitor is often prescribed. Note that ibuprofen is also available in lower doses (Advil, Nuprin, Midol, etc.) without prescription.

Pelvic examination is often unrewarding and sometimes may not be performed. However, if endometriosis is suspected, the pelvic exam should be done during the pre-menstrual phase of the menstrual cycle.

In cases of heavy bleeding, dilatation and curettage, or "D and C," may be required. Hysterectomy should not be performed for this complaint alone. If a tumor is found, surgery will sometimes be required; but the common fibroid tumor will often stop growing by itself, and surgery may not be needed. Such tumors often grow slowly and stop growing at menopause, so an operation can be avoided by waiting. If the Pap smear is positive, however, surgery is often indicated.

# Menopause

Margaret Mead once said, "The most creative force in the world is the menopausal woman with zest." But many pre-menopausal women expect that menopause will be a time of difficulties and unhappiness. Understanding menopausal changes and what you can do about the problems that may come up is the best way to minimize the negative side of the menopause. You may even find that, on balance, menopause is a positive experience.

Menopause occurs because ovaries' production of estrogen and progesterone, the female hormones, is greatly decreased quite suddenly. The ovaries do continue to produce low levels of androgens, hormones that help maintain muscle strength and sexual drive. The decrease in estrogen is responsible for the menopausal changes of most concern.

## Changes in the Body

Menstrual periods usually become lighter and irregular before they stop altogether. The end of menstrual periods also means the end of fertility and with it the need for any form of contraception that may have been used. These menopausal events are the ones that are most often considered to be positive.

**Hot flashes**—sudden feelings of intense heat usually lasting for two or three minutes—are most likely to occur in the evening but may happen at any time of the day. They may be aggravated by caffeine or alcohol, and some doctors believe that they are lessened by exercise. For most women, hot flashes gradually decrease over a period of about two years and eventually disappear altogether.

Estrogen hormones are responsible for stimulating the production of the natural lubricants in the vagina, so that the loss of estrogen can cause **vaginal dryness**. This may lead to irritation and itching as well as soreness during and after intercourse.

The thinning of bones, **osteoporosis**, that begins with menopause usually causes no symptoms for years. Unfortunately, the first symptom is usually a fracture, often of the hip. These fractures are especially serious because they may cause prolonged physical inactivity, a risk in itself. Furthermore, once the bone has become thin enough to fracture easily, it is difficult to reverse the process and actually strengthen the bones.

## The Emotional Side

Many women also experience unexpected mood swings. Although it is logical to assume that these changes are also related to the decrease in hormone production, the link is less clear than with other menopausal changes. More important, there seems to be an important difference between the mood changes that are actually experienced by women during menopause and those anticipated by pre-menopausal women. Many people, including men, expect that menopause will be characterized by unhappy and angry moods that come without warning and can't be avoided or ameliorated.

In fact, the medical literature suggests that the mood changes are not necessarily unpleasant, just unexpected. For example, a feeling of wakefulness in the middle of the night may be unusual for an individual but not uncomfortable; however, it might cause some worry if it is not understood as a normal part of the menopause. Most experts now believe that the menopause itself is not a cause of depression.

Aging and wrinkling of the skin cannot be blamed on menopause. Exposure to the sun and smoking are the most significant negative influences on the health of your skin.

## HOME TREATMENT

Keeping cool is the rule for hot flashes. Keep the home or office cool, dress lightly, drink plenty of water. Go easy on alcohol and caffeine, and maintain a regular exercise program. You don't have a fever, and there is no need for medicines such as aspirin or acetaminophen.

Lubricants such as water-based gels (Lubifax, K-Y, etc.), unscented creams (Albolene, etc.), vegetable oils, or a host of over-the-counter preparations (Lubrin, etc.) provide relief from vaginal dryness for many women. Many women also find that regular sexual activity actually decreases the problems of soreness with intercourse.

Regular exercise and adequate calcium in the diet are important in preventing osteoporosis. A regular aerobic exercise program (30 minutes a day, 4 days a week) is the foundation of a good program, but all types of activity—walking, climbing stairs rather than riding the elevator, and the like—will help maintain strong bones. Some studies have shown that the usual loss of calcium over these years can be almost entirely blocked by weight-bearing exercise. Swimming probably does not help.

Current recommendations are for post-menopausal women to obtain 1200 to 1500 milligrams (mg) of calcium per day. This is the equivalent of 4 or 5 eight-ounce glasses of skim milk. A calcium supplement may be indicated if the required amount cannot be obtained through dairy products.

Finally, understanding and acceptance of the unexpected mood changes is the best approach to these events.

Hot flashes, vaginal dryness and osteoporosis can be treated with estrogen. Such treatment requires a doctor's prescription and some careful consideration by you before you request or accept such a prescription.

**MENOPAUSE**

Are you over age 42?

**no** → Menopause usually occurs between ages 45 and 55 with an average at about age 51. Consider another problem.

**yes** ↓

Is one or more of the following present?

- Decreasing menstrual periods
- Hot flashes
- Vaginal dryness
- Unexpected mood changes

**no** → Consider another problem.

**yes** ↓

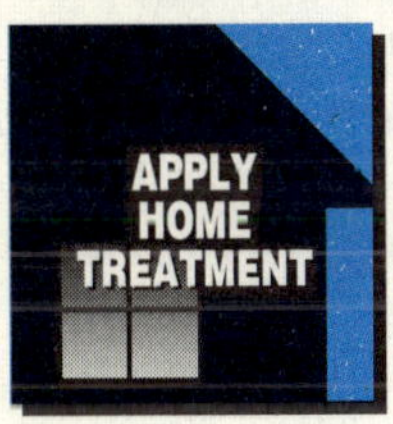


## WHAT TO EXPECT AT THE DOCTOR'S OFFICE

The doctor will interview and examine you to confirm that the symptoms are associated with menopause. The major question will then be whether to use estrogen replacement therapy. Current research suggests that pills consisting of estrogen alone may increase the risk of uterine cancer very slightly so that the estrogen should be combined with a progesterone. Such combinations appear to eliminate the increased risk and might even be protection against breast cancer. However, there is some indication that this combination approach might increase the risk of high blood pressure, heart disease, and stroke and that there is an interaction with smoking that increases these risks dramatically. A careful discussion of these risks with your doctor is required before embarking on estrogen replacement; most doctors believe the risks are minimal. Recently, many doctors have begun to recommend estrogen skin patches, which have a low dose and appear to have very few side effects; these may not have enough estrogen to strengthen the bones, however. Remember that estrogen replacement therapy will not make you young again or prevent aging.

Vaginal dryness can be treated with vaginal creams or suppositories that contain estrogen. This is effective, and because only a very little of the estrogen is absorbed, it may be a safer way of using estrogen for this problem than the taking of pills.

Osteoporosis is a more difficult question because of the silent nature of the condition until it causes a major problem in the form of a fracture. Almost all doctors emphasize exercise and adequate calcium intake. Many recommend estrogen supplements. We believe this is a reasonable approach.

# Missed Periods

Although pregnancy is often the first thought when a period is missed, there are many reasons for being late. Obesity, excessive dieting, strenuous exercise, and stress may cause missed or irregular periods. Diseases such as hyperthyroidism that upset the hormonal balance of the body may also be the source of missed periods, but these diseases are relatively infrequent causes of this problem. And, of course, menopause means the end of menstrual periods and it is normal for periods to be irregular before they stop completely.

## Pregnancy Tests

Testing for pregnancy has become faster, easier, and more sensitive in the last decade. Home test kits are now available that provide a reasonable degree of accuracy and may show a positive result as early as two weeks after the missed period. The most sophisticated laboratory test available through your doctor's office may turn positive within a few days after the period should have started. In both instances, a negative result is less reliable when the test is used soon after the period is missed. Thus, it is common to repeat the test after a negative result if periods do not resume.

Because a positive result is less likely to be misleading than a negative one, the rule is to believe a positive test, but not to trust a negative test until it has been repeated at least once.

## Other Causes

Two opposites, obesity and starvation, often lead to irregular periods. If either of these conditions is severe and persistent, it can cause the complete cessation of periods. At the other end of the health spectrum, women who are undergoing rigorous athletic training often have irregular periods. The missed periods themselves do not harm the athlete, but there is some concern that the hormonal imbalance that causes the missed periods may also lead to loss of calcium from bones. Currently, it is not possible to determine if this poses any real risk to women athletes.

Emotional as well as physical stress may result in irregular periods. Indeed, anxiety over possible pregnancy may cause a missed period, thereby increasing the anxiety even further.

If you've reached the age when menopause is possible or likely, then this inevitable event must move to the top of your list of possible causes for the missed period. You may have already experienced some of the other symptoms of menopause. Your periods

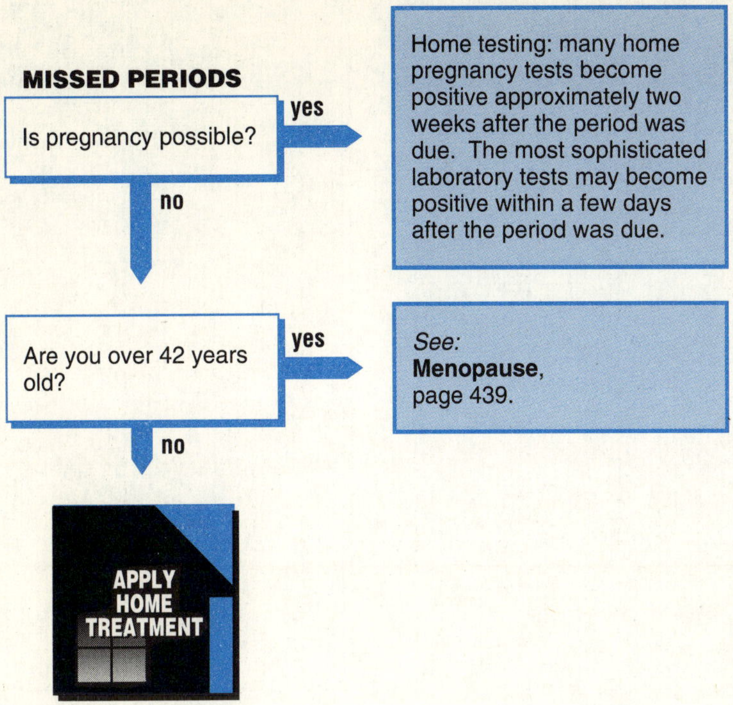


may also be irregular for a considerable period of time before they cease altogether. (See page 439 for more information.)

## HOME TREATMENT

In this instance, home treatment consists of giving yourself some time to consider the various causes of missed periods. You can do something about obesity (see Chapter 1). If you are dieting to the point of starvation, you may have a condition known as **anorexia nervosa**, and you should consult a doctor or a psychotherapist. If you are following a course of strenuous physical exercise, be alert for further information concerning the possible harmful effects of hormonal imbalance associated with missed periods. Finally, knowing that emotional stress may lead to missed periods will help you focus on the cause of the stress rather than a potential symptom.

If you feel that there is no satisfactory explanation for the missed period or are unable to develop a plan for dealing with the cause on your own, a phone call to your doctor should provide the advice you need.

## WHAT TO EXPECT AT THE DOCTOR'S OFFICE

Because diseases are relatively infrequent causes of missed periods, most doctors will not rush into a series of tests in an effort to detect these diseases. The doctor will consider the common causes of missed periods discussed above; this is best done with a careful history and physical examination. If pregnancy is the only real possibility, the doctor may refer you by phone to the laboratory for a pregnancy test so that you can avoid an unnecessary office visit.

CHAPTER Q

# *Sexual Problems and Questions*

# Sexually Transmitted Diseases

If you think you might have a sexually transmitted disease (STD), you need the help of the doctor. The only noteworthy exception to this rule is when you are sure that you have **genital herpes** and you have chosen to manage the problem without the use of acyclovir. Other than this, home treatment consists of prevention only. Consult Table Q for further information.

If you think your problem might be genital herpes, see page 448, **Genital Herpes Infections**. For information on AIDS and the prevention of STDs, see **AIDS and Safer Sex**, page 451.

**TABLE Q1** *Sexually Transmitted Diseases*

| *Disease* | *Type of Infection* | *Symptoms* |
|---|---|---|
| *Chlamydia* | Bacterial | When present, symptoms similar to those of gonorrhea |
| Genital warts | Virus | Small, fleshy growths, called "condylomas," in the genital or anal area; soft, reddish internal growths; firmer, darker external growths |
| Pubic lice | Parasite | Itching that is worse at night; lice visible in pubic hair; eggs, called "nits," attached to pubic hair |
| Acquired immunodeficiency syndrome (AIDS) | Virus | Unusual susceptibility to illness; development of rare, opportunistic diseases; persistent fatigue; fever; night sweats; unexplained weight loss; swollen glands; persistent diarrhea; dry cough |
| Gonorrhea | Bacterial | Males—discharge from penis, burning upon urination<br>Females—usually none; sometimes vaginal discharge and abdominal discomfort |
| Syphilis | Bacterial | Initially a sore called a "chancre," usually located in the genital or anal area, or mouth; later a rash, slight fever, and swollen joints |
| Genital herpes | Virus | Painful sores, or blisters, in the genital area; sometimes fever, enlarged lymph glands, and flu-like illness; sores heal, but tend to recur. |

*Adapted with permission from Pfeiffer, G. J.* Taking Care of Today and Tomorrow. *Reston, Va.: The Center for Corporate Health Promotion, 1989.*

| *Diagnosis* | *Treatment* | *Special Concerns* |
|---|---|---|
| Microscopic examination of vaginal discharge; culture | Can be cured with antibiotics. | *Chlamydia* that is not cured can lead to pelvic inflammatory disease, infertility in women, and complications in pregnancy. |
| Physical examination | Large condylomas may be removed surgically. A caustic preparation may be applied to burn off condylomas. | Genital warts can recur following treatment. |
| Physical examination | Medication is given to kill lice. | None |
| Blood test to check for antibodies to the AIDS virus; medical history | Several drugs now available can help fight the virus and slow the progression of this disease; there is no cure and no vaccine. | AIDS is a fatal illness. AIDS-related complex, a less serious set of symptoms, will generally develop into AIDS over time. |
| Microscopic examination of vaginal discharge or culture from a suspected infection | Can be cured with antibiotics. | If left untreated, gonorrhea can develop into pelvic inflammatory disease—a serious condition in women—or cause infertility, arthritis, as well as other problems. |
| Examination of fluid from a chancre; blood test. | Penicillin or other antibiotics are given. | If syphilis is not treated, it can cause severe problems many years later, including blindness, brain damage, and heart disease. |
| Physical examination; Pap smear; laboratory tests | Medications can ease symptoms, but there is no cure. | Genital herpes is most contagious during an outbreak. Avoid sexual contact at these times. Genital herpes can cause complications during pregnancy and may be passed on to an infant during vaginal birth. For this reason, a cesarean delivery may be advised. |

# Genital Herpes Infections

Herpes infections of the genitalia (herpes progenitalis) are well on their way to occupying a unique place in medicine as the first popular venereal disease. Certainly, herpes progenitalis is the only sexually transmitted disease with its own membership organization, complete with newsletter and telephone hotline. With an estimated 20 million Americans having a recurrent problem with herpes, the prospects for building the membership of this organization seem to be excellent.

There are two types of herpes simplex virus. Infections of the genitalia are usually caused by type 2, but may be due to type 1 viruses, especially in children. Herpes type 1 is responsible for the all too frequent fever blisters and cold sores of the lips and mouth (see **Mouth Sores**, page 257). Whereas type 1 infections are usually spread by kissing and other similar contact, herpes type 2 infections are almost always spread by sexual contact. The virus takes up a permanent home in about one-third of the people it infects and causes recurrent outbreaks of painful, red blisters. These recurrences may be triggered by other illnesses, trauma, or emotional distress. The blisters usually last from five to ten days.

### Not Infecting Others

Herpes is most contagious during and just before the period when the blisters are present. Many people with recurrent herpes can tell a day or two before an outbreak actually occurs. They develop an itchy or tingling feeling called a **prodrome**. The key to preventing transmission of herpes is to avoid sexual contact when the prodrome or blisters are present. **Condoms** probably give some protection against transmitting the disease but may be painful when sores are present, and they are not complete protection.

### Medication

There is no drug that cures herpes, but acyclovir (Zovirax) ointment may make an initial attack go away in 10 to 12 days rather than 14 to 16 days with no treatment. Recurrent attacks seem resistant to the ointment.

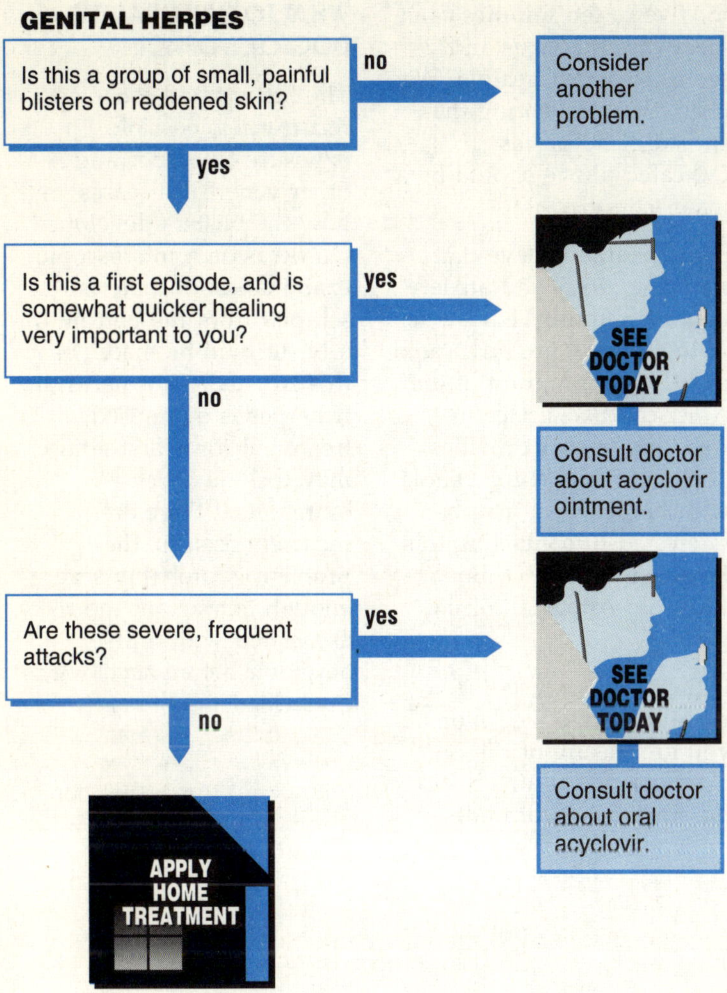


Oral acyclovir also speeds healing of initial attacks and is somewhat less effective with a recurrence. Oral acyclovir will decrease the number and severity of recurrence if taken continuously, but attacks return when the drug is stopped, sometimes worse than before. Oral acyclovir is associated with many side effects including nausea, vomiting, diarrhea, dizziness, joint pain, rash, and fever. Its long-term safety has not been established.

### Dangers of Herpes

The painful, reddened, grouped blisters of herpes are seldom mistaken for the painless shallow ulceration (chancre) that is the initial sign of syphilis. However, if you are unsure about the problem you are dealing with, you should not assume that it is herpes. A call or a visit to your doctor may be necessary.

Several studies have indicated that herpes infections are associated with cancer of the cervix, but it is not known if herpes is involved in causing this cancer. If you have recurrent herpes infections, this is another reason for a Pap smear. However, you should have Pap smears taken anyway, and it is not known if the presence of herpes indicates a need for more frequent Pap smears.

## HOME TREATMENT

The painful truth is that the treatment of herpes primarily consists of "grin and bear it." Various salves such as calamine lotion, alcohol, and ether have been tried; they may provide some relief in individual cases, but none have been remarkably successful. A hot tub bath for five to ten minutes can inactivate the virus and seems to speed healing. We think that preventing the spread of herpes as indicated above should be a major concern.

Some people believe that reducing stress and anxiety may be helpful. This is one of the approaches advocated by HELP, a program of the American Social Health Association that provides personal support for people with herpes. You may be interested in contacting this organization at P.O. Box 100, Palo Alto, California 94302.

If the problem lasts for more than two weeks or you are unsure of the diagnosis, a call or visit to the doctor is indicated.

## WHAT TO EXPECT AT THE DOCTOR'S OFFICE

The history will focus on recurrences, possible exposure to herpes and other venereal diseases, and how the blisters developed. On occasion a microscopic examination of material scraped from the bottom of a blister will be made, but this is usually not necessary. If herpes is diagnosed, treatment for a first attack may include acyclovir ointment. If there are recurrent attacks, the problem is probably severe enough to warrant the risks associated with oral acyclovir before acyclovir is prescribed.

# AIDS and Safer Sex

AIDS and its prevention are also discussed in Chapter 1. We think that much of that information warrants repeating here along with more detail on prevention and testing.

AIDS is caused by the human immunodeficiency virus (HIV). This suppresses the immune system and leaves the body susceptible to normally rare disorders, including *Pneumocystis pneumonia*, Kaposi's sarcoma (a form of skin cancer), and other opportunistic diseases (diseases that take advantage of the body's low immune defenses).

The symptoms of AIDS include:

- Persistent fatigue
- Unexplained fever
- Drenching night sweats
- Unexplained weight loss
- Swollen glands
- Persistent diarrhea
- Dry cough

However, it can take many years before any of these symptoms appear.

## MODES OF TRANSMISSION

The AIDS virus is transmitted through sexual intercourse—oral, vaginal, or anal—when semen or vaginal fluids are exchanged and the virus finds an entry into the bloodstream, usually through a tear in the mucous membrane.

A second mode of transmission is through sharing needles or syringes with an infected person.

The AIDS virus has not been shown to be spread from saliva, sweat, tears, urine, or feces. You will not get AIDS from casual contact, such as working with someone with AIDS. A kiss, a telephone, a toilet seat, or a swimming pool will not spread AIDS. However, babies of infected women may be infected during pregnancy or through breast-feeding.

Some hemophiliacs and surgical patients have become infected because of transfusions of contaminated blood. However, with the development of HIV-screening techniques, the probability of receiving infected blood is now very small. There is absolutely *no* risk in donating blood.

## WHO'S AT RISK?

As of 1993, the majority of AIDS cases in this country were concentrated among male homosexuals, bisexuals, and intravenous drug users. Approximately 4% of the cases have been attributed to heterosexual contact.

The extent to which AIDS is spreading within the heterosexual community is not clear. However, there is an alarming increase among intravenous drug abusers. Experts believe that this may be the main means of transmission within the heterosexual population in the future. It is important to stress that though AIDS has been pre-dominant in certain groups (that is, gay men and intravenous drug abusers), it's not who you are, it's what you do, that increases your risk of infection. Casual sex, whether homosexual or heterosexual, is the biggest threat for most people; promiscuity can be very dangerous, even when condoms are used. Therefore, reducing risky behavior is the first step to preventing and controlling the spread of AIDS.

Risky behaviors are the following:

- Having sex with multiple partners
- Sharing drug needles and syringes
- Anal sex with or without a condom
- Vaginal or oral sex with someone who shoots drugs or engages in anal sex
- Sex with a stranger (pick-up or prostitute) or with someone who is known to have multiple sex partners
- Unprotected sex without a condom

## AIDS TESTING

Here are some ground rules for AIDS testing.

**WHO:** Men or women who have had sex with many partners or with prostitutes, who use intravenous drugs, who have gonorrhea or syphilis, who have had sex with anyone who has engaged in these behaviors, or anyone who has received a blood transfusion or blood products between 1978 and 1985.

**WHEN:** Every three to six months for as long as the behavior creating the risk continues.

**WHY:** To detect infection with the AIDS virus (human immunodeficiency virus or HIV). If you test positive, there are now certain treatments that can reduce the risks of complications in some patients. You do need to know.

Current tests for AIDS, made with a sample of blood, are not able to identify the HIV virus that causes AIDS. Rather, they look for antibodies manufactured by the body in response to the infection. The standard screening test is the enzyme-linked immunosorbent assay, or ELISA. When an ELISA is positive, the finding is always confirmed with the more accurate, more expensive test known as the Western Blot.

Although these tests accurately diagnose HIV infection in high-risk groups, their performance falls woefully short in populations that are not at high risk. A study conducted by the Congressional Office of

Technology Assessment found that when HIV-antibody tests are performed under ideal conditions, fully one-third of the positive results in a low-risk group—such as blood donors from downstate Illinois—could be expected to be falsely positive. Worse yet, if the test conditions resembled those that actually prevail in U.S. laboratories, almost nine out of ten positive tests in this low-risk group would be false positives.

AIDS testing is further complicated by a number of other issues. Testing needs to be accompanied by counseling with respect to prevention of AIDS as well as interpretation of results. Keeping results confidential may require special strategies, but notification of sexual partners is essential when results are positive.

## PREVENTING AIDS

Currently, a number of researchers are testing AIDS vaccines. However, a vaccine for mass inoculation is not on the immediate horizon. Some experts believe that it may be extremely difficult to provide an effective vaccine because HIV is a retro-virus. This means that it periodically changes its genetic code, thus requiring a different vaccine for each new strain.

Therefore, the primary means of prevention are:

- Celibacy
- Maintaining a monogamous relationship with an uninfected person
- Practicing safer sex in relationships where risk of infection is possible
- Not sharing needles and/or syringes, or better yet not shooting drugs

Although some controversy remains, the risk of AIDS is probably decreased by using a **latex condom** before, during, and after oral, anal, and vaginal intercourse.

Safety is increased by using a water-based lubricant such as K-Y jelly, Gynol II, Today, and Corn Husker's Lotion. Do not use petroleum jelly, cold cream, or baby oil as a lubricant. These products weaken the latex and can cause it to break.

A recent study has shown that the use of a **spermicide** containing nonoxynol-9 in conjunction with a condom may provide further protection from HIV infection if the condom breaks.

## TREATMENT

More than 70 drugs are currently being tested that are designed to slow or stop the AIDS virus or help bolster the body's immune response. To date, zidovudine (AZT) is the most promising drug and has shown positive results in extending the longevity of AIDS victims. Two newer drugs that have substantial promise are ddI and ddC. However, there is no cure. Drugs like inhaled pentamidine and Septra can reduce the frequency of some AIDS infections.

For the foreseeable future, the best way to prevent AIDS is to avoid risky behavior and practice safer sex when in doubt of your partner's status. Individuals who engage in risky behavior should consider having a blood test to detect the presence of HIV antibodies. Confidential HIV testing is offered through county health departments, hospitals, blood banks, sexually transmitted disease clinics, and your personal doctor.

### PREVENTION OF OTHER STDs

The rules for AIDS prevention also decrease the risk of developing other STDs. Again, the effectiveness of condoms as a barrier to infection is not complete, but can be substantial if properly used.

# Preventing Unwanted Pregnancy

Every woman must decide to abstain from sex, have babies, or use a contraceptive technique. Ideally, the male partner participates in this decision, but through a well-known quirk of nature, he does not participate in the most direct consequences. This chapter is concerned with the *medical* considerations involved in making decisions about contraception and childbearing. These decisions have a major effect on your health, both directly and indirectly, whether you are male or female. Childbearing and every form of contraception has a definite risk.

Few women will pursue one course of action for all their childbearing years. Abstention is most effective, but will be a reasonable choice for only a few. For most it is neither a practical nor healthy suggestion. The majority of women employ some form of contraception except for specific periods when they are attempting to get pregnant or are not engaging in sexual intercourse.

## FORMS OF CONTRACEPTION

If you are sure that you do not want any more children, the surgical methods of tubal ligation or vasectomy are the safest methods for ensuring this. Here are brief descriptions of the most popular forms of contraception:

**Birth control pills**. "The pill" uses hormones to prevent pregnancy and must be taken on a daily basis. When used safely, they are very effective in preventing pregnancy. However, they may cause blood clots, which have been fatal on occasion. They may also contribute to high blood pressure. There are also less dangerous but annoying side effects such as weight gain, nausea, fluid retention, migraine headaches, vaginal bleeding, and vaginal yeast infections.

**Intrauterine device (IUD).** This device is inserted into the uterus by a doctor and remains there until removed or expelled. If the IUD is expelled, it may not be noticed. In such cases, some pregnancies have resulted. The IUD may also cause bleeding and cramps. In rare instances, it is associated with serious infections of the uterus, although the type most frequently associated with these uterine infections—the Dalkon Shield—has been removed from the market.

**Diaphragm.** A diaphragm is a rubber membrane that fits over the opening to the uterus in the vagina. It must be inserted before intercourse and kept in place for a number of hours thereafter. There are no side effects or complications from diaphragms. They are best used with a spermicidal foam or jelly.

**Foams, jellies, and suppositories.** These forms contain chemicals that kill or immobilize the man's sperm. In the past they have been used by themselves but now are almost always used in conjunction with a diaphragm. Side effects are unusual and consist of some irritation to the walls of the vagina. Their effect lasts only about 60 minutes, and many people find these preparations inconvenient and just plain messy.

**Condoms.** These are enjoying a resurgence of popularity. If used correctly, they are 90% effective in preventing pregnancy. There are no side effects, they are inexpensive and widely available, and they give some protection against sexually transmitted diseases, including AIDS. However, remembering to use them seems to be a problem, and they do result in decreased sensitivity for the male.

**The rhythm method.** Intercourse is avoided during the time when ovulation is expected. This method requires fairly regular periods and a willingness to carefully take daily temperatures in order to predict the time of ovulation. Under the best of circumstances, it is only moderately effective. Some currently taught techniques of "natural family planning," based on frequent measurement of the pH of the cervical mucus, are a slight improvement, but require highly motivated people.

**TABLE Q2** *Expected Pregnancies: Percentage of Married Women Who Become Pregnant Within the First Year of Contraceptive Use*

| *Method* | *Age Group* 15–19 | *20–24* | *25–29* | *30–34* | *35–39* | *40–44* |
|---|---|---|---|---|---|---|
| **Pill** | 2.3 | 1.5 | 1.2 | 0.8 | 0.8 | 0.8 |
| **IUD** | 4.5 | 2.9 | 2.3 | 1.5 | 1.5 | 1.5 |
| **Condom** | 10.7 | 15.4 | 5.7 | 0.9 | 0.9 | 0.9 |
| **Diaphragm and spermicide** | 17.9 | 11.7 | 9.6 | 6.3 | 6.3 | 6.3 |
| **Rhythm** | 23.3 | 15.4 | 12.6 | 8.3 | 8.3 | 8.3 |

* *Percentages shown are the lowest rates for each age group in A.L. Shirm, J. Trussell, J. Menken, and W.R. Grady, "Contraceptive Failure in the United States: The Impact of Social, Economic and Demographic Factors,"* Family Planning Perspectives, *Vol. 14, Table 2, p. 68, 1982.*

**Coitus interruptus.** Here the male withdraws from the vagina just before ejaculation. Because there are sperm present in the secretions of the penis *before* ejaculation occurs and because withdrawal at just the right time is a tricky business at best, this method reduces the chances of pregnancy by reducing the number of sperm deposited in the vagina, but rather frequently fails to prevent pregnancy.

**Douche.** Douching after intercourse also decreases the number of sperm in the vagina and therefore decreases the chance of pregnancy somewhat. It is far from reliable.

Table Q2 gives information on the effectiveness of contraceptives.

**Relative Risks**

Tables Q3 and Q4 present information on the risks women face in using different forms of birth control or no birth control at all (thus increasing the chance that they become pregnant). The risks in Table Q3 were calculated by measuring the number of women who died from giving birth after trying, or not trying, contraception and the number who died from fatal complications, if any, due to their contraceptive method. The higher the number, the greater the risk.

Note the results:

- The risk to women who smoke and take birth control pills is substantially higher than the risk to non-smokers—yet another good reason to stop smoking
- Unprotected intercourse is one of the most hazardous choices women can make because of the maternal mortality rates associated with pregnancy or childbirth.
- The least hazardous techniques for women, aside from sterilization, require the availability of abortion.

As far as your health is concerned, it seems clear that you should consider "mechanical" forms of contraception (IUD, condom, diaphragm with foam) and assure yourself of access to facilities for abortion. We present this information not to promote any particular method, but to ensure that you can make an informed decision. To risk your health unknowingly is the truly tragic choice.

**TABLE Q3** *Risks of Pregnancy and Contraceptive Methods by Age: Annual Number of Deaths Associated with Birth Control per 100,000 Women*

| *Method of Control and Outcome* | *Age Group 15–19* | *20–24* | *25–29* | *30–34* | *35–39* | *40–44* |
|---|---|---|---|---|---|---|
| **No birth control** | | | | | | |
| BIRTH-RELATED | 7.0 | 7.4 | 9.1 | 14.8 | 25.7 | 28.2 |
| **Abortion** | | | | | | |
| METHOD-RELATED | 0.5 | 1.1 | 1.3 | 1.9 | 1.8 | 1.1 |
| **Pill/non-smoker** | 0.5 | 0.7 | 1.1 | 2.1 | 14.1 | 32.0 |
| BIRTH-RELATED | (0.2) | (0.2) | (0.2) | (0.2) | (0.3) | (0.4) |
| METHOD-RELATED | (0.3) | (0.5) | (0.9) | (1.9) | (13.8) | (31.6) |
| **Pill/smoker** | 2.4 | 3.6 | 6.8 | 13.7 | 51.4 | 117.6 |
| BIRTH-RELATED | (0.2) | (0.2) | (0.2) | (0.2) | (0.3) | (0.4) |
| METHOD-RELATED | (2.2) | (3.4) | (6.6) | (13.5) | (51.1) | (117.2) |
| **IUD only** | 1.3 | 1.1 | 1.3 | 1.3 | 1.9 | 2.1 |
| BIRTH-RELATED | (0.5) | (0.3) | (0.3) | (0.3) | (0.5) | (0.7) |
| METHOD-RELATED | (0.8) | (0.8) | (1.0) | (1.0) | (1.4) | (1.4) |
| **Diaphragm and spermicide** | | | | | | |
| BIRTH-RELATED | 1.9 | 1.2 | 1.2 | 1.3 | 2.2 | 2.8 |
| **Condom** | | | | | | |
| BIRTH-RELATED | 1.1 | 1.6 | 0.7 | 0.2 | 0.3 | 0.4 |
| **Condom and abortion** | | | | | | |
| METHOD-RELATED | 0.1 | 0.1 | 0.1 | * | * | * |
| **Rhythm** | | | | | | |
| BIRTH-RELATED | 2.5 | 1.6 | 1.6 | 1.7 | 2.9 | 3.6 |

**Fewer than 0.1*

*From Howard W. Ory, "Mortality Associated with Fertility and Fertility Control: 1983,"* Family Planning Perspectives, *Vol. 15, No. 2, March/April 1983.*

### Deciding to Give Birth

You may decide to become pregnant for the best of reasons—your own reasons. Choosing a method of contraception is one of the most intensely personal decisions, and the rest of us should respect your right to make up your own mind. Ideally, your choice depends on you and your partner.

One of the most popular reasons to have sex without birth control is that you wish to raise a family, a desire that can easily outweigh the health risks. Many women have ethical or religious objections to abortion—or to other forms of contraception, for that matter. A pregnant woman who will not be able to care for her baby but cannot accept an abortion has the option of allowing the newborn to be adopted.

Another common reason not to use contraception is simply not wanting to bother with it. Remember that deciding to have sex without birth control is, over the long run, the same as deciding to become pregnant. Make a choice for yourself.

In any case, a woman who chooses to give birth to a child deserves good medical care. This lowers the health risks of pregnancy and childbirth, and provides for a healthier, happier baby. We and Dr. Robert Pantell discuss pregnancy and birth in detail in *Taking Care of Your Child.*

**TABLE Q4** *Cumulative Risk of Mortality per 100,000 Women, Ages 15–44*

| | |
|---|---|
| **No birth control** | 462 |
| **Abortion** | 41 |
| **Pill/non-smoker** | 251 |
| **Pill/smoker** | 977 |
| **IUD** | 45 |
| **Condom** | 23 |
| **Diaphragm and spermicide** | 53 |
| **Condom and abortion** | 1 |
| **Rhythm** | 68 |

*From Howard W. Ory, "Mortality Associated with Fertility and Fertility Control: 1983."* Family Planning Perspectives, *Vol. 15, No. 2, March/April 1983.,*

# Questions About Sex

Sex is an area in which we all experience some insecurity. Every individual has anxieties and fears; everyone thinks that friends and colleagues are free from such problems. There are no personal experts in sex. No personal experience can constitute both a broad sampling of individual differences and probe the depths of a long-standing, profoundly intimate relationship. Because everyone knows only his or her own activities, and for the most part imagines what others are up to, myths abound.

Each generation and most people discover anew the exhilaration of a good sexual experience. In a perverse game played between the generations, a variety of contradictory rules for the conduct of sexual relationships are dogmatically advocated. Accusations are formulated, anxieties created, and health disturbed.

Good feelings are what sex is all about. But the good feelings go beyond the pleasurable physical sensations of sexual arousal. Feeling good about yourself, your partner, intimacy—these are feelings you need for sex to be its most satisfying and pleasurable. A number of factors may undercut these good feelings; only a few factors are related to sexual function itself. Anxiety or depression from any cause may result in problems with sex.

## MYTHS AND ANXIETIES

Attitudes toward sex create problems, usually unnecessarily. Anxiety about sex, especially in the learning stage, must be counted as normal simply because it is a universal phenomenon. But this anxiety has been compounded by the two dominant contemporary approaches toward sex.

The first approach considers sex as unspeakable. Moralistic fantasies develop. A feature of the human mind is that fantasies cannot be suppressed by thinking about them. If you avoid feeling guilty about your fantasies, you promote your sexual health.

We are equally concerned with an emerging view of the sexual partner as an orgasm machine, a preoccupation with technique rather than feeling, and with the resulting depersonalization of the sexual relationship. Between them, these attitudes have given rise to many myths about sex without allowing sensible answers to be discussed.

**Virility** is one major area of myth. We frequently encounter patients who have fears that their sexual activity is too frequent or too infrequent. Part of this problem stems from publication of average figures from large-scale sex surveys. People who find that their practices are distant from the averages are often concerned. Relax. It may be eight times a day or eight times a year. The only rule worth remembering is that in a stable relationship, the frequency of sexual activity should be a workable compromise between the desires of the partners.

Another area of anxiety concerns the **sexual equipment**. Men worry about the size of their penis. Women worry that their breasts are too big or too small, their legs too fat or too thin. Men worry about a pigeon chest, no hair on their chest, or too much hair on their chest. Women are concerned that their hair does not properly frame their face, that they have hairs around the nipples, or that their total image is too dowdy, too awkward, or too cheap. There is little that is worthwhile in such concerns.

Some individuals are more attractive than others. Some are more sensual than others. However, the breadth of taste runs from thick to thin. Somebody likes you the way you are. Men may like large women or slender women who wear clothes well. Women may be excited by broad shoulders or by a thoughtful gesture. Whether this whole business is due to cultural indoctrination or to innate differences between individuals, the point is the same. Usually, the sexual equipment is the least important part of the problem! If you fear that you were not created as the most attractive of creatures to the opposite sex, you will find that this obstacle can be reduced by warmth, affection, and humanity. In sex, how you feel *about* each other is more important than how you feel *to* each other.

The man frequently worries unnecessarily about penis size. In fact, there is little difference in size of the erect penis between different men, although there are significant differences in the resting state. Moreover, the vaginal canal, which accommodates birth, is potentially much larger than the thickest of penises. The size and rigidity of the penis will vary for the same man at different times. Some factors affecting erect penile size are physical—such as the length of time since previous intercourse—and some are psychological.

**Impotence** is seldom due to disease of genitalia, nerves, or blood vessels. No male is equally potent at all times, and all males are, on some occasions, impotent. Chronic impotence implies chronic anxiety, at least partially compounded by worry over the impotence.

**Premature ejaculation**, while physically the opposite of impotence, has the same cause. Again, relaxation is usually a solution. There are some other potential aids. A firm pinch on the tip of the penis will delay ejaculation. A condom usually decreases sensation so that ejaculation is delayed. Seldom are such measures necessary for more than a few occasions.

**Female orgasm** is the most written-about sexual phenomenon in recent years. This subject has been linked inseparably to aspects of the women's movement. It has been pointed out that some women are multi-orgasmic and may climax several times during a single intercourse. It has been held that equality of orgasm is a principal requirement for sexual equality. On the other hand, it has been observed that a large number of women do not have orgasms with regularity. The emerging sexual myth is that these women are in some way abnormal. In fact, many women relating deep and satisfactory sexual experiences do not report frequent orgasms as a significant feature. If you let others tell you what you should be doing and then allow guilt to develop when you don't meet false "norms," you are promoting these myths. Of all human activities, sexual activity, more than any other, should be directed by the individual at his or her own pace and style.

## SEXUAL PRACTICES

A variety of sexual practices have been recently re-emphasized. These include sex with the aid of various appliances, oral sex, and sex in a virtual infinity of positions. Such practices are recorded in all eras of human literature, but advocates of sexual variety were discouraged by legal and ethical barriers until recently.

Medically, there is no reason either to encourage or discourage sexual variety and experimentation. The problems presently seen are a reaction to earlier attitudes. They come from the second dominant approach to sexuality; all must now meet a perfect hedonistic norm. People now feel guilty that their sex life has insufficient variety.

For example, the majority of heterosexual activity takes place in the "male-superior" position. This position is often the most satisfactory for both partners because it allows the deepest penetration and the sensitivity value of being face to face. Recent derogation of this technique as the "missionary position" illustrates ignorance of history and anatomy. The accusatory tone of the phrase suggests an attempt to arouse guilt and anxiety about a normal practice.

Other individuals, for equally good reasons, prefer many different positions or find their greatest satisfaction with a particular alternative technique. There is no right way and no standard pattern for sexual expression. Averages are meaningless in a personal relationship between two individuals. Such relationships may be physically expressed in a wide variety of ways, none of which have any superiority to the others. You have personal freedom to be either ordinary or exotic—with pleasure, and without guilt.

There are sexual practices that do have risk, of course. Having multiple partners increases the risk of all sexually transmitted diseases including AIDS. The risk is raised when the selection of these partners is indiscriminate or when you have sex with those who are indiscriminate (such as prostitutes). Finally, anal sex increases the risk of AIDS transmission for several reasons. The current public discussions of safer sex emphasize these points and the methods by which you may protect yourself (see page 451).

Sex is not a competitive sport. Sexual health, for the great majority of individuals, comes down to common sense. If it feels good to both partners, do it. If it doesn't feel good, don't do it. Don't allow the fear of being "hung up" to become the major hang-up. Individuals should not allow other individuals, equally non-expert, to define their satisfaction for them. There remain "different strokes for different folks."

PART V

# *Family Records*

# *Immunizations: A Family Record*

**DPT** = Diphtheria, pertussis (whooping cough), and tetanus (lockjaw)
**DT** = Diphtheria and tetanus (lockjaw)
**HIB** = *Hemophilus* influenza type B
**Measles** = Measles
**Mumps** = Mumps
**OPV** = Oral polio virus
**Rubella** = German measles (three-day measles)
**T(d)** = Tetanus and adult diphtheria
**Hepatitis B** = Hepatitis B

| *Name:* | | | | | | |
|---|---|---|---|---|---|---|
| ***Recommended Age*** | ***Date*** | ***Date*** | ***Date*** | ***Date*** | ***Date*** | ***Date*** |
| **Newborn** | | | | | | |
| Hepatitis B | | | | | | |
| **2 months** | | | | | | |
| DPT #1 | | | | | | |
| OPV #1 | | | | | | |
| HIB #1 | | | | | | |
| **4 months** | | | | | | |
| DPT #2 | | | | | | |
| OPV #2 | | | | | | |
| HIB #2 | | | | | | |
| **6 months** | | | | | | |
| DPT #3 | | | | | | |
| OPV #3 | | | | | | |
| HIB #3 | | | | | | |
| **15 months** | | | | | | |
| Measles #1 | | | | | | |
| Mumps #1 | | | | | | |
| Rubella #1 | | | | | | |
| HIB #4 | | | | | | |
| **18 months** | | | | | | |
| OPV #4 | | | | | | |
| DPT #4 | | | | | | |
| **4–6 years** | | | | | | |
| OPV #5 | | | | | | |
| DT | | | | | | |
| **5–18 years** | | | | | | |
| Measles #2 | | | | | | |
| Mumps #2 | | | | | | |
| Rubella #2 | | | | | | |

*NOTE: Tetanus and diphtheria [T(d)] is recommended every 10 years for life, with an additional tetanus booster for contaminated wounds more than 5 years after the last booster.*

# *Childhood Diseases*

## *Whooping Cough*

| **Name** | **Date** | **Place** | **Remarks** |
|---|---|---|---|
| | | | |
| | | | |
| | | | |
| | | | |

## *Chicken Pox*

| **Name** | **Date** | **Place** | **Remarks** |
|---|---|---|---|
| | | | |
| | | | |
| | | | |
| | | | |

## *Measles*

| **Name** | **Date** | **Place** | **Remarks** |
|---|---|---|---|
| | | | |
| | | | |
| | | | |
| | | | |

## *Mumps*

| **Name** | **Date** | **Place** | **Remarks** |
|---|---|---|---|
| | | | |
| | | | |
| | | | |
| | | | |

*German Measles (Rubella)*

| Name | Date | Place | Remarks |
|---|---|---|---|
| | | | |
| | | | |
| | | | |
| | | | |

*Hepatitis*

| Name | Date | Place | Remarks |
|---|---|---|---|
| | | | |
| | | | |
| | | | |
| | | | |

*Other Diseases*

| Name | Date | Place | Remarks |
|---|---|---|---|
| | | | |
| | | | |
| | | | |
| | | | |

| Name | Date | Place | Remarks |
|---|---|---|---|
| | | | |
| | | | |
| | | | |
| | | | |

| Name | Date | Place | Remarks |
|---|---|---|---|
| | | | |
| | | | |
| | | | |
| | | | |

| Name | Date | Place | Remarks |
|---|---|---|---|
| | | | |
| | | | |
| | | | |
| | | | |

## *Family Medical Information*

| Name | Blood Type | RH Factor | Allergies (Including drug allergies) |
|---|---|---|---|
| | | | |
| | | | |
| | | | |
| | | | |
| | | | |
| | | | |
| | | | |
| | | | |
| | | | |
| | | | |

# *Hospitalizations*

Name ______________ Date ______________ Hospital ______________
Address ______________ Reason ______________

Name ______________ Date ______________ Hospital ______________
Address ______________ Reason ______________

Name ______________ Date ______________ Hospital ______________
Address ______________ Reason ______________

Name ______________ Date ______________ Hospital ______________
Address ______________ Reason ______________

Name ______________ Date ______________ Hospital ______________
Address ______________ Reason ______________

Name ______________ Date ______________ Hospital ______________
Address ______________ Reason ______________

Name ______________ Date ______________ Hospital ______________
Address ______________ Reason ______________

Name ______________ Date ______________ Hospital ______________
Address ______________ Reason ______________

Name ______________ Date ______________ Hospital ______________
Address ______________ Reason ______________

Name ______________ Date ______________ Hospital ______________
Address ______________ Reason ______________

Name ______________ Date ______________ Hospital ______________
Address ______________ Reason ______________

# Additional Reading

## Books

American College of Obstetrics and Gynecologists. *Planning for Pregnancy, Birth, and Beyond*. Washington, D.C., 1990.

Dubos, R. *Mirage of Health: Utopias, Progress, and Biological Change*. New York: Harper & Row Publishers, 1959.

Farquhar, J. W. *The American Way of Life Need Not Be Hazardous to Your Health*. Reading, Mass: Addison-Wesley, 1987.

Ferguson, T. *Medical Self-Care: Access to Health Tools*. New York: Summit Books, 1980.

Frank, J. F. *Persuasion and Healing*. New York: Schocken Books, 1963.

Fries, J. F. *Aging Well*. Reading, Mass.: Addison-Wesley Publishing Co., 1989.

Fries, J. F. *Arthritis: A Comprehensive Guide*. Rev. ed. Reading, Mass.: Addison-Wesley Publishing Co., 1990.

Fries, J. F., and L. Crapo. *Vitality and Aging*. San Francisco, Calif.: W. H. Freeman and Co. Publishers, 1981.

Fries, J. F., and G. E. Ehrlich. *Prognosis: A Textbook of Medical Prognosis*. Bowie, Md.: The Charles Press Publishers, 1983

Fuchs, V. R. *How We Live*. Cambridge, Mass.: Harvard University Press, 1983.

Knowles, J. H. *Doing Better and Feeling Worse: Health in the United States*. New York: W. W. Norton & Co., 1977.

Lorig, K., and J. F. Fries. *The Arthritis Helpbook*. Menlo Park, Calif.: Addison-Wesley Publishing Co., 1990, Revised edition.

Lowell, S. L., A. H. Katz, and E. Holst. *Self-Care: Lay Initiatives in Health*. New York: Prodist, 1979.

McKeown, T. *The Role of Medicine: Dream, Mirage, or Nemesis?* Princeton, N.J.: Princeton University Press, 1979.

Pantell, R., J. F. Fries, and D. M. Vickery. *Taking Care of Your Child*. 4th ed. Reading, Mass.: Addison-Wesley Publishing Co., 1993.

Riley, M. W. *Aging from Birth to Death: Interdisciplinary Perspectives*. Boulder, Col.: Westview Press, 1979.

Silverman, M., and P. R. Lee. *Pills, Profits and Politics*. Berkeley, Calif: University of California Press, 1974.

Sobel, D. S., and T. Ferguson. *The People's Book of Medical Tests*. New York: Summit Books, 1985.

Totman, R. *Social Causes of Illness*. New York: Pantheon Books, 1979.

Urquhart, J., and K. Heilmann. *Risk Watch. The Odds of Life*. New York: Facts on File Publications, 1984.

U. S. Department of Health and Human Services. Healthy People 2000: National Health Promotion and Disease Prevention Objectives. 1991. DHHS No. 91-50213. U. S. Government Printing Office, Wash., D.C. 20402.

Vickery, D. M. *Taking Part: A Consumer's Guide to the Hospital*. Reston, Va.: The Center for Corporate Health Promotion, Inc., 1986.

Vickery, D. M. *Lifeplan: Your Personal Guide to Maintaining Health and Preventing Illness*. Reston, Va.: Vicktor, 1990.

## *Articles*

American Cancer Society. *The Cancer-Related Health Checkup*. 8 February 1980.

Betz, B. J., and C. B. Thomas. "Individual Temperament as a Predictor of Health or Premature Disease." *Johns Hopkins Med. J.* 144(1979):81–89.

Breslow, L., and A. R. Somers. "The Lifetime Health-Monitoring Program." *N. Engl. J. Med.* 296(1977):601–08.

Brody, D. S. "The Patient's Role in Clinical Decision Making." *Ann. Intern. Med.* 93(1980):718–22.

Camargo, Jr., C. A., P. T. Williams, K. M. Vranizan, J. J. Albers, and P. D. Wood. "The Effect of Moderate Alcohol Intake on Serum Apolipoproteins A-I and A-II." *JAMA* 253(1985):2854–57.

Creagan, E. T., et al. "Failure of High-Dose Vitamin C (Ascorbic Acid) Therapy to Benefit Patients with Advanced Cancer." *N. Engl. J. Med.* 301(1979):687–90.

Delbanco, T. L., and W. C. Taylor. "The Periodic Health Examination: 1980." *Ann. Intern. Med.* 92(1980):251–52.

Dinman, B. D. "The Reality and Acceptance of Risk." *JAMA* 244(1980):1226–28.

Farquhar, J. W. "The Community-Based Model of Life Style Intervention Trials." *Am. J. Epidemiol.* 108(1978):103–11.

Fletcher, S. W., and W. O. Spitzer. "Approach of the Canadian Task Force to the Periodic Health Examination." *Ann. Intern. Med.* 92(1980):253.

Franklin, B. A., and M. Rubenfire. "Losing Weight Through Exercise." *JAMA* 244(1980):377–79.

Fries, J. F. "Aging, Natural Death, and the Compression of Morbidity." *N. Engl. J. Med.* 303(1980):130–35.

Fries, J. F. "Compression of Morbidity: Near or Far?" *Milbank Quarterly* 67(1990):208–232.

Fries, J. F., S. T. Fries, C. L. Parcell, and H. Harrington. "Health Risk Changes with a Low-cost Individualized Health Promotion Program: Effects at up to 30 Months. *Am. J. Health Promotion* 6(1992):364–371.

Fries, J. F., L. W. Green, and S. Levine. "Health Promotion and the Compression of Morbidity." *Lancet* 1(1989):481–483.

Glasgow, R. E., and G. M. Rosen. "Behavioral Bibliotherapy: A Review of Self-Help Behavior Therapy Manuals." *Psych. Bull.* 85(1978):1–23.

Goldman, L., and E. F. Cook. "The Decline in Ischemic Heart Disease Mortality Rates." *Ann. Int. Med.* 101(1984):825–36.

Greco, P. J., K. A. Schulman, R. Lavizzo-Mourey, and J. Hansen-Fluscher. "The Patient Self-determination Act and the Future of Advance Directives." *Ann. Int. Med.* 115(1991):639–643.

Hayward, R.S.A., E. P. Steinberg, D. E. Ford, M. F. Roizen, and K. W. Roach. "Preventive Care Guidelines, 1991." *Ann. Int. Med.* 114(1991):758–783.

Herbert, P. N., D. N. Bernier, E. M. Cullinane, L. Edelstein, M. A. Kantor, and P. D. Thompson. "High-Density Lipoprotein Metabolism in Runners and Sedentary Men." *JAMA* 252(1984):1034–37.

Huddleston, A. L., D. Rockwell, et al. "Bone Mass in Lifetime Tennis Athletes." *JAMA* 244(1980):1107–09.

Huttenen, J. K., et al. "Effect of Moderate Physical Exercise on Serum Lipoproteins." *Circulation* 60:(1979):1220–29.

Kaplan, N. M. "Non-Drug Treatment of Hypertension." *Ann. Int. Med.* 102(1985):359–73.

Kromhout, D., E. B. Bosschieter, and C. DeLezenne Coulander. "The Inverse Relation Between Fish Consumption and 20-Year Mortality from Coronary Heart Disease." *N. Engl. J. Med.* 312(1985):1205–09.

Lane, N. E., D. A. Bloch, H. B. Hubert, H. Jones, U. Simpson, and J. F. Fries. "Running, Osteoarthritis, and Bone Density." *Am. J. Med.* 88(1990):452–459.

Langford, H. G., et al. "Dietary Therapy Slows the Return of Hypertension After Stopping Prolonged Medication." *JAMA* 253(1985): 657–64.

Leigh, J. P., and J. F. Fries. "Health Habits, Health Care Utilization, and Costs in a Sample of Retirees." *Inquiry* 29(1992):44–54.

Leigh, J. P., N. Richardson, R. Beck, C. Kerr, H. Harrington, C. L. Parcell, and J. F. Fries. "Randomized Controlled Study of a Senior Health Promotion Program: The Bank of America Study." *Arch. Int. Med.* 152(1992):1201–1206.

Lipid Research Clinics Program. "The Lipid Research Clinics Coronary Primary Prevention Trial Results. I. Reduction in Incidence of Coronary Heart Disease." *JAMA* 251(1984):351–64.

Lipid Research Clinics Program. "The Lipid Research Clinics Coronary Primary Prevention Trial Results. II. The Relationship of Reduction in Incidence of Coronary Heart Disease to Cholesterol Lowering." *JAMA* 251(1984):365–74.

Lorig, K., R. G. Kraines, B. W. Brown, and N. Richardson. "A Workplace Health Education Program Which Reduces Outpatient Visits." *Medical Care* 23(1985):1044–1054.

Moore, S. H., J. LoGerfo, and T. S. Inui. "Effect of a Self-Care Book on Physician Visits." *JAMA* 243(1980):2317–20.

Multiple Risk Factor Intervention Trial Research Group. "Multiple Risk Factor Intervention Trial. Risk Factor Changes and Mortality Results." *JAMA* 248(1982):1465–501.

Nash, J. D., and J. W. Farquhar. "Community Approaches to Dietary Modification and Obesity." *Psychiatric Clinics of No. Amer.* 1(1978):713–24.

Paffenbarger, R. S., and R. T. Hyde. "Exercise as Protection Against Heart Attack." *N. Engl. J. Med.* 302(1980):1026–27.

Paffenbarger, R. S., et al. "A Natural History of Athleticism and Cardiovascular Health." *JAMA* 252(1984):491–95.

Phelps, C. E. "Illness Prevention and Medical Insurance." *J. Human Resources* 13(1978):183–207.

Phillipson, B. E., et al. "Reduction of Plasma Lipids, Lipoproteins, and Apoproteins by Dietary Fish Oils in Patients with Hypertriglyceridemia." *N. Engl. J. Med.* 312(1985):1210–16.

Relman, A. S. "The New Medical-Industrial Complex." *N. Engl. J. Med.* 303(1980):963–70.

Remington, P. L., et al. "Current Smoking Trends in the United States. The 1981–1983 Behavioral Risk Factor Surveys." *JAMA* 253(1985):2975–78.

Rosen, G. M. "The Development and Use of Nonprescription Behavior Therapies." *Amer. Psych.* (February 1976):139–41.

Stallones, R. A. "The Rise and Fall of Ischemic Heart Disease." *Scientific Amer.* 243(1980):53–59.

Taylor, W. C., and T. L. Delbanco. "Looking for Early Cancer." *Ann. Intern. Med.* 93(1980):773–75.

Vickery, D. M. "Medical Self-care: A Review of the Concept and Program Models. *AJHP* 1(1986):23–28.

Vickery, D. M. and T. Golaszewski. "A Preliminary Study on the Timeliness of Ambulatory Care Utilization Following Medical Self-Care Interventions." *AJHP* (Winter 1989):Vol. 3, No. 3, 26–31.

Vickery, D. M., T. Golaszewski, et al. "The Effect of Self-Care Interventions on the Use of Medical Service Within a Medicare Population." *Medical Care* (June 1988):580–588.

Vickery, D. M., T. Golaszewski, et al. "Life-Style and Organizational Health Insurance Costs." *JOM* 28(Nov. 1986):1165–1168.

Vickery, D. M., H. Kalmer, D. Lowry, M. Constantine, E. Wright, and W. Loren. "Effect of a Self-Care Education Program on Medical Visits." *JAMA* 250(1983):2952–56.

Weinstein, M. C. "Estrogen Use in Postmenopausal Women—Costs, Risks, and Benefits." *N. Engl. J Med.* 303(1980):308–16.

Zook, C. J., and F. D. Moore. "High-Cost Users of Medical Care." *N. Engl. J. Med.* 302(1980):996–1002.

# Index

**F**or advice on a common medical problem, look up the primary symptom in this index. Numbers in **boldface** indicate the pages where you can find the most information on each subject. These are usually the pages with decision charts and advice on home treatment and when to see a doctor.

To find specific advice on a common medical problem, look up the main symptoms in the Index on page 477, or follow this decision chart to the appropriate chapter.

## HOW TO USE THE DECISION CHARTS

Does the patient show any of these Emergency Signs?

- Major injury
- No pulse or breath
- Unconsciousness
- Active bleeding
- Stupor or drowsiness
- Disorientation
- Shortness of breath while resting
- Cold sweats
- Severe pain

**yes** → Go to the emergency room or call for help immediately. Turn to Emergencies, page 144, for more instructions.

**no** ↓

Is the patient choking, and unable to speak or cry out?

**yes** → Turn to page 149 for instructions in the abdominal-thrust maneuver.

**no** ↓

Has the patient swallowed poison?

**yes** → Identify the poison, call the Poison Control Center, and turn to page 153 for more instructions.

**no** ↓

Read the list of problems below and turn to the appropriate chapter:

| | |
|---|---|
| Common Injuries | Turn to Chapter D, p. 155. |
| Fever, Headache, and Other Common Problems | Turn to Chapter E, p. 190. |
| Eye Problems | Turn to Chapter F, p. 210. |
| Ears, Nose, and Throat Problems | Turn to Chapter G, p. 221. |
| Allergies | Turn to Chapter H, p. 261. |
| Skin Problems | Turn to Chapter I, p. 271. |
| Childhood Diseases | Turn to Chapter J, p. 321. |
| Bones, Joints, and Muscles | Turn to Chapter K, p. 337. |
| Stress, Mental Health, and Addiction | Turn to Chapter L, p. 383. |
| Chest Pain, Shortness of Breath, and Palpitations | Turn to Chapter M, p. 399. |
| Digestive Tract Problems | Turn to Chapter N, p. 406. |
| Men's Health | Turn to Chapter O, p. 423. |
| Women's Health | Turn to Chapter P, p. 426. |
| Sexual Problems and Questions | Turn to Chapter Q, p. 444. |